MW01051860

OSPF AND IS-IS

OSPF AND IS-IS

Choosing an IGP for Large-Scale Networks

Jeff Doyle

✦ Addison-Wesley

Upper Saddle River, NJ • Boston • Indianapolis • San Francisco
New York • Toronto • Montreal • London • Munich • Paris
Madrid • Capetown • Sydney • Tokyo • Singapore • Mexico City

Many of the designations used by manufacturers and sellers to distinguish their products are claimed as trademarks. Where those designations appear in this book, and the publisher was aware of a trademark claim, the designations have been printed with initial capital letters or in all capitals.

The author and publisher have taken care in the preparation of this book, but make no expressed or implied warranty of any kind and assume no responsibility for errors or omissions. No liability is assumed for incidental or consequential damages in connection with or arising out of the use of the information or programs contained herein.

The publisher offers excellent discounts on this book when ordered in quantity for bulk purchases or special sales, which may include electronic versions and/or custom covers and content particular to your business, training goals, marketing focus, and branding interests. For more information, please contact:

U. S. Corporate and Government Sales
(800) 382-3419
corpsales@pearsontechgroup.com

For sales outside the U. S., please contact:

International Sales
international@pearsoned.com

Visit us on the Web: www.awprofessional.com

Library of Congress Cataloging-in-Publication Data

Doyle, Jeff.
  OSPF and IS-IS : choosing an IGP for large-scale networks / Jeff
Doyle.
    p. cm.
  ISBN 0-321-16879-8
    1. Open Shortest Path First (Computer network protocol) 2. IS-IS
(Computer network protocol)   I. Title.
  TK5105.578.D69 2006
  004.6'2--dc22
                              2005020444

Copyright © 2006 Pearson Education, Inc.

All rights reserved. Printed in the United States of America. This publication is protected by copyright, and permission must be obtained from the publisher prior to any prohibited reproduction, storage in a retrieval system, or transmission in any form or by any means, electronic, mechanical, photocopying, recording, or likewise. For information regarding permissions, write to:

Pearson Education, Inc.
Rights and Contracts Department
One Lake Street
Upper Saddle River, NJ 07458

ISBN 0-321-16879-8
This product is printed digitally on demand.

*This book is dedicated to my parents,
L.H. and Louise Doyle, with much love.*

CONTENTS

ABOUT THE AUTHOR

Specializing in IP routing protocols, MPLS, and IPv6, Jeff Doyle has designed or assisted in the design of large scale IP service provider networks throughout North America, Europe, Japan, Korea, and the People's Republic of China. Jeff is the author of *CCIE Professional Development: Routing TCP/IP*, Volumes I and II, and is an editor and contributing author of *Juniper Networks Routers: The Complete Reference*. Jeff has presented numerous corporate seminars for Juniper Networks, and has also spoken at NANOG, JANOG, APRICOT, and at IPv6 Forum conferences.

Prior to joining Juniper Networks, Jeff was a Senior Network Systems Consultant with International Network Services, where he also specialized in IP routing protocol design. Jeff holds a Bachelor of Arts degree from Memphis State University, and studied electrical engineering at the University of New Mexico. Jeff lives in Denver, Colorado, with his wife and four children.

PREFACE

This book is an expansion of a PowerPoint presentation I have used for years in design meetings for IP carrier and service provider networks, comparing and contrasting OSPF and IS-IS. The PowerPoint presentation in turn grew from numerous informal chalk talks I had done for years before that, to address the concerns of engineers who had worked extensively with OSPF but had little or no experience with IS-IS and therefore wondered whether that protocol might be a better fit for their network.

With the growth of large-scale networks, the demand for information on OSPF and IS-IS—and how they compare—continues to increase. To enhance the ability of engineers to access, retain, and reference this information, creating a book was a logical next step in the evolution of my live presentations and seminars. The information in this book certainly reflects the questions, concerns, and challenges that audiences have consistently articulated. I trust readers will find their own business and technical interests addressed herein.

Audience

I have written this book primarily for those engineers and network architects who know OSPF but would like to learn more about IS-IS. For this reason, you will find that for each chapter or section topic I almost always discuss OSPF first, and then IS-IS: The idea is to start you off on familiar ground, discussing how the topic at hand is implemented in OSPF, and then showing how it is implemented in IS-IS.

The book will also be helpful to those who do not already have a rich understanding of OSPF. Perhaps you know OSPF or IS-IS or both at an intermediate level, and you want to deepen your understanding of both protocols. Or perhaps you are one of those rare engineers who knows IS-IS but not OSPF. I have detailed both protocols equally to meet any of these needs.

You will also find the book educational if you are a beginning-level networker who wants to expand your knowledge of link state protocols. Chapter 2 in particular is written for you, to get you through the essential concepts of routing protocols in general and link state protocols in particular, so that you are prepared to tackle the remainder of the book. The chapters are arranged so that they take you from foundation concepts to increasingly more complex ones.

Finally, if you are preparing for a network certification such as Cisco Systems' CCIE or
Juniper Networks' JNCIE, you will gain in these pages the essential conceptual understanding of OSPF and IS-IS needed to do well on the test. Configuration and troubleshooting exer-
cises are beyond the scope of this book, however, and you will need to practice solving them
via another resource to prepare fully for a certification exam. Review questions are included
at the end of each chapter of this book to help you test your comprehension and retention of
concepts before moving on to the next chapter. Because the answers are well documented in
the body of the chapter, a separate answer sheet is not included.

What Is a Large-Scale Data Communications Network?

OSPF and IS-IS are uniquely appropriate routing protocols for large-scale data communication networks. But how exactly do we characterize such a network? It might be useful to
approach a definition by remembering that data communication networks and ideas about
them have been around since long before the advent of computers.

For example, when Alexander Graham Bell and Theodore Vail founded American Telephone and Telegraph Company (AT&T) in 1885, they had no intention of providing telegraph services. But they understood that the network they were building could be used for
transmitting more than just telephony signals. They had no clear vision of what those other
signals might be, other than knowing that they would be, like telephony signals, representa-
tions of information. "Telegraph" reflected Bell's and Vail's anticipation of data communication networks within the understanding of their time.

Wide-area data communication has been around for as long as man has had a need to
share information over a range greater than voice can cover. Many ancient civilizations used
signal fires to communicate quickly over a long distance. In feudal Japan, villages sent paper
lanterns aloft in the evenings, rising on hot air created by the same fire that illuminated them,
to notify nearby villages of their safety. Throughout the southwestern United States you can
find petroglyphs—carvings of figures and symbols on the sides of rocks—created by hunting,
warring, or traveling parties of Native Americans over the centuries. Although some might
have been intended as merely decorative, many petroglyphs are thought to be signals and
messages left by one party for other parties expected to pass that way. These carvings put an
interesting twist on data communications: The signal remains stationary while the transmitting and receiving nodes move around.

Telegraph networks were the first data communications networks using electrical, digital
signals. And although they were certainly wide-area—connecting countries and even spanning continents via transoceanic cables—they did not entail the complexity that we assume
today when we talk about large-scale networks. Signals were easily originated, routed, and
received by human operators, and the network was maintained through human monitoring
and intervention.

How, then, do we define a large-scale network? Although the number of nodes and links certainly influences the definition, a definition based solely on numbers is too narrow. Instead, the scale of a network is defined by its complexity. A small-scale network is one that can be easily managed by direct human intervention; hence early telegraph networks could be considered small-scale even though they covered a very large geographic area. In terms of IP networks, a small-scale network is one that can be routed statically and requires no automated management systems. Notice I say *can be*: A given small-scale network might in fact run a routing protocol or automated management software; just because it can be routed statically does not mean it must be.

As a network grows in complexity, automation becomes more necessary. A mid-sized network is one in which static routing and management by direct human monitoring and intervention are no longer practical. In IP networks, a routing protocol such as RIP is required to maintain forwarding over many paths.

As the network continues to grow, however, the capabilities of automated systems themselves become an issue. As Chapter 2 explains, simple routing protocols such as RIP present problems in complex networks with many routing variables. A large-scale network, then, is one in which the automated network systems must be able to manage the network as a single entity rather than managing individual connections between nodes. Factors to consider in a large-scale network include the following:

- Complex interactions between individual nodes
- Complex path diversity requiring load balancing, traffic monitoring and distribution, and strong loop avoidance
- Complex link metrics
- Diverse data transport requirements
- Stringent requirements for security and reliability

OSPF and IS-IS can easily be run in a network of any size. But their true value is in their capability to perform consistently as their network domain grows large. No other IGP for IP networks can reliably route the world's largest networks.

A Word on IOS and JUNOS

The examples used throughout this book are provided in either Cisco Systems IOS or Juniper Networks JUNOS. In the early chapters, I occasionally provide examples from both operating systems. However, my intention is to provide you with an understanding of the protocols themselves, not to attempt to teach you a specific operating system. I have used IOS and JUNOS simply because they are the router operating systems I know and have access to. Armed with the information in this book you should be able to pick up a manual from any router vendor and easily configure and troubleshoot OSPF and IS-IS on that vendor's system.

ACKNOWLEDGMENTS

I first and foremost want to thank Catherine Nolan and all of the editorial, production, and marketing staff at Addison-Wesley for the extraordinary patience they had with me and with my long string of missed deadlines. I also want to thank my development editor, Laurie McGuire. This is not the first book Laurie and I have worked on together, and as usual she has made me appear to be a much better writer than I am.

Thanks to my technical reviewers: Eural Authement, Hannes Gredler, Dave Humphrey, Pete Moyer, Mike Shand, and Rena Yang. The experience and depth of knowledge this group represents are incomparable, and no author could ask for a better review team. I would also like to thank Ross Callon, Vint Cerf, Steve Crocker, Paul Goyette, Matt Kolon, Chelian Pandian, and Russ White, and all of my colleagues in the Professional Services group of Juniper Networks, for comments and advice on specific sections of the book.

My wife, Sara, and my children, Anna, Carol, James, and Katherine, are my bedrock. Their support and encouragement have been essential to the success of this book project; and the love, teasing, and laughter they bring into my life is priceless. Without them, I would be adrift.

Finally, I want to thank all of the readers of my previous books. I am honored by the kind comments and generous compliments I have received from around the world, and I hope you find this book to be equally useful.

CHAPTER 1

The Roots of Link State Protocols

It's a terrible way to start off a book: telling you that you can skip this first chapter if you want to. If all you care about is the technical aspects of OSPF and IS-IS, proceed directly to Chapter 2: The little technical content in this chapter is not prerequisite reading. Nonetheless, I'm compelled to tell the story of link state protocols for the very simple reason that one of the few subjects I love more than networking technology is history. The study of history is essential for understanding our world and culture, and for avoiding being hoodwinked by marketeers, politicians, and other nefarious characters who would like to sell us something other than the truth. So too with technology. Knowing how a protocol works is fine, but knowing the history of the protocol deepens your understanding of it and helps you put it in a larger context. That in turn might make choosing the right protocol for your network easier. If nothing else, history is just so much more entertaining than fiction.

The history of link state protocols is inextricably intertwined with the history of the Internet and its predecessor, the ARPANET. The emergence of these large-scale networks drove the need for and evolution of link state protocols. So, this chapter is really a brief history of the Internet and how OSPF and IS-IS fit into it.

1.1   An Intergalactic Network

Pages could be filled by listing all the people who have made significant contributions to the origin and evolution of the modern Internet. But one person laid the intellectual foundation: J. C. R. Licklider, a remarkably modest man who insisted on being called "Lick" rather than "Dr. Licklider" and who was comfortable letting others take credit for his ideas. Licklider had both a wide-ranging curiosity and (according to him) a short attention span. Combined with a gift for problem solving, these characteristics made him a generalist with deep insights into a number of fields. The fact that he was a psychologist, not an engineer, explains why his early ideas about computing and networking centered more on their cultural role than on technology.

While researching psychoacoustics at MIT in the mid-1950s, Licklider developed an intense interest in computers as a tool for modeling human cognition. During this time, and later as a vice president of Bolt Baranek and Newman (BBN), a consulting firm specializing in acoustic engineering, he and his protégés began fomenting ideas on computers as cognitive and communications tools. So deep was his immersion that by the very early 1960s Licklider, who had known little about computers before 1955, had become a widely recognized leader in computer science.[1] His seminal ideas were presented in various memos and later in two important papers, "Man-Computer Symbiosis" and "The Computer as a Communication Device."[2]

One of the key ideas promulgated by Licklider, discussed in "Man-Computer Symbiosis," was real-time, interactive computer processing. In the 1950s, computations were done by batch processing: You formulated the problem and worked out a program to compute the solution to the problem. The difficulty with batch processing is that the very process of solving a complex problem can change the original question. Unforeseen alternatives mean going back to the beginning and creating another batch program. Licklider quoted Poincare: "The question is not, 'What is the answer?' The question is, 'What is the question?'" Real-time interaction between human and computer allows the question to be modified to accommodate new information discovered during the problem-solving process.

Batch processing also means that the computer runs one program at a time; everyone must wait his turn. If interaction with the computer is to take place in real time, multiple people should be able to use the computer concurrently. An extension to the idea of real-time interactive computing, then, is time sharing.

Another idea discussed in the same paper is the concept of a computer as a supplemental component in the human thought process. Using his own typical workday as an example, Licklider determined that most of his activities were clerical or mechanical: "About 85 percent of my 'thinking' time was spent getting into a position to think, to make a decision, to learn something I needed to know. Much more time went into finding or obtaining information than into digesting it." Computers are much faster at finding and coordinating information than we are; the symbiosis of man and computer applies the computer to the drudgery of information retrieval and data processing, leaving us free to direct the problem-solving process as new information presents itself.

Out of these ideas springs yet another, that of "thinking centers." If a computer is to be used for information retrieval, it might need access to vast amounts of data––more than a single computer can hold. Licklider's idea of a thinking center was multiple computers interconnected over a wide area, comprising a new kind of library. A user at any computer had

---

[1] Lick foresaw home computers, graphical user interfaces, point-and-click input devices, and many other aspects of the modern computing. His work also made him the father of artificial intelligence.

[2] J. C. R. Licklider, "Man-Computer Symbiosis," *IRE Transactions of Human Factors in Electronics*, Volume HFE-1, March 1960, and "The Computer as a Commmunication Device," *Science and Technology*, April 1968.

Reprints of both papers, with an introduction by Bob Taylor, can be found on the Web as "In Memoriam: J.C.R. Licklider, 1915–1990," gatekeeper.dec.com/pub/DEC/SRC/research-reports/SRC-061.pdf, published by the Systems Research Center of Digital Equipment Corporation, August 1990.

access to the information on any computer in the thinking center. This, of course, brings us to the core concept of a WAN-based internetwork.

The idea put forth in "The Computer as a Communication Device" is not just that networked computers can link humans over wide areas, but that they can assist in the basic psychology of communication. "Creative, interactive communication requires a plastic or moldable medium that can be modeled, a dynamic medium in which premises will flow into consequences, and above all a common medium that can be contributed to and experimented with by all." Licklider saw the computer as this medium, creating models that the human mind does not: "By far the most numerous, most sophisticated, and most important models are those that reside in men's minds. In richness, plasticity, facility, and economy, the mental model has no peer, but, in other respects, it has shortcomings. It will not stand still for careful study. It cannot be made to repeat a run. No one knows just how it works. It serves its owner's hopes more faithfully than it serves reason. It has access only to the information stored in one man's head. It can be observed and manipulated only by one person." This concept builds on the earlier ideas of man-computer symbiosis, but takes us well into the basic concepts of using a wide-area network for distributed data processing.

In October 1962, Licklider was hired by the U.S. Department of Defense Advanced Research Projects Agency (ARPA)[3] to head both its Command and Control Research division and its Behavioral Sciences division. Command and Control Research was soon renamed the Information Processing Techniques Office (IPTO). Licklider brought with him not only his ideas about time sharing and man-computer symbiosis; he also attracted many of the top computer scientists of the era to ARPA. He called this tight-knit group of scientists the Intergalactic Computer Network, an inside joke reflecting his most significant ideas of a globally connected computer network.

Although Licklider stayed at IPTO only until 1964, his ideas were inseminated in the Intergalactic Computer Network. These scientists became some of the key figures in the development of the ARPANET.

An Early Vision of the Web

Licklider's early thoughts about man-computer symbiosis were influenced by those of another visionary: Vannevar Bush. Bush conceptualized a machine he called a "memex," which could be used to augment the cognitive process.

Bush published his thoughts about the memex in 1945 in an article called "As We Might Think."[4] The memex Bush envisioned would be used to retrieve information stored on microfilm: "A memex is a device in which an individual stores all his books, records, and communications, and which is mechanized so that it may be consulted with exceeding speed and flexibility. It is an enlarged intimate supplement to his memory. It consists of a desk… On the top are slanting translucent screens, on which material can be projected… There is a keyboard, and sets of buttons and levers… As he [the user] has

---

[3] In 1972, ARPA was somewhat unnecessarily renamed *Defense* Advanced Research Projects Agency, or DARPA.

[4] Vannevar Bush, "As We Might Think," *The Atlantic Monthly*, July 1945.

several projection positions, he can leave one item in position while he calls up another. He can add marginal notes and comments..."

What is so forward thinking is not the information-retrieval mechanism, but a proposed mechanism for linking information being called up, tying multiple pieces of information together: "When the user is building a trail, he names it, inserts it in his code book, and taps it out on his keyboard. Before him are the two items to be joined, projected onto adjacent viewing positions... The user taps a single key, and the items are permanently joined... Thereafter, at any time, when one of these items is in view, the other can be instantly recalled... Moreover, when numerous items have been thus joined together to form a trail, they can be viewed in turn, rapidly or slowly... It is exactly as though the physical items had been gathered together to form a new book. It is more than this, for any item can be joined into numerous trails."

Thus in 1945, and within the limitations the technology of the time, Vannevar Bush foresaw the information-linking capabilities of hypertext and the information-retrieval capabilities of the World Wide Web.

1.2 ARPANET

ARPA was created by the Eisenhower administration in 1958 in reaction to the Soviet Union's orbiting of the Sputnik satellites—perceived in the United States as a clear sign that the Soviets were outpacing the United States in science and technology. The motivation was to fund and manage research and development projects—primarily through universities—in hopes of avoiding another such national embarrassment. Famously wary of the military-industrial complex and the sometimes-intense competition among the branches of the military, Eisenhower made ARPA an independent agency under a civilian director with liberal funding and with wide leeway in the projects they undertook.

J. C. R. Licklider's successors as director of ARPA's IPTO were first Ivan Sutherland and then Bob Taylor; both were influenced by Licklider's "Intergalactic Network" concepts, connecting communities of interest by networking time-sharing computers. Interestingly, Taylor was, like Licklider, a psychologist whose research in psychoacoustics led him to an interest in computer science.

Much of the early research at ARPA dealt with satellite and missile technology, and such related technologies as command and control systems. Obviously, computers were a central part of the research both as tools and as objects of research. And because much of the research funded by ARPA was performed at universities around the United States, the computers involved were also scattered around the country. Bob Taylor's own office was connected to three computers, at MIT, the University of California at Berkley, and System Development Corporation (SDC) in Santa Monica, California. Each computer required a separate terminal in Taylor's office and separate login procedures. Taylor, inspired by Licklider's ideas, wondered why there could not be a single terminal connecting him to all three computers. More important, Taylor was seeing a growing inefficiency as work was duplicated among the researchers using computers around the country. If UCLA developed a program that researchers at MIT found useful, for instance, MIT would have to write a version of it for their own, different computer. Wouldn't it be better if the researchers at MIT could use the UCLA program right on UCLA's computer? Further, if researchers could access remote computers the need for an expensive computer of their own could be reduced. Licklider's ideas about time sharing were already being implemented; it was time for his ideas about networking communities of interest to be implemented.

So, in 1966, Bob Taylor proposed a project to develop such a network, and received funding. The ARPA Network—ARPANET, as it was eventually called—was begun.

Taylor's first step was to hire a manager and principal architect for the network. For this he chose Larry Roberts, a respected young computer scientist at MIT. In Taylor's view, Roberts was the only candidate for the position: In addition to his computer science background, he had excellent management skills and had already run on a small networking project connecting MIT's Lincoln Labs computer to the SDC computer in Santa Monica.[5]

Among Roberts's roles was bringing together key individuals and ideas for ARPANET implementation. Three people in particular developed the fundamental architectural concepts of the ARPANET: Leonard Kleinrock, Paul Baran, and Donald Davies. In the early 1960s, these three had developed similar ideas without knowledge of each other's work.

Len Kleinrock, a close friend and gambling buddy of Roberts from MIT, had done his doctoral thesis, "Information Flow in Large Communication Nets," in 1962. The focus of the research, later published in a book,[6] was on queuing theory in store-and-forward networks. This research formed the foundation of packet switching. Eventually, Kleinrock would work directly on the ARPANET project, developing performance analysis methods for it.

Paul Baran joined the RAND Corporation in 1959 and spent the next five years researching network survivability.[7] His focus was not on computer networks per se, but on the command and control networks for ballistic missile systems and how to ensure that if some nodes were destroyed in a nuclear attack, the other nodes would continue functioning. Baran understood that human neural networks are tremendously robust: If a part of the brain is damaged, the neural net can build new pathways to bypass the damaged cells. So once again, networking ideas sprung from the study of human cognition. A centralized communication network, such as shown in Figure 1.1(a), can be easily destroyed by eliminating the central node. A decentralized network, as shown in Figure 1.1(b)—such as a typical telephone system—provides a bit more redundancy but not enough. Baran proposed a distributed network as shown in Figure 1.1(c) in which there is no centralized switch and which therefore can build paths around any nodes destroyed by enemy attack.

---

[5] The project was proposed by Tom Marill, yet another psychologist who found his way into computer research. Marill created the procedures the computers used to exchange messages, and was the first to call such procedures a "protocol."

[6] Leonard Kleinrock, *Communication Nets: Stochastic Message Flow and Design*, McGraw-Hill, 1964.

[7] Baran later helped originate the packet voice technology developed by StrataCom and which evolved into ATM.

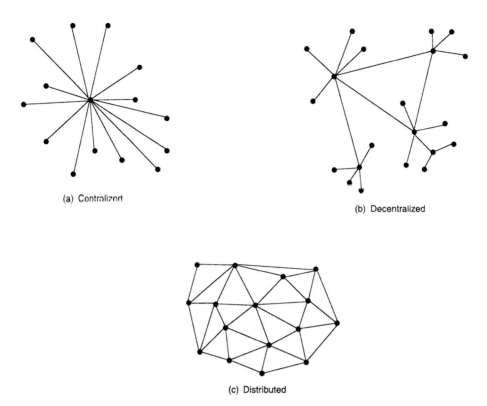

(a) Centralized

(b) Decentralized

(c) Distributed

Figure 1.1   Paul Baran introduced the concept of a distributed network that was far more resilient than centralized or decentralized networks.

Baran further proposed that the messages sent across the decentralized network should themselves be broken into segments, which he called "message blocks." Because data communication is inherently bursty, Baran theorized that message blocks allowed more efficient use of the available bandwidth between nodes by allowing the interleaving of message blocks from multiple sources. The nodes themselves would be store-and-forward switches that determined the best route to the destination for each message block and forwarded it quickly—Baran called it "hot-potato routing"—and if a node had been destroyed, the message block could be routed around the destruction. Baran's ideas gave rise to dynamic routing.

Larry Roberts learned of Paul Baran's work in 1967 and met with him in 1968. Afterward, Baran became informally involved in the ARPANET in an advisory capacity.

At the same time that Roberts learned of Baran's work, he also learned of the work being done by Donald Davies, a physicist at the British National Physical Laboratory (NPL) in London. Without knowing of Baran's work, Davies proposed a similar concept of routing segmented messages dynamically, although his proposals did not have the level of redundancy of Baran's distributed network. However, Davies was interested not in military command and control systems but in a new form of public communication. He saw the routing of message segments through the network as analogous to the postal service routing small packages through its system; for this reason, he called the message segments not message blocks, as had Baran, but "packets." And the routing of the packets through the network he called "packet switching."

Another significant contribution from Davies came when he realized that different machines were likely to speak different computer languages, and therefore have difficulty communicating directly. Davies proposed using smaller, dedicated "interface computers," speaking a common language across the network, between the host systems and the network.

When Larry Roberts proposed the ARPANET concept to the researchers at the various host sites, the concept was well received but not the practical implementation. Computer resources were always at a premium, and few wanted to have a part of their time-sharing computers' resources used for the routing and processing of packets. Wesley Clark, an engineer at Washington University in St. Louis who, in the mid-1950s while at MIT had given J. C. R. Licklider his first serious exposure to computers, suggested placing small computers between the hosts and the network. These small computers would perform the dynamic routing. At the time, Clark did not know of Donald Davies's almost identical idea.

Roberts adopted this suggestion and called the small computers "Interface Message Processors" (IMPs). These were the precursors to modern routers.

Roberts issued a Request For Proposal for building the IMPs, and the contract was awarded to BBN in Cambridge, Massachusetts, where Licklider had earlier served as a vice president. Licklider had been responsible for purchasing the first computer for BBN, and as a result the company evolved from being just an acoustics engineering consultancy to being a leading computer research firm.

Frank Heart, BBN's director of the IMP project, selected a "hardened" version of the Honeywell DDP-516 minicomputer[8] on which to build the IMP. Although the 516 was built to military specifications to withstand battlefield and naval deployment conditions, it was not enemy actions that Heart feared. Rather, it was the unwanted attention of graduate students. In the spirit of a highly reliable network, the IMP developers counted on the hardened 516 to be sufficiently resistant to tinkering.

By October 1969, the first two IMPs were installed at UCLA and at Stanford Research Institute (SRI), connecting the mainframe hosts at those sites over a 50kbps link, and the first packets were exchanged. By early December, two more host sites at the University of California Santa Barbara and the University of Utah were added to the network. Early the following year, a cross-country 50kbps link connecting BBN in Cambridge to UCLA was added. By April 1971, there were 15 sites:

1. UCLA
2. SRI
3. UCSB

---

[8] Minicomputers of the time were "mini" only in relation to mainframes. The Honeywell 516 was the size of a refrigerator, weighed almost 1000 pounds, and cost around $100,000.

4. University of Utah

5. BBN

6. MIT

7. RAND Corporation

8. System Development Corporation

9. Harvard University

10. MIT Lincoln Labs

11. Stanford University

12. University of Illinois at Urbana

13. Case Western Reserve University

14. Carnegie Mellon University

15. NASA Ames Research Center

The ARPANET was not only up and running, it was growing steadily. [9]

The first public demonstration of ARPANET was held at the International Conference on Computer Communication (ICCC) at the Washington Hilton Hotel in October 1972. Robert Kahn, one of the BBN IMP researchers who had been instrumental in developing the IMP-to-host protocol, architecting the ARPANET, and improving its reliability, had spent more than a year organizing the event. Approximately 40 terminals of different makes and models were connected to a Terminal Interface Processor, or TIP, [10] which in turn was connected to the ARPANET over two 50kbps lines. Conference attendees were invited to come in and play with applications of all sorts, running on computers all over the country. The ICCC event was a huge success, demonstrating to the computer and telecommunications industry that packet switching networks are viable and convincing many that the industry was about to change significantly.

The feasibility of the network had been proven, but a large hurdle remained: When the first few ARPANET sites were connected, instruction sets were improvised at and unique to each host, allowing it to speak to other hosts—mainly by making the host think its peer was actually a "dumb" terminal. A common host-to-host protocol still needed to be developed.

ARPANET and the Bomb

One of the most enduring myths about the origins of the ARPANET is that its was designed to withstand a nuclear attack. The myth is undoubtedly rooted in Paul Baran's work at the RAND Corporation. But nuclear attack was the furthest thing from the

---

[9] For a good set of diagrams of the ARPANET as it grew, plus some hand-drawn sketches by Larry Roberts and others, see www.cybergeography.org/atlas/historical.html.

[10] BBN had developed the TIP a year earlier to connect sites that had no local host. The IMPs had only 4 host interfaces and no terminal interfaces; so the TIP was an IMP with interfaces for up to 64 terminals.

minds of Larry Roberts and his scientists. Baran's network survivability ideas influenced the construction of the ARPANET for the much more immediate reason that switching nodes and the links connecting them were at the time notoriously unreliable. (According to a famous story, when Charley Kline sent the first packets on the ARPANET in 1969, from UCLA to Stanford Research Institute, he got as far as the g in "login" before the system crashed.) Redundant packet switches and links, and a dynamic routing protocol, were for routing packets around failed links and nodes, not radioactive craters.

1.3   The Network Working Group

UCLA was not chosen randomly as the site for the first IMP installation in 1969. Len Kleinrock was there. Kleinrock had done key work on analytical models for data flows, and had influenced his friend Larry Roberts's ideas about store-and-forward switching networks during their time together at MIT. At UCLA, Kleinrock established the Network Measurement Center (NMC), and in October 1968 Roberts awarded the NMC the contract for performance analysis of the ARPANET. Kleinrock put together a team of some 40 graduate students to help him.

Approximately a year before the first IMP was installed, graduate students from the first four planned sites began meeting; Steve Crocker represented the NMC. Their agenda was open, with the objective of discussing the many development and application tasks that lay ahead of them. "We had lots of questions," Crocker recalls. "How IMPs and hosts would be connected, what hosts would say to each other, and what applications would be supported. No one had any answers, but the prospects seemed exciting. We found ourselves imagining all kinds of possibilities—interactive graphics, cooperating processes, automatic database query, electronic mail—but no one knew where to begin."[11] Out of these discussions emerged a working group of three people: Steve Carr from the University of Utah, Jeff Rulifson from SRI, and Steve Crocker from UCLA, who became the chairman. They called themselves the Network Working Group (NWG). Because they had no official charter or assignment from BBN, the group felt free to discuss a wide range of networking topics: "Our earliest meetings," Crocker said, "were unhampered by knowledge of what the network would look like or how it would interact with the hosts. Depending on your point of view, this either allowed us or forced us to think about broader and grander topics."[12]

A prime topic for the NWG was the yet-to-be-specified host-to-host protocol. They began developing their own ideas about how it should work, keeping notes on their agreements. They were acutely aware that they were just a bunch of grad students and that there must be a real design team back at BBN hard at work on the real protocol. But BBN had their hands full just getting the IMPs to pass bits reliably. There was no protocol design team.

[11] Stephen D. Crocker, "The Origins of RFCs," in Joyce Reynolds and Jon Postel, "The Request for Comments Reference Guide," RFC 1000, August 1987.

[12] Steve Crocker, "The First Pebble: Publication of RFC 1," in RFC Editor et al., "30 Years of RFCs," RFC 2555, April 1999.

"I remember having great fear that we would offend whomever the official protocol designers were, and I spent a sleepless night composing humble words for our notes," Crocker said. "The basic ground rules were that anyone could say anything and that nothing was official." To emphasize that the notes were "the beginning of a dialog and not an assertion of control," Crocker called the notes "Requests For Comments." Crocker himself wrote RFC 1, on their early ideas for a host-to-host protocol.

Responsibility for managing and editing the RFCs was soon taken over by Jon Postel, another of Kleinrock's graduate students at the NMC. Postel remained the RFC editor until his untimely death in 1998.

Among the first developments of the NWG was the Decode-Encode Language (DEL) for encapsulating and unencapsulating messages—RFC 5 called it "packing" and "unpacking"—and the Network Interchange Language (NIL), for telling a receiver how to interpret information to be sent. Over the spring and summer of 1969, Crocker's NWG struggled to develop working protocols. "Although we had a vision of the vast potential for intercomputer communication, designing usable protocols was another matter ... It would have been convenient if we could have made the network simply look like a tape drive to each host, but we knew that wouldn't do." The delivery date of the first IMP was fast approaching. "With the pressure to get something working and the general confusion as to how to achieve the high generality we all aspired to, we punted and defined the first set of protocols to include only Telnet and FTP [File Transfer Protocol] functions. In particular, only asymmetric, user-server relationships were supported." The Telnet part, for remote login, was ready in time for the first connection to SRI in October, and it was this function that was used to pass the first packets on the ARPANET.

But the host-to-host protocol was still to be done. "In December of 1969," Crocker writes, "we met with Larry Roberts in Utah, and suffered our first direct experience with 'redirection'. Larry made it abundantly clear that our first step was not big enough, and we went back to the drawing board."

By December 1970, a host-to-host protocol called the Network Control Protocol (NCP) was ready for deployment, and by 1972 NCP had been implemented throughout the ARPANET. When the NWG was first considering the overall architecture of the host-to-host protocol, they chose to use a layered structure. As Crocker put it, "Along with the basic host-to-host protocol, we also envisioned a hierarchy of protocols, with Telnet, FTP, and some splinter protocols as the first example. If we had only consulted the ancient mystics, we would have seen immediately that seven layers were required." Layered protocol architectures have been accepted wisdom ever since.

One of the key NWG designers that produced NCP was yet another of Kleinrock's graduate students from the NMC and a close friend of Crocker's since high school days named Vinton Cerf.

1.4   The Birth of the Internet

Bob Kahn had for some time during the development of the IMP been worrying about congestion in the network. He theorized that the flow control algorithms would, in some circumstances, allow the queues in an IMP to fill to capacity, causing upstream IMPs to in turn fill their queues. Such cascading congestion would cause the network to lock up. But his colleagues at BBN, despite Kahn's nagging, were too busy with engineering to spend time on abstractions. They just wanted to get the network up and running; refinement could come later.

So in January 1970, after the first four sites were up, Kahn made a trip to the NMC to test his theories. There he met Vint Cerf, who along with Crocker, Postel, and others helped with the testing. In Cerf's words: "Bob came out to UCLA to kick the tires of the system in the long-haul environment, and we struck up a very productive collaboration. He would ask for software to do something, I would program it overnight, and we would do the tests."[13]

Kahn was able to easily push the fledgling ARPANET into congestive failure in exactly the ways he predicted. He returned to Cambridge with his theories vindicated, and the problems were quickly corrected. But much more significantly, a collaborative friendship with Vint Cerf had begun; within a few years, that friendship would have a profound impact on networking.

Larry Roberts had for some time been interested in packet radio networks; the military applications were obvious. Kahn moved from BBN to DARPA in 1972, and Roberts put him to work studying packet radio networks. Kahn began looking at a network called ALOHANET.

In 1969, ARPA had funded an experimental packet radio network at the University of Hawaii, directed by Professor Norman Abramson. ALOHANET[14] connected sites spread around the Hawaiian Islands to a central time-sharing computer on the U of H campus. Abramson whimsically named his version of an IMP Menehune (a mischievous Hawaiian elf). ALOHANET users could connect to the ARPANET through a TIP attached to the Menehune. But this access through the TIP meant that from the ARPANET perspective ALOHANET was just a terminal connection. Kahn was interested in finding a way to make ARPANET and ALOHANET, or any diverse networks, full peers with transparent access between hosts. From this, DARPA's Internetting Project was begun to explore open network architectures.

While this was happening, the first public demonstration of the ARPANET at the ICCC that Kahn had organized took place in October 1972. At that event, a new working group called the International Network Working Group (INWG) was organized. Several packet switching projects had sprung up in Europe, and the mission of the INWG was to find a way

---

[13] Vinton Cerf, as told to Bernard Aboba, "How the Internet Came to Be," *The Online User's Encyclopedia*, Addison-Wesley, 1993.

[14] Steve Crocker exposed his friend Bob Metcalfe to Abramson's work. Metcalfe was intrigued by the ALOHANET's procedures for random access to a broadcast medium, particularly the retransmit procedures when packets collide. These ideas led Metcalfe and David Boggs to invent Ethernet.

to connect ARPANET and these other diverse networks, making an international network of networks. Vint Cerf was the INWG chairman.

Cerf and Kahn began a lengthy series of discussions to find a solution to their mutual challenges. Their model was an internetworking of the ARPANET with a packet radio network and a satellite network (SATNET)—each of which used different protocols and different interfaces, optimized for that particular network's needs.

Early in 1973, Cerf proposed linking the three networks by adding a routing computer he called a "gateway" between each network. The gateway would understand the protocols and procedures of each of the attached networks and be able to pass packets between them by providing the correct interfaces, procedures, and packet encapsulations to each connected network.

But there were other challenges. ARPANET was designed for a very high degree of reliability, and NCP depended upon that. Packet radio and satellite links could not guarantee that kind of reliability. Another problem was addressing. NCP addressed only next-hop nodes, something like modern MAC addresses, and could not address on a wider—much less global—scale. Also, each network had its own maximum packet sizes, and adjusting packet sizes from one network to another was required. So Kahn undertook the development of a new host-to-host protocol with global addressing, the ability to recover from lost packets, fragmentation and reassembly, end-to-end checksums, and host-to-host flow control. He asked Cerf, who was by this time a professor at Stanford University, to help because of his experience designing NCP. Cerf ran a series of seminars at Stanford for students and visitors to discuss and challenge their ideas as they formed.

Cerf and Kahn presented their first version of the new protocol at a meeting of the INWG at Sussex University in the United Kingdom in September 1973.[15] They called it the Transmission Control Protocol (TCP).

Over the next five years, the protocol went through four iterations, with modifications such as the addition of a three-way handshake and a lengthening of the address from the originally proposed 24 bits to 32 bits. The term *datagram* also comes into usage during these modifications.

The first demonstration of the new protocol came in July 1977. A van driving on the San Francisco Bayshore Freeway was linked into a packet radio system, which linked through a gateway to the ARPANET. The ARPANET was then linked through another gateway to a point-to-point transatlantic satellite link to Norway and then by land line to the University College London. Packets then recrossed the Atlantic on another SATNET link, and back through the ARPANET to a host at the University of Southern California's Information Sciences Institute (ISI). Cerf writes, "Since the Defense Department was paying for this, we were looking for demonstrations that would translate to militarily interesting scenarios. So the packets were traveling 94,000 miles round trip, as opposed to what would have been an 800-mile round trip directly on the ARPANET. We didn't lose a bit!"

---

[15] Vinton G. Cerf and Robert E. Kahn, "A Protocol for Packet Network Intercommuication," *IEEE Transactions on Communications*, Volume COM-22, Number 5, pp. 627–641, May 1974.

In August 1977, Jon Postel wrote: "We are screwing up in our design of internet protocols by violating the principle of layering. Specifically we are trying to use TCP to do two things: serve as a host level end to end protocol, and serve as an Internet packaging and routing protocol. These two things should be provided in a layered and modular way."[16] Postel proposed moving the hop-by-hop portion of TCP into a separate protocol called Internet Protocol (IP). In the same paper, he proposed the IP header as we know it today. Cerf and Postel then wrote the specifications for splitting TCP, and TCP/IP came into being.[17] User Datagram Protocol (UDP) was then specified by Postel to provide direct access to IP, when best-effort service is desired.

In 1980, the U.S. military adopted TCP/IP as a networking standard, and a "flag day" transition from NCP to TCP/IP was scheduled for the ARPANET on January 1, 1983. The transition went reasonably smoothly, and marks the beginning of the Internet and the beginning of the end for the ARPANET.

Al Gore Invents the Internet

A recent bit of Internet mythology is U.S. Vice President Al Gore's supposed claim that he invented the Internet. The story started with an interview with Wolf Blitzer on CNN's *Late Edition*. Gore was campaigning for the Democratic nomination for president, and Blitzer asked Gore why voters should support him rather than Bill Bradley. As part of Gore's reply, he said, "During my service in the United States Congress, I took the initiative in creating the Internet. I took the initiative in moving forward a whole range of initiatives that have proven to be important to our country's economic growth and environmental protection, improvements in our educational system."[18]

Although his choice of words was clumsy (taking the initiative on initiatives?), Gore was trying to get across that as a congressman and senator he had been a leader in addressing a range of important issues.

Reporters were quick to pick up on the gaffe. At first, most simply tried to point out that the Internet was "invented" in 1969 (which is not true either), long before Gore came to Congress. But the news media soon morphed Gore's unfortunate choice of words into a claim that he had invented the Internet. Comedians and political opponents happily repeated the misquote until it became accepted truth. Even Gore himself began making jokes about it.

The reality is that Gore's legislative efforts from the 1970s on did indeed help create the Internet we now enjoy (or hate). Republican leader Newt Gingrich stated, "Gore is the person who, in the Congress, most systematically worked to make sure that we got to an Internet."[19]

---

[16] Jon Postel, "Comments on Internet Protocol and TCP," IEN #2, August 1977.

[17] Some early documents called it IP/TCP.

[18] "Transcript: Vice President Gore on CNN's 'Late Edition'," www.cnn.com/ALLPOLITICS/stories/1999/03/09/president.2000/transcript/gore/, March 9, 1999.

[19] Quoted in James Gerstenzang, "Gore Can Mispeak, and That's No Exaggeration," *Los Angeles Times*, September 22, 2000.

Vint Cerf and Bob Kahn also weighed in on the subject: "We don't think, as some people have argued, that Gore intended to claim he 'invented' the Internet. Moreover, there is no question in our minds that while serving as senator, Gore's initiatives had a significant and beneficial effect on the still-evolving Internet. The fact of the matter is that Gore was talking about and promoting the Internet long before most people were listening."[20] After enumerating his contributions, they conclude: "No one in public life has been more intellectually engaged in helping to create the climate for a thriving Internet… The vice president deserves credit for his early recognition of the value of high-speed computing and communication and for his long-term and consistent articulation of the potential value of the Internet to American citizens and industry and, indeed, to the rest of the world."

1.5   Routing in the ARPANET

By the time of the NCP-to-TCP/IP transition at the beginning of 1983, two communities were using the ARPANET: military operations and university/corporate researchers. Particularly in the second community, a tremendous number of graduate students was learning to appreciate and use the network in ways that would quickly influence the business community. They were also using the network for some distinctly nonresearch activities such as gaming. As a result of this large and growing user population, the Department of Defense became concerned about security, and decided to move their nodes to a separate network called the MILNET. But they wanted to continue to have access to the ARPANET nodes, so the two networks remained connected through a gateway. The separation was really just one that provided separate administrative control; the users on both networks didn't notice the difference. The transition to TCP/IP made such a split possible.

Other networks also began cropping up and interconnecting, both in the United States and in Europe. The one with the most important long-range impact was the NSFNET, begun by the National Science Foundation in 1985. Originally intended to interconnect five supercomputer sites over 56kbps links, the network links were upgraded to T1 in 1988 and then T3 (45Mbps) beginning in 1990. NSFNET connected universities and corporations all around the country; more important, it offered free connectivity to the regional networks cropping up around the country. ARPANET's slow links and its old IMPs and TIPs, plus its restrictive access polices, meant that by the late 1980s most users were connected to other networks. DARPA decided it was time to decommission the 20-year-old network. One by one, its sites were transferred to one of the regional networks or to the MILNET, so that by 1990 the ARPANET ceased to exist.

But as this short historical overview has shown, almost all of the internetworking technologies we use to this day had their start with the ARPANET. That includes the topic of this book, routing. By the mid-1980s, a number of companies had sprung up to sell commercial versions of gateways, called routers: 3Com, ACC, Bridge, Cisco, Proteon, Wellfleet, and

---

[20] Robert Kahn and Vinton Cerf, "Al Gore and the Internet," e-mail to Declan McCullaugh and Dave Farber, September 28, 2000.

others. They all used routing algorithms first explored in the ARPANET. Interestingly, engineers at BBN had tried to encourage the company to get into commercial routers, but their marketing department decided that there was no future in it.

The first routing protocol used in the ARPANET was designed in 1969 by Will Crowther, a member of the original IMP team at BBN. Like all routing protocols, it was based on mathematical graph theory—in this case, the algorithms of Richard Bellman and Lester Randolph Ford. The Bellman-Ford algorithm forms the basis of most of a class of routing protocols over the years called distance vector protocols. Crowther's protocol was a distributed adaptive protocol—that is, it was designed to adapt to quickly changing network characteristics by adjusting the link metrics it used (adaptive), and the routers cooperate in calculating optimal paths to a destination (distributed).

Crowther's routing protocol used delay as its metric. The delay was estimated at each IMP by counting, every 128 milliseconds, the number of packets queued for each attached link. A constant, representing a minimum cost, was added to the counts to avoid an idle link being given a metric of zero.[21] The more often the queue length was measured, the more quickly each IMP could detect and adapt to changing link delays. The result, it was theorized, was that traffic distribution should be fairly balanced on all outgoing trunks to a given destination.

At each new count, the IMP's routing table was updated, and then the routing table was advertised to its neighbors. Neighbors, on receiving the table, estimated the delay to the advertising IMP, added the results to the information in the received table, and used the sums to update the information in their own tables about destinations reachable via the advertising IMP. Once updated, the neighbors advertised their own tables to their neighbors. The distributed nature of the routing calculation, then, came from the iterative advertising and updating of tables across the network.

This original protocol served the ARPANET well for its first decade of life. Under light traffic loads, the routing decisions were determined mainly by the constant added to the estimated delay. Under moderate loads, congestion might arise in isolated areas of the network; the measured queue lengths in these areas became a factor, and traffic was shifted away from the congestion.

But the protocol began showing increasing problems as the ARPANET grew larger and traffic loads grew heavier. Some of the problems had to do with the way the metric was determined:

- The queued packet count is an instantaneous measurement. In a busy network, queue lengths can vary quickly and regularly, causing extreme fluctuations in the metric and hence oscillations in routing tables.

- Counting queued packets does not take into consideration differences in available link speeds. Even with more queued packets, a high-speed link might have less delay than a low-speed link.

---

[21] Although probably irrelevant to routing, one advantage that the Bellman-Ford algorithm has over the Dijkstra algorithm is that Bellman-Ford can account for negative cost values on branches of a graph, whereas Dijkstra cannot.

- Queuing delay is not the only factor influencing overall delay. Packet lengths, processing time in the IMP, and other factors can contribute to delay.

Additionally, problems with the distance vector approach itself began arising:

- As the number of network nodes grew, the exchange of routing tables was expected to begin consuming a significant fraction of the available bandwidth.
- The rate of measuring delays and updating tables, coupled with the instantaneous queue measurement, could restrict the network from reacting fast enough to true congestion but also cause it to react too fast to minor or insignificant queue changes.
- The distributed calculation, which by nature is slow to converge (related to the last bullet, bad news travels fast but good news travels slow), was susceptible to persistent routing loops and inaccuracies. (Chapter 2 discusses the typical vulnerabilities of distance vector protocols.)

In 1979, BBN deployed a new ARPANET routing protocol, developed by John McQuillan, Ira Richer, and Eric Rosen.[22] The new protocol introduced three significant changes from the original:

- Although the protocol still used an adaptive metric based on measured delay, the metric was both more accurate and less instantaneous.
- Update frequency and the size of the updates were sharply reduced, requiring less bandwidth.
- The routing algorithm changed from a distributed calculation based on advertised databases to a local calculation at each IMP based on advertised metrics.

The improved metric determination meant less thrashing of routes. Rather than counting queued packets, the IMP timestamped each arriving packet with an arrival time. Then when the first bit of the packet was transmitted, the packet was stamped with its transmit time. When an acknowledgement of the packet was received, the arrival time was subtracted from the transmit time. Then a constant (called a bias)[23] representing the propagation delay of the line on which the packet was transmitted and a variable representing the transmission delay (based on packet length and line speed) were added to the difference between the arrival and transmit times. The resulting value was a more accurate measure of true delay. Every 10 seconds, the average of these measured delays for each attached link was taken, and this average became the metric for the link. By taking an average, the problems associated with using an instantaneous measurement were avoided.

---

[22] John M. McQuillan, Ira Richter, and Eric C. Rosen, "The New Routing Algorithm for the ARPANET," *IEEE Transactions of Communications*, Vol COM-28, No. 5, pp. 711–719, May 1980.

[23] As with the previous protocol, the constant prevents the possibility of attributing a cost of zero to an idle link.

The second change, reduced update frequency, was accomplished by setting a threshold that began at 64 milliseconds. When the 10-second average delay was calculated, the result was compared with the previous result. If the difference did not exceed the threshold, no update was sent, and the threshold was reduced by 12.8ms for the next comparison. If the threshold was exceeded, an update was sent, and the threshold was reset to 64ms. This decaying threshold ensured that big metric changes were advertised quickly and small changes were advertised slower. If no metric change occurred, the threshold would decay to 0 in 50 seconds causing an update to be sent even if no metric change had occurred. As a result of this new algorithm, the frequency of updates and the associated bandwidth consumption was sharply reduced.

Also important was what was in the update. Rather than sending the routing table to neighbors, each IMP sent only the metrics of its local links; the update would be sent throughout the network (the designers called the procedure "flooding"), and each IMP would keep a copy in a database. An IMP did not have to perform its local calculation before forwarding the update. This had two beneficial effects: The updates themselves were small—averaging 176 bits—further reducing bandwidth consumption; and because the updates were flooded to all IMPs quickly—within 100ms—the network could react to changes more quickly. Using sequence numbers, ages, and acknowledgments ensured accuracy and reliability of the flooded metrics.[24]

The third significant change, and the one most important to this book, is that instead of the Bellman-Ford algorithm the protocol calculated routes based on an algorithm created by graph theorist Edsger Dijkstra. Each IMP used its database of metrics flooded from all IMPs to calculate locally the shortest path to all other IMPs. This procedure sharply reduced the looping that had begun plaguing the ARPANET under the previous routing protocol. McQuillan, Richer, and Rosen called their Dijkstra-based algorithm a shortest-path-first (SPF) algorithm. It was the first link state protocol widely used in a packet switching network.

The second routing protocol was used in the ARPANET for eight years, until once again problems arose due to the inability of the algorithms to scale to the continued network growth. But this time, the SPF algorithms were unchanged; it was only the adaptive metric calculation that was problematic.

The three factors that the previous protocol used to calculate delay were queuing delay (represented by the difference between transmit time and arrival time), link propagation delay (based on the constant), and link transmission delay (based on packet length and line speed). Under low traffic loads, the effect of the queuing delay was negligible. Under medium loads, the queuing delay becomes a more significant factor but results in reasonable shifts in the traffic flows. Under heavy loads, however, the queuing delay becomes the major factor in the computation of the metric. At this point, the queuing delay could cause route oscillations.

---

[24] This protocol used circular sequence numbering, as described in Section 2.2.2. For a facinating story of how a simple corruption of a couple of sequence number bits brought down the ARPANET on October 27, 1980, read Eric C. Rosen, "Vulnerabilities of Network Control Protocols: An Example," RFC 789, 1981.

Take, for example, the network of Figure 1.2. Two links, A and B, connect two regions of the network; all traffic between the "east" and "west" regions must use one of these two links. If most routes use link A and the load across the link is heavy, the queuing delay for that link becomes high, and a high delay value will be advertised to all the other nodes. Because the other nodes run their SPF calculations more or less simultaneously, they will simultaneously come to the same conclusion: that A is overloaded and B is a better path. All traffic then shifts to B, causing B to have a high delay; at the next measurement, B's high delay is advertised and all routes shift back to the now underutilized A. A is now seen as overloaded, traffic switches again to B, and so on; the oscillations could go on indefinitely. At each shift, the load causes a large change in the link metrics and as a result as soon as the shift occurs the metrics that caused the shift become obsolete.

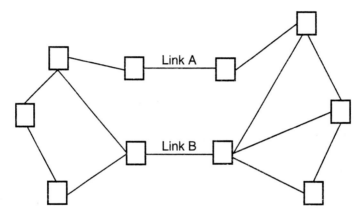

Figure 1.2   The original adaptive metric calculation of the second ARPANET routing protocol could cause
route oscillations between parallel links such as A and B shown here.

To address the problem, in 1987 a new metric calculation algorithm designed by Atul Khanna, John Zinky, and Frederick Serr of BBN was deployed.[25] The new algorithm was still adaptive, and still used a 10-second average delay measurement. Under light to medium loads, its behavior was not very different from the previous metric algorithm. The improvement was seen in how the algorithm operated under heavy loads. The metric is no longer delay but a function of delay, and the range of metric variation is confined so that in a homogeneous network the relative metrics between two otherwise equal paths cannot vary by more than two hops—that is, traffic cannot be routed around a congested link over more than two hops. All this is a function of link utilization; when utilization is light, the algorithm behaves as if the metric is delay based, and as utilization increases it behaves as if the metric is capacity based.

While the metric calculation algorithm for the ARPANET was changed, the SPF algorithm underwent only a minor change: Calculations were performed in such a way that

[25] Atul Khanna and John Zinky, "The Revised ARPANET Routing Metric," *Proceedings of the ACM SIGCOMM Symposium*, pp. 45–56, September 1989.

routes were moved off of an overutilized link gradually rather than all at once, reducing the potential for heavy route oscillations.

A description of the metric calculation algorithm itself is impractical for the needs of this book, and that says something about adaptive routing algorithms in general: Distributed adaptive algorithms involve significant complexity to be effective. As a result, most adaptive algorithms used in modern packet switching networks for functions such as traffic engineering are centralized rather than distributed. The link state routing protocols that grew out of the early ARPANET experiences have used fixed rather than adaptive metrics.

Does the Internet Have a Father?

I've always been a little irked when fellow Americans call George Washington the "father of our country." As an ardent admirer of John Adams, I think that his revolutionary and, later, diplomatic efforts earn him the title (although admittedly Adams wasn't a very good president). Others might feel as strongly about Franklin or Jefferson. If we must use paternalistic language at all, "Founding Fathers" is more fair. The sobriquet justly recognizes that the United States was born of the efforts of many people, not one.

So too with the Internet. Vint Cerf is probably called "the father of the Internet" more often than anyone else, but J. C. R. Licklider, Larry Roberts, Len Kleinrock, Bob Kahn, Jon Postel, and others have also been pegged with solitary fatherhood. But singling out the efforts of any one person unfairly belittles the efforts of many, many others. The Internet has no one father but a rather large group of Founding Fathers—and a few Mothers.

In the short history I have presented in this chapter, more of the Internet's founders have gone unmentioned than mentioned. I have drawn from many sources in writing this history, but my most useful reference was the book by Katie Hafner and Matthew Lyon, *Where Wizards Stay Up Late: The Origins of the Internet*.[26] If you want to know more about the birth of the Internet, and who gets credit, I highly recommend this entertaining and informative book.

1.6   The European Invasion

The Network Working Group set the tone for the development of most protocols and procedures associated with the Internet and TCP/IP to this day. From its beginning as a group of graduate students and staffers working at the first four ARPANET sites, worried that their junior status and audacity at suggesting protocol solutions would offend the "real" protocol designers, Internet protocol development has been open, driven from the bottom up, with anyone allowed to participate in the process. RFCs were their means of documentation.

---

[26] Katie Hafner and Matthew Lyon, *Where Wizards Stay Up Late: The Origins of the Internet*, Simon & Schuster, 1998.

"When the RFCs were first produced," Vint Cerf writes, "they had an almost nineteenth-century character to them—letters exchanged in public debating the merits of various design choices for protocols in the ARPANET."[27]

The NWG grew large over the years, and in 1986 they became the Internet Engineering Task Force (IETF). Over the years, the IETF has grown to become the de facto standards body for IP and related protocols. Yet in spite of this, the IETF has never had an official charter; it still operates as a loose organization of kindred spirits dedicated to creating and improving Internet and networking protocols. And although vendors often play a big role in protocol development these days, they still must participate in the IETF working groups, come to the meetings, and present their work for review and criticism just like everyone else.

But the ad hoc spirit of the IETF did not sit well with everyone. Governments, which are (with a few disastrous exceptions) highly structured bureaucracies, prefer that highly structured bureaucracies set their standards. The IETF was hardly that. But, the International Organization for Standardization (ISO) was.[28] The ISO, headquartered in Geneva, was founded in 1946 by the union of two earlier standardization bodies. Its mission is to enhance international manufacturing and trade through agreement on industrial standards, and it sets standards for industries ranging from construction and agriculture to medicine and electronics. ISO standards define screw threads, credit cards, tool safety, and the pictorial symbols seen in airports, along highways, and on toilet doors worldwide.

As experimental packet switching networks began cropping up not only in the United States but in Europe in the 1970s, many governments began to see the need for standardization but wanted the standards to come from a more official body than the IETF. In 1977, the British Standards Institute proposed that the ISO standardize an architecture for communications infrastructures. The ISO set up Subcommittee 16 under Technical Committee 97, and in 1978 the subcommittee proposed the establishment of a reference model to be called the Open Systems Interconnection (OSI) model.[29] The American representative to the ISO, the American National Standards Institute (ANSI), was tasked with developing proposals for the OSI reference model.

At about this same time, Mike Canepa and Charlie Bachman at Honeywell had been working on an architecture for distributed databases. Drawing from work done by IBM in 1974 on their Systems Network Architecture, which had seven layers, the Honeywell team proposed in 1978 a seven-layer architecture for interconnecting computers called the Honeywell Distributed Systems Architecture (HDSA). When ANSI met in Washington in March 1978 to consider proposals for the OSI model, Canepa and Bachman presented HDSA. It was the only proposal presented, and ANSI adopted their model as the now-famous seven-layer OSI reference model.

---

[27] Vint Cerf, "RFCs—The Great Conversation," in RFC Editor et al., "30 Years of RFCs," RFC 2555, April 1999.

[28] You might notice that the acronym ISO does not match the English name. That is because it is not actually an acronym; it is a name. ISO is derived from the Greek *isos*, meaning "equal." This was chosen so that the acronym would not vary from language to language. The organization is always ISO, in any country.

[29] ISO/TC97/SC16, "Provisional Model of Open Systems Architecture," Doc. N34, March 1978.

Work then began to establish protocols compliant to the OSI model. European governments and the European Commission put their weight behind the ISO work rather than the IETF; in the United States, although the military had adopted TCP/IP, the civilian sector under the Department of Commerce was expected to support the ISO protocols. And when the ISO finally produced a preliminary set of protocols in 1988, the U.S. government adopted the OSI protocols even though TCP/IP had been in operation for five years and the OSI protocols had yet to be implemented.[30]

With massive government backing, it seemed inevitable that the OSI protocols would replace TCP/IP. Throughout the late 1980s and early 1990s, the OSI community viewed TCP/IP as nothing more than an academic experiment. Yet in the end TCP/IP became the Internet standard, and OSI died on the vine.

The prevalence of TCP/IP can be partly attributed to the widespread popularity of the UNIX operating system, versions of which began including TCP/IP as early as 1981. But the biggest reason for the acceptance of TCP/IP has to do with the personalities of the IETF and the ISO. The IETF was interested in practical solutions, whereas the ISO was trying to develop protocols that would fit into a predetermined reference model. As the IETF merrily surged ahead under its credo of "rough consensus and running code," implementing first and then standardizing what worked and abandoning what didn't, the ISO committees plodded along developing standards before getting to implementation. Throughout Europe, supposedly the bastion of OSI, universities became impatient with waiting for the ISO and increasingly adopted TCP/IP.

However, one protocol arose out of the OSI work that remains important to the Internet to this day: IS-IS.

1.7   Separate But Equal

OSI appealed to governments, telcos, and other organizations that were much more comfortable with established standards bodies than with the freewheeling style of the IETF. And because such organizations represented major customer bases, the computer and networking vendors of the time set to work developing OSI-compliant protocol suites. Novell (NetWare), Banyan (VINES), General Motors (MAP and TOP), Apple (AppleTalk), and others scrambled to show how their network operating systems fit into the OSI reference model (sometimes a tight squeeze).

But the company that made the most progress on OSI, and whose protocols became synonymous with OSI protocols, was Digital Equipment Corporation (DEC). DEC had already established their Digital Network Architecture (DNA) in the mid-1970s and had developed four versions of their DECnet software as implementations of DNA. They called each version a phase, specifically DECnet Phases I through IV. In 1987, DEC introduced DECnet Phase V, and began selling products supporting Phase V in 1991.[31] This newest version moved sharply

---

[30] The Government Open Systems Interconnection Profile (GOSIP) was outlined in the Federal Information Processing Standard (FIPS #146), developed by the National Institute of Standards and Technology (NIST).

[31] James Martin and Joe Leben, *DECnet Phase V: An OSI Implementation*, Digital Press, 1992.

away from the earlier versions of DECnet to comply with the OSI model. In 1987, the ISO adopted the work done by DEC, and so DECnet Phase V is mostly indistinguishable from what we now call the OSI protocol suite.

The network routing protocol used by DECnet Phase V, developed at DEC by Radia Perlman, Mike Shand, Dave Oran, and others, was adopted in its entirety by the ISO as IS-IS. "ISO's standard for routing CLNP is known as IS-IS," Perlman writes, "because all the other names (e.g., 10589: 'Intermediate system to Intermediate system Intra-Domain routing information exchange protocol for use in Conjunction...') are worse."[32]

Around the same time in 1987 that the ISO adopted IS-IS, the IETF recognized the need for a link state interior gateway protocol. The NSFNET backbones and the regional networks at the time were either using static routes or, where dynamic routing was needed, RIP. Static routes did not scale for simple management reasons, and RIP was showing many of the vulnerabilities at scale that the early ARPANET Bellman-Ford protocol showed. With the experience gained from developing and operating the ARPANET's SPF protocol, developing a link state IGP for use at larger scales seemed logical.

But this move created two camps in the IETF. One camp looked at IS-IS and decided that it made little sense to develop a new link state protocol when one was already at hand. Why not just extend IS-IS to support TCP/IP? The other camp did not want a protocol that was controlled by an outside body, particularly one as rigidly bureaucratic as the ISO. The IETF approach was proven and familiar, so why not develop an open, nonproprietary version of the ARPANET's SPF—OSPF—to better coexist with the open TCP/IP? A visceral resentment of the ISO's arrogance in dismissing TCP/IP also fed the second camp; IS-IS was unacceptable simply because it was an ISO protocol.

Rather than choose between the competing camps, the IETF decided to compromise by accepting both an extended IS-IS and a home-grown OSPF as separate but equal protocols. An IS-IS Working Group and an OSPF Working Group were formed.

The IS-IS Working Group finished extending IS-IS to support IP in 1990 and called the extended version "Integrated" or "Dual" IS-IS. The IP extensions were published in RFC 1195, authored by Ross Callon, a Digital Equipment Corporation engineer who had previously worked at BBN.[33]

The OSPF Working Group produced their first version of OSPF in October 1989. However, this first version (OSPFv1) revealed several operational problems and some areas where the protocol could be optimized; it was never deployed. The working group revised the protocol, and OSPFv2 was published in RFC 1247, authored by John Moy, in July 1991.[34] Moy worked at Proteon, Inc., an early router manufacturer, and like Callon was an ex-BBN engineer.

OSPF was deployed successfully in several regional networks in 1990, and was demonstrated successfully at INTEROP in October 1991. "It is difficult," Moy wrote, "to create a

[32] Radia Perlman, *Interconnections: Bridges and Routers*, page 268, Addison-Wesley, 1992.

[33] Ross Callon, "Use of OSI IS-IS for Routing in TCP/IP and Dual Environments," RFC 1195, December 1990.

[34] John Moy, "OSPF Version 2," RFC 1247, July 1991.

flashy demonstration of a routing protocol. When the routing protocol is working, one does not really notice that it is there at all."[35]

Throughout the development process, the two working groups borrowed from each other. The concept of a designated router on broadcast networks, for instance, which is used by both OSPF and IS-IS, was first developed for IS-IS. They also both used lessons learned from the ARPANET's SPF protocol. For example, the surprising meltdown of the ARPA-NET on October 27, 1980, described in RFC 789, was partially due to the protocol's circular sequence number space. Both IS-IS and OSPF adopted a linear sequence number space (described in Chapter 2). The working groups also recognized the complexity of adaptive metrics, and specified configurable, nonadaptive metrics.

By the mid-1990s Cisco Systems was well on its way to becoming the dominant commercial supplier of routers for the Internet backbone and regional networks. Cisco began supporting both OSPF and the OSI version of IS-IS in 1991; the following year, they released an implementation of Integrated IS-IS for IP support. But the significant event for IS-IS, leading to its use in service provider networks worldwide, happened in 1994 when Cisco began supporting NLSP.

Novell Networks had some years earlier begun developing a link state protocol for its NetWare network operating system. Under the direction of Neil Castagnoli,[36] Novell released their NetWare Link Services Protocol (NLSP). NLSP was essentially IS-IS adapted for routing Novell IPX. (Radia Perlman joined Novell shortly after NLSP was released, leading to the myth that she created NLSP from IS-IS.)

When Cisco Systems implemented NLSP, it decided to rewrite its IS-IS code to merge the two very similar protocols internally in IOS wherever possible. Dave Katz conducted the rewrite, and the result was a reliable, robust IS-IS implementation. The Cisco OSPF implementation at the time was less refined, and service providers were becoming dissatisfied with it. Partly spurred by the OSI mania of the time, many switched to IS-IS and have been convinced IS-IS users ever since. The Cisco OSPF code has of course become just as reliable, but those experiences in 1994 through 1996 led many to argue even today that IS-IS is a more reliable protocol.

1.8 Conclusion

The ARPANET experiences of the 1970s demonstrated that distance vector protocols—at least those based on Bellman-Ford—do not scale to large networks. Currently, OSPF and IS-IS are the only two open IP protocols that are proven and reliable in large-scale networks. In fact, any router vendor expecting to sell to carriers and Internet service providers must be able to demonstrate carrier-grade implementations of these two protocols.

---

[35] John Moy, *OSPF: Anatomy of an Internet Routing Protocol*, Addison-Wesley, 1998.

[36] Hannes Gredler and Walter Goralski, *The Complete IS-IS Routing Protocol*, Springer, 2005, page 5.

Now that you know something about their origins, the remainder of this book delves into IS-IS and OSPF in depth, comparing and contrasting them, in the hope that you will come away with a deeper knowledge of both and be able to make informed decisions about which protocol is right for your network.

CHAPTER 2

Link State Basics

All current IP routing protocols belong to one of two classes: *vector* protocols or *link state* protocols. RIP, RIPv2, RIPng, Cisco Systems' IGRP and EIGRP, and BGP are vector protocols, whereas OSPF and IS-IS are link state. This chapter presents the fundamental concepts of link state protocols. With these concepts firmly understood, the remaining chapters can then demonstrate how OSPF and IS-IS implement each concept similarly or differently.

The objective of a routing protocol is to create, in each router in a network, a database of reachable destination addresses for the purpose of forwarding packets. Each address in the database is associated with the router interface closest to the destination and possibly the address of the next router on the path toward the destination. This database is called the routing information database (RIB), or simply the routing table. Two mechanisms must be defined for a routing protocol to create the RIB:

- A procedure by which destination addresses and their associated information are communicated between routers
- An algorithm that uses shared information to calculate the shortest path to each destination in the database

The fundamental difference between vector and link state is in how the two classes of protocols implement these two mechanisms. To understand the possible advantages of link state protocols, we first briefly examine vector protocols.

2.1 Vector Protocol Basics

A vector is defined as a quantity that has both magnitude and direction. An IP route is a vector, in which the direction is some egress interface or a next-hop address. How the route's magnitude is defined varies from one protocol to another. It might be a distance measured in router hops (RIP), autonomous system hops (BGP), or a sum of interface characteristics (IGRP and EIGRP). The magnitude might also be a sum of dimensionless interface metrics (OSPF and IS-IS). But stating that a route is a vector is not really useful in differentiating vector protocols from link state protocols. A route derived by either is a vector.

My friend Paul Goyette points out that in virology, a vector is a means of propagation of some pathogen. In fact, the Latin root of the word, *vectus*, means "bearer" or "carrier." For example, a mosquito is a vector that carries malaria from one organism to the next: Mosquito A picks up the malaria virus from organism X and deposits it in organism Y. Mosquito B picks up the virus from organism Y and deposits it in organism Z.

This definition gets us closer to understanding a vector protocol: Update message A picks up route data from router X and deposits it in router Y. Update message B picks up route data from router Y and deposits it in router Z (Figure 2.1).

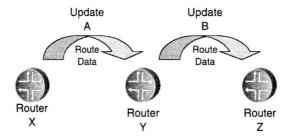

Figure 2.1   Update A and Update B are vectors—carriers of information from one router to another.

Getting back to mosquitoes, the virus that mosquito B takes away from organism Y is not the same virus that mosquito A deposited in organism Y. The deposited virus multiplies and possibly even mutates within the organism before some copy of it is picked up by mosquito B.

Similarly, the route data update message B picks up from router Y is not the same route data that update message A deposited in router Y, even though the route data pertains to the same destination. An algorithm modifies the deposited route data in router Y in such a way that the data reflects that router's position in the network relative to the route's destination.

We have now defined, at a very high level, both the procedure used by vector protocols to communicate destination addresses and their associated information between routers, and the algorithm that uses the information to calculate shortest paths to the destination addresses. Moving with all due prudence away from malarial mosquitoes, let's add more focus to the definitions.

Information for a particular destination prefix originates in some router. The router learns the information in one of three ways:

- The destination prefix is associated with one of the router's attached interfaces.
- The router is manually configured to originate the destination prefix.
- The router learns the destination prefix from another routing protocol.

A vector protocol transmits the destination prefix to its directly connected neighbors. Each neighbor, when it receives the route information, modifies the information in such a way that the route information indicates the distance from that router to the originating router. For example, RIP increases the router hop count by one. The modified route is then added into the router's routing table. Only then is the route sent to that router's own directly connected neighbors, to be modified again by those neighbors.

2.1.1 Vector Protocol Convergence

Figure 2.2 shows how route information is vectored from the originating routers.[1] At time t_0, the only entries in the four routers' routing tables are their directly connected networks, indicated by a hop count of 0. No other information has yet been communicated by the routing protocol.

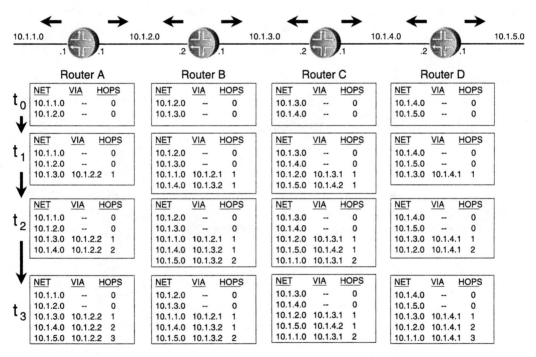

Figure 2.2 Routing information converges in a hop-by-hop manner in a network using a distance vector protocol.

At time t_1, the first updates have been received and processed by the routing protocol, and the results have been entered into the routing tables. Each new time increment represents a new update period, until at time t_3 all four routing tables have all the information needed

[1] Adapted from Jeff Doyle, *CCIE Professional Reference: Routing TCP/IP*, Volume I, Cisco Press, 1998, p. 149–150, with permission from Cisco Press.

to reach all subnets in the network. At this time the routes to all subnets in the network are said to be *converged*.

Processing of the update messages involves two steps. First, the advertised hop count is incremented by one. If router B tells router A that a destination prefix is two hops away from itself, router A increments the hop count to three to indicate its own distance to the destination.

In the second step, the routing protocol compares the received routes and their newly incremented hop counts with the existing routing table entries. If there is no entry for the particular destination address, an entry is made. The entry includes the destination prefix, the distance (hop count), and the address of the neighboring router that sent the advertisement. If the route table already contains an entry for the processed route, the hop counts are compared. If the newly incremented hop count of the received route is equal to or greater than the hop count of the existing entry, no change is made. But if the hop count of the received route is less than the hop count of the existing entry, the entry is replaced by the new route. In this way, the shortest route to each destination is maintained in the routing table.

For example, at time t_1, router B advertises prefixes 10.1.2.0 and 10.1.3.0 to router A, both with a hop count of 0 because the prefixes are directly connected to B. Router A increments the hop counts of both prefixes to 1, and then looks at the entries in its routing table. There is already an entry for 10.1.2.0, and the hop count of the entry is 0. That is less than the route received from B, which now has a hop count of 1, so the received route is dropped. However, there is no entry for 10.1.3.0, so that route is entered into the table along with the hop count and router B's interface address.

The basic vector algorithm described here is more officially called the Bellman-Ford or Ford-Fulkerson algorithm.

2.1.2   Common Characteristics of Vector Protocols

Three important characteristics of all vector protocols can be observed from the preceding example:

- Each router along a path plays a part in the route calculation.
- A router cannot update its neighbors about a route until it has performed its own route calculation.
- If a destination is not directly connected, all a router knows about the destination is what a directly connected neighbor tells it.

Each of these characteristics bears examining, because each can be a disadvantage of vector protocols.

Each router along a route plays a part in the route calculation. Look at router D's entry for subnet 10.1.1.0 in Figure 2.2. The entry indicates that the subnet is three hops away, via router C (10.1.4.1). This entry is the result of A advertising the prefix with a hop count of

0 at time t_0, B advertising the prefix with a hop count of 1 at time t_1, and C advertising the prefix with a hop count of 2 at time t_2. As a result, the calculation of the route to 10.1.1.0 from router D is a *distributed* calculation—several routers play a role in deriving the route. If any router makes a mistake in its calculation, all subsequent routers inherit the mistake.

A router cannot update its neighbors about a route until it has performed its own route calculation. Router C could not tell D about prefix 10.1.1.0 until it had first incremented the hop count advertised by B, compared the result with its own routing table, and made the appropriate entry for the shortest route. That shortest route entry is then what is advertised to D. This is significant because the processing at each router takes some finite amount of time. If the processing time at each router is t, then the time for a route to be processed across three routers is $3t$, and across six routers $6t$. If the route includes many router hops, the *convergence time*—the time for the last router on the path to correctly enter the route into its routing table—can be unacceptably long.

If a destination is not directly connected, all a router knows about the destination is what a directly connected neighbor tells it. All of us have had the experience of having to ask someone for directions. With vector routing protocols, the neighboring router is the guy giving the directions: "You go this-a-way for eight hops. You can't miss it." (I always cringe when someone says I can't miss it, because it invariably means I will.) You have no other information; you must trust that the neighbor giving the directions, whether to an IP subnet or to an antique store in the country, is giving you accurate information. The neighbor might be mistaken, or might even give you intentionally incorrect information.

Two of these characteristics—that all routers along a route participate in the calculation and that a given router only knows what its upstream neighbor tells it—combine to exacerbate the potential for inaccuracy. As a child, you might have played the game variously known as Gossip or Rumor. The game works best with 10 or more participants. Everyone lines up, and the person at one end of the line whispers some statement into the ear of the next person in line. That person whispers what was heard into the next person's ear, and so on, until the last person in line gets whispered to. That person then says out loud what he or she was told, and the first person says out loud what the original statement was. The end statement is almost always different from the beginning statement, often in very funny ways. "My uncle has three mean hogs" might arrive at the end of the line as "Jeff's uncle is a green tree frog." Slight changes at several hops compound, causing extreme corruption of the original message.

Vector protocols are susceptible to the same sorts of incremental corruption of information, although the end result is seldom funny.

2.1.3 Routing Loops

Distance vector protocols are susceptible to routing loops because of the way routing information converges—each router knows only its directly connected links and what its neighbors tell it. It cannot "see" the entire network topology. This section looks at several tactics used by vector protocols for avoiding routing loops and the limitations of those tactics.

2.1.3.1   Split Horizon

Because vector protocols process updates hop by hop, the updates for a particular destination should always flow *downstream*—that is, away from the destination. Updates should not flow upstream toward a destination; partly because it just does not make sense for a route update to go backward along a route, and more important, because doing so can cause incorrect route calculations.

Suppose router D in Figure 2.3 advertises subnet 10.1.1.0 toward router C. Router C then thinks it has an alternative route to 10.1.1.0, via router D. Under stable conditions, this is harmless. But suppose the real route to 10.1.1.0 becomes invalid. In that case, router C installs an entry in its routing table to 10.1.1.0 with a distance of four hops and pointing toward router D. A packet with a destination on the 10.1.1.0 subnet is then mistakenly forwarded to router D, which of course forwards the packets right back to router C. A single-hop routing loop has formed, and the packet will continue bouncing back and forth between the two routers until its TTL expires. Presumably there would not be just one packet going to the same destination, but a flow of packets. And when each packet in the flow expires in the loop, the packet is retransmitted. You can easily see that such a loop, aside from gobbling up packets, can cause a possibly serious depletion of link and router resources. Many types of packets in modern networks can have quite high TTL values, making the impact of a routing loop that much worse.

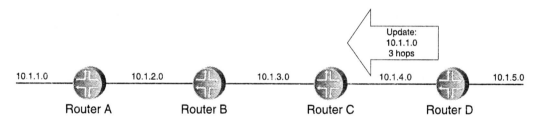

Figure 2.3   A potential one-hop routing loop can develop if updates flow upstream.

Single-hop loops in the simple, linear network of Figure 2.3 are easily prevented with update rules such as *split horizon*, which dictates that an update for a destination must not be sent to the neighbor from which the destination was learned. That is, updates must never be sent upstream, only downstream.

But what about the network in Figure 2.4? Links have been rearranged so that routers B, C, and D and their links form a physical loop. Physical loops in a network are good because they almost always add redundancy. But loops can also be a challenge for vector protocols. When router A advertises subnet 10.1.1.0, its only neighbor is B, and so the update is clearly sent downstream. B advertises the subnet to its neighbors C and D, which are also downstream. But things become murky at routers C and D. As the figure shows, C and D send updates to each other over their shared link. Are the updates being sent downstream from subnet 10.1.1.0 or upstream toward the subnet?

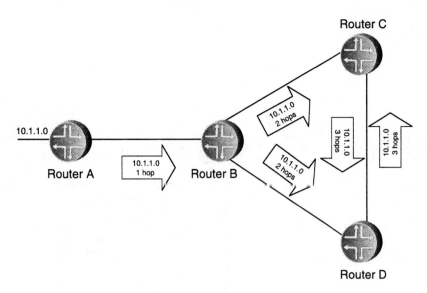

Figure 2.4   Physical loops in a network introduce the possibility of routing loops in distance vector protocols.

Perhaps a sufficient, if not satisfactory, answer is that the updates between C and D are being sent "parallel" to subnet 10.1.1.0. The reality is that in most cases the split horizon rule will take care of any ambiguities in this network. Both C and D will have already made an entry into their routing tables indicating 10.1.1.0 as two hops away via router B. When C receives D's update, and D receives C's update, each router will increment the hop count to 3, see that it is a longer distance than the existing route to 10.1.1.0, and drop the update.

In Figure 2.5, the link between router B and router C is broken. This is where the redundancy of physical loops pays off. Router C knows from the link's Layer 2 protocol that the link has failed and that therefore the route to 10.1.1.0 via next-hop router B is no longer useable. C can then select the next-best route to 10.1.1.0, via router D.

How router C learns of the next-best route depends on the specific vector protocol. RIP and IGRP send periodic unsolicited updates to their neighbors, so C will learn that D has an alternate route at the expiration of D's next update period. If the routers in Figure 2.5 are running BGP, each router stores alternate routes in a table. So C will find the next-best route to 10.1.1.0 via D in its BGP table. If the network is running EIGRP C either has the alternate route in a topology table or will actively query D for a route to 10.1.1.0.[2]

---

[2] If you want to learn more about EIGRP feasible successors and neighbor queries, see Jeff Doyle, *CCIE Professional Development: Routing TCP/IP*, Volume I, Chapter 8, Cisco Press, 1998, or Alvaro Retana, Russ White, and Don Slice, *EIGRP for IP: Basic Operation and Configuration*, Addison-Wesley, 2000.

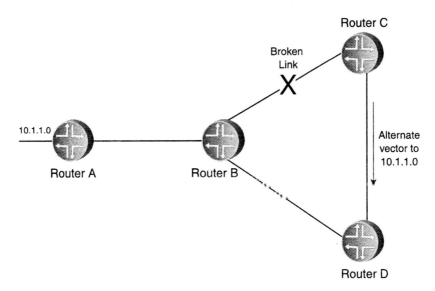

Figure 2.5   Router C can learn an alternate route to 10.1.1.0 when the link between B and C fails.

2.1.3.2   Counting to Infinity

In Figure 2.6, the link between router A and router B has failed. This presents a more interesting case than the failure in Figure 2.5 because it introduces the possibility of some vector protocols becoming confused about the network topology. As with the previous case, router B invalidates the route to 10.1.1.0 as soon as it learns from the Layer 2 protocol that the link to A has failed. All modern IP vector protocols update their neighbors as soon as such a change is detected (called a *triggered* or *flash* update). So, B sends updates to C and D telling them that the route it previously advertised to 10.1.1.0 is no longer valid. Most of the time, these triggered updates cause a reasonably fast network reconvergence. But given the right circumstances, things can go wrong.

Imagine a very small time period in which two things happen (Figure 2.7):

- D sends a periodic unsolicited update to C before it processes the update from B.
- C receives and processes the update from B before receiving the update from D.

Router C has already processed the update from B and knows that 10.1.1.0 is no longer reachable through that neighbor. But then it receives the update from D, claiming it can reach 10.1.1.0 2 hops away. C assumes this information is accurate (remember, a vector protocol only knows what its neighbors tell it), and makes an entry in its routing table indicating that the previously unreachable 10.1.1.0 is now reachable via D, three hops away.

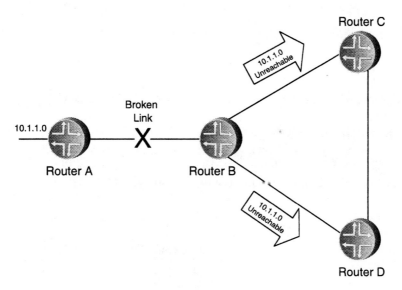

Figure 2.6 Router B notifies C and D that 10.1.1.0 is unreachable when the link between A and B fails.

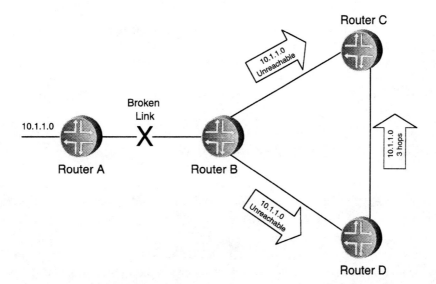

Figure 2.7 When a link is broken in a vector protocol network, routing complications can result because of the timing of updates.

The new route at C triggers an update to B, which now thinks 10.1.1.0 is reachable from C, four hops away. B updates D, which records the subnet reachable via B, five hops away. D then sends this information to C. When C receives this new update, the route is compared with the existing route table entry. The existing entry says that 10.1.1.0 is three hops away, whereas the new route shows the same subnet six hops away. However, both the existing route and the new route came from router D. Therefore, C must assume that the new entry describes the same route, and that the distance has increased for some unknown reason. So, C replaces the existing route with the new one. Another consequence of "I only know what my neighbors tell me."

C then updates B, which increments its route to seven hops and updates D, which increments its route to eight hops and updates C, and so on. Because this circular pattern of updates could go on, theoretically, until the hop count reaches to infinity, the problem is called *counting to infinity*. The ill effects of counting to infinity can be limited by defining a finite value at which a route is considered unreachable. RIP, for example, defines an unreachable route as being 16 hops. In our example, the first router to increment the route to 16 hops marks the route as unreachable and then updates its downstream neighbor that the route is unreachable. Such a procedure eventually stops the counting to infinity loop, but it does not prevent the loop. Any packet with a destination address belonging to subnet 10.1.1.0 that arrives at any one of the three routers in Figure 2.7 is routed in a loop until the routers conclude that the route is unreachable.

2.1.3.3   Holddown Timers

A solution for preventing the counting to infinity problem is a holddown timer. If a router learns a route from a neighbor and then hears from that same neighbor that the route has become unreachable, a holddown timer is set for the route. Until the timer expires, the router will not accept any new information about that destination unless either

- The information comes from the same neighbor that announced that the route was unreachable; or
- Another neighbor advertises a route to the destination with a distance that is equal to or less than the distance of the original route.

In our example, C would have set a holddown timer on the route to 10.1.1.0, and would not have accepted the update with a higher hop count from D. By the time the timer expired, D would know that 10.1.1.0 is unreachable.

The problem with holddown timers is that they come with a price. The holddown period is 180 seconds for RIP, and 280 seconds for IGRP. As a result, holddown timers can drastically increase network convergence time. Suppose the same link failure happened in the network shown in Figure 2.8. Here, router D actually does have an alternate route to 10.1.1.0. Because the alternate route through D has a higher hop count that the broken route through B, however, C will not accept D's route for at least three minutes. 10.1.1.0 is unreachable to any hosts or additional network segments connected through C for the duration of the holddown period.

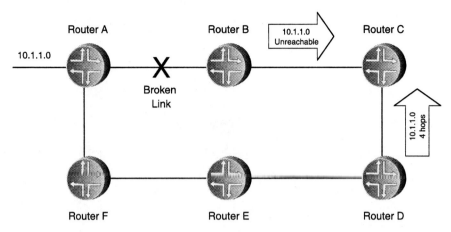

Figure 2.8   Router C will not accept Router D's alternate route to 10.1.1.0 until the holdown timer
has expired.

2.1.3.4 EIGRP Tactics

EIGRP uses an alternative convergence algorithm known as the diffusing update algorithm
(DUAL) that is specifically designed to perform distributed routing calculations while maintaining freedom from loops at every instant. EIGRP does not send periodic updates, which
was the core cause of the loop in the previous example. Instead, it maintains a topology table
in which routes from neighbors, within certain distance limits, are kept. The best of these
feasible routes is selected and added to the routing table. If the router learns that a route has
become invalid, it looks in the topology table for an alternate route. Keeping a set of alternative routes at the ready means that EIGRP can often reconverge faster than protocols that
must wait for an update.

A route advertised by a neighbor is only considered feasible and added to the topology
table if the distance from the neighbor to the destination is shorter than the router's own
shortest distance to the destination. This selection rule, called the *feasibility condition*, is key
to loop avoidance: If my neighbor's advertised distance to a destination is less than my own
shortest distance to the destination, the neighbor's route cannot possibly loop through me.
The feasibility condition is applied in Figure 2.9. Router A has chosen the route through B,
at a cost of 20 (B's advertised distance of 15 plus the link cost of 5) as its shortest path to
destination X. Router A has also selected the route through router C as a feasible route and
placed it into the EIGRP topology table, because C's advertised distance of 18 is lower than
A's distance of 20.

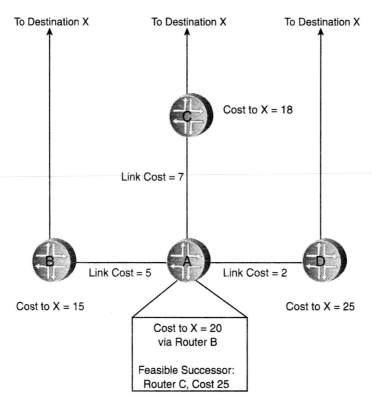

To Destination X   To Destination X   To Destination X

Cost to X = 18

Link Cost = 7

B   Link Cost = 5   A   Link Cost = 2   D

Cost to X = 15   Cost to X = 25

Cost to X = 20
via Router B

Feasible Successor:
Router C, Cost 25

Figure 2.9   With EIGRP, router A selects route B as its shortest path to destination X, and router C as a feasible route to be used as an alternative if the route through B becomes invalid.

The absence of an alternative route in the topology table does not necessarily mean that no alternative route exists. Router D in Figure 2.9 also has a valid route to destination X. But because D's distance to X is 25, which is higher than A's distance to X, the route is not considered feasible and is not added to the topology table. But what happens if the route through B fails, and either the alternate route through C also fails or does not exist? If A looks into its topology table and finds no feasible successor to the failed route through B, it sends a query to each of its downstream neighbors asking them for a route to X. The neighbor then looks into its own topology table for a feasible successor. If it finds one, it sends a reply to the querying router with the route information. If it does not find a feasible successor, it in turn queries its own downstream neighbors. If it has no downstream neighbors, it sends a reply saying so.

So when a router queries its neighbors for a route to a destination, either it will receive one or more replies with alternative routes or, if there are no alternative routes, the queries will reach the edges of the EIGRP domain where there are no more neighbors to query and replies will come back empty. A querying router waits until it has received a reply from every queried neighbor before choosing a new route or declaring that the destination is unreachable.

DUAL makes EIGRP a decided improvement over RIP and IGRP, but it has two possible drawbacks. The first is that EIGRP is a proprietary protocol, so an EIGRP domain is an all-Cisco domain. Whether this is an issue varies from one network operator to another, depending on their preferences.

The second drawback is that although EIGRP works well in small to medium networks, it can begin to exhibit scalability problems as a network grows very large. Queries can take a long time to return, causing slow convergence. And in extreme cases, a query might take so long to return that the querying router will decide that the query is lost, and declare the neighbor to whom the query was sent *stuck in active* (SIA). When that happens, the router clears its adjacency to the neighbor and drops all routes learned from the neighbor, resulting in sometimes serious network stability problems.

There are two solutions to an EIGRP network prone to SIAs. The first is to increase the time that a router waits for replies to queries. This works as long as queries are just slow and not actually being lost, but it increases convergence time. The second solution is to break up the network into areas. However, EIGRP has no facility for easily doing this. Instead, multiple EIGRP processes must be used, and careful design and operational procedures are needed to control traffic in such a network.

Are Link State Protocols Better Than EIGRP?

EIGRP is a fine protocol in networks up to a medium size. In fact, some theoretical studies done by J. J. Garcia-Aceves Luna argue that DUAL converges faster than link state protocols, and with less processing required. I do not know whether this has ever been demonstrated in an operational network, but the fact is that EIGRP does converge quickly in small to medium-sized networks and without loops. The real deciding factor is that it is proprietary to Cisco Systems. This might be important to some, and not to others.

2.1.3.5 BGP Tactics

BGP has a very simple loop-avoidance mechanism. Its basic measure of distance is the autonomous system hop. But rather than measure this distance in autonomous system (AS) hop counts, it associates with each destination prefix a route attribute called AS_PATH. This attribute is a list, sequenced or unsequenced, of the AS numbers of all autonomous systems that a route passes through. To find a shortest path to a given destination, the router selects the route to the destination with the least AS numbers in the AS_PATH.[3] AS numbers are globally unique, so no two numbers for different autonomous systems should be the same. As a router receives a route update from a BGP neighbor, it examines the AS_PATH of each route the update contains. If the router sees its own AS number in a route's AS_PATH, it knows that the route has already passed through its AS once. The route therefore represents a loop, and is dropped.

---

[3] This is a simplification of the actual BGP path selection process, which considers a number of path attributes associated with a given route.

But BGP is designed for advertising routes between autonomous systems, not for advertising routes within a single AS. In other words, BGP is an external gateway protocol, not an internal gateway protocol (IGP). BGP can run internally within an AS, but this is only to communicate routes from one external-facing router at the edge of the AS to another external-facing router at another edge of the AS. It is not used for discovering routes between two destinations within the same AS.

Distance Vector and Path Vector

All of the vector protocols with the exception of BGP are commonly called distance vector protocols. BGP is called a path vector protocol, because it tracks not paths through routers but paths through autonomous systems. Is there really any difference between distance vector and path vector? At least one acquaintance likes to differentiate them by saying that a distance vector route is a sum of quantities, whereas path vector is a sequence of quantities. My own opinion is that it is all semantics. Although BGP has a different application than an IGP, and does indeed describe its routes as a series of AS numbers, it is still a distance vector protocol.

2.2   Fundamental Link State Concepts

To recap, the two most serious problems with most vector protocols are:

- They sometimes converge slowly.
- They are vulnerable to loops.

This section looks at the basics of link state routing, with emphasis on how it avoids these two problems.

Slow convergence in vector protocols is due to the hop-by-hop, distributed calculation of routes. The more routers on a route—the larger the network is—the longer the convergence time. Suppose that instead of having to perform a route calculation before passing along the results of the calculation, a router could pass an update along to its downstream neighbors as soon as it is received, and then perform its route calculation on a copy of the update afterward? The improvement in convergence time is apparent: Routing information can be sent throughout the routing domain almost as fast as the routers can forward it. Convergence can then happen in all routers at almost the same time.

What is the nature of the shared routing information used in such a forward-then-calculate scheme? If the routing information is received and forwarded before a calculation is performed, the information must be independent of the calculation. In other words, each router along a route is performing a local calculation independent of any other router's calculation, and the result of each router's calculation is not shared with other routers. If the calculations are local, it is imperative that all routers along a route derive the same conclusions so that packets are forwarded consistently. Therefore, the information must be exactly the same for each router. No router can alter the information in any way as it is passed along.

But the information must be originated somewhere. A route always pertains to some destination address, so it makes sense that the originator of the information is the router directly attached to the destination. It makes sense for another reason, too: If no router is sharing the results of its route calculations with any other router, the only thing it can know before any calculation is itself and its directly connected links.[4]

So, then, the shared information is an announcement[5] by a router identifying itself in some way, and identifying the addresses of the links attached to it.

It is not enough, however, for some router a number of hops away from the destination to receive an announcement of, "I am router A, and I have a directly connected subnet of X." The receiving router must still know how to reach router A. Therefore, every router in the network must send an announcement identifying itself, its links, and the cost associated with each link.

One final piece of information must be included in the individual announcements for everything to work properly: Each router must not only identify itself and its directly connected links, but must also identify any directly connected neighboring routers on those links. Neighbors are easily identified if every router transmits messages—Hello messages—on its links announcing its presence, and listening for Hellos from neighboring routers on the links. As long as the Hellos are never forwarded off of a local link, receiving routers can be sure Hellos are from neighbors.

We now have enough details to begin describing a high-level framework for a link state routing protocol:

- Every router in a network sends Hello messages on its local links and listens for Hellos, to discover neighboring routers.
- Every router sends an announcement identifying itself, its directly connected links, and its directly connected neighboring routers.
- Every router receiving an announcement keeps a copy of the announcement in a database, and forwards the announcement to its downstream neighbors.
- When a router has a copy of an announcement from every other router in its database, it can accurately calculate routes to destinations.

Figure 2.10 shows how a router might use the database of announcements to determine a route to a destination. The database shown contains the announcements each of the four routers has originated. The announcement from A, for example, shows that it has directly connected links 10.1.1.0 and 10.1.2.0, and a neighbor B. Because all four announcements

---

[4] The router might also know about routes it has learned from other routing protocols.

[5] OSPF calls these announcements link state advertisements (LSAs), whereas IS-IS calls them link state protocol data units (LSPs).

have been forwarded to all four routers, each of the four routers has a database that looks exactly like the one shown.

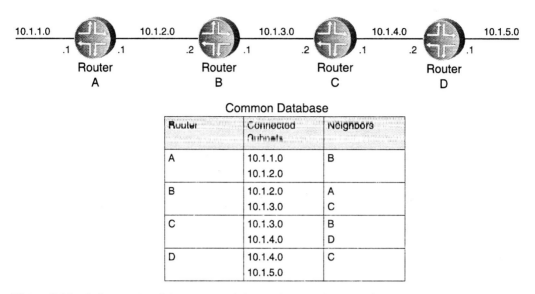

Figure 2.10   Each router in a link state network has the identical database of routes.

The information in the database is like pieces of a jigsaw puzzle. Without looking at the diagram of the network at the top of Figure 2.10, you can deduce what the network looks like. Router A announced that it has a neighbor B, and B announced that it has a neighbor A. They each are directly connected to subnet 10.1.2.0, so you know that they are connected on this subnet. In the same way, you can look at the announcements of B and C and see that they are connected on subnet 10.1.3.0.

Using such deductions, each router can use the database to form a picture of the entire network. From the picture, the router can make entries into its routing table. Router D, for instance, can not only immediately see that subnet 10.1.1.0 is attached to router A, it can see all the routers on the path to A. Therefore, it can make an entry in its database that 10.1.1.0 is reachable via router C, three hops away.

This "picture" of the network also reduces the problem of loops. Vector protocols are vulnerable to loops because all a vector protocol router knows about a network is its directly connected links and what its neighbors tell it. But a link state router, because it knows the complete topology of the network, is much less susceptible to these kinds of loops.[6]

Because the routers use the database to maintain state concerning the links and routers in the network, the protocol is called *link state*.

---

[6] Link state protocols can be susceptible to looping or other routing inaccuracies while announcements of topology changes are being flooded but the announcements have not yet reached all databases, because during this transition time the rule that all databases must be identical is broken.

Having described how a link state protocol works at a simplistic level, it is now time to describe the four fundamental concepts of link state protocols. Those concepts are:

- **Adjacencies**—How two link state routers discover each other and agree to exchange routing information.
- **Flooding**—How routing information is forwarded reliably to all routers in a network.
- **The link state database**—How routing information is stored and kept accurate.
- **SPF calculations**—How a router actually uses the information in the link state database to calculate routes.

2.2.1   Adjacencies

Before link state routers can begin sending and receiving announcements and building their databases, they must be able to identify their neighbors. And it is not enough to just identify directly connected routers; in some networks, routers might be speaking several routing protocols. A router running a specific link state protocol must be able to find just those directly connected routers running the same protocol. And even this requirement is not good enough. Within the domain of a single routing protocol, there can be constraints on which routers are allowed to exchange route information.

So far I have used the term *neighbor* loosely, but now I will give you a tighter definition: Two routers are neighbors if they should be exchanging route information using a common protocol. If two routers have identified each other as neighbors, each has verified that the other is aware of it, and both have verified that no condition exists that would prevent the exchange of route information,[7] the neighbors are *adjacent*.

Prerequisite to the operation of a link state protocol is the ability for every router to identify itself. Therefore, each link state router has a router ID (RID), which is an address unique to each router within a single routing domain. The router ID can be administratively assigned, or it can be automatically derived by some means such as using an interface address. The only requirement is that it must be different from the ID used by any other router in the domain, and it must be consistent—a router cannot identify itself differently to different neighbors.

To identify itself and to discover neighbors, a link state protocol uses *Hello* messages (an appropriately cheerful name for a protocol used between neighbors). At the least, a Hello message includes the ID of the router that originated the message. The Hello also includes information specific to the routing protocol and relevant to the sending router such as timer settings, interface parameters, and authentication information. Such information is used to ensure, before forming an adjacency, that the two routers are in agreement:

---

[7]   An example of a condition in which neighbors recognize each other as speaking the same routing protocol but cannot exchange information is one in which authentication is used but the routers do not have the same passwords. Chapter 9, "Security and Reliability," discusses protocol authentication.

- About how to exchange information and maintain their adjacency,
- That the information can be exchanged reliably,
- And that the neighbors can trust each other.

When a routing protocol is enabled on a router, there is usually some method of specifying which connected links—from one link to all links—are to be included in the protocol operations. Link state protocols then transmit Hello messages on these links at some regular interval. The messages must be broadcast or multicast, so that any as-yet-undiscovered neighbors will hear them. Because the Hello protocol is used to discover only directly connected neighbors, it is important that no Hello message is ever forwarded beyond the link on which it is transmitted. The originating router can ensure this by methods such as setting the TTL of the IP packet containing the message to 1 or using a multicast address that is specifically scoped to a single link.

When a router receives a Hello from a neighbor, it cannot assume that the neighbor has also received its Hellos. If I am router A, and receive Hellos from router B, before I can establish an adjacency I need some indication that B is also receiving my Hellos. Even though I am receiving B's Hellos, it is possible that some sort of half-break in the link is preventing my Hellos from arriving at B. Or, B might be receiving my Hellos and rejecting them for reasons such as packet corruption, incompatible link parameters, or unacceptable protocol parameters within the Hello. Therefore, there must be a procedure by which two-way communication can be verified by both routers. This procedure is called *handshaking*.

An easy way to verify two-way communication is for each router to include in its Hellos on a link a list of all routers from which it has received Hellos on that link. Router A in Figure 2.11 has received a Hello from router B. In its next Hello, A includes B's router ID. When router B receives this Hello, it sees its ID and knows that A is aware of it. Router B responds in kind by including A's ID in its Hellos. When A sees its ID in B's Hellos, it knows B is aware of it. Now both routers have verified two-way communication, and are adjacent. This method of handshaking is called *three-way handshaking*.

After an adjacency is formed, Hellos serve as keepalives for the adjacency. One of the protocol parameters that a router can include in its Hello messages is a specification of how often it sends Hellos. A receiving router then knows how often to expect Hellos from that neighbor. If the specified time period elapses without the reception of a Hello (allowing some extra time for lost Hellos), a router can assume that the neighbor is no longer active on the link and therefore the adjacency with that neighbor is invalid. Depending on the link state protocol, the Hello period between routers might be predetermined and non-negotiable, the routers might be able to negotiate a Hello period, or the Hello periods of the two routers might be independent (each router just accepts its neighbor's period).

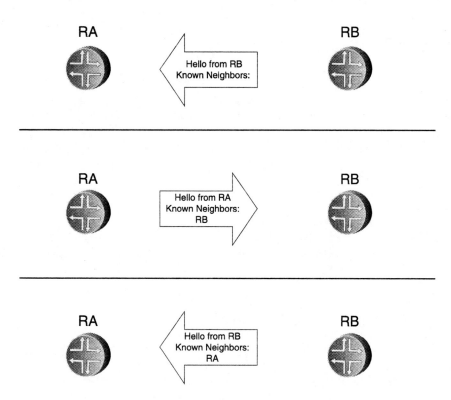

Figure 2.11   Three-way handshaking is used to verify two-way communication.

Are Link State Protocols Always Better than Distance Vector Protocols?

In large networks, there is little question that link state protocols perform better, converge faster, and offer more tools for scaling the network. But writing a stable implementation of OSPF or IS-IS is difficult, and a new implementation might take years to mature. Some implementors might never get it right. RIP, on the other hand, is very easy to implement. This makes the protocol useful at the edges of OSPF and IS-IS networks, for speaking to old routers or routers with poor link state implementations, or where you only need simple routing and do not want to expose your link state protocol to certain routers. And, of course, in a network with just a few routers and a simple topology, RIP will serve your needs quite well.

2.2.2   *Flooding*

Within a network of adjacent routers, each router originates an announcement of its directly connected links and neighbors. As you have already seen, every router in the network must receive every announcement and record a copy in its database. The process of getting the announcement to every router is called *flooding*. Flooding in the network shown in Figure 2.10 is an easy process: Each router sends its announcement to all of its adjacent neighbors, and each of these neighbors forwards a copy of the announcement to each of its own adjacent neighbors. If split horizon is practiced (no router sends an announcement back to the neighbor it received the announcement from), every router gets a copy of every announcement and the flooding then stops.

The network in Figure 2.12 presents more of a challenge for flooding because of all the loops. Just as split horizon rules are insufficient to stop the looping of vector protocol updates in such a topology, split horizon rules are insufficient to control the flooding of link state announcements. A better process is needed to stop the flooding of an announcement after all routers have a copy.

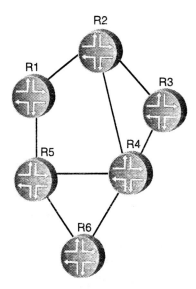

Figure 2.12   A well-meshed network poses challenges for flooding.

There are other considerations beyond just knowing when to stop flooding. If a router originates an announcement and then fails, how do the other routers know that its announcement no longer is valid? If a router receives differing announcements from the same router, which announcement should be believed? If an announcement becomes corrupted either in transit or in a database, how can a router detect the corruption?

Three mechanisms used to create a more reliable flooding process are aging, sequence numbers, and checksums.

2.2.2.1 Timely Flooding: Aging

One of the essential concepts of a link state protocol is that the information in every router's database must be the same as the information in every other router's database. To guarantee "sameness," no router can modify another router's announcement. That means that every router is responsible for its own announcements.

What happens, then, if a router fails after flooding an announcement? If the failure is due to a link problem, the neighbors on the link will detect the failure through the Layer 2 protocol. If the failure is a protocol daemon or the router itself, neighbors will detect the failure through the loss of Hello messages. In either case, the effected neighbors send new announcements indicating the change.

But now there can be a dilemma. If router A fails, nonadjacent routers receive announcements from A's adjacent neighbors indicating the loss of A. But these routers also still have A's link announcement in their databases. What should be done with those announcements? Can the other routers safely deduce that A has failed and remove A's announcement? Is this a violation of the rule that no router can modify another router's announcement? And more important, how can each router be confident that all other routers have removed the announcement, to preserve database consistency?

To help resolve this dilemma, link state protocols include an age field in each link announcement. When a router originates an announcement, it sets a value in the age field. This value is changed (either incremented or decremented)[8] by other routers during flooding, and by every router as the announcement resides in its database. Some absolute value is specified in the protocol at which, if the age reaches this value, the announcement is declared invalid or "aged out," and is deleted from the database. The originating router is responsible for sending a new copy of the announcement at some time prior to this age expiration. The origination of a new announcement is called a *refresh*. In our example scenario, router A's announcement ages out in all databases because A is no longer refreshing the announcement. Every router in the network then has some assurance that as it deletes A's announcement, all of the other routers are also deleting the announcement.

An age counter can be either up-counting or down-counting. An up-counting age is less flexible because it is set between two absolutes: zero and the maximum age specified in the protocol design. On the other hand, a down-counting age can start at some arbitrary value, bounded at the upper end only by the size of the age field, and counts down to zero. This flexibility has some implication for protocol scalability, and discussed further in Chapter 8.

2.2.2.2 Sequential Flooding: Sequence Numbers

Whenever a router receives a link announcement, it sends a copy out each of its downstream interfaces. It is obvious in a well-meshed[9] network such as the one depicted in Figure 2.12 that an announcement will be replicated numerous times during flooding, and as a result some routers will receive multiple copies of the same announcement. If all announcements arrive at the same time, any announcement can be chosen. Of course, delays across different

---

[8] OSPF increments the age, whereas IS-IS decrements it.

[9] A well-meshed network is one in which no single link or interface failure can isolate a router.

network paths back to the originator are going to vary, so in most cases the multiple copies of the same announcement arrive at different times. In this case, the router might simply accept the announcement with the lowest age, on the grounds that the lowest age indicates the newest announcement.

However, accepting the announcement with the lowest age assumes that the multiple announcements contain the same information. Suppose that very soon after a router originates an announcement a link changes state, prompting a new announcement. It is entirely possible that delay variations in the network could cause the second announcement to arrive with a greater age than the first announcement, causing the second announcement to be incorrectly dropped. Therefore, age is not a reliable determinant for choosing the most recent announcement. A second value, the sequence number, specifies the most recent version of a router's announcement. Given two announcements from the same router, the announcement with the higher sequence number is newer.

As with aging, the design of the sequence counter is important. The simplest sequence numbering scheme is a linear one: A sequence number starts at zero, and increments up to some maximum. For example, a 32-bit sequence number (used by both OSPF and IS-IS) can range from zero to 2^{32}, or about 4.3 billion. If a router always starts numbering its announcements at sequence number one, this many available numbers should last far beyond the lifetime of the router. Even if a router produces a new announcement every second—a sign of a very unstable link— the maximum sequence number would not be reached for more than 130 years. Presumably someone would repair the instability before then.

What if a router does, for some reason, reach the maximum sequence number? In such a case the router must go back to sequence number 1. The problem is that the last announcement with a high sequence number still resides in databases across the network. If a new announcement is sent with a sequence number of 1, that announcement will be viewed by other routers as an older announcement and will be rejected. To avoid this situation, the router must wait until the existing announcement ages out of all databases. This is unacceptable, because while waiting for the age timer to expire—which can be one hour or longer—a possibly incorrect announcement continues to be used for route calculations.

There are several possible approaches to this potential problem. One approach is to just do nothing, trusting that with a large enough sequence number space the maximum sequence number will never be reached. The trust here is not that no router or routing protocol is going to remain in uninterrupted service for more than a century, but that no glitches in the protocol daemon will cause the generation of a very high sequence number, introducing the possibility of counting up to the maximum number soon after.

A better approach is for the router cycling its sequence numbers back to the beginning to first cause its previous announcement to be deleted from all databases. The router can do this by issuing another copy of the announcement with the maximum sequence number, but with the age set to a value indicating that the announcement's age has expired (MaxAge or 0, depending on whether the age counter is up-counting or down-counting). But remember that when comparing two otherwise identical announcements, the router chooses the one with the lower age. Therefore, the rules must be modified a bit, so that an "aged-out" announcement is always accepted over an identical announcement of any other age.

Of course, there is still a period between when the artificially aged-out announcement is sent and the time the new announcement is installed in all databases. Certainly, it is a far smaller period than just waiting for the announcement to age out normally, but it is still a period during which the originating router is not correctly accounted for in the databases.

So, a third approach to prevent reaching the end of the sequence number space is to create a space in which there is no end: a circular sequence number space. For example, if there is a 32-bit sequence number space, the number after 4,294,967,295 is 0. However, there is the potential for confusion in this scheme. Suppose two announcements are received from a router, one of which has a sequence number of 0xFFFFFFFC and one with a sequence number of 0xFFF10D69. The sequence numbers are not contiguous; so is the first announcement newer, or has the sequence number wrapped, making the second number higher?

A couple of rules can reduce the chance of such confusion. Given some sequence number space of n and two sequence numbers a and b, a is considered larger under either of the following conditions:

- $a > b$, and $(a - b) < n/2$
- $a < b$, and $(b - a) > n/2$

Figure 2.13 shows a diagram of a 6-bit sequence number.[10] A 6-bit space means that

$$n = 2^6 = 64$$

and

$$n/2 = 32.$$

Given two sequence numbers 48 and 18, 48 is more recent because by the first rule

$$48 > 18 \text{ and } (48 - 18) = 30, \text{ and } 30 < 32.$$

Given two sequence numbers 3 and 48, 3 is more recent because by the second rule

$$3 < 48 \text{ and } (48 - 3) = 45, \text{ and } 45 > 32.$$

Given two sequence numbers 3 and 18, 18 is more recent because by the first rule

$$18 > 3 \text{ and } (18 - 3) = 15, \text{ and } 15 < 32.$$

---

[10] This example originally was used by the author in *CCIE Professional Development: Routing TCP/IP*, Volume I, Cisco Press, 1998, pp. 167–168.

You can see by comparing the relative positions of the numbers on the graph in Figure 2.13 how the two rules enforce circularity when there is a discontinuity between two sequence numbers.

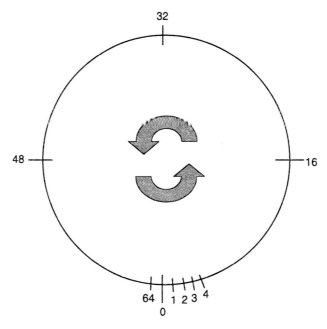

Figure 2.13   Sequence numbers in link state protocols could follow a circular number space.

Although a circular sequence number space seems better than a linear one, an odd series of simultaneous errors in a circular sequence number space can cause a network outage much worse than what sequence number rollover in a linear space causes. This determination is based on a meltdown of the ARPANET on October 27, 1980, when an early link state protocol with a 6-bit circular sequence number space was being used.[11] As a result of that experience, both OSPF and IS-IS use linear sequence numbers.

The last issue with sequence numbers is what happens when a router or protocol restarts and loses all memory of what its last sequence number was. It cannot start again at the beginning, because other routers are likely to have an old announcement from the router in their databases with a higher sequence number, in which case the other routers would reject the new announcement with the lower sequence number. Therefore, another rule is added. When a link state protocol starts, the router sends its announcement with a sequence number of 1 (or whatever the beginning sequence number is for that protocol). If a neighbor has an announcement from the router in its database with a more recent sequence number, it sends a copy of the announcement to the router. The router can then look at the sequence number and begin numbering its new announcements one higher than that number.

---
[11] Eric C. Rosen, "Vulnerabilities of Network Control Protocols: An Example," *Computer Communication Review*, July 1981.

2.2.2.3   Reliable Flooding: Checksums

The importance of having consistent information in all databases within a link state network has been emphasized throughout this chapter. Yet in networks a link state announcement can become corrupted in many ways. An announcement can be changed due to noise on a link, or it can be corrupted while it resides in a router's database. Because of the possibility of the announcement being altered, there should be a mechanism for checking to ensure that the announcement is accurate.

The concern over information corruption certainly extends beyond link state protocols. Most IP packets and messages include error checking, most often in the form of a checksum. A checksum is performed over the entire contents of a link state announcement with the exception of the age field. Because the age changes as the announcement passes through routers during flooding, including it in the checksum would mean recalculating the checksum every time the age changes.

2.2.3   Announcement Headers

We have now discussed several kinds of identifiers associated with a link state announcement. Some identifiers, such as the router ID, are used to differentiate the announcement from other routers' announcements.[12] Other identifiers, such as the sequence number, age, and checksum, are used to differentiate between specific instances of an announcement from the same router.

All of these identifiers are included in a header that precedes the actual route information of the announcement. This way, none of the information in the announcement itself must be examined during the flooding process—only the header must be examined.

There is also another benefit to having such identifiers in a header. When a router must describe to a neighbor what announcements it has in its database, or when a router must request a copy of an announcement from a neighbor, the announcements can be fully described by sending just the header rather than the entire announcement. Why routers would need to describe announcements to or request announcements from neighbors is explained in the next section.

2.2.4   Database Synchronization

You should, by now, have a good understanding of a link state database. Announcements from all routers in the network are flooded, and every router keeps a copy of the most recent announcement from every router (including itself) in the database. You also saw how aging is used to ensure that "orphaned" announcements from missing routers are not kept in the database forever. The age of every announcement is tracked, and if the originating router does not refresh the announcement before the age limit is reached, the announcement is deleted from the database.

---

[12] You will see in later chapters that there are other announcement identifiers, such as a link state ID and link state type.

There is one other procedure concerning the link state database that must be explained. When a new link state router becomes active in a network, it floods its announcement to update the other databases. But how does the router build its own database? Requiring the other routers to reflood their announcements when they see a new router's announcement might be one way, but it is not very efficient or scalable.

Remember that for a link state protocol to work, every router must have exactly the same database. As you saw in the previous section on flooding, extensive safeguards are implemented to ensure that all databases are identical. This fact can be exploited to allow a new router to build its database without requiring extensive reflooding. After the router forms adjacencies with one or more neighbors, it initiates a *database synchronization*. When two routers synchronize their databases, they describe the contents of their databases to each other. If a router sees through its neighbor's descriptions that the neighbor has one or more announcements that are not in its own database, the router can request that the neighbor send it a full copy of the announcement. With the assurance that the new router's neighbors have the exact same database as everyone else's, if the router synchronizes with its neighbor it too now has a complete and consistent database.

This is where the announcement headers discussed in the preceding section come in. Because an announcement is completely differentiated by its header, only the header needs to be sent during the phases of synchronization in which a neighbor is describing the announcements in its database and when a router is requesting a copy of the announcements it does not have.

2.2.5   SPF Calculations

With a complete database, the router can begin calculating a shortest path to all other routers in the network. When a path to all routers is known, a path to any of the routers' connected subnets is also known. In the example of Figure 2.10, it was easy to see how the information in a database is used to visualize a network. But it is easy because we are visual creatures. A database describing a more complex topology, such as the one that was shown in Figure 2.12, is not so easy to visualize. But a router's route processor is not visual, it is a computer and thus needs a well-defined set of mathematical rules for calculating shortest paths from the database.

This set of rules comes from graph theory and was formulated by Edsger W. Dijkstra. A network is viewed as a graph of nodes, in which the routers are the nodes. Keep in mind that we are calculating *shortest* paths, so we need some way to assign a cost to each link connecting two nodes. The sum of the costs across a route is the distance of the route. We could, if we wanted, just use router hops. In this case, each link would have a cost of one hop. But router hops limits us in the ways we can define and control traffic patterns in the network. A better scheme is to assign a dimensionless number to each link, as shown in Figure 2.14. Each number then represents the *cost* of sending a packet out the interface connected to the link. A shortest path is the one in which the total cost of all outgoing interfaces from the source to the destination is the lowest (or "cheapest").

We can now influence the choice of shortest paths and, consequently, traffic flows by manipulating the cost of each link. Notice, too, in Figure 2.14 that the costs assigned to the links do not have to be the same at both ends of the links. The costs are assigned to the router interfaces connecting to the links, and apply to outgoing traffic on those interfaces. This way, traffic flows between two routers across the network can be made asymmetric.

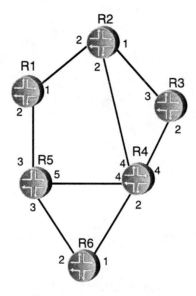

Figure 2.14   A link cost on each path in the network will factor into Dijkstra's algorithm for calculating the shortest-path routing tree in a link state network.

The clearest description of the Dijkstra algorithm for computing shortest paths in a graph of n nodes comes from Dijkstra himself. Do not worry if the set of rules do not make much sense to you; it will be clearer when we apply it to calculating a shortest-path tree.

Construct [a] tree of minimum total length between the n nodes. (The tree is a graph with one and only one path between every two nodes.)

In the course of the construction that we present here, the branches are divided into three sets:

    I. the branches definitely assigned to the tree under construction (they will be in a subtree);

    II. the branches from which the next branch to be added to set I, will be selected;

    III. the remaining branches (rejected or not considered).

The nodes are divided into two sets:

  A. *the nodes connected by the branches of set I,*

  B. *the remaining nodes (one and only one branch of set III will lead to each of these nodes).*

We start the construction by choosing an arbitrary node as the only member of set A, and by placing all branches that end in this node in set II. To start with, set I is empty. From then onwards we perform the following two steps repeatedly.

  Step 1: *The shortest branch of set II is removed from this set and added to set I. As a result, one node is transferred from set B to set A.*

  Step 2: *Consider the branches leading from the node, that has just been transferred to set A, to the nodes that are still in set B. If the branch under construction is longer than the corresponding branch in set II, it is rejected; if it is shorter, it replaces the corresponding branch in set II, and the latter is rejected.*

We then return to step 1 and repeat the process until sets II and B are empty. The branches in set I form the tree required.[13]

Now we can adapt Dijkstra's rules for routers and networks. First, we define the sets. Dijkstra defines three sets of branches: I, II, and III. We define these three sets as follows:

- **Set I: The tree database**—Links (branches) are added to the shortest-path tree by adding them to this database. When the algorithm is finished, this database will contain the shortest-path tree.
- **Set II: The temporary database**—Links are copied from the link state database to this list in a prescribed order, where they become candidates to be added to the tree. When this database becomes empty, we know the calculation is finished.
- **Set III: The link state database**—This is the complete routing database for the network, containing the shortest path to each destination.

Dijkstra also specifies two sets of nodes, A and B, as follows:

- **Set A**—The routers connected to the links in the tree database.
- **Set B**—All other routers. When the calculation is finished, this set will be empty. In other words, all routers will be accounted for in the tree database.

Figure 2.15 shows the network of Figure 2.14 along with the link state database for the network. Each of the entries is in the form [originating router – neighbor, cost to neighbor]. The way to read this database is, for instance, that router R1 has sent an announcement indicating two neighbors: neighbor R2, at a cost of 1, and R5, at a cost of 2. R2 has announced

---

[13] E. W. Dijkstra, "A Note on Two Problems in Connexion with Graphs," *Numerische Mathematik*, Vol. 1, 1959, pp. 269–271.

three neighbors: R1 with a cost of 2, R3 with a cost of 1, and R4 with a cost of 2. Comparing the entries in the database with the diagram of the network, you can see that all adjacencies are accounted for from the perspective of all routers.

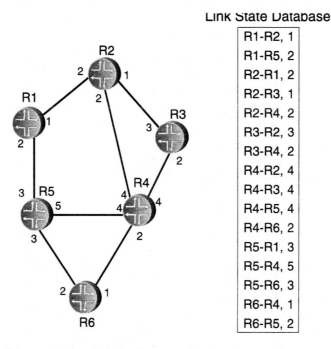

Link State Database

R1-R2,	1
R1-R5,	2
R2-R1,	2
R2-R3,	1
R2-R4,	2
R3-R2,	3
R3-R4,	2
R4-R2,	4
R4-R3,	4
R4-R5,	4
R4-R6,	2
R5-R1,	3
R5-R4,	5
R5-R6,	3
R6-R4,	1
R6-R5,	2

Figure 2.15   The link state database includes all router adjacenies and a cost for each.

Each router then creates a tree database and a candidate database, and performs the following steps:

1. The router adds itself to the tree database as the root of the tree. It shows itself as its own neighbor, with a cost of 0.

2. All entries in the link state database describing links from the root to its neighbors are added to the candidate database.

3. The cost from the root to each node in the candidate database is calculated. The link in the candidate database with the lowest cost is moved to the tree database, along with the cost from the root. If two or more links are an equally low cost from the root, choose one. If any entries are left in the candidate database with a link to the neighbor just moved to the tree, those entries are deleted from the candidate database.

4. The router ID of the neighbor on the link just added to the tree is examined. Entries originated by that neighbor are added to the candidate database, except for entries in which the ID of the neighbor is already in the tree database.

5. If entries remain in the candidate database, return to Step 3. If the candidate database is empty, terminate the calculation. At this time every router in the network
   should be represented as a neighbor on one of the links in the tree database, and
   every router should be represented just once.

For the example network in Figure 2.15, we focus on the Dijkstra calculation that R2
would perform. Figure 2.16 shows the link state database from Figure 2.15, along with the
candidate and tree databases. R2 has added itself to the tree as the root, with a cost of 0,
completing Step 1. R2 then looks into its link state database for all links to neighbors, and
adds those to the candidate database. R2's neighbors are R1, R3, and R4, so these three
entries are added to the candidate list. This completes Step 2.

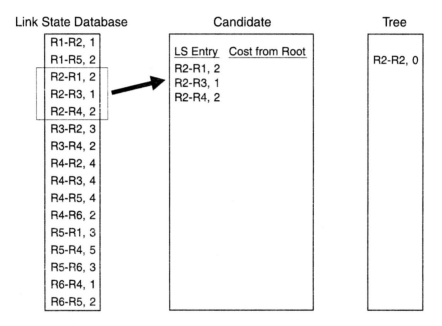

Figure 2.16   R2 begins building its shortest-path tree.

Figure 2.17 shows the completion of the first iteration of Step 3. The cost from the root
to each of the neighbors on the link is calculated. In this case, because the neighbors are
directly connected, the cost is just the cost of the link. The entry with the lowest cost from
the root is then selected, which in this case is the link to R3. This entry is moved from the
candidate list to the tree.

Step 4 is performed in Figure 2.18. Because the link to R3 was added to the tree in the
preceding step, all of the entries in the database showing links to R3's neighbors are examined. R3 has links to R2 and to R4. Because a link to R2 is already in the database, that entry
is ignored. Only the link to R4 is added to the candidate list.

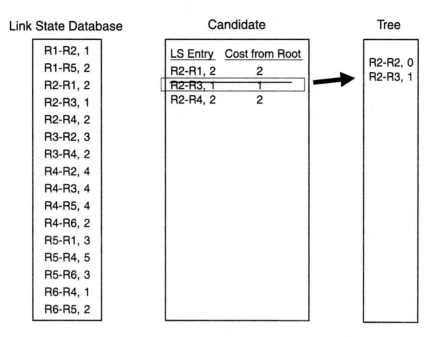

Figure 2.17   When the entry with the lowest path is added to the tree, it is removed from the candidate list.

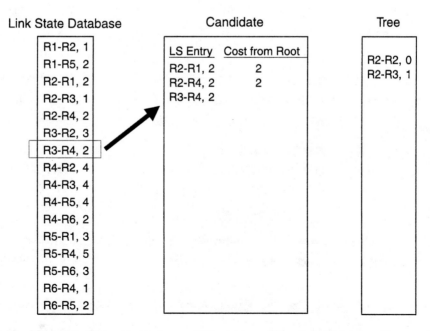

Figure 2.18   R3's path to R4 is added to the candidate database; R3's path to R2 is ignored because a path to R2 already exists in the tree.

Step 5 says that if there are entries in the candidate database, return to Step 3. So, Step 3 is repeated in Figure 2.19. The cost from the root to the neighbor in the new entry is calculated, which is the cost of the link from R2 to R3, shown in the tree database to be 1, and the cost from R3 to R4, which is 2, for a total of 3. The lowest cost from the root in the candidate database is then selected. This time, there are two lowest costs: R2-R1, and R2-R4. Step 3 says that if two or more costs are equal, just select one. So we select R2-R1 and move it from the candidate list to the tree.

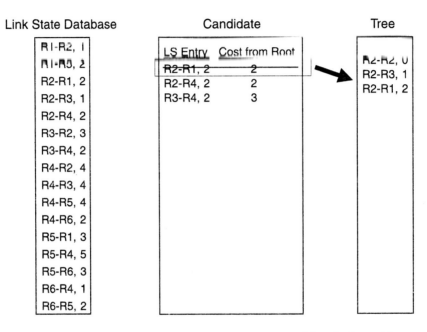

| Link State Database | Candidate | | Tree |

Link State Database:
| R1-R2, 1 |
| R1-R3, 2 |
| R2-R1, 2 |
| R2-R3, 1 |
| R2-R4, 2 |
| R3-R2, 3 |
| R3-R4, 2 |
| R4-R2, 4 |
| R4-R3, 4 |
| R4-R5, 4 |
| R4-R6, 2 |
| R5-R1, 3 |
| R5-R4, 5 |
| R5-R6, 3 |
| R6-R4, 1 |
| R6-R5, 2 |

Candidate:
LS Entry	Cost from Root
R2-R1, 2	2
R2-R4, 2	2
R3-R4, 2	3

Tree:
| R2-R2, 0 |
| R2-R3, 1 |
| R2-R1, 2 |

Figure 2.19   When there are two or more lowest cost entries in the candidate database, pick one to move to the tree database.

Figure 2.20 shows the second iteration of Step 4. R1 was added to the tree in the previous step, so the link state database entries for R1's neighbors, R1-R2 and R1-R5, are examined. R2 is already on the tree, so only the R1-R5 entry is added to the candidate list.

We cycle back to Step 3 again in Figure 2.21. The cost from the root to R5 is 4, which is the cost from R2 to R1 plus the cost from R1 to R5. The costs from root are again examined, R2-R4 is found to have the lowest cost, and it is moved from the candidate list to the tree. Because the shortest path to R4 is now on the tree, the longer R3-R4 link on the candidate list is removed from the candidate list.

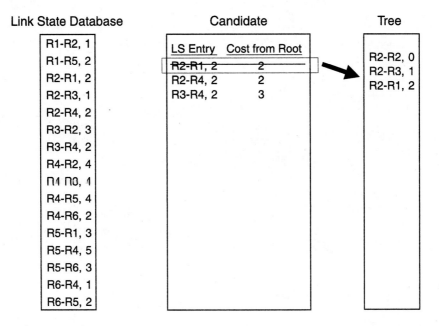

Figure 2.20   R1's path to R5 is added to the candidate database. R1's path to R2 is ignored because a path to R2 already exists in the tree.

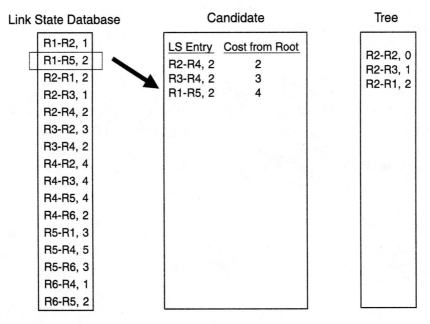

Figure 2.21   The cost from the root to R5 is the cost of R2 to R1 (2) plus the cost of R2 to R5 (2).

R4's four entries in the database are examined next. R2 and R3 are already on the tree, so only the entries for links from R4 to R5 and R6 are added to the candidate list.

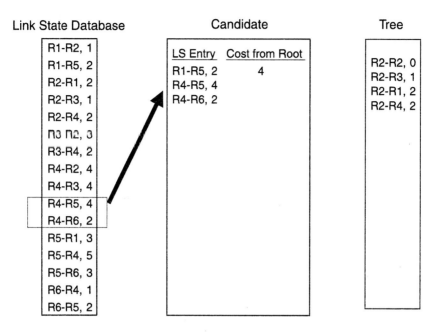

Figure 2.22   R4's paths to R4 and R5 are added to the candidate database. R4's paths to R2 and R3 are ignored because paths to R2 and R3 already exist in the tree.

Costs to the root are again calculated. The cost to R5 through R4 is 6 (R2-R4 plus R4-R5), and the cost to R6 through R4 is 4 (R2-R4 plus R4-R6). There are two entries with a low cost of R4, so we arbitrarily choose the R1-R5 entry and move it to the tree. There is a longer link to R5 via R4 on the candidate list, so this entry is removed.

Back to Step 3 again in Figure 2.24. The only entry from R5 that does not have a neighbor that is already on the tree is R5-R6, so this one entry is added to the candidate list.

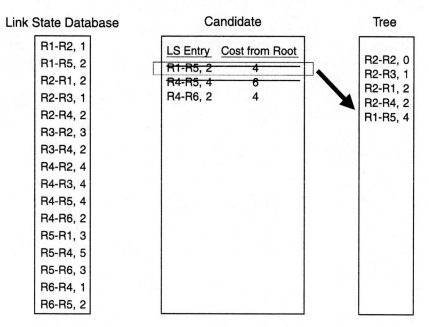

Figure 2.23 Choose one of the two lowest-cost paths to move to the tree. Delete the longer path from the root to R5 from the candidate database.

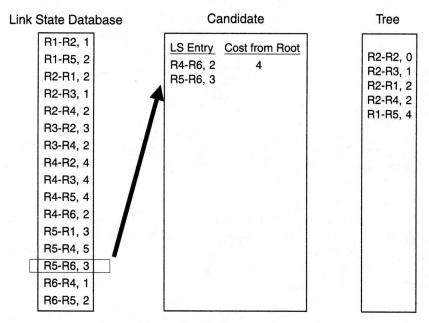

Figure 2.24 Of R5's neighbors, only R6 is not yet on the tree, so add R5-R6 to the candidate database.

In Figure 2.25 the cost from the root to R6 through R5 is 7 (R1-R5 plus R5-R6). The R4-R6 entry, with a cost of 4, is moved to the tree. And because R6 is now on the tree, the R5-R6 entry is removed from the candidate list. At this time, when we go to Step 4, we find that there are no entries in the link state database from R6 that lead to a neighbor that is not already on the tree. Therefore, the candidate list is empty, which Step 5 says is the indication that the computation is complete.

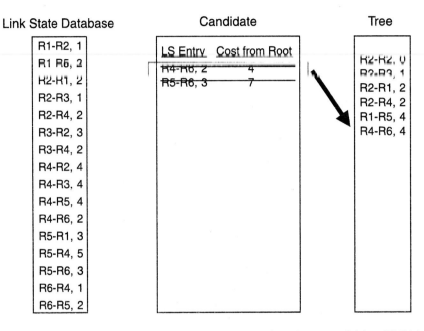

Figure 2.25   From the candidate database, add the smaller cost path to the tree and delete R5-R6 because a shorter path already exists in the tree.

The tree database now describes the shortest path from R2 to every other router in the network. Figure 2.26 shows the tree database and the network diagram, with only the links of the tree showing.

An important detail of the calculation that was just performed has to do with loops. The tree from the root—the router doing the calculation—is built branch by branch, and at no point during the calculation was there a loop on the tree. This is because no entry is added to the tree that has a neighbor already on the tree, and any entry on the candidate list that has a neighbor already on the tree is removed from the list before the next iteration of the calculation is performed. This is a major advantage of link state protocols over vector protocols using a Bellman-Ford algorithm: There is no point during this calculation when loops might occur. Link state protocols are therefore more stable in times of network transition.

Tree

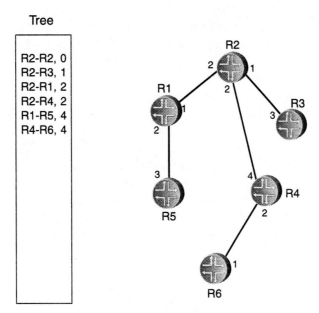

R2-R2, 0
R2-R3, 1
R2-R1, 2
R2-R4, 2
R1-R5, 4
R4-R6, 4

Figure 2.26   The shortest path from the node (R2) to each other router in the network now resides in the tree database.

2.2.6   Areas

If a link state network grows very large, the flooding procedures and the link state database can begin presenting scaling problems. Flooding is a problem because as more routers are added to the network, announcement refresh activity becomes more and more frequent. Although the refresh interval is set by protocol parameters, the times at which each router's refresh timer expires are randomly distributed throughout the network. This is a good thing. You would not want all routers' refresh timers expiring at the same time, creating a massive flood of announcements and a corresponding spike in traffic and processing load.

The link state database can become a scalability problem in large networks because all announcements from all routers must be stored and then used in the Dijkstra SPF calculation. I took a long time and much page space to describe the Dijkstra calculation in the preceding section, but a router can perform the calculations extremely fast. But if the number of entries in the link state database is in the thousands rather than in the tens or hundreds, the corresponding SPF calculations might become burdensome.

Another factor in the scalability of link state protocols is the fact that all routers in the network must maintain and process exactly the same database as every other router. So, if you have a network built with dozens of high-memory, high-powered core routers and one low-memory, low-powered router, the performance of your entire network is bounded by the capabilities of this one small router.

These basic link state scaling problems are countered by breaking up the network into areas. With areas, the database and flooding rules are modified as follows:

- All routers in one area must have an identical link state database, rather than all routers in the entire routing domain.
- The flooding of individual router announcements is limited to the boundaries of an area.

Some routers must connect areas, and are called (in OSPF, anyway) area border routers. The modified link state database rule says that all routers within an area must have the same link state database, so area border routers must maintain separate link state databases for each area to which they are attached. The scope of the trees calculated by the routers internal to an area is the area boundary. Area border routers calculate multiple trees, one for each of its attached areas.

The entire reason for flooding is to ensure that all link state databases have the same entries. If the databases must now only be identical within an area, the scope of flooding is also defined by the area boundaries.[14] Area border routers know all destinations within an attached area, and send an announcement into its other attached areas listing these destinations. So rather than have all announcements from the routers in an area flooded throughout a routing domain, the area is represented by a single announcement from each of its border routers. Areas also help reduce the problem of one router imposing limitations on the entire domain. Small, low-powered routers can be placed in small areas, thereby keeping the link state database size and flooding traffic well within the capabilities of the small routers.

Review Questions

1. What does it mean when a network is converged?
2. What is a distributed route calculation?
3. What three general characteristics of vector protocols make the protocls susceptible to problems such as corrupted route data, loops, and slow convergence?
4. What is split horizon?
5. What is counting to infinity, and how are its adverse effects reduced?
6. How does a holddown timer help prevent routing loops? Does it have any negative effects on the network?
7. What are the four fundamental concepts of link state protocols?
8. What purposes does a Hello protocol serve?
9. How is a Hello protocol ensured to discover only directly connected neighbors?

---

[14] You will see in subsequent chapters that this rule is modified so that certain kinds of flooding—particularly of information about destinations external to the routing domain—can still cross area boundaries.

10. What is handshaking? What is the purpose of a three-way handshake?

11. What three mechanisms are used to make flooding reliable?

12. What is database synchronization?

13. What is an area? Define it in terms of the link state database and the SPF tree, and its general benefit to a link state network.

14. What is an area border router? In what way does its link state database differ from that of other routers? In what way does its SPF processes differ from those of other routers?

CHAPTER 3

Message Types

Comparing the respective message types of OSPF and IS-IS seems like a good starting point for beginning a broader comparison of the two protocols. I find myself with something of a chicken-or-egg problem, however. To describe either protocol's messages requires also describing the functions they support, but those functions themselves call for extensive description, and often entire chapters of their own. I trust that the preceding chapter gave you enough of a general understanding of the basic link state functions that I can now refer to the OSPF or IS-IS versions of those functions without yet giving you the details. I therefore lay a few eggs for you in this chapter and hatch the chickens later.

3.1   Comparative Terminology

This first section has nothing to do with messages, but it has to go somewhere. So here you are. OSPF is a child of the IETF, whereas IS-IS is born of the ISO, and they frequently use different terms to describe the same things. So before getting into messages, I want to spend a short time listing these redundant terms.

The most obvious terminology difference is between the IETF term *router* (or, that relic of earlier times, *gateway*) and the ISO term *intermediate system* (IS). Similarly, an IETF *host* is in ISO terms an *end system* (ES), and ES-IS is a protocol spoken between end systems and intermediate systems (hosts and routers). ES-IS is only used for CLNP, never for IP, so it is not mentioned again in this book. It is relevant here as a point of contrast to IS-IS, a protocol spoken between intermediate systems: a routing protocol. With few exceptions, I use the term *router* in this book to refer to both OSPF and IS-IS nodes, and I always use the term *host*, rather than ES.

A router identifies itself by a *router ID*, whereas an intermediate system identifies itself by a *system ID*, often abbreviated to sys ID. Functionally a router ID and a sys ID are the same thing, but I use both terms to differentiate OSPF and IS-IS routers.

IS-IS defines a term *subnetwork point of attachment* (SNPA), which is a point at which subnetwork services are provided by a device to a subnetwork. You can think of an SNPA as a logical (not physical) interface connected to a data link, and represented by a data link address such as a MAC address.

IETF terminology defines a network layer data unit as a *packet* or, less frequently, *datagram*. At the data link layer, a data entity is a *frame*. ISO uses the more flexible *protocol data unit* (PDU) to describe data units at all layers: subnetwork PDUs, network PDUs, and so on. I like the term *PDU*, and often use it even in the context of OSPF.

The basic unit of link state routing information that we called, in the previous chapter, a link state announcement is in OSPF a *link state advertisement* (LSA) and in IS-IS a *link state PDU* (LSP). Although they serve the same fundamental purpose of populating the link state database, the difference between LSAs and LSPs is one of the more distinct differences between the two protocols. LSAs and LSPs are introduced in Section 3.5 in this chapter, and are detailed in Chapter 5.

The IETF concept of *autonomous system* (AS) is, in ISO terms, a *routing domain*. I much prefer the second term. These days, an AS has a specific meaning in BGP networks, to differentiate one area of autonomous administrative control from another, and as entities interconnected by EBGP. Within a single AS, multiple IGPs can be running. In contrast, a routing domain is always the scope of a single set of routers speaking the same routing protocol to each other, unbroken by any other routing protocol. In this book, I use *routing domain* to describe either an OSPF or an IS-IS domain except where specific IETF terminology is required (such as the OSPF term *autonomous system boundary router*).

Finally, there are some differences in area terminology. Both OSPF and IS-IS use a two-level area hierarchy, as introduced in the preceding chapter. OSPF calls the higher-level area a *backbone* area, or simply *area 0* based on the area ID that always signifies the OSPF backbone. Lower-level OSPF areas are designated by the unwieldy term *nonbackbone* area. IS-IS identifies the higher-level area as *level 2* (L2), and the lower-level areas as *level 1* (L1) areas. IS-IS does not actually refer to the L2 area as an area—instead, it is called the L2 *subdomain*. Chapter 7 discusses the nuances of the differences between an area and a subdomain.

Table 3.1 summarizes the most common terminology differences between OSPF and IS-IS. With the basic jargon explained, we are ready to begin looking at message types.

Table 3.1   ISOspeak 101

IETF or OSPF Term	ISO or IS-IS Term
Router	Intermediate System (IS)
Host	End System (ES)
Router ID (RID)	System ID (Sys ID)
MAC Address	Subnetwork Point of Attachment (SNPA)
Packet	Network Protocol Data Unit (NPDU)
Frame	Subnetwork Protocol Data Unit (SNPDU)

IETF or OSPF Term	ISO or IS-IS Term
Link State Advertisement (LSA)	Link State PDU (LSP)
Autonomous System (AS)	Routing Domain
Backbone area	Level 2 (L2) Subdomain
Nonbackbone area	Level 1 (L1) Area

3.2 Message Encapsulation

OSPF operates directly over IP, with a protocol number of 89. The source address of all OSPF messages is always the local end of an adjacency, and all messages are either multicast to one of two reserved multicast addresses, 224.0.0.5 and 224.0.0.6, or unicast to the distant end of an adjacency. At no time does OSPF broadcast its messages. The rules for when to multicast and when to unicast, and what the two reserved multicast addresses signify, are discussed in context in later chapters. For now, it is enough to know how the messages are sent.

IS-IS operates not over the network layer like OSPF, but over the data link layer. But like OSPF, IS-IS messages are either unicast or multicast—never broadcast. The source address of IS-IS messages is always the data link layer address (the MAC address, for example) of the local end of the adjacency, and the destination address is either the data link layer address of the distant end of the adjacency or, on broadcast media such as Ethernet, one of two reserved multicast MAC addresses: 0180:c200:0014 or 0180:c200:0015. As with OSPF, the rules for when to unicast and when to multicast, and how the two reserved multicast addresses are used, is explained in context in the appropriate chapters.

Encapsulating messages at the IP layer or at the data link layer each presents both advantages and disadvantages. One point of contrast is security. Because it runs over IP, OSPF can be—and has been—the target of spoofing and denial-of-service (DoS) attacks. Several tools are openly available for both snooping and attacking OSPF, such as IRPAS and Nemesis. Because of this vulnerability, both authentication and careful filtering are strongly recommended on OSPF networks with exposure to untrusted sources. IS-IS is not vulnerable to IP-based external attacks because it is not an IP protocol and runs over the data link layer. Attacking IS-IS requires direct access to a network link or router. Securing OSPF and IS-IS is detailed in Chapter 9.

Another issue arising from the choice of encapsulation layer is message prioritization. In times of congestion, when packets cannot be sent immediately on a link, routers put the packets in a queue. The problem is that if the congestion is severe, the queue can fill up, and subsequent arriving packets are dropped. Some applications are more sensitive to packet loss than others, so many routers support the creation of multiple queues on an interface, and the assignment of each packet to one of the multiple queues based on one or more parameters. The queues are then serviced in such a way that the packets in some queues are given a better chance of being transmitted than packets in other queues. This procedure of classifying packets, sorting them into queues according to their classification, and then servicing the queues with differing levels of preference is called class of service (CoS).

Obviously, in times of congestion routing protocol packets should receive the best preferential treatment because if routing messages do not get through the routing protocol can fail, and then no other packets will be routed. OSPF marks the precedence field in the IP header of all its messages as "network control" (binary 110), so that if a router is set up for CoS queuing these packets are placed into the highest-priority queue. Some router manufacturers implement a high-priority queue by default and place packets marked for network control into this queue.

Because IS-IS is not an IP protocol, prioritizing its messages is more problematic. Some router manufacturers, such as Juniper Networks and Cisco Systems, use proprietary internal mechanisms to tag IS-IS messages in such a way that they can be added to the same network control queue as OSPF. In any IS-IS network, using routers that either prioritize IS-IS messages automatically and internally or allow configured prioritization of IS-IS traffic by some manual means is essential to the stability of network routing.

Finally, IS-IS can potentially present a problem in some ATM environments. Specifically, AAL5MUX encapsulation (also called null encapsulation or VC multiplexing) limits each virtual circuit (VC) to a single Layer 3 protocol. Because IS-IS messages are not IP packets, they cannot be sent over the same VC as the IP traffic being routed. To send IS-IS and IP traffic over the same VC, AAL5SNAP encapsulation (also called LLC/SNAP encapsulation) or AAL5NLPID encapsulation must be used.

The problem is this: SNAP and NLPID encapsulation add a header to the packet being encapsulated in the AAL5 frame, which identifies the enclosed protocol type, so that the receiving system can read the SNAP or NLPID header and send the encapsulated packet to the correct protocol stack. Approximately 40 percent of normal IP traffic consists of small 40-byte TCP acknowledgements. The AAL5 header adds 8 bytes to make each TCP ACK 48 bytes, exactly the payload size of one ATM cell. But an LLC/SNAP header adds another 8 bytes, and an NLPID header adds 2 bytes, bringing the size of each TCP ACK encapsulated in either AAL5SNAP or AAL5NLPID to either 56 or 50 bytes. That means two ATM cells are required to carry each TCP ACK, and most of the second cell is empty. The result is that when using AAL5SNAP or AAL5NLPID encapsulation, the number of cells required to carry some 40 percent of normal IP traffic doubles, adding greatly to the overall cell tax.

AAL5MUX drops the packet and AAL5 header directly into a cell with no other headers. For TCP ACKs, this means that with the AAL5 header each ACK is 48 bytes long and fits exactly into the payload of a single cell, improving overall efficiency. But this also means that the receiving system has no header information to identify the encapsulated protocol. Instead, a single protocol is identified implicitly by the VC itself. As a result, IS-IS and IP cannot be carried in the same VC, because the receiving system does not have enough information to demultiplex the two protocols to their individual stacks.

Henk Smit of Cisco Systems proposed a solution to this problem.[1] Although AAL5MUX does not provide a header for the end system to identify the encapsulated message, what if

---

[1] Henk Smit, "IS-IS and IP over the Same ATM VC with AAL5MUX Encapsulation," draft-hsmit-isis-ip-aalmux-00.txt. Draft expired December 1999.

the end system just looked at the first part of the message itself? The first octet in every IP header is the 4-bit version number and the 4-bit header length. Depending on the length of the options field in the IPv4 header, this first byte is always between 0x45 and 0x4f inclusive. The first byte of every IS-IS message is the Intradomain Routing Protocol Discriminator, which is always 0x83. So, the receiving system can look at the first byte of the message and distinguish between IP and IS-IS, without depending on the ATM layer to demultiplex. As it turns out, no one has implemented this solution primarily because there has been no demand for it. IS-IS for IP is seldom found outside of large Internet service provider networks, and most of these networks, over the past few years, have been migrating their cores away from ATM. You can draw the conclusion that if there has been no demand, the IS-IS over AAL5MUX problem has apparently not been a problem for many users.

3.3   Message Architecture

OSPF messages and LSAs are all structured on 32-bit boundaries. The original intention was to make the messages easier to parse. But in these times of high-speed processors and abundant memory, such architecture does not matter much any more. The format of OSPF messages is fixed, so the protocol can only be extended by creating new LSAs.

IS-IS does not adhere to set boundaries, and all messages are constructed of type-specific headers followed by type/length/value (TLV) structures.[2] The type and length fields are each one octet, and specify the type and length (in bytes) of the data in the value field. Because the length field is one byte, the value field can vary from 0 to 254 bytes. They can also be nested—that is, a TLV can exist inside another TLV.

Extensibility of the Message Architecture

Because OSPF messages are built of set-length, well-defined fields, only the LSAs are extendable—and these only by defining new LSAs when needed. As a result, OSPF can be difficult to extend. Not only must new LSAs be defined, but the OSPF processes on all routers where the new LSAs are used must be able to negotiate the acceptance of these LSAs. And in one case—extending OSPF to support IPv6—an entirely new version of OSPF is required. Opaque LSAs, discussed in Chapter 10, help alleviate this extensibility problem in some cases.

The use of TLVs in both IS-IS messages and LSPs make IS-IS much more easily extendable. IPv6 support, for example, requires the simple addition of two TLVs to the existing messages. The comparative extensibility of the two protocols is discussed in more detail in Chapter 10, and specific extensions are covered in Chapters 11 through 13.

---

[2] ISO terminology calls this construct a code/length/variable (CLV). The acronym TLV is much better known, and so is used throughout this book.

Figure 3.1 compares the general structure of OSPF and IS-IS messages. The types of messages depicted here, and the meanings of the fields in each message, are not important yet. For now, you only need to know that the formats shown are the same ones used throughout this book for depicting the messages of each protocol. OSPF messages are always depicted on their 32-bit boundaries, whereas IS-IS messages are always shown with labels to the right indicating the length in bytes of the variable-length fields. As Dave Katz says, OSPF's 32-bit alignment is mostly useful these days in that it provides tidy packet pictures.

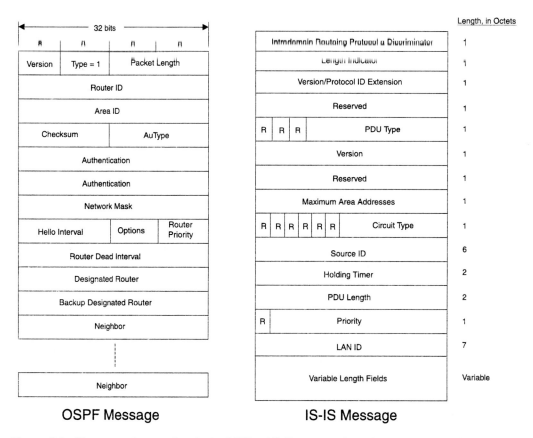

OSPF Message   **IS-IS Message**

Figure 3.1   The conventions used to depict OSPF and IS-IS messages throughout this book.

3.4 Message Types

OSPF uses five message types:

- Hello
- Database Description (DD)
- Link State Request
- Link State Acknowledgement
- Link State Update

IS-IS uses four basic message types:

- IS-IS Hello (IIH)
- Complete Sequence Number PDU (CSNP)
- Partial Sequence Number PDU (PSNP)
- Link State PDU (LSP)

Unlike OSPF, IS-IS messages have subtypes. There are LAN and Point-to-Point Hellos, used as the names imply on either broadcast or point-to-point media. The LAN Hellos are also subdivided into level 1 and level 2 types and are sent over level 1 and level 2 adjacencies. Likewise, Sequence Number PDUs (CSNPs and PSNPs) and LSPs are also subdivided into level 1 and level 2 types. So although there are only four basic types of IS-IS messages, when divided by function, there are nine actual types:

- Level 1 LAN IIH
- Level 2 LAN IIH
- Point-to-Point IIH
- Level 1 CSNP
- Level 2 CSNP
- Level 1 PSNP
- Level 2 PSNP
- Level 1 LSP
- Level 2 LSP

Hello messages serve the same three purposes in both OSPF and IS-IS. They are used to discover neighbors, to negotiate adjacencies, and, on established adjacencies, serve as keep-alives. Although IS-IS Hellos are officially assigned the acronym IIH, as shown in the previous two lists, in this book I use the term *Hello* to refer to both OSPF and IS-IS Hellos for the sake of simplicity. Chapter 4 discusses the formats of the Hello messages and a detailed comparison of their use by the two protocols.

OSPF Database Description, Link State Request, and Link State Acknowledgement packets are used for the OSPF database synchronization process. Similarly, IS-IS sequence number PDUs are used for the IS-IS database synchronization process. The formats of these messages, and a comparison of their uses, are found in Chapter 6.

Table 3.2 associates the OSPF and IS-IS message types by function. The most interesting comparison in the table is that between OSPF Updates and IS-IS LSPs. Earlier in the section on comparative terminology, I equated LSPs to LSAs, yet here I equate LSPs to Updates. This seeming inconsistency is at the heart of the difference between LSAs and LSPs, and is explained in the following section.

Table 3.2   A Comparison of OSPF and IS-IS Messages by Function

OSPF Message	IS-IS Message	Function
Hello	Hello	Neighbor discovery
		Adjacency negotiation
		Adjacency keepalive
Database Description	Complete Sequence Number PDU (CSNP)	Database synchronization
Link State Request	Partial Sequence Number PDU (PSNP)	Database synchronization
Link State Acknowledgement	No equivalent message, although PSNPs are used as ACKs in some cases	Database synchronization
Link State Update	Link State PDU	Database synchronization and flooding

3.5   LSAs and LSPs

OSPF LSAs are, as you already know, the building blocks of OSPF link state databases. That is, an OSPF router's LS database is just a collection of all LSAs the router has either originated itself or has heard from other routers. LSAs are sent from one router to its adjacent neighbors in Update messages, and an Update can carry many LSAs. Figure 3.2 shows an example of LSAs in an OSPF link state database, and Figure 3.3 shows the complete contents of one of the LSAs in the database.

```
jeff@Juniper7> show ospf database

    OSPF link state database, area 0.0.0.0
 Type       ID            Adv Rtr        Seq        Age  Opt  Cksum   Len
 Router   192.168.254.5  192.168.254.5  0x80000007  809  0x2  0xf59e   36
 Router   192.168.254.6  192.168.254.6  0x80000006  881  0x2  0xfe53   72
 Router  *192.168.254.7  192.168.254.7  0x80000005 1280  0x2  0xeba3   36
 Network  192.168.3.2    192.168.254.5  0x80000003 1034  0x2  0x9e02   32
 Network  192.168.4.1    192.168.254.6  0x80000002  886  0x2  0xb1ec   32
 Summary  192.168.1.0    192.168.254.5  0x80000005 1634  0x2  0x8df2   28
 Summary  192.168.2.0    192.168.254.5  0x80000005 1409  0x2  0x82fc   28
 Summary  192.168.254.2  192.168.254.5  0x80000004 1334  0x2  0x91ef   28
 Summary  192.168.254.4  192.168.254.5  0x80000003 1709  0x2  0x7f01   28
 Summary  192.168.254.5  192.168.254.5  0x80000004  134  0x2  0x6916   28
 Summary *192.168.254.7  192.168.254.7  0x80000003 1788  0x2  0x4b31   28

    OSPF link state database, area 0.0.0.10
 Type       ID            Adv Rtr       Seq         Age  Opt  Cksum   Len
 Router  *192.168.254.7  192.168.254.7  0x80000007 1188  0x2  0x7388   36
 Summary *172.16.1.0     192.168.254.7  0x80000004  980  0x2  0x140e   28
 Summary *192.168.1.0    192.168.254.7  0x80000004  888  0x2  0x97e5   28
 Summary *192.168.2.0    192.168.254.7  0x80000004  680  0x2  0x8cef   28
 Summary *192.168.3.0    192.168.254.7  0x80000004  588  0x2  0x7705   28
 Summary *192.168.4.0    192.168.254.7  0x80000004  380  0x2  0x621a   28
 Summary *192.168.254.2  192.168.254.7  0x80000004  288  0x2  0x99e3   28
 Summary *192.168.254.4  192.168.254.7  0x80000004   80  0x2  0x85f5   28
 Summary *192.168.254.5  192.168.254.7  0x80000003 2088  0x2  0x7309   28
 Summary *192.168.254.6  192.168.254.7  0x80000003 1880  0x2  0x5f1d   28
    OSPF external link state database
 Type       ID            Adv Rtr       Seq         Age  Opt  Cksum   Len
 Extern  *192.168.100.0  192.168.254.7  0x80000002 1580  0x2  0xafe4   36
 Extern  *192.168.200.0  192.168.254.7  0x80000002 1488  0x2  0x5fd0   36
```

Figure 3.2 This display shows a summary of all LSAs in an OSPF LS database.

```
jeff@Juniper7> show ospf database router lsa-id 192.168.254.5 extensive

    OSPF link state database, area 0.0.0.0
 Type       ID            Adv Rtr       Seq         Age  Opt  Cksum   Len
 Router   192.168.254.5  192.168.254.5  0x80000007 1264  0x2  0xf59e   36
  bits 0x1, link count 1
  id 192.168.3.2, data 192.168.3.2, type Transit (2)
  TOS count 0, TOS 0 metric 1
  Aging timer 00:38:56
  Installed 00:21:00 ago, expires in 00:38:56, sent 12w1d 10:01:09 ago
```

Figure 3.3 The complete contents of the first LSA in the database of Figure 3.2.

IS-IS LS databases consist of LSPs the local router has either originated or has heard from other routers. LSPs are in this sense the equivalent of OSPF LSAs. But a single OSPF router can generate several types of LSA, whereas an IS-IS router generates at most two LSPs: a single LSP for its L1 adjacencies and a single LSP for its L2 adjacencies.[3] If a router needs to communicate different types of information, the types are encoded in different TLVs within the single LSP. Figure 3.4 shows an example of an IS-IS LS database, and Figure 3.5 shows the complete contents of one of the LSPs in the database. The most fundamental types of LSAs and IS-IS TLVs, and why they are needed, are explained in Chapter 5.

Also, IS-IS has no Update message like OSPF. Instead, the LSP is itself a message. So, in this sense LSPs are the equivalent of OSPF Updates. You might also argue that the TLVs in LSPs are the actual equivalent of LSAs, in that just as there are different types of LSAs for carrying different kinds of information, there are also different types of TLVs. But this comparison is not as close: IS-IS LS databases are built from complete LSPs, not TLVs alone. The moral of the story is that a clear one-for-one comparison cannot be made between every aspect of OSPF and IS-IS.

```
jeff@Juniper7> show isis database
IS-IS level 1 link-state database:
LSP ID                    Sequence Checksum Lifetime Attributes
Juniper7.00-00                 0xa    0x84c1     1056 L1 L2 Attached
  1 LSPs

IS-IS level 2 link-state database:
LSP ID                    Sequence Checksum Lifetime Attributes
Juniper5.00-00                 0x8    0xaec6      652 L1 L2
Juniper5.04-00                 0x7    0xf9a3      737 L1 L2
Juniper6.00-00                 0xb    0xd8e8      866 L1 L2
Juniper7.00-00                 0xa    0x21d6     1193 L1 L2
Juniper7.02-00                 0x7    0x5841      440 L1 L2
  5 LSPs
```

Figure 3.4   This display shows a summary of all the LSPs in an IS-IS LS database.

---

[3] This description is admittedly simplistic. IS-IS fragments large LSPs, and during flooding the fragments are treated as separate LSPs. But the fragments are reassembled by receiving IS-IS processes and are again treated as a single LSP. LSP fragmentation is discussed in detail in Chapter 8.

```
jeff@Juniper7> show isis database Juniper5.00-00 extensive
IS-IS level 1 link-state database:

IS-IS level 2 link-state database:

Juniper5.00-00  Sequence: 0xa, Checksum: 0xaac8, Lifetime: 842 secs
    IS neighbor:                Juniper5.04  Metric:        10
    IP prefix:           192.168.254.5/32 Metric:       0 Internal
    IP prefix:           192.168.3.0/24 Metric:       10 Internal
    IP prefix:           192.168.2.0/24 Metric:       10 Internal
    IP prefix:           192.168.1.0/24 Metric:       10 Internal

  Header: LSP id: Juniper5.00-00, Length: 177 bytes
     Allocated length: 177 bytes, Router ID: 192.168.254.5
     Remaining lifetime: 842 secs, Level: 2,Interface: 3
     Estimated free bytes: 0, Actual free bytes: 0
     Aging timer expires in: 842 secs
     Protocols: IP

  Packet: LSP id: Juniper5.00-00, Length: 177 bytes, Lifetime : 1196
        secs
     Checksum: 0xaac8, Sequence: 0xa, Attributes: 0x3 <L1 L2>
     NLPID: 0x83, Fixed length: 27 bytes, Version: 1, Sysid length: 0
          bytes
     Packet type: 20, Packet version: 1, Max area: 0

  TLVs:
     Area address: 47.0002 (3)
     Speaks: IP
     Speaks: IPv6
     IP router id: 192.168.254.5
     IP address: 192.168.254.5
     Hostname: Juniper5
     IP prefix: 192.168.1.0/24, Internal, Metric: default 10
     IP prefix: 192.168.2.0/24, Internal, Metric: default 10
     IP prefix: 192.168.3.0/24, Internal, Metric: default 10
     IP prefix: 192.168.254.5/32, Internal, Metric: default 0
     IP prefix: 192.168.1.0/24 metric 10 up
     IP prefix: 192.168.2.0/24 metric 10 up
     IP prefix: 192.168.3.0/24 metric 10 up
     IP prefix: 192.168.254.5/32 metric 0 up
     IS neighbor: Juniper5.04, Internal, Metric: default 10
     IS neighbor: Juniper5.04, Metric: default 10
        IP address: 192.168.3.2
No queued transmissions
```

Figure 3.5   The complete contents of one of the LSPs in the database.

3.6   Subnetwork Dependent and Independent Functions

ISO 10589[4] organized all IS-IS functions into one of two classes: *subnetwork dependent functions* and *subnetwork independent functions*. The functional organization might be a handy way of remembering whether the differences in data links can influence a particular routing function—for troubleshooting, perhaps. But the organization certainly is not necessary for understanding IS-IS. Nevertheless, because it is a central part of the IS-IS documentation, I am obliged to present it. You are not obliged to read it. All of the functions listed and discussed briefly in this section are covered in more detail in subsequent chapters.

Although the functional organization is only found in the IS-IS documentation, most of the organization applies equally to OSPF.

RFC 1195, which describes the extension of IS-IS for routing IP, defines a more comprehensive list of functions than ISO 10589, and also defines some IP-specific functions not defined in the original ISO document. The organization shown in the following two subsections therefore comes from both ISO 10589 and RFC 1195.

3.6.1   Subnetwork Dependent Functions

Subnetwork functions are functions between two neighboring routers that can differ depending on the particular data link protocol connecting the routers, as follows:

- Link demultiplexing
- Multiple IP addresses per interface
- LANs, designated routers, and pseudonodes
- Maintaining router adjacencies
- Forwarding to incompatible routers

Link demultiplexing concerns the fact that IS-IS is an ISO protocol, not an IP protocol. The type of link connecting two neighbors must have some facility for identifying IS-IS messages and IP packets, so that the receiving router can distinguish between the two and send traffic to the correct process. You have already encountered an IS-IS demultiplexing problem in Section 3.2, where AAL5MUX has no facility for distinguishing two protocols on the same virtual circuit. Although not much is said about link demultiplexing in this book, the more general classification of link types by OSPF and IS-IS is discussed in Chapter 4.

Multiple IP addresses per interface applies to the fact that IS-IS permits multiple IP addresses to be assigned to a single interface. Or in the case of point-to-point links, there may be no IP address at all assigned. Routers must have a method for communicating the assigned addresses to its neighbors. This is also discussed in Chapter 4.

---

[4]   The official designation is ISO/IEC 10589 (International Organization for Standardization/ International Electrotechnical Commission standard 10589).

LANs, designated routers, and pseudonodes refer to the function of representing broadcast networks and all routers connected to the network as a single node on the SPF tree to reduce flooding load and control adjacencies. The designated router processes for OSPF and IS-IS are discussed in Chapter 4.

Maintaining router adjacencies is a subnetwork dependent function primarily for IS-IS, where a different type of Hello is sent on point-to-point links than the type of Hello sent on broadcast media. However, there are also some OSPF adjacency functions that can change for certain media types, such as demand circuits (Chapter 8). Adjacencies and their maintenance are covered in Chapter 4.

Forwarding to incompatible routers deals, in RFC 1195, with the actions that must be taken in a dual IS-IS environment when an IP packet is forwarded to an OSI-only router or vice versa. Because this book deals only with IS-IS as it applies to IP, this function is not of interest to us. But this function can also apply to how OSPF and IS-IS deal with the situation when one router supports certain timer values or extensions that a neighbor does not support. These functions are dealt with primarily in Chapter 4, and briefly in Chapter 10.

3.6.2 Subnetwork Independent Functions

Subnetwork independent functions are those functions that operate the same no matter what type of subnetwork they are operating over.

ISO 10589 defines the following subnetwork independent functions:

- Addresses
- The decision process
- The update process
- The forwarding process
- Routing parameters

All of these are the basic functions of any routing protocol, and do not need to be defined further. RFC 1195 adds more functions to the list, some of which do need to be defined:

- Exchange of routing information
- Hierarchical abbreviation of IP reachability information
- Addressing routers in IS-IS packets
- External links
- Type of service routing
- IP-only operation
- Encapsulation
- Authentication
- Order of preference of routes/ Dijkstra computation

Exchange of routing information is the function of including the necessary IP routing information in IS-IS messages. This information is covered in multiple chapters, wherever LSAs and LSPs are described.

Hierarchical abbreviation of IP reachability information is the function of summarizing the reachability information in a lower-level area (L1 or OSPF nonbackbone) into a higher-level area (L2 or OSPF backbone). Chapter 7 covers this topic.

Addressing routers in IS-IS packets defines how routers are identified. Because IS-IS is an ISO protocol, NSAP addresses are used to identify the router. This function, if you eliminate the IS-IS reference in the name, also applies to OSPF, which uses a 32-bit IP address[5] as its router ID. The procedures for defining router IDs are discussed in Chapter 4.

External links defines how routing information learned from protocols external to the OSPF or IS-IS routing domain is distributed into the domain in a form understandable by the internal protocol. Chapter 5 covers this topic.

Type of Service routing is the function of assigning metrics to routes, and is discussed in Chapter 5.

IP-only operation only applies to IS-IS routers, and deals with TLVs defined in ISO 10589 for OSI routing that have no relevance to IP routing, and can therefore be omitted from IS-IS routers in IP-only mode. The OSI TLVs that have no relevance to IP are "End Systems Neighbors" and "Prefix Neighbors" TLVs. Again, because this book is only concerned with IP routing, the omission of these TLVs is not mentioned elsewhere.

Encapsulation issues are dealt with in this chapter, in Section 3.2.

Authentication of IS-IS and OSPF messages is covered in Chapter 9.

Order of preference of routes deals with the procedures for selecting routes based on longest prefix matches, metrics, type of service values, and area origination. Chapters 5 and 6 cover this topic.

Review Questions

1. What is OSPF's IP protocol number?
2. What is the fundamental difference between the way OSPF messages are encapsulated and the way IS-IS messages are encapsulated?
3. What is the fundamental difference between the source and destination addresses of an encapsulated OSPF message and the source and destination addresses of an encapsulated IS-IS message?
4. What are the five OSPF message types?
5. What OSPF message types are used for database synchronization?

---

[5] Although the 32-bit OSPF RID does not actually have to be an IP address (it can be manually specified as any dotted-decimal 32-bit number), it almost always is an IP address configured somewhere on the router.

6. What OSPF message type is used for flooding?

7. What are the four basic IS-IS message types? How are these four types divided into nine subtypes?

8. What IS-IS message types are used for database synchronization?

9. What IS-IS message type is used for flooding?

10. What is the difference between a subnetwork dependent function and a subnetwork independent function?

CHAPTER 4

Addressing, Neighbor Discovery, and Adjacencies

Finally, after three chapters, we leave concepts and generalities behind and begin examining the mechanics of the two protocols. The best place to begin is where the protocols themselves begin, which is to look at what they do when they first start up. First, the protocol must discover essential information about itself and the router it is running on, such as router IDs, area configurations, interface parameters, and the links the interfaces are connected to. Next, neighbors must be discovered; a routing protocol is not much good if it has no one to talk to. And with the discovery of neighbors, adjacencies must be established, so that the protocols know what to talk about.

4.1 Router and Area IDs

An essential requirement for the proper functioning of a link state protocol, as you saw in Chapter 2, is that each router must be able to uniquely identify itself within the routing domain. This is the purpose of the OSPF router ID (RID) and the IS-IS system ID (SysID). In addition, the router must be able to identify its general position within the routing domain. This is the purpose of the area ID (AID).

4.1.1 OSPF Router IDs

OSPF uses a 32-bit number for its RID, represented in the same dotted-decimal format as an IP address. A router can find its RID in one of two ways: The RID can be administratively specified in the OSPF configuration, or an IP address configured on one of the router's interfaces can be used as the RID. The second option is made possible because the RID format is the same as the IP address format, and because there is an assumption that an interface address is unique within the routing domain.

Which option is used to acquire a RID depends on the particular OSPF implementation. And in some cases, both options are available. For example, both Juniper Networks' and Cisco Systems' OSPF implementations have a prioritized RID selection process:

1. If a RID is administratively configured, that value is used.
2. If no RID is administratively configured, an IP address configured on a loopback interface is used.
3. If no IP address is configured on a loopback interface, an address is taken from a physical interface.
4. If no IP address is configured on any interface and no RID is administratively configured, OSPF cannot start.

The original logic behind Step 2, taking an address from a loopback interface, was that because a loopback interface is a logical interface—it exists only in software and has no physical presence on the router—it is not susceptible to physical failures. So, there is no risk that an interface failure or shutdown on a router could force OSPF to find a new RID and re-advertise its LSAs using the new RID, which in turn causes SPF runs on routers throughout the area and contributes to network instability.

There are two approaches by which a particular OSPF implementation could handle the loss of a RID. One approach is that the failure of an interface will have no effect on the RID. After all, the OSPF process just needs to know some 32-bit value, with some confidence that the value is unique within the OSPF routing domain, to use as its RID at start-up. Once the value is known, it can be remembered, and the subsequent failure of the interface from which the RID was derived is irrelevant. The problem with this approach is that the loss of an IP address on an interface might not have been accidental. What if the IP address is intentionally removed from an interface and is reused on another router, and that router selects that IP address as its own RID? If the first router retains the same address as its RID, you now have duplicate RIDs in your network.

The second approach avoids the problem just described and is therefore the lesser of two evils. This approach to the loss of an IP address from which the RID is derived is to force the router to acquire a new RID from its remaining IP addresses.

4.1.2 Troubleshooting: Duplicate Router IDs

Allowing more than one router in a network to use the same RID results in serious network outages, and the symptoms can be misleading. For example, in Figure 4.1, two routers—R4 and R7—have both been configured with the RID 192.168.254.7. The physical interfaces for R6 are shown, as are the interface addresses for R6 and its neighbors. We will observe the results of the duplicate RIDs from that router.

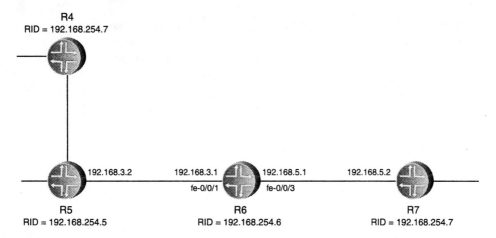

Figure 4.1   R4 and R7 are using the same RID.

Figures 4.2 through 4.6 show the OSPF entries in the routing table of R6, observed within a time span of just a few minutes. The differences are obvious. The OSPF entries in Figure 4.2 look normal. The network diagram in Figure 4.1 does not show the larger network, so we do not know where most of the destination networks are actually located; we can only assume the entries in Figure 4.2 are correct. (In fact, some of the entries have the correct next hop and some do not.)

```
jeff@R6> show route protocol ospf

inet.0: 19 destinations, 19 routes (18 active, 0 holddown, 1 hidden)
+ = Active Route, - = Last Active, * = Both

192.168.1.0/24      *[OSPF/10] 00:00:00, metric 3
                     > to 192.168.5.2 via fe-0/0/3.0
192.168.2.0/24      *[OSPF/10] 00:00:00, metric 2
                     > to 192.168.3.2 via fe-0/0/1.0
192.168.4.0/24      *[OSPF/10] 00:00:00, metric 2
                     > to 192.168.5.2 via fe-0/0/3.0
192.168.6.0/24      *[OSPF/10] 00:00:00, metric 2
                     > to 192.168.5.2 via fe-0/0/3.0
192.168.100.0/24    *[OSPF/150] 00:00:00, metric 0, tag 0
                     > to 192.168.5.2 via fe-0/0/3.0
192.168.200.0/24    *[OSPF/150] 00:00:00, metric 0, tag 0
                     > to 192.168.5.2 via fe-0/0/3.0
192.168.254.2/32    *[OSPF/10] 00:00:00, metric 2
                     > to 192.168.5.2 via fe-0/0/3.0
192.168.254.5/32    *[OSPF/10] 00:16:27, metric 1
                     > to 192.168.3.2 via fe-0/0/1.0
192.168.254.7/32    *[OSPF/10] 00:00:00, metric 1
                     > to 192.168.5.2 via fe-0/0/3.0
224.0.0.5/32        *[OSPF/10] 2w3d 06:59:07, metric 1
```

Figure 4.2   The first display of the OSPF route entries appears normal.

Figure 4.3 shows our first indication of trouble (aside from the complaints of network users). This display of the OSPF entries in the routing table was taken just moments after the display in Figure 4.2, but most of the route entries have disappeared. After a few more moments, some but not all of the route entries have returned, as Figure 4.4 shows. But then, in Figure 4.5, most of the entries have again disappeared. This fluctuation continues, with the routing table changing almost as fast as it can be repeatedly displayed.

```
jeff@R6> show route protocol ospf

inet.0: 11 destinations, 11 routes (10 active, 0 holddown, 1 hidden)
+ = Active Route,    - = Last Active,  * = Both

192.168.254.5/32    *[OSPF/10] 00:16:36, metric 1
                    > to 192.168.3.2 via fe-0/0/1.0
224.0.0.5/32        *[OSPF/10] 2w3d 06:59:16, metric 1
```

Figure 4.3   Here, most of the OSPF entries have disappeared from the route table.

```
jeff@R6> show route protocol ospf

inet.0: 15 destinations, 15 routes (14 active, 0 holddown, 1 hidden)
+ = Active Route,  - = Last Active,  * = Both

192.168.4.0/24      *[OSPF/10] 00:00:02, metric 2
                    > to 192.168.5.2 via fe-0/0/3.0
192.168.100.0/24    *[OSPF/150] 00:00:02, metric 0, tag 0
                    > to 192.168.5.2 via fe-0/0/3.0
192.168.200.0/24    *[OSPF/150] 00:00:02, metric 0, tag 0
                    > to 192.168.5.2 via fe-0/0/3.0
192.168.254.5/32    *[OSPF/10] 00:16:49, metric 1
                    > to 192.168.3.2 via fe-0/0/1.0
192.168.254.7/32    *[OSPF/10] 00:00:02, metric 1
                    > to 192.168.5.2 via fe-0/0/3.0
224.0.0.5/32        *[OSPF/10] 2w3d 06:59:29, metric 1
```

Figure 4.4   Some of the entries have returned, but not all.

```
jeff@R6> show route protocol ospf

inet.0: 11 destinations, 11 routes (10 active, 0 holddown, 1 hidden)
+ = Active Route,  - = Last Active,  * = Both

192.168.254.5/32    *[OSPF/10] 00:16:55, metric 1
                    > to 192.168.3.2 via fe-0/0/1.0
224.0.0.5/32        *[OSPF/10] 2w3d 06:59:35, metric 1
```

Figure 4.5   Most of the entries have disappeared again.

Such fluctuations in the routing table might be interpreted by a troubleshooter as a symptom of a flapping link somewhere in the network. But among the many changes observed in the routing table is the one shown in Figure 4.6. Here, some of the entries have again reappeared in the table, but this time the next-hop addresses have changed. The next hop of all the prefixes in Figure 4.6 is 192.168.3.2, or router R5 in Figure 4.1. In the routing tables of Figures 4.2 and 4.4, several of the prefixes indicated 192.168.5.2, router R7, as the next hop. This behavior might lead you to suspect a routing loop.

```
jeff@R6> show route protocol ospf

inet.0: 17 destinations, 17 routes (16 active, 0 holddown, 1 hidden)
+ = Active Route, - = Last Active, * = Both

192.168.1.0/24       *[OSPF/10] 00:00:00, metric 4
                      > to 192.168.3.2 via fe-0/0/1.0
192.168.2.0/24       *[OSPF/10] 00:00:15, metric 2
                      > to 192.168.3.2 via fe-0/0/1.0
192.168.6.0/24       *[OSPF/10] 00:00:00, metric 3
                      > to 192.168.3.2 via fe-0/0/1.0
192.168.254.2/32     *[OSPF/10] 00:00:00, metric 3
                      > to 192.168.3.2 via fe-0/0/1.0
192.168.254.4/32     *[OSPF/10] 00:00:00, metric 2
                      > to 192.168.3.2 via fe-0/0/1.0
192.168.254.5/32     *[OSPF/10] 00:22:08, metric 1
                      > to 192.168.3.2 via fe-0/0/1.00
192.168.254.7/32     *[OSPF/10] 00:00:00, metric 2
                      > to 192.168.3.2 via fe-0/0/1.0
224.0.0.5/32         *[OSPF/10] 2w3d 07:04:48, metric 1
```

Figure 4.6   Some of the entries have returned again, but with a different next-hop address.

As this example demonstrates, the impact of duplicate RIDs on a network is severe, and the symptoms can be misleading. Quickly finding the true cause of the problem depends on how well you know your network and usually involves careful analysis of the OSPF link state database. Therefore, exercise extreme care to ensure that such a problem never arises through misconfiguration or use of unreliable OSPF code.

RID Configuration Tips

Although it is common practice to configure the RID on a loopback interface, my own preference is to administratively configure the RID—even if it is the same number as the loopback interface address. This ensures beyond a doubt that the RID is exactly what you intend it to be, and anyone else reading the router's configuration file can quickly determine the RID. Other network architects can and do disagree. What is important is not so much how you do it, but that you do it consistently. That is, you must have an established and well-documented network standard for setting the RID. The standard should be part of your addressing plan, and ensures that the same RID is not assigned to more than one router.

Another practice I like to stress is making certain that the RID is visibly different from any IP address used in the domain. For example, some octet of the RID might be 255, such as 192.168.255.X or 10.255.X.Y. Setting leading octets to 0, such as 0.0.0.X, is also useful. All that is important is that it is consistent and that it is understood by your operations personnel. With such a standard, a RID is readily recognized and easily distinguished from IP addresses during troubleshooting. Obviously, such an approach eliminates the use of IP addresses as RIDs that are otherwise legitimate within the domain.

4.1.3   OSPF Area IDs

The OSPF area ID (AID) is also a 32-bit number. It can be expressed in dotted-decimal format or, with most implementations, as a simple decimal number such as 1, 55, 218, and so on. If the OSPF implementation supports the latter case, the router just fills in the leading bits with 0s. Some implementations will fill in the leading 0s in configuration displays, whereas others display the configuration exactly as typed. In Figure 4.7, for example, the entry of the same OSPF area configuration is shown for Juniper Networks' JUNOS and for Cisco Systems' IOS. Notice that the resulting JUNOS configuration has filled in the leading 0s, but the IOS configuration shows the area IDs as typed. Do not let this fool you, however. The OSPF messages created by both the Juniper and Cisco routers contain the exact same area ID.

If the decimal number entered for the AID is greater than 255, JUNOS expresses the binary equivalent of the number in dotted-decimal format. The third entry in Figure 4.7, for instance, specifies an AID of 1547. 1547 in binary is 11000001011, which converts to the dotted-decimal number 0.0.6.11.

The OSPF backbone area is always represented with an ID of all 0s (0.0.0.0). No other configuration is necessary to designate the backbone area, because this ID is reserved and recognized by OSPF. As with other AIDs, and as shown in Figure 4.7, the backbone AID can also be expressed simply as 0.

AID Configuration Tip

If you have a well-designed IP address architecture, in which a single prefix represents all the IP addresses in an area, it is convenient and useful to use the prefix as the AID. For example, if all IP addresses in an area come from the prefix 10.1.8.0/21, the AID can be 10.1.8.0. This is a common practice and contributes to a tidy, easily understood network design.

```
JUNOS CONFIGURATION:

[edit]
jeff@Juniper6# set protocols ospf area 145 interface fe-0/0/0

[edit]
jeff@Juniper6# set protocols ospf area 0 interface so-1/2/0

[edit]
jeff@Juniper6# set protocols ospf area 1547 interface fe-1/0/0

[edit]
jeff@Juniper6# show protocols ospf
area 0.0.0.145 {
    interface fe-0/0/0.0;
}
area 0.0.0.0 {
    interface so-1/2/0.0;
}
area 0.0.6.11 {
    interface fe-1/0/0.0;
}


IOS CONFIGURATION WITH SAME AREA IDs:

Cisco5#conf t
Enter configuration commands, one per line.  End with CNTL/Z.
Cisco5(config)#router ospf 1
Cisco5(config-router)#network 192.168.1.254 0.0.0.0 area 145
Cisco5(config-router)#network 192.168.2.1 0.0.0.0 area 0
Cisco5(config-router)#network 192.168.3.0.0.0.0 area 1547
Cisco5(config-router)#^Z
Cisco5#

Cisco5#wr t
Current configuration:
!
[Non-OSPF portions of configuration not shown]
!
router ospf 1
 network 192.168.1.254 0.0.0.0 area 145
 network 192.168.2.1 0.0.0.0 area 0
 network 192.168.3.150 0.0.0.0 area 1547
!

Cisco5#
```

Figure 4.7   The router automatically expresses the AID in dotted-decimal format and fills in the leading 0s when a single decimal number is specified for the AID.

4.1.4   IS-IS System and Area IDs

In contrast to the OSPF AID and RID, which are expressed separately, the IS-IS AID and SysID are specified together in the *Network Entity Title* (NET). The NET is a special version of an ISO network service access point (NSAP) address, familiar to anyone who has worked with ISO protocols or with ATM. Figure 4.8 shows the basic format of a NET.

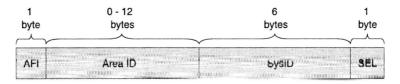

Figure 4.8   The format of a Network Entity Title.

As Figure 4.8 indicates, there are a few rules for configuring a NET:

- The AFI must be 1 byte.
- The remaining Area ID can be from 0 to 12 bytes.
- The SysID must be 6 bytes.
- The SEL must be 1 byte.

The NET is always specified in hexadecimal.

The *Authority and Format Identifier* (AFI) is actually a part of the Area ID, but is identified separately because of its special configuration rule. In ISO addresses, the AFI identifies the assigning authority of the address and the format of most of the rest of the address. But when the NET is assigned to a router in an IP-only network, the AFI has no real meaning separate from the rest of the AID.

The last byte, the *NSAP Selector* (SEL), is used in ISO protocols to identify an upper-layer function to which the address points—something like a port number in IP protocols. The SEL value 0x00 specifies the router itself. In an IP-only network, where there are no upper ISO protocol layers, a router never examines the SEL, which therefore can be set to any 1-byte value. Nonetheless, common practice is to always set the SEL to 0x00.

NET Configuration Tips

Unlike some OSPF implementations, there are no automatic selection mechanisms for the NET—it is always manually configured. Although the NSAP format provides the possibility of some complex NET configurations,[1] it is best in IP-only networks to keep it as simple as possible.

---

[1]   R. Colella, E. Gardner, and R. Callon, "Guidelines for OSI NSAP Allocation in the Internet," RFC 1237, July 1991, gives you some examples of complex NSAP addresses. Such complexity is seldom if ever necessary for NETs.

The simplest approach to configuring an area ID is to use only the AFI field for the AID. For example, the following NET specifies an AID of 05, a SysID of 00d0.b775.ff31 and a SEL of 00:

```
05.00d0.b775.ff31.00
```

Alternatively, many network operators prefer to stay in compliance with NSAP format standards by specifying an AFI of 49, which is the NSAP AFI indicating a locally assigned address, and then specifying the AID after the AFI. The following NET uses an AFI of 49, and an AID of 0005, with the SysID and SEL the same as the last example:

```
49.0005.00d0.b775.ff31.00
```

There are several frequently used approaches to specifying a SysID. The first is to select the MAC address of an interface on the router the NET is to be configured on. Because both the MAC address and the SysID are 48 bits, the MAC address is perfectly adaptable as the SysID. And because the interface MAC is globally unique, you are guaranteed that the SysID based on it meets the requirements of being unique within the IS-IS domain. A possible liability of this approach is if the interface that the SysID is taken from is removed from the router and reused on another router. In this case, the MAC address of the same interface could be used inadvertently as the SysID on more than one router. Another problem with this approach is that some routers might not have any broadcast interfaces and so no MAC addresses to use.

Another common approach to configuring the SysID is to encode the 32-bit, IP-based loopback address or RID into a 48-bit SysID. For example, the loopback address 192.168.255.15 might be used as the SysID:

```
1921.6825.5150
```

The IP address 192.168.255.15 could also be expressed in hexadecimal:

```
c0a8.ff0f.0000
```

or perhaps:

```
0000.c0a8.ff0f
```

However, changing the dotted-decimal address to hex adds an unnecessary complexity to the NET configuration, and can make record keeping and troubleshooting more difficult.

The simplest of all techniques is to assign SysID values sequentially, starting with 1:

```
0000.0000.0001
0000.0000.0002
0000.0000.0003
```

.

.

.

```
0000.0000.0157
```

.

.

.

Assuming that you document and assign the SysIDs in your network as carefully as you do IP addresses and 32-bit RIDs, the potential of assigning duplicate SysIDs is minimized. The consequences of duplicate SysIDs is the same as with the OSPF example in Section 4.1.2: thrashing routes and rapidly increasing LSP sequence numbers.

Some would argue that during troubleshooting the utility of having the IP-based RID encoded in the SysID outweighs the simplicity of sequential numbering. Dynamic Hostname Exchange, described later in this chapter, also eases troubleshooting. Only you can determine the right scheme for your network.

4.2   The Hello Protocol

When the OSPF or IS-IS protocol process starts on a router, neighbors must be discovered and adjacencies established. Both protocols send and listen for Hello messages to discover neighbors. Functionally, the Hello protocol is the same for both OSPF and IS-IS; they differ only in the details. As you learned in Chapter 3, the Hello protocol performs several functions:

- It discovers neighboring OSPF or IS-IS routers.
- It performs three-way handshaking to ensure bidirectional communication between the neighbors.
- It communicates information necessary for establishing whether an adjacency can be formed with a neighboring router.
- After an adjacency is formed, it serves as a keepalive mechanism to detect failed neighbors or adjacencies.

The Hello protocol also performs other functions such as the discovery and election of Designated Routers. The remainder of this chapter examines the similarities and differences in how OSPF and IS-IS implement the Hello protocol and defines functions that rely on the protocol such as the designated router function.

4.2.1 OSPF Hello Protocol Basics

Figure 4.9 diagrams the OSPF Hello message.

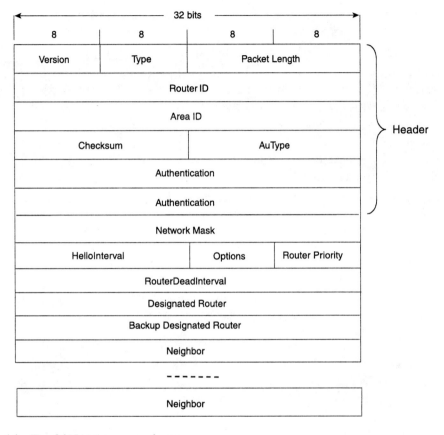

Figure 4.9 The OSPF Hello message format.

■ **Network Mask** is a 32-bit field that identifies, in 1s, the prefix length of the subnet on which the message is sent. For example, if the Hello is sent on subnet 192.168.18.0/24, the value of the Network Mask field is 0xffffff00 (24 ones, specifying a 24-bit prefix length). If the subnet is 10.1.0.0/16, the Network Mask field is 0xffff0000, and so on.

■ **Hello Interval** specifies, in seconds, the interval at which the originating router sends Hellos. RFC 2328 does not specify a default Hello interval, but it suggests a value of 10 seconds for LANs and 30 seconds for nonbroadcast networks such as X.25. Both Cisco Systems and Juniper Networks use the suggested default of 10 seconds for broadcast networks. However, the default for nonbroadcast networks varies: Cisco uses 30 seconds, whereas Juniper uses 120 seconds. The reason for the longer intervals on nonbroadcast networks is an artifact of the days when it could be assumed that the links associated with such networks had less bandwidth to spare for Hello traffic.

- **Options** specifies any optional capabilities the originating OSPF router might have. The Options field is described in Section 4.3.

- **Router Priority** is used by the Designated Router election process.

- **RouterDeadInterval** specifies the time that the originating router's neighbors should wait for a Hello before declaring it dead. As with the Hello interval, RFC 2328 does not specify a default value but suggests a value of four times the Hello interval. Both Cisco Systems and Juniper Networks use that suggested default.

- **Designated Router** and **Backup Designated Router** are, like the Router Priority, used in the Designated Router election and maintenance mechanism. This mechanism is described in Section 4.4.

- **Neighbor** lists the RIDs of the OSPF neighbors the originating router has received Hellos from on the subnet. This list is used in the three-way handshaking process before an OSPF adjacency is established.

When an OSPF router receives a Hello from an OSPF neighbor, it stores the information contained in the Hello in a neighbor database. The first output in Figure 4.10 displays one such database. As you can see from the first display, the router has three neighbors. The second output in Figure 4.10 displays the information from the neighbor whose RID is 192.168.254.2. In this second display, you can observe all the information learned from that neighbor's Hellos: the Priority, the remaining time before the advertised Router Dead Interval expires, the RID and AID from the packet header, the value of the Options field, and the addresses of the Designated Router and Backup Designated Router. Chapter 6 details the neighbor database, along with the various neighbor states.

```
jeff@Juniper5> show ospf neighbor
  Address       Interface       State     ID              Pri  Dead
  192.168.3.1   fe-0/0/3.0      Full      192.168.254.6   128   34
  192.168.1.1   fe-0/0/1.0      Full      192.168.254.2   128   39
  192.168.2.1   fe-0/0/2.0      Full      192.168.254.4   128   39

jeff@Juniper5> show ospf neighbor 192.168.254.2 extensive
  Address       Interface       State     ID              Pri  Dead
  192.168.1.1   fe-0/0/1.0      Full      192.168.254.2   128   37
    area 0.0.0.2, opt 0x42, DR 192.168.1.1, BDR 192.168.1.2
    Up 5w3d 02:09:26, adjacent 5w3d 02:09:26
```

Figure 4.10 OSPF routers store the information they learn in neighbors' Hellos in the OSPF neighbor database.

4.2.2   IS-IS Hello Protocol Basics

Unlike OSPF, which uses a single form of Hello message, IS-IS has three. First, a different form of Hello is used depending on whether it is being originated on a point-to-point (non-broadcast) link or a LAN (broadcast) link. On LAN links, the type of Hello varies depending upon whether a potential neighbor is in the same area (level 1) or in a different area (level 2). Which type of Hello is sent on a particular LAN link depends on the configuration of the router interface connecting to the link. The interface can be configured as L1-only, in which case Level 1 LAN Hellos are sent, or as L2-only, in which case Level 2 LAN Hellos are sent. A LAN interface can also be both L1 and L2, in which case both types of Hellos are sent. The reason for this is that a router might find multiple neighbors on a single broadcast link. Some of the neighbors might have the same area ID, in which case an L1 adjacency will be established. Other neighbors might have different area IDs, in which case L2 adjacencies will be established. Point-to-point links have, by definition, only a single neighbor, so there will only be an L1 or L2 adjacency or, at most, one L1 and one L2 adjacency. An interface connecting to a point-to-point link should be configured accordingly. A single Point-to-Point Hello is used for both L1 and L2 adjacencies.

Figure 4.11 shows the format of the IS-IS LAN Hello. Note that the Type field in the header indicates whether the LAN Hello is level 1 or level 2. L1 LAN Hellos are type 15 (0x0f), and L2 LAN Hellos are type 16 (0x10).

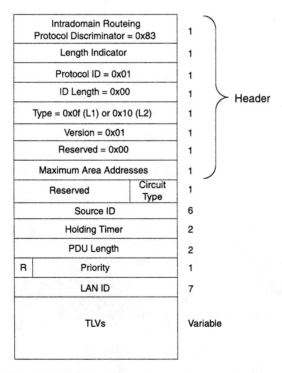

Figure 4.11   The IS-IS LAN Hello PDU format.

- **Circuit Type** is a 2-bit field indicating the types of adjacencies the originating router will accept. Table 4.1 lists the meanings of the circuit type values. The 6 bits preceding the Circuit Type field are reserved and are always set to 0. Receiving routers ignore these 6 bits.

Table 4.1   Circuit Type Values

Value*	Circuit Type
0	Reserved value. If set to this value, the entire PDU is ignored.
1	Level 1 only.
2	Level 2 only.
3	Both L1 and L2. (Originator is a level 2 intermediate system and will use this link for both L1 and L2 adjacencies.)

* A Level 1 LAN Hello must have a circuit type value of either 1 or 3. A Level 2 LAN Hello must have a circuit type value of either 2 or 3.

The values shown in Table 4.1 have some interesting implications. The first is that a router sending L2 LAN Hellos can establish both L1 and L2 adjacencies. The second is that two L2-only neighbors with the same AID (and therefore in the same area) can establish an L2 adjacency, so that only L2 information is exchanged. Chapter 7 discusses these capabilities in the context of IS-IS area design.

- **Source ID** is the 6-bit SysID of the originating router.
- **Holding Timer** specifies the maximum time a neighbor should wait for another Hello before declaring the originator dead. While the Holding Timer is functionally the same as the OSPF Router Dead Interval, you can see in Figure 4.11 that there is no equivalent field to the OSPF Hello interval. This is an indication that IS-IS is more flexible in its handling of Hello intervals than OSPF, a fact that is discussed more fully later in Section 4.3. Hello intervals are configured on the IS-IS router, but a neighbor does not really need to know this period—it only needs to know the maximum time it should wait for a subsequent Hello. Typically, the holding timer defaults to three times the configured or default Hello interval, but it can be configured separately.
- **PDU Length** specifies the length of the Hello PDU in bytes, including the header. This field is important because the TLVs included in the PDU are variable.
- **Priority** is a 7-bit value used in the election of a designated router, as discussed in Section 4.4. Functionally, it is the same as the Router Priority field in the OSPF Hello. The bit immediately preceding the Priority field is reserved and always set to 0, and is ignored by receiving routers.
- **LAN ID** is a 7-octet field consisting of the 6-byte SysID of the designated router on the broadcast network, plus an additional 1-byte identifier assigned by the designated router. Section 4.4 discusses the use of the LAN ID.

Figure 4.12 shows the format of the IS-IS Point-to-Point Hello (type 17, or 0x11, in the Type field). The Hello looks very similar to the LAN Hello, with just two exceptions:

- There is no Priority field as in the LAN Hello, because designated routers are not elected on point-to-point links.
- Rather than the 7-byte LAN ID field, there is a 1-byte Local Circuit ID field, which carries the ID by which the circuit is known by the routers at each end. Each router assigns a Local Circuit ID, unique among the router's interfaces, to the link. The Local Circuit ID assigned by the router with the lowest source ID becomes the ID by which the circuit is known by both routers.

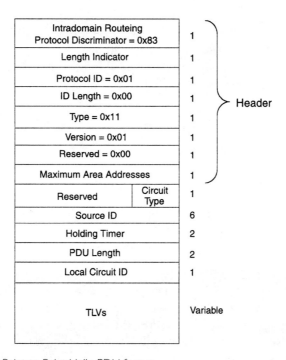

Figure 4.12 The IS-IS Point-to-Point Hello PDU format.

4.2.2.1 TLVs

Following the common fields in the IS-IS Hello PDUs are several possible TLVs. The TLVs that can be included in the Hello PDUs, and their type numbers, are:

- Area Addresses TLV (type 1)
- Intermediate System Neighbors TLV (type 6)
- Protocols Supported TLV (type 129)

- IP Interface Address TLV (type 132)
- Authentication Information TLV (type 10)
- Padding TLV (type 8)

The LAN Hello PDU can carry any or all of these TLVs, and the Point-to-Point Hello can carry any of them with the exception of the IS Neighbors TLV. Two of the TLVs, Protocols Supported and IP Interface Address, are IP extensions to IS-IS and are described in RFC 1195. The others are standard IS-IS TLVs described in the original specifications. A few other TLVs might also appear in IS-IS Hellos; they are discussed later in this book in relevant chapters on extensions to the protocol.

The Area Addresses TLV, shown in Figure 4.13, contains in its Variable part a list of AIDs configured on the originating router that must be advertised to neighbors. The fact that more than one AID can be listed in this TLV tells you that an IS-IS router can be configured with more than one AID. The multiple AID capability of IS-IS can be used for smoothly changing AIDs during a network transition. Chapter 7 discusses the use of multiple AIDs.

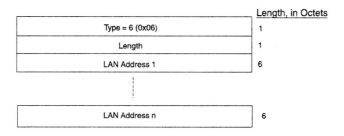

Figure 4.13   The Area Addresses TLV.

The Intermediate System Neighbors TLV, in Figure 4.14, lists neighbors on the link, by the MAC addresses of their attached interfaces—or subnetwork points of attachment (SNPAs), in IS-IS language. In this function, the IS Neighbors TLV serves something of the same purpose as the Neighbor list in the OSPF Hello, to create a three-way handshake for verifying bidirectional communication. For an originating router to include a neighbor's MAC address in this TLV, the originator must have received a LAN Hello from the neighbor during the last holding time. In that case, the state of the adjacency to the neighbor will be either "Up" or "Initializing." (See Section 4.4 for more details.) Level 1 LAN Hellos list L1 neighbors and level 2 LAN Hellos list L2 neighbors. Point-to-Point Hellos do not carry this TLV, which means some other mechanism must be used for three-way handshaking. Section 4.4 discusses the other means.

The Protocols Supported TLV, shown in Figure 4.15, specifies, as the name implies, which protocols the originating router supports. It lists one or more Network Layer Protocol Identifiers (NLPIDs), which are defined in ISO/TR 9577 and in several extension documents. Because IS-IS originally was designed to route just CLNP, this TLV was added when the protocol was extended to support IP. With it, the originator can advertise whether it supports

CLNP only, IPv4 only, or both. With the subsequent extension of IS-IS to support IPv6, as described in Chapter 13, that protocol also is listed in the Protocols Supported TLV when the originator uses IS-IS to route IPv6. The NLPID of IPv4 is 129 (0x81), and the NLPID of IPv6 is 142 (0x8e).

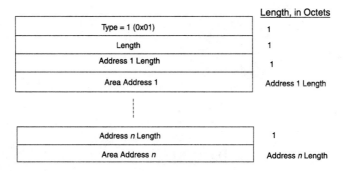

Figure 4.14 The Intermediate System Neighbors TLV.

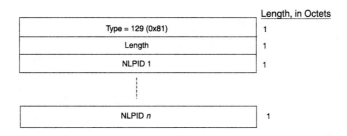

Figure 4.15 The Protocols Supported TLV.

The IP Interface Address TLV, in Figure 4.16, lists all the IP addresses of the interface from which the Hello was originated. Although in most cases an interface will have only one address, it is possible to configure multiple IP addresses on an interface. Because the length field of the TLV, which specifies the byte length of the value field, is 1 byte, and because each listed IP address is 4 bytes long, the maximum number of IP addresses that can be listed in the TLV is 63.

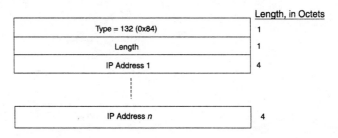

Figure 4.16 The IP Interface Address TLV.

The Authentication Information TLV carries information to be used when the router is configured to authenticate PDUs to and from its IS-IS neighbors. This TLV is illustrated in Chapter 9, which discusses protocol security.

After two neighbors have discovered each other, one of the parameters they must verify before they can become adjacent is that the maximum transmission units (MTUs)[2] of their two interfaces are compatible. For example, if one interface has an MTU of 1000 bytes and the other 1500 bytes, the router with the 1500-byte MTU might send routing messages larger than the router with the smaller MTU can receive. The result would be dropped messages, lost information, and probably broken adjacencies. So, there must be a way for two neighbors to verify that their MTUs are compatible before forming an adjacency. OSPF routers advertise their interface MTUs in their Database Description messages, as described in Chapter 5, and refuse adjacencies unless the MTU values of the two neighbors match. IS-IS tests the link MTU between neighbors by padding their Hello packets out to a maximally acceptable size, using Padding TLVs (Figure 4.17).

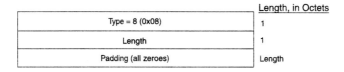

Figure 4.17   The Padding TLV.

The value of the Padding TLV consists of some quantity of 0s, which are ignored by receiving routers. The only purpose of the TLV is to increase the size of the PDU containing it. ISO 10589 specifies that IS-IS routers must be capable of receiving PDUs of at least 1492 bytes in length—a value it calls ReceiveLSPBufferSize. When a router sends Hellos, it uses the Padding TLV to increase the size of the Hello PDU either to this size, or to the MTU of the connecting link, whichever is greater. As a result, if the neighboring router has a lower interface MTU, it drops the padded Hellos, and an adjacency is never established.

Because of the 1-byte length field in the TLV, the maximum size of the value field is 255. Because of this, IS-IS routers will add multiple Padding TLVs to their Hellos to reach the needed size. Also note that padded Hellos are needed only when an adjacency is first being negotiated. After it is established, continuing to pad the Hellos between adjacent neighbors is just a waste of bandwidth. As a result, smart IS-IS implementations pad only the first few Hellos. When the adjacency is established, padding is discontinued.

Figure 4.18 shows an IS-IS neighbor table, functionally analogous to the OSPF neighbor table shown in Figure 4.10. The first display shows that the router has three IS-IS neighbors.

---
[2]   In another disconnect between IETF and ISO terminology, ISO 10589 calls the MTU the *dataLinkBlocksize*. This book uses MTU whether talking about OSPF or IS-IS, because it is the more well-known term.

The second display focuses on one of those neighbors, and you can observe information learned from the neighbor's Hellos:

- The adjacency is L1.
- The Holding Timer expires in 22 seconds.
- The Priority is 64.
- The Circuit Type is 1 (level 1 only).
- The protocols supported are IPv4 and IPv6.
- The MAC address learned from the IS Neighbors TLV is 0·90·27·9d·f2·69
- The LAN ID is "Juniper5.02."
- The neighbor's interface IP address, learned from the IP Interface Address TLV, is 192.168.1.1.

```
jeff@Juniper5> show isis adjacency
Interface          System        L State    Hold(secs)      SNPA
fe-0/0/1.0         Juniper2      1 Up            25        0:90:27:9d:f2:69
fe-0/0/2.0         Juniper4      1 Up            24        0:90:27:5b:87:f8
fe-0/0/3.0         Juniper6      2 Up            20        0:90:27:9f:34:2d

jeff@Juniper5> show isis adjacency Juniper2 extensive
Juniper2
 Interface: fe-0/0/1.0, Level: 1, State: Up, Expires in 22 secs
 Priority: 64, Up/Down transitions: 1, Last transition: 8w0d 14:29:16
          ago
 Circuit type: 1, Speaks: IP, IPv6, MAC address: 0:90:27:9d:f2:69
 Topologies: Unicast
 Restart capable: No
 LAN id: Juniper5.02, IP addresses: 192.168.1.1
 Transition log:
 When                   State        Reason
Tue Mar  8 23:13:25     Up           Seenself
```

Figure 4.18   IS-IS routers store the information they learn from neighbors' Hello PDUs.

4.2.3 IS-IS Dynamic Hostname Exchange

A perhaps surprising detail in Figure 4.18 is that where you would expect a SysID to be displayed—under the System heading in the first output and as the first part of the LAN ID in the second output—there is instead a host name. This is the result of an extension to IS-IS called the Dynamic Hostname Exchange Mechanism, described in RFC 2763. The RFC defines a new TLV, called the Dynamic Hostname TLV (type 137), which a router can add to its LSPs. The value field of the TLV contains an ASCII text name of the router, which is usually just the configured host name of the router. When other routers in the IS-IS domain receive the LSP, they can map the name contained in the TLV with the SysID of the originating router, and store the information in a host name mapping table.

Figure 4.19 shows a host name mapping table taken from the same router as the display in Figure 4.18. You can see that this router contains five SysID-to-name mappings, including its own (indicated as a static, rather than dynamic, mapping). The advantages for network operations, maintenance, and troubleshooting of having an easily understood name in the place of cryptic hex-based SysIDs in displays such as the one in Figure 4.18 are readily apparent.

```
jeff@Juniper5> show isis hostname
IS-IS hostname database:
System ID       Hostname                                  Type
0192.0168.0002 Juniper2                                   Dynamic
0192.0168.0004 Juniper4                                   Dynamic
0192.0168.0005 Juniper5                                   Static
0192.0168.0006 Juniper6                                   Dynamic
0192.0168.0007 Juniper7                                   Dynamic
```

Figure 4.19   SysIDs are mapped to symbolic names in an IS-IS host mapping table.

4.2.4   OSPF Domain Name Lookup

Some OSPF implementations support a feature similar to IS-IS Dynamic Host Name Lookup. Although the benefits are the same—providing names rather than addresses in OSPF displays to simplify activities—the feature operates very differently. Instead of carrying configured names as ASCII text in messages, the router attempts to resolve the IP addresses of OSPF displays in DNS. If you have entered all loopback addresses, RIDs, and interface addresses in your local DNS, this utility can show these by name instead of numerically. However, there is no IETF extension of OSPF to support this feature, as there is for IS-IS dynamic host names. Rather, if it is supported it is a feature added by an implementer.

A potential liability of this OSPF feature, when it is supported, is that the DNS lookup is independent of OSPF itself and dependent upon the availability of a DNS server. So if a name cannot be resolved quickly, or the DNS server becomes unavailable, your router might become slow to respond to requests for OSPF displays as it waits for DNS. The very time you most need OSPF information displays from a router—during network outages—is also a time that a DNS server is likely to become unavailable. This scenario should be a consideration in whether to use the utility. In most cases, the day-to-day usefulness of OSPF name lookups outweighs possible problems with it. And, if the feature should create problems for you, DNS name lookups can be easily disabled on the router until the DNS server is again available.

4.3 Adjacencies

As you progress through this book, you will learn that IS-IS and OSPF have quite a few optional capabilities—particularly OSPF. Before two neighbors that have discovered each other can begin exchanging routing information, they must ensure that they understand each other's capabilities. Otherwise, some of the information exchanged might be misunderstood, or interpreted differently between the two neighbors, resulting in inaccurate or broken routing. Additionally, the neighbors must ensure that they agree on some basic parameters such as that they are on the same IP subnet, that their interface MTUs are the same, how often each neighbor should expect a Hello message from the other, and so on.

To ensure that two IS-IS or OSPF neighbors can reliably exchange routing information, they form an adjacency. An adjacency can be thought of as a negotiated agreement between neighbors that essential subnet parameters match and that the information they exchange will be correctly interpreted. If the two neighbors cannot agree on a defined set of parameters and options, they do not become adjacent and they do not consider each other as valid next hops toward other routers.

4.3.1 OSPF Adjacencies

After discovering a neighbor, an OSPF router must verify that bidirectional communication is possible with the neighbor, through a mechanism called three-way handshaking. Figure 4.20 expands on the basic example of three-way handshaking you saw in Chapter 2. RB has just become active on the subnet shared with RA, and is not yet aware of RA. So, in its first Hello, the neighbor list is empty. RA, having received that first Hello from RB, sends a Hello of its own. Notice that it includes RB's RID in its neighbor list. RB, when it receives the Hello, not only has discovered RA but sees its RID in the neighbor list and knows that there is two-way communication with RA. In the third Hello shown, RB has added RA's RID to the neighbor list. When RA receives this Hello, it likewise knows that two-way communication with RB is established.

After two-way communication is established, and if the network type connecting the two neighbors is broadcast or nonbroadcast multi-access (NBMA), a designated router and backup designated router election is performed. Section 4.4 covers the mechanics of DR and BDR election.

Next, the neighbors decide whether an adjacency should be formed between them. If the network type connecting them is point to point, point to multipoint, or a virtual link (discussed in Section 4.2.3), the routers should form an adjacency. If the network type is broadcast or NBMA, an additional consideration is made: An adjacency is formed only if one of the neighbors is a DR or BDR.

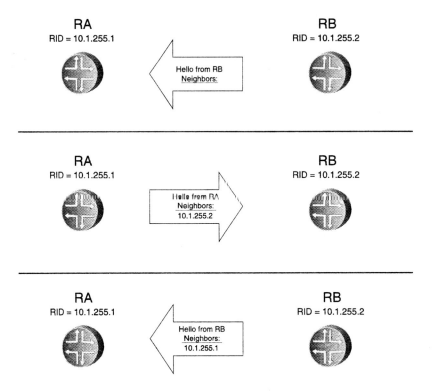

Figure 4.20   Three-way handshaking verifies two-way communication.

If the two neighbors decide that an adjacency should be formed, they begin synchronizing their link state databases. Only after the databases are synchronized are OSPF neighbors *fully adjacent*. In OSPF, both the neighbor relationships and the database synchronization are driven by state machines. The neighbor state machine and database synchronization are detailed in Chapter 6.

Throughout the OSPF adjacency formation process, from neighbor discovery to database synchronization, certain parameters must be verified as matching. If any of them do not, the adjacency is not established. Most of these parameters are in the Hello messages, and are checked when a neighbor's Hello is received. First, the IP header and OSPF headers of the Hello packet are checked for validity. Next, the values in the Hello Interval and Router Dead Interval fields are checked. If these values do not match the values of the receiving interface, no adjacency is formed. On all network types except point-to-point and virtual links, the Network Mask is also checked and must match the mask configured on the interface. On point-to-point networks and virtual links, the Network Mask field is ignored.

In addition to such standard parameters that must match between any two OSPF neighbors, certain optional capabilities, if supported by one neighbor, must be supported by the other neighbor. A router indicates which optional capabilities it supports in the Options field, which was shown in Figure 4.9. The Options field appears not only in the Hello message header, but also in the headers of Database Description packets and all LSAs. As this varied appearance might indicate, flags in this field are examined at various points during the database synchronization and adjacency process. Some options must match for a neighbor's Hello packets to be accepted at all, whereas other mismatched options can be ignored or negotiated between the neighbors. Full use of the Options field is explained in Chapter 6, but for now it is sufficient to say that some of the options flags in the Hello header are examined during the initial neighbor discovery.[3]

After examining the parameters carried in the Hello message, a decision is made whether to continue attempting to form an adjacency. If the decision is positive, the Hello messages provide input events to the OSPF neighbor state machine and the adjacency process continues.

So, When Are OSPF Neighbors Adjacent?

The use of the term *adjacent* can be confusing in OSPF documentation. In some places, neighbors are called adjacent as soon as they discover each other. In others, you are told that successful database synchronization is prerequisite to an adjacency. Which is right?

Neighbors are adjacent when they discover each other, but are not *fully adjacent* until they complete the database synchronization process as described in Chapter 6. It is a subtle difference in terminology for what is in practice a big difference in the state of the neighboring routers, but that is what we are given.

4.3.2 IS-IS Adjacencies

Defining IS-IS adjacencies can be a bit confusing if you try to glean the definition from the documentation. ISO 10589 defines an adjacency as "The subset of the local routing information base pertinent to a single neighbor." And it defines the routing information base as the combination of the link state database and the forwarding database. This implies that two IS-IS neighbors are adjacent only after their databases have been synchronized, just as with OSPF. However, when you read further in the spec, it becomes apparent that operationally, IS-IS neighbors consider themselves adjacent when two-way communication has been established and *before* database synchronization has taken place. But ISO 10589 is not self-contradictory in its definitions. As you will see in Chapter 6, OSPF uses a complex, state-machine-driven process to synchronize its databases, whereas IS-IS database synchronization is a much simpler process. There is an assumption that if two neighbors have two-way communication, they can synchronize their databases. Much of this assumption has to do with

---

[3] If you simply cannot wait until Chapter 6 to find out, the E (External Routing Capability) in the Hello's Options field must match. This flag is used to enforce the rules of stub areas (see Chapter 7), and if the flags do not match between neighbors the Hello messages are rejected.

the fact that the rules for accepting IS-IS LSPs are more flexible and forgiving than those for accepting OSPF LSAs.

Therefore, it is proper to say that IS-IS neighbors are adjacent after they establish bidirectional communication.

Two kinds of adjacency can be formed by IS-IS: L1 adjacencies, between two neighbors whose area IDs are the same, and L2 adjacencies, between two neighbors that have the same or different AIDs. Recall from the discussion accompanying Table 4.1 earlier in this chapter that the Circuit Type field on the IS-IS Hello can be one of three values:

- 1 means the originator accepts only L1 adjacencies.
- 2 means the originator accepts only L2 adjacencies.
- 3 means the originator accepts both L1 and L2 adjacencies.

Recall also that IS-IS uses two types of Hello messages: LAN Hellos and Point-to-Point Hellos. Routers treat these two types somewhat differently, so we will examine adjacencies on broadcast networks first, and then look at adjacencies on point-to-point networks.

4.3.2.1 IS-IS Adjacencies on Broadcast Networks

A LAN Hello, as you read earlier, can be either an L1 or L2 Hello. A router's IS-IS interface can be configured as L1 only, L2 only, or both. This determines what kind of Hello the router originates, and whether the router listens for messages whose destination LAN address is AllL1ISs (0180.c200.0014), AllL2ISs (0180.c200.0015), or both.

Two TLVs included in LAN Hellos are essential for forming adjacencies: the IS Neighbors TLV (Figure 4.14) and the Area Addresses TLV (Figure 4.13). The IS Neighbors TLV is used for three-way handshaking, and the Area Addresses TLV is used along with the Circuit Type field to determine the type of adjacency to form.

IS-IS routers keep track of adjacencies in an adjacency database, and reference them by SysID. The initial state of an adjacency is "Down." In this state, the router is sending LAN Hellos on the interface but has not heard any Hellos from neighbors. When a LAN Hello is received, the source MAC address of the LAN Hello is recorded in the adjacency database as the SNPA, and the adjacency state is changed to "Initializing." This state signifies that the neighbor is known, but that bidirectional communication has not yet been verified. The router then includes the neighbor's SNPA in the IS Neighbors TLV in its own LAN Hellos. When the router sees its own interface MAC address in the IS Neighbors TLV of the neighbor's Hellos, it knows that bidirectional communication has been verified. It can then change the state of the adjacency to "Up." But before that can happen, the two neighbors must agree on the type of adjacency to establish.

When an L1 LAN Hello is received, the router checks the AIDs listed in the Area Addresses TLV against its own configured AIDs. If one or more AIDs match, the router accepts an L1 adjacency to the originating neighbor. If no AIDs match, the adjacency is rejected. When an L2 LAN Hello is received, the router does not check the AID list; it just accepts an L2 adjacency to the originating neighbor.

These variables open up several possible results, based on the interface configurations of the originator and receiver of the Hellos and the configured AIDs of the originator and receiver. To demonstrate the possible results, suppose two routers R1 and R2 are connected over an Ethernet link. In the first example, the routers are both configured as L1-only and with the same AIDs. The result is an L1 adjacency:

```
jeff@R1> show isis adjacency
Interface       System         L State      Hold (secs)     SNPA
fe-0/0/2.0      R2             1 Up          19              0:90:27:5b:88:51
```

If one of the AIDs is changed so that they no longer match, the L1 adjacency is no longer valid:

```
jeff@R1> show isis adjacency
Interface       System         L State      Hold (secs)     SNPA
fe-0/0/2.0      R2             1 Rejected    22              0:90:27:5b:88:51
```

But, if the routers are changed to L2 only, and the conflicting AIDs remain, an L2 adjacency is established:

```
jeff@R1> show isis adjacency
Interface       System         L State      Hold (secs)     SNPA
fe-0/0/2.0      R2             2 Up          19              0:90:27:5b:88:51
```

If the AIDs are changed so that they again match, and the routers remain L2 only, an L2 adjacency remains:

```
jeff@R1> show isis adjacency brief
Interface       System         L State      Hold (secs)     SNPA
fe-0/0/2.0      R2             2 Up          20              0:90:27:5b:88:51
```

If one router is L1 only while the other is L2 only, an adjacency is not established, whether the AIDs match or not:

```
jeff@R1> show isis adjacency
Interface       System         L State      Hold (secs)     SNPA
fe-0/0/2.0      R2             2 Down        23              0:90:27:5b:88:51
```

Next, the routers are given the same AIDs, but R1 is L1 only whereas R2 is configured to accept both L1 and L2 adjacencies. R2 receives only an L1 LAN Hello from R1, and so accepts just an L1 adjacency:

```
jeff@R2> show isis adjacency
Interface       System      L State       Hold (secs)    SNPA
fe-0/0/2.0      R1          1 Up           8              0:90:27:9d:f1:38
```

But because R2 is configured for both L1 and L2, it sends both L1 and L2 LAN Hellos. R1, which is configured as L1 only, reflects this in its adjacency database by accepting the L1 adjacency and rejecting the L2 adjacency:

```
jeff@R1> show isis adjacency
Interface       System      L State       Hold (secs)    SNPA
fe-0/0/2.0      R2          1 Up           23             0:90:27:5b:88:51
fe-0/0/2.0      R2          2 Rejected     18             0:90:27:5b:88:51
```

Using the same configuration as before but with mismatched AIDs, no adjacencies are accepted. R1 cannot accept an L1 adjacency because the AIDs are different, and cannot accept an L2 adjacency because it is configured as L1 only:

```
jeff@R1> show isis adjacency
Interface       System      L State       Hold (secs)    SNPA
fe-0/0/2.0      R2          1 Rejected     8              0:90:27:5b:88:51
fe-0/0/2.0      R2          2 Rejected     9              0:90:27:5b:88:51
```

The next example is similar to the previous two, except that R1 is now configured as L2 only. Again, R2 is sending out both L1 and L2 LAN Hellos. R1 rejects the L1 adjacency, whether the AIDs are mismatched or not, but accepts the L2 adjacency in both cases:

```
jeff@R1> show isis adjacency
Interface       System      L State       Hold (secs)    SNPA
fe-0/0/2.0      R2          1 Rejected     12             0:90:27:5b:88:51
fe-0/0/2.0      R2          2 Up           22             0:90:27:5b:88:51
```

If R1 and R2 are both configured to accept both L1 and L2 adjacencies, and the AIDs match, both L1 and L2 adjacencies are accepted:

```
jeff@R1> show isis adjacency
Interface       System      L State       Hold (secs)    SNPA
fe-0/0/2.0      R2          1 Up           21             0:90:27:5b:88:51
fe-0/0/2.0      R2          2 Up           21             0:90:27:5b:88:51
```

However, if the AIDs do not match, the L1 adjacency is again rejected:

```
jeff@R1> show isis adjacency
Interface      System        L State        Hold (secs)    SNPA
fe-0/0/2.0     R2            1 Rejected      10             0:90:27:5b:88:51
fe-0/0/2.0     R2            2 Up            25             0:90:27:5b:88:51
```

Table 4.2 summarizes the results of all these examples.

Table 4.2 Summary of Different L1/L2 and Area ID Combinations

R1 Type	R1 AID	R2 Type	R2 AID	Adjacency
L1-only	47.0001	L1-only	47.0001	L1
L1-only	47.0001	L1-only	47.0002	None
L2-only	47.0001	L2-only	47.0002	L2
L2-only	47.0001	L2-only	47.0002	L2
L1-only	47.0001	L2-only	47.0002	None
L1-only	47.0001	L2-only	47.0001	None
L1-only	47.0001	Both	47.0001	L1
L1-only	47.0001	Both	47.0002	None
L2-only	47.0001	Both	47.0001	L2
L2-only	47.0001	Both	47.0002	L2
Both	47.0001	Both	47.0001	L1 and L2
Both	47.0001	Both	47.0002	L2

All of the examples you have seen here concern the relationship between just two routers. But an Ethernet network, or other type of LAN network, can have many routers attached to the same broadcast medium. It is possible for a set of routers sharing a common link to be configured with a variety of Circuit Type values and AIDs, resulting in several different adjacency relationships on the same link. A very diverse set of IS-IS configurations on a single link is unusual in practice, but it could happen. To understand such a network, it is necessary to understand how each router sees its adjacencies in relation to every other router in the link.

4.3.2.2 IS-IS Adjacencies on Point-to-Point Networks

The rules for forming adjacencies between two neighbors across point-to-point links are almost identical to the rules between any two neighbors on a LAN link, with one difference: Unlike LAN Hellos, Point-to-Point Hellos do not have an IS Neighbors TLV for verifying bidirectional communication. The original IS-IS specification in ISO 10589 simply forgoes the three-way handshake and requires that the underlying point-to-point medium be reliable.

This is hardly a safe bet, so an extension that allows IS-IS three-way handshaking on point-to-point links has been specified in RFC 3373. This extension uses a Point-to-Point Three-Way Adjacency TLV, shown in Figure 4.21.

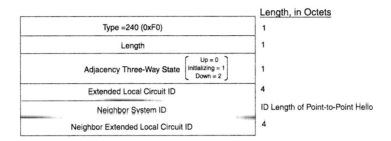

Figure 4.21   The Point-to-Point Three-Way Adjacency TLV.

When an IS-IS router supports the three-way option, it looks for the Three-Way Adjacency TLV in the Hellos of its neighbors. The absence of this TLV means that the neighbor does not support the option; in this case, the router reverts to the standard ISO two-way handshake. Normal behavior for IS-IS is to ignore TLVs it does not understand. So, if an IS-IS router that does not support the three-way option receives a Point-to-Point Hello from a router that does, the Three-Way Adjacency TLV is just ignored.

If a router that supports the option has not received a Point-to-Point Hello containing a valid Three-Way Adjacency TLV on a particular interface, the three-way adjacency state of the interface is "Down." In its Hellos transmitted on that interface it indicates the three-way state of "Down" with a value of 2 in the Adjacency Three-Way State field, and includes its circuit ID for the connected circuit in the Extended Local Circuit ID field.

When the router receives a Hello that includes a valid Three-Way Adjacency TLV, but the router does not see its System ID in the Neighbor System ID field and its local circuit ID in the Neighbor Extended Local Circuit ID field, it changes the three-way state for that interface to "Initializing." The router makes note of the neighbor's SysID from the Source ID field in the Hello, and the neighbor's local circuit ID from the relevant field in the Hello or the Extended Local Circuit ID in the TLV. These values are then included in the Neighbor System ID and Neighbor Extended Local Circuit ID fields of its own subsequent Hellos, and the value of the Adjacency Three-Way State field is changed to 1, indicating the Initializing state.

When the router receives a Hello with its own SysID in the Neighbor System ID field and its local circuit ID in the Neighbor Extended Local Circuit ID field, it changes the three-way adjacency state to Up. The Up state is also signaled in subsequent Hellos with a value of 0 in the Adjacency Three-Way State field.

You surely noticed that the three possible states of the three-way adjacency, Down, Initializing, and Up, seem to be the same three states in the standard ISO-prescribed adjacency. They are not the same states. An IS-IS router can have both an adjacency state and a three-way state, to be backward compatible with neighbors that do not support the three-way option. So, a router that receives a Point-to-Point Hello with no Three-Way Adjacency TLV will transition its adjacency state to Up, while its three-way adjacency remains Down.

You probably are wondering about the word *extended* that is associated with the Local Circuit ID fields in the TLV. Notice that the fields in the TLV are 4 bytes long. This is a byproduct of the new TLV that overcomes a limitation of the original IS-IS specification, in which a router could only support 256 interfaces, because of the 1-byte Local Circuit ID field in the point-to-point Hello (Figure 4.12). Chapter 8 discusses this extended capability in more detail.

And, one last detail you might be puzzling over: Why is it necessary for the two neighbors to advertise their local circuit IDs in the TLV, when an exchange of SysIDs should suffice for three-way handshaking? Consider a case where the point-to-point link is moved to another interface, either on the same router or on a different router, and the move happens in such a way that no link-down condition is reported by the link's physical layer. Suppose further that the new interface has the same Circuit ID as the previous interface, or the new router has the same SysID as the previous router. Such a circumstance is highly unlikely, but if you have worked with large networks for any time, you know that "unlikely" does not mean "impossible." By including both the SysID and the local Circuit ID in the TLV, such changes are more likely to be detected and cause a proper break in the existing adjacency.

When an adjacency is established, the local router sets the holding time for the adjacency to the value of the holding time in the neighbor's Hello. On broadcast networks the neighbor priority also is set according to the value of the Priority field in the LAN Hello. And, the area addresses in the Area Addresses TLV are associated with the neighbor in the adjacency database. If any of these three variables changes in subsequent Hellos received from the neighbor, the adjacency database is updated to reflect the changes. This is a significant difference from OSPF: Two IS-IS neighbors can have different advertised holding times, priorities, and lists of area addresses.

In OSPF, the hello times and router priorities must match for the adjacency to be accepted. Perhaps more important, with IS-IS these values can change from one Hello to the next. Because of this variability, the IS-IS values can be changed "on-the-fly," whereas OSPF adjacencies fail until the changes are made on both sides of the adjacencies, requiring scheduled downtime to make such changes.

4.4   Designated Routers

Broadcast network media such as Ethernet presents interesting problems for link state protocols, both in terms of database synchronization and SPF calculations. Think of six routers sharing a broadcast link, as in Figure 4.22. If each of the six routers forms an adjacency with each of its neighbors in the link, there will be a total of 15 adjacencies, as shown in the illustration. In fact the number of adjacencies that will be formed under such a scenario, given some number of routers n, is $.5(n^2 - n)$. What this formula tells you is that as the number of routers sharing a broadcast link increases, the number of adjacencies increases exponentially.

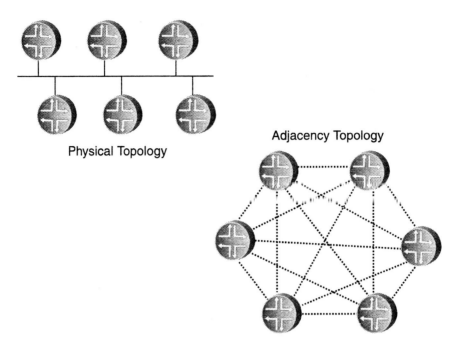

Figure 4.22   Under the procedures described so far, all routers sharing a broadcast network will form adjacencies with each other.

The number of adjacencies is usually not a problem by itself. In any sane network design, a large number of routers are not likely to share a single link, and modern routers can maintain a reasonably large number of adjacencies. The real problem is inefficiency. For each adjacency shown in Figure 4.22, the routers at each end must synchronize their databases. You already know that the information must be the same in every link state database within an area, so a single router on the network could provide the database information to all the other routers, as depicted in Figure 4.23. If all routers on the link were to form an adjacency to this one router, the number of synchronizing adjacencies can be reduced from an exponential $.5(n^2 - n)$ to a linear $n - 1$.

The other problem with the network in Figure 4.22 is how it is represented in SPF calculations, where the shortest path from every node to every other node is determined. If each of the routers (nodes) in Figure 4.22 advertises itself and each of its five adjacencies to the larger network (routers not connected to the broadcast network), a large amount of redundant information is flooded and the SPF calculation becomes unnecessarily complicated.

Instead, the network can be represented as a *pseudonode*,[4] as shown in Figure 4.24. Rather than each router advertising the attached broadcast network and its adjacent neighbors on the link, a single advertisement can be flooded that specifies the link and lists the nodes attached to the link. The attached routers then advertise just an adjacency to the pseudonode rather than adjacencies to the other attached routers.

---

[4] *Pseudonode* is an IS-IS term, and does not appear in OSPF RFCs. But the term is useful and descriptive, so I use it when talking about both IS-IS and OSPF.

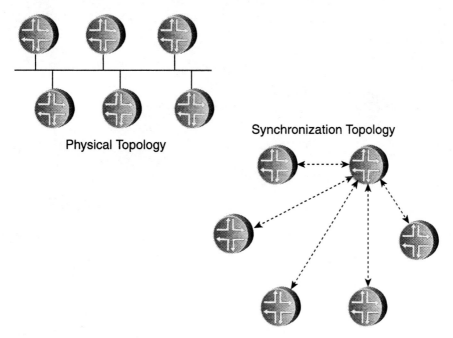

Figure 4.23   Exchange of redundant information across the broadcast network is reduced if one router is the database synchronization neighbor for all the other routers.

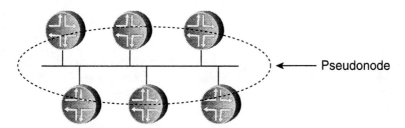

Figure 4.24   A pseudonode allows the SPF process to view a broadcast link and its attached nodes as a single node.

Figure 4.25 shows how the pseudonode figures into the SPF calculation. Each of the routers connected to the broadcast network on the left (routers B, C, D, E, F, and G) send their normal link state advertisements, and in these advertisements they show their normal interface cost to the broadcast link. But a link state advertisement is also generated by one router for the pseudonode itself. This link state advertisement has its own ID, which in the example of Figure 4.25 is H. "Node" H indicates that routers B, C, D, E, F, and G are directly connected neighbors, at a cost of 0. The SPF process in all routers then sees H as just another node, and calculates the tree shown in the right side of the illustration.

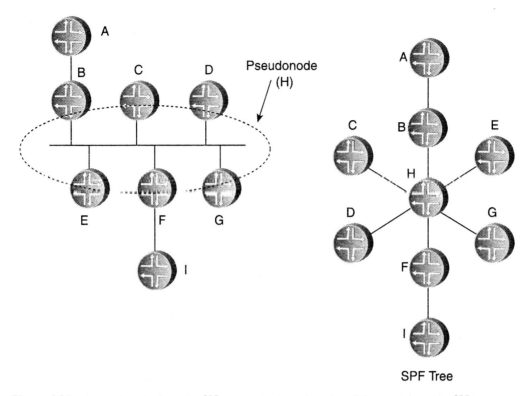

Figure 4.25   A pseudonode allows the SPF process to view a broadcast link as a node on the SPF tree.

You can see from Figure 4.25 how a pseudonode simplifies the SPF tree. However, although the pseudonode is seen as a node on the tree, it should not be seen as an extra router hop—that is why the pseudonode's link state advertisement shows a cost of 0 to the node's directly connected neighbors. Suppose all routers in Figure 4.25 advertise an interface cost of 1. The route from A to I, then, would be a cost of 3: 1 from A to B, 1 from B to H, 0 from H to F, and 1 from F to I. H is seen as a node but does not effect the physical route costs.

Key to making both the simplified database synchronization and the pseudonode possible is the selection of a *designated router*. The designated router is one of the routers on the broadcast link to which all other routers on the link synchronize their databases, and the designated router is responsible for originating the link state advertisement that represents the pseudonode. OSPF and IS-IS both use designated routers, although their implementations of the concept vary in significant ways. The remainder of this section examines how the two protocols select and use designated routers.

4.4.1   OSPF Designated Routers

OSPF elects a designated router (DR) on all multi-access links: broadcast and NBMA. The DR forms an adjacency with all other OSPF routers on the network, and the other routers synchronize their LS databases only with the DR. The DR represents the network to the rest of the OSPF area by producing a special LSA called a Network LSA, which is described in detail in Chapter 5 along with the other basic OSPF LSA types.

When routers are synchronizing their databases with the DR over a broadcast link, it would be a waste of bandwidth and interface resources for the DR to produce duplicate Update packets for each and every adjacency. To avoid this inefficiency, multicast addresses are used. The DR sends packets to the other routers on the network using a destination address of 224.0.0.5 (called *AllSPFRouters*); the other routers communicate with the DR by sending packets to the multicast address 224.0.0.6 (called *AllDRouters*). By definition, NBMA networks do not support broadcasting and multicasting, so on these networks the DR and its adjacent routers must communicate using unicast on every adjacency. (This sounds like a worse problem than it actually is. In reality, the DR election happens very fast.)

The broadcast or NBMA network represented by the DR is seen by the SPF process and the graph of nodes it derives as a single node—a pseudonode, as described in the previous section. The OSPF pseudonode is represented by the address of the DR's interface attached to the network. This means that if the DR fails, a new DR must be elected, the other routers must synchronize their LS databases to this new DR, and the new DR must advertise its own Network LSA indicating that the pseudonode is now represented by its own interface address. The problem is that until a new DR is elected, adjacencies formed with it and databases resynchronized, and until a new Network LSA is advertised, the network might appear as unreachable to the rest of the OSPF domain.

To minimize the impact of a failed DR, OSPF elects a backup designated router (BDR) in addition to the DR. Routers that are neither the DR nor the BDR (called *DROthers* in OSPF parlance) form adjacencies with both the DR and the BDR. The DR and BDR are also adjacent, and the BDR synchronizes with the DR just like the DROthers. Figure 4.26 illustrates this relationship. The BDR also listens to the ALLDRouters multicast address on broadcast links. Beyond that, the job of the BDR is like that of a vice president: to read the obituaries. That is, it quietly monitors the DR and if it detects that the DR has failed, it immediately takes over the job. The DROthers are already adjacent with the BDR, and because the BDR has synchronized to the DR just as the DROthers have, everyone should have the same LS database—resynchronization is not necessary. As a result, recovery from a DR failure should be faster.

Looking back at the Hello packet in Figure 4.9, notice the Router Priority, Designated Router, and Backup Designated Router fields. These are the specific fields used for the election of DRs and BDRs. Every broadcast and NBMA interface is assigned a priority value, which can be any number between 0 and 255. The value of the priority can be manually specified, and if it is not specified most routers will use some predetermined default value. However, RFC 2328 does not specify what the default should be, so it might vary from implementation to implementation. The default priority of Cisco Systems routers, for example, is 1, whereas the default for Juniper Networks routers is 128. If an interface has an assigned priority value of 0, the router is ineligible to be a DR or BDR on the connected network. The Designated Router and Backup Designated Router fields carry the IP address of the DR and BDR, if they are known. If the addresses of either or both of these routers are not known, the corresponding field is set to 0.0.0.0.

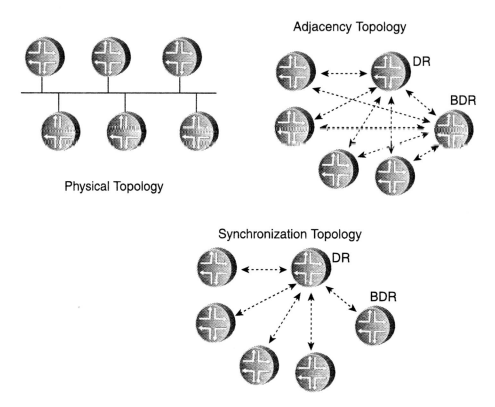

Figure 4.26   Both the DR and the BDR have adjacencies to all other routers on a multi-access network, but the routers only synchronize with the DR.

The steps preceding the OSPF DR election process are as follows:

1. When an OSPF router interface becomes active on a multi-access network, it sets the DR and BDR values in the interface data structure to 0.0.0.0 to indicate that the DR and BDR are unknown. It also starts a wait timer with the value of the interface router dead interval.

2. The router begins the neighbor-discovery process. It sends Hellos with the DR and BDR fields set to 0.0.0.0.

3. If the received Hellos indicate an existing DR and BDR, the wait timer is stopped and the DR/BDR advertised in the Hellos is accepted.

4. If the wait timer expires without a DR being discovered, the DR election process begins.

The steps of the DR election are:

1. Of all the neighbors on a link with which bidirectional communication has been established, list the neighbors that are eligible to become the DR or BDR (neighbors whose advertised priority is greater than 0). The router includes itself in this list unless its interface priority is 0.

2. From this list, create a subset of routers that includes all routers except the ones listing their own address in the DR field of their Hellos (thus claiming to be the DR).

3. Select from the subset all routers who claim to be the BDR by including their own address in the BDR field of their Hellos. From this subset, the router with the highest priority value becomes the BDR. If the priority values are equal, the router with the highest RID becomes the BDR.

4. If no router in the list claims to be the BDR, the router on the list with the highest priority becomes the BDR. Again, if the priorities are equal, the router with the highest RID becomes the BDR.

5. From the original list, select all routers claiming to be the DR. Using the same qualifications as are used for selecting the BDR (highest priority value with the highest RID used as a tie breaker), select the DR.

6. If no router claims to be the DR, the newly elected BDR becomes the DR and Steps 2 through 4 are repeated to elect another BDR.

This procedure is used not only when the network first becomes active, but also when the DR fails. It provides for an orderly promotion from BDR to DR, and also takes into account the rare situation in which a misbehaving router claims to be the DR when it should not.

Most interesting, in light of the complexity of the procedure, is that it is unlikely to be invoked very often. When a new router becomes active on a multi-access link on which a DR and BDR already exist, no election process takes place even if the new router has a higher priority. In other words, existing DRs and BDRs are not preempted. This rule makes the multi-access link more stable by preventing an election process from taking place whenever a new router joins. On the other hand, it means that the OSPF DR election process has little meaning on a stable multi-access network: The first two DR-eligible routers to become active on the link will be the DR and BDR.[5]

4.4.2 IS-IS Designated Intermediate Systems

IS-IS designated routers—or, in IS-IS parlance, *designated intermediate systems* (DIS)—serve the same purpose as OSPF DRs. They are elected on all broadcast networks (IS-IS does not recognize NBMA network types), originate a pseudonode LSP to represent the pseudonode, and all other routers sharing the broadcast link synchronize their LS databases with that of

---

[5] This assumes that two or more routers do not become active on a broadcast network within the same wait time. If multiple routers become active in the same wait time (as might happen after a network reboot or link restoration), the election process occurs as described.

the DIS. Although multicast is used for communication between the DIS and other routers on the broadcast network, there is not, as with OSPF, a special multicast address for the DIS. But underlying these functional similarities are some distinct differences in how the functions are performed.

IS-IS DISs differ from OSPF DRs in several significant ways:

- There is no backup DIS.
- An IS with a higher priority will preempt the existing DIS.
- Setting a priority of 0 does not mean the router is ineligible to become the DIS.
- A full mesh of adjacencies is established on a broadcast network, rather than just with the DIS.
- On a given broadcast network, separate DISs can exist for L1 and L2 adjacencies.

As with OSPF, IS-IS broadcast interfaces are assigned a priority. You can see in the format of the IS-IS LAN Hello in Figure 4.11 that the Priority field is 7 bits, so the priority value can be any number between 0 and 127. (The default for both Cisco Systems and Juniper Networks routers is 64.) The priority value is set separately for level 1 and level 2, so it is possible for one router to be elected as the level 1 DIS and a different router on the same broadcast network to be elected as the level 2 DIS. If a router's interface is L1 only, then it participates only in the election of an L1 DIS, and likewise if the interface is L2 only, it participates only in the election of the L2 DIS. If the interface is L1/L2, the router participates in both election processes.

When a router runs an L1 DIS election, it includes all neighbors with which it has an L1 adjacency, plus itself. Likewise, when a router runs an L2 DIS election, it considers all neighbors with which it has an L2 adjacency, plus itself. Remember that IS-IS considers two neighbors to be adjacent as soon as bidirectional communication is confirmed, whereas OSPF does not consider neighbors to be fully adjacent until their databases have been synchronized. This accounts for the difference in the prerequisite neighbor states for DIS/DR election.

If a router is attached to a broadcast network but does not find any adjacent neighbors, it does not consider itself the DIS. This eliminates the possibility of a router that can transmit packets but cannot receive them—either because of a network component defect or some network configuration—from erroneously declaring itself the DIS.

The election process is simple: Select the router within the L1 or L2 set with the highest priority to be the DIS. If the priority values are all the same, select the router whose interface connecting to the network has the numerically highest SNPA (MAC address). Unlike OSPF, a priority of 0 does not eliminate a router from the election process; it only means that the router will not be the DIS as long as another router has a higher priority. It also means that unlike OSPF you cannot accidentally create a situation in which no router on the link is eligible to become DIS.

Another dissimilarity from OSPF is that there is no wait timer and no association with neighbor state changes. An IS-IS router runs this election process every time a LAN Hello is received from an adjacent neighbor and every time it transmits its own LAN Hello as long as there is at least one adjacent neighbor. The need to ensure an orderly transition from the BDR to DR contributes to much of the complexity of the OSPF DR election process. The absence of any sort of "backup" DIS is a major factor in the simplicity of the IS-IS DIS election process, and is a reasonable tradeoff: The election process happens so fast that the benefit of a backup is negligible.

Running the election process whenever a LAN Hello is received means that whenever a Hello is received that has a higher priority than the existing DIS (or higher MAC address if the priority is equal to the DIS priority) the originator of the Hello becomes the DIS. Whenever the DIS is preempted (or resigns by lowering its priority to below that of another router on the link) the new DIS purges the pseudonode LSP generated by the old DIS and originates its own, and all other routers synchronize to the new DIS's LS database. At first look, this might seem to be a source of network instability—something good network engineers constantly strive to minimize. But you can answer that concern yourself. How often is a router likely to be added or removed from a broadcast network shared with other routers? The answer is "once in a while, at the most." Even during transition projects, DIS preemption is not going to have a noticeable impact on network stability.

Point-to-Point Adjacencies over Ethernet

Ethernet interfaces, whether 10M, 100M, 1G, or 10G, are consistently cheaper than other interfaces of equivalent speed. Accordingly, Ethernet is often used as a point-to-point connection between devices in the same equipment room, building, campus, or metro area. When used to connect only two devices, a DR or DIS serves no purpose. Yet because OSPF and IS-IS classify Ethernet interfaces as broadcast by default, one of the two devices is going to be elected as a DR or DIS.

Conscientious network engineers like to keep their networks as simple, efficient, and uncluttered as possible. To us, allowing unnecessary DRs or DISs means unnecessary network traffic, unnecessary information in the link state databases, and unnecessary nodes on the SPF tree. If nothing else, it offends our sense of network aesthetics. Although some might argue that this is fastidiousness run amok, when you manage a very large network you find yourself constantly on the lookout for inefficiencies. And some large networks can have hundreds or even thousands of point-to-point Ethernet links. To add to the complexity, some Ethernet links carry Virtual LAN (VLAN) logical links. If OSPF or IS-IS is run over these links, DR/DIS functions can again contribute to undesirable complexity.

Some router vendors provide you with the option of changing the Ethernet interface network type for OSPF or IS-IS or both from its default broadcast to point-to-point. In addition to making the overall network simple and hence more manageable, configuring point-to-point Ethernet links to the OSPF or IS-IS point-to-point network type enables the use of IP unnumbered for address conservation.

4.5   Media Types

The preceding discussion on DRs and DISs makes it clear that both OSPF and IS-IS behave differently for different physical media. Understanding these differences is important not only for correctly designing your networks but also for troubleshooting problems on your network.

4.5.1   OSPF Network Types

OSPF classifies all interfaces, physical or logical, into one of five network types:

- Broadcast networks
- Point-to-point networks
- Nonbroadcast multi-access (NBMA) networks
- Point-to-multipoint networks
- Virtual links

Broadcast networks might be more accurately named broadcast multi-access networks. More than two devices can connect to the network, and packets sent by one device can be seen by all connected devices. These days, broadcast networks almost always means Ethernet. Token Ring and FDDI, nowadays considered obsolete LAN technologies, are also broadcast networks. OSPF procedures assume bidirectional communication capabilities for all neighbors on broadcast networks, and hence that a single packet sent to one of the two OSPF multicast addresses AllSPFRouters (224.0.0.5) and AllDRouters (224.0.0.6) will be received by all neighbors on the network. A DR is always elected on a broadcast network.

Point-to-point networks always connect just two neighbors. The physical topology directly corresponds to a branch on the SPF tree, so there is no need for a DR, and no DR is elected. If IP addresses are configured on the router's physical interfaces connecting to the link, all OSPF packets are sent to the AllSPFRouters multicast address. However, the very nature of a point-to-point network is that if a packet is transmitted onto the link, it has nowhere to go except to the router at the other end. So, OSPF will operate over unnumbered point-to-point links—that is, point-to-point links with no IP addresses assigned.

NBMA networks include Frame Relay and ATM and, if you are operating an ancient network, X.25. Common to all of these media is that the network is comprised of *virtual circuits* (VCs) connecting the attached devices. As with broadcast networks, OSPF assumes that NBMA networks are represented by a single IP subnet and that more than two routers can be connected to the subnet. The key difference is that there is no assumption that a packet sent by one router will be seen by all other routers on the subnet. If the network consists of a full mesh of VCs, as shown on the left of Figure 4.27, any router can send packets directly to all other routers on the network. But economy often—if not usually—limits the number of VCs to a partial mesh, as shown on the right. "Nonbroadcast" means that a single packet cannot be seen by all connected devices. Therefore, OSPF unicasts a separate packet to each of its known neighbors on NBMA networks.

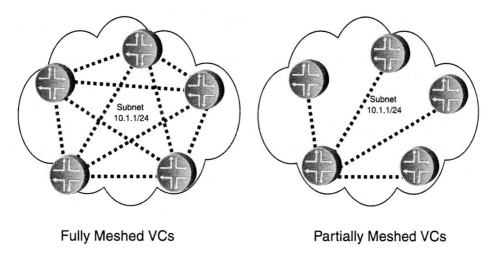

Fully Meshed VCs   **Partially Meshed VCs**

Figure 4.27   The virtual circuits comprising a NBMA network can be a full mesh or a partial mesh, so there is no guarantee that every connected device has a direct VC to every other device.

Because an NBMA network is assumed to be a single IP subnet with possibly more than two routers attached, OSPF elects a DR and BDR. But because there is no assurance of a full VC mesh, the DR election process must be carefully managed. There are two choices:

* Ensure that there is a full mesh of VCs, so that each router sends packets to every other router. This is an expensive approach, in terms of both cost and complexity of VCs. And as more routers are added to the network, the number of VCs increases exponentially. There is also a risk that a full mesh can become a partial mesh due to failures or misconfiguration, possibly causing problems for the pseudonode. Most Frame Relay and ATM networks use a hub-and-spoke VC topology rather than a full mesh.

* Select a router that has VCs to all other routers to be the DR, and then ensure that this router is elected as the DR by manipulating OSPF router priority values so that all other routers are ineligible to be the DR.

Another factor to consider when working with a partially meshed NBMA network is that some interfaces, such as Frame Relay, do not by default support broadcast and multicast packets. As a result, OSPF cannot multicast Hellos onto the network to discover neighbors and cannot unicast Hellos without knowing who the neighbors are. There are, again, two solutions to this problem:

- Manually specify, at each router, the address and router priority of each of its neighbors and the data link identifier (such as Frame Relay DLCI) on which each neighbor address is found.

- If your router software supports it, you can change the interface to support broadcast and multicast, and then change the OSPF network type from NBMA to broadcast.

Figure 4.28 shows an example of the first option, using Cisco Systems IOS to perform the configuration. The interface configuration includes statements that map three neighbor IP addresses to the Frame Relay DLCIs that connect to the neighbors. Under the OSPF section, you can see that the addresses and the router priorities of the three neighbors are manually provided to OSPF. The priority of all three neighbors is 0, which means they are ineligible to become DRs. The router on which this configuration resides has a default priority, and the configurations on all of the neighbors referring to this router will assign a priority value greater than 0. As a result, this router becomes the DR.

```
interface Serial0
    encapsulation frame-relay
    ip address 10.1.1.1 255.255.255.0
    frame-relay map ip 10.1.1.2 17
    frame-relay map ip 10.1.1.3 19
    frame-relay map ip 10.1.1.4 18
!
router ospf 1
    network 10.1.1.0 0.0.0.255 area 0
    neighbor 10.1.1.2 priority 0
    neighbor 10.1.1.3 priority 0
    neighbor 10.1.1.4 priority 0
```

Figure 4.28   An OSPF configuration for a Frame Relay network, manually identifying neighbors and the neighbors' router priority values.

Figure 4.29 shows the second option, in which broadcast (and by extension, multicast) support is added to the neighbor-to-DLCI mappings, allowing the OSPF network type to be changed to broadcast. Because Hellos can be exchanged using this configuration, router priorities are assigned only on the routers to which the priority applies. A priority of 50 is assigned to this router, and a priority of 0 is again configured for the neighbors so that this router will become the DR.

```
interface Serial0
   encapsulation frame-relay
   ip address 10.1.1.1 255.255.255.0
   ip ospf network broadcast
   ip ospf priority 50
   frame-relay map ip 10.1.1.2 17 broadcast
   frame-relay map ip 10.1.1.3 19 broadcast
   frame-relay map ip 10.1.1.4 18 broadcast
!
router ospf 1
   network 10.1.1.0 0.0.0.255 area 0
```

Figure 4.29   An OSPF configuration for a Frame Relay network, in which the OSPF network type is broadcast rather than NBMA.

A simpler alternative to running OSPF over NBMA networks is to use the fourth OSPF network type, point-to-multipoint. OSPF point-to-multipoint treats the NBMA VCs as a collection of point-to-point links, and as a result no DR election takes place. Figure 4.30 shows an example using this network type. Notice that no router priority is assigned, because none is needed. There are also no static mappings of neighbor addresses to DLCIs; instead, Frame Relay uses inverse ARP to map dynamically the network to data link addresses.

```
interface Serial0
   encapsulation frame-relay
   ip address 10.1.1.1 255.255.255.0
   ip ospf network point-to-multipoint
!
router ospf 1
   network 10.1.1.0 0.0.0.255 area 0
```

Figure 4.30   An OSPF configuration for a Frame Relay network, using an OSPF point-to-multipoint network type.

The simplest approach to OSPF over NBMA networks springs directly from the way most VCs are configured in modern NBMA networks. Rather than treating the network as a single subnet attached to the routers' physical interfaces, multiple logical interfaces (also called subinterfaces) are configured on the physical interface, and each VC attaches to a logical interface. Each VC is then treated as a separate point-to-point link, either with its own subnet address or as an IP unnumbered link. With this underlying configuration, you simply specify the logical interfaces as OSPF point-to-point network types (see Figure 4.31).

```
interface Serial0
  no ip address
  encapsulation frame-relay
interface Serial 0.17 point-to-point
  ip address 10.1.1.1 255.255.255.254
  frame-relay interface-dlci 17
interface Serial 0.18 point-to-point
  ip address 10.1.1.5 255.255.255.254
  frame-relay interface-dlci 18
interface Serial 0.19 point-to-point
  ip address 10.1.1.9 255.255.255.254
  frame-relay interface-dlci 19
!
router ospf 1
  network 10.1.1.0 0.0.0.255 area 0
```

Figure 4.31   An OSPF configuration for a Frame Relay network, in which each VC is treated as a point-to-point link with its own subnet.

The fifth OSPF network type, virtual link, cannot be easily described until OSPF area issues are discussed in more detail. Therefore, Chapter 7 describes virtual links.

4.5.2   IS-IS Network Types

IS-IS, in contrast to OSPF, supports only two network types (or *subnetwork types*, in IS-IS terminology):

■ Broadcast (LAN) networks
■ General topology networks

Broadcast networks are the same in IS-IS as they are in OSPF: networks to which more than two devices can attach, and over which a single PDU can be received by all attached devices. As with OSPF, the primary characteristic of an IS-IS broadcast network type is that a DIS is elected to represent the network as a pseudonode. Also as with OSPF, there is an assumption that a single PDU sent to one of the two IS-IS multicast MAC addresses AllL1ISs (0180.c200.0014) or AllL2ISs (0180.c200.0015) can be received by all attached IS-IS routers.

General topology networks are point-to-point links. The IS-IS spec breaks this network type down into several subtypes, but for our purposes it is sufficient to say that this second network type is point to point. IS-IS PDUs are unicast on general topology networks.

ISO 10589 includes a specification for virtual links, but unlike OSPF IS-IS does not classify virtual links as a separate network type. The distinction is irrelevant for us anyway, because commercial implementations of IS-IS do not support the virtual links option. Chapter 7 says a bit more about IS-IS virtual links.

The most noticeable difference from OSPF is that IS-IS has no equivalent of the OSPF NBMA and point-to-multipoint network types for NBMA support. But, as discussed in the preceding section, modern implementations of Frame Relay and ATM networks with very few exceptions treat each VC either as a distinct subnet or as an IP unnumbered link, rather than treating the entire NBMA "cloud" as a single subnet. As a result, both IS-IS and OSPF are normally configured to treat NBMA VCs as point-to-point network types.

Figure 4.32 shows an example of an IS-IS configuration on a NBMA network. In this example, the network is ATM and the configuration is JUNOS rather than IOS. But the concept of configuring each VC as an individual subnet is the same as the example in Figure 4.31.

```
interfaces {
        at-3/1/0 {
            atm-options {
                vpi 0 maximum-vcs 512;
            }
            unit 101 {
                encapsulation atm-snap;
                point-to-point;
                vci 0.101;
                family inet {
                    address 10.1.1.1/30;
                }
                family iso;
            }
            unit 102 {
                encapsulation atm-snap;
                point-to-point;
                vci 0.102;
                family inet {
                    address 10.1.1.5/30;
                }
                family iso;
            }
            unit 103 {
                encapsulation atm-snap;
                point-to-point;
                vci 0.103;
                family inet {
                    address 10.1.1.9/30;
                }
                family iso;
            }
        }
    }
protocols {
    isis {
        interface at-3/1/0.101;
        interface at-3/1/0.102;
        interface at-3/1/0.103;
    }
}
```

Figure 4.32   An IS-IS configuration for an ATM network, in which each VC is treated as a point-to-point link with its own subnet.

4.6   Interface Databases

There are two databases in which an OSPF or IS-IS router stores information about its immediate environment: the interface and the neighbor database. The OSPF or IS-IS interface database records all the router interfaces on which the protocol is enabled and the interface parameters relevant to the protocol. The neighbor database likewise records all known neighbors and neighbor parameters, mostly based on the information from received Hello messages.

This section examines interface databases for OSPF and IS-IS. IS-IS neighbor databases could also be examined in this chapter, because IS-IS neighbors are adjacent after bidirectional communication is established. But OSPF neighbors are not fully adjacent until after database synchronization, and many of the states recorded in its neighbor database refer to steps in the synchronization process. For that reason, neighbor databases are described in Chapter 6, which discusses link state database synchronization.

4.6.1   The OSPF Interface Data Structure

Each router interface running OSPF has an interface data structure associated with it, and the collection of those structures comprises the interface database. Figure 4.33 shows most of the database entry for an OSPF interface.

```
jeff@Juniper6> show ospf interface fe-0/0/2.0 extensive
Interface       State      Area        DR ID           BDR ID         Nbrs
fe-0/0/2.0      BDR        0.0.0.0     192.168.254.7   192.168.254.6    1
Type LAN, address 192.168.4.1, mask 255.255.255.0, MTU 1500, cost 1
DR addr 192.168.4.2, BDR addr 192.168.4.1, adj count 1, priority 128
Hello 10, Dead 40, ReXmit 5, Not Stub
```

Figure 4.33   The data for an OSPF interface from the interface database.

Although the format in which the router displays such information varies from vendor to vendor (Figure 4.33 is taken from a Juniper Networks router), in each case the interface data structure contains the same essential information:

- **Type** indicates the OSPF network type to which the interface is attached (broadcast, nonbroadcast, NBMA, point to multipoint, or virtual link). In Figure 4.33, you can see that the network type is LAN (broadcast).

- **State** is the functional level of the interface, as described in the next chapter. The router decides whether adjacencies can be formed on the interface state. The state of the interface in Figure 4.33 is BDR (backup), indicating that this router is the BDR on the network to which this interface is attached.

- **IP Interface Address** is the IP address assigned to the interface, and the source address of all OSPF packets sent out the interface. If the interface is unnumbered, of course, no IP address is assigned to it and this entry is empty. The address of the interface in Figure 4.33 is 192.168.4.2.

- **IP Interface Mask** indicates the portion of the IP interface address that is the IP prefix for the attached network. On virtual links and some point-to-point links, an address mask is not defined and so will not appear as a part of the interface data. The IP interface mask in Figure 4.33 is 255.255.255.0.

- **Area ID** specifies the area to which the attached network belongs. OSPF messages originated on the interface will include this AID. In Figure 4.33, the AID is 0.0.0.0.

- **Hello Interval** is the configured or default OSPF hello interval for the interface. The routers send Hellos on the attached network at this interval, and include this value in the Hello Interval field of each Hello sent. In Figure 4.33, the hello interval is 10 seconds.

- **RouterDeadInterval** is the configured or default value advertised in Hello packets sent from this interface. In Figure 4.33 the router dead interval is 40 seconds.

- **InfTransDelay** is the estimated number of seconds it takes to transmit a link state Update packet over the interface. The LSAs contained in the Update packet will have their age incremented by this amount before the packet is transmitted. (Use of the InfTransDelay value and LSA aging is discussed in Chapter 5.) No InfTransDelay is displayed in Figure 4.33, but it is nonetheless a part of this data structure. In almost all common OSPF implementations, the InfTransDelay is 1.

- **Router Priority** is the value set in the Hello packets transmitted on this interface, to be used in the DR election. The router priority in Figure 4.33 is 128, the default value used by Juniper Networks routers.

- **Hello Timer**, which is 10 seconds in Figure 4.33, is the interval between Hellos transmitted to the attached network. The hello interval in the transmitted Hellos is set to this value.

- **Wait Timer** is the time the router listens, after first becoming active on the attached network, for the presence of a DR (advertised on neighbors' Hellos). No wait timer value is displayed in Figure 4.33 because it is not a configurable value. It is, as it is in all common OSPF implementations, the same as the router dead interval.

- **List of Neighboring Routers** is the addresses of all neighbors learned from received Hellos. The router might or might not be adjacent with all the neighbors in this list. The JUNOS display in Figure 4.33 does not explicitly show this list, and instead just shows that there is one known neighbor (Nbrs) on the attached network. You can see the list with the JUNOS `show ospf neighbors` command. Cisco IOS does display the list along with its `show ip ospf interface` command.

- **Designated Router** is both the RID and the interface address of the DR for the attached network (if there is one). Figure 4.33 shows that the DR RID is 192.168.254.7, and its interface address is 192.168.4.2.

■ **Backup Designated Router** is the RID and interface address of the BDR of the attached network, if there is one. Figure 4.33 shows that the BDR RID is 192.168.254.6, and its interface address is 192.168.4.1. As you already know from the interface state in the display, the displaying router is the BDR, which you can also see from the fact that the BDR interface address and the IP interface address match.

■ **Interface Output Cost** is the outgoing cost of the interface. This metric, which is 1 for the interface in Figure 4.33, is advertised in Router LSAs originated by this router.

■ **RxmtInterval** specifies the time the router waits, after sending LSAs on this interface, for an acknowledgement. If no acknowledgement is received after the number of seconds specified by this value, the router retransmits. The interface in Figure 4.33 has a RxmtInterval (ReXmit in the display) of 5 seconds, which is the default for both Juniper and Cisco routers.

■ **AuType** is the type of OSPF authentication used on the interface. OSPF authentication is discussed in Chapter 9.

■ **Authentication Key** is the secure information used for authentication when either simple password or cryptographic authentication is enabled, as described in Chapter 9. No authentication is configured for the interface in Figure 4.33.

4.6.2   OSPF Interface States

Like so many OSPF components, there is a state machine for determining what state each interface should be in, based on prescribed events. The possible OSPF interface states are:

■ Down
■ Loopback
■ Waiting
■ Point-to-Point
■ DR Other
■ Backup
■ DR

■ The interface is in the **Down** state when the underlying link media is unusable, either as a result of an indication from the physical or data link protocols or because the interface has been administratively disabled. No OSPF packets are sent or received on an interface in this state, all parameters are in their initial values, all timers are disabled, and no adjacencies exist.

■ **Loopback** indicates that the interface is looped back either in hardware or software, usually for maintenance purposes. OSPF does not transmit any packets on an interface in this state, but it does include the interface address in the Router LSAs flooded from other interfaces to facilitate monitoring and maintenance functions such as pinging the interface.

■ **Waiting** indicates that the router is attempting to determine whether a DR or BDR exists on the attached network, as indicated by received Hello packets. As discussed earlier in this chapter, the interface stays in the waiting state for a period equal to the router dead interval. The router sends Hellos (with the DR and BDR fields set to 0.0.0.0), but cannot attempt to start a DR/BDR election for the attached network while the interface is in this state.

■ **Point-to-point** indicates that the OSPF network type is point-to-point or point-to-multipoint and that the interface is fully operational. OSPF packets are sent and received, and if a neighbor is detected on the link the router attempts to establish an adjacency with it.

■ **DR Other** indicates that the interface is fully operational on a broadcast or NBMA network and that it is neither the DR nor the BDR. OSPF packets are sent and received, the router forms adjacencies with the DR and BDR if they exist, and it attempts to synchronize its link state database with the DR.

■ The interface is in the **Backup** state when it is fully operational on a broadcast or NBMA network and the router has been elected as the BDR. In this state, the router established adjacencies with all other routers on the network but does not perform database synchronization.

■ The interface state is **DR** when the interface is fully operational on a broadcast or NBMA network and the router has been elected the DR for the network. The router attempts to become adjacent with all other routers on the network, synchronizes its link state database with all adjacent routers, and originates a Network LSA to represent the network as a pseudonode.

Figure 4.34 shows a diagram of the OPSF interface state machine. The events causing an interface state change are:

■ **InterfaceUp**—Lower-level protocols have indicated that the interface is up. Or, in the case of virtual links, this event is triggered by the SPF calculation.

■ **WaitTimer**—The wait timer has expired.

■ **BackupSeen**—A Hello packet is received from a neighbor with which bidirectional communication has been established, and which either lists itself as the BDR or which lists itself as the DR and indicates that there is no BDR.

- **NeighborChange**—An event caused by one of the following:
  - ◆ Bidirectional communication has been established with a neighbor.
  - ◆ Bidirectional communication is lost with a neighbor.
  - ◆ A bidirectional neighbor is newly declaring itself the DR or BDR.
  - ◆ A bidirectional neighbor is no longer declaring itself the DR or BDR.
  - ◆ The router priority value in a bidirectional neighbor's Hello has changed.
  - ◆ A NeighborChange event triggers a DR/BDR election.
- **LoopInd**—The interface is looped back.
- **UnLoopInd**—The interface loopback has been dropped.
- **InterfaceDown**—Lower-level protocols indicate that the interface is down. The interface can be in any state prior to this event.

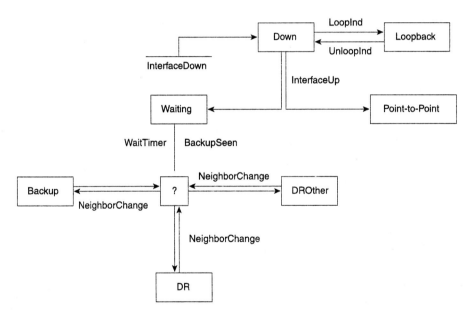

Figure 4.34   The OSPF interface state machine.

A detailed description of the events causing OSPF interface state changes, and the results of those changes, is provided in RFC 2328, Section 9.3.

Figure 4.35 shows a log file capture of an interface that failed and then was restored (by means of the author removing and replacing its Ethernet connector). The interface becomes the DR after the WaitTimer event indicates that the wait timer expired without another DR or BDR being detected on the network. Notice from the timestamps that the WaitTimer event happens exactly 40 seconds—the default router dead interval—after the interface state changed from down to waiting.

```
jeff@Juniper6> show log interface_state
Nov 22 22:40:13 OSPF Interface fe-0/0/3.0 event Down
Nov 22 22:40:13 OSPF interface fe-0/0/3.0 state changed from DR to Down
Nov 22 22:40:17 OSPF Interface fe-0/0/3.0 event Up
Nov 22 22:40:17 OSPF interface fe-0/0/3.0 state changed from Down to Waiting
Nov 22 22:40:57 OSPF Interface fe-0/0/3.0 event WaitTimer
Nov 22 22:40:57 OSPF interface fe-0/0/3.0 state changed from Waiting to DR
```

Figure 4.35 JUNOS traceoptions log entries of state changes on an OSPF interface.

Figure 4.36 shows another example of state changes, due to the same mischief with Ethernet connectors. This time, there is a neighbor on the interface, so there are two NeighborChange events due to bidirectional communication being lost and then established with the neighbor. A Hello is seen from the neighbor causing a BackupSeen event just 1 second after the interface enters the Waiting stage, and the router becomes the BDR on this network. Notice that the expiration of the wait timer again causes a WaitTimer event exactly 40 seconds after the interface enters the Waiting state; because the interface is already in the BDR state, however, the event causes no state change.

```
Nov 22 22:41:44 OSPF Interface fe-1/1/1.0 event Down
Nov 22 22:41:44 OSPF interface fe-1/1/1.0 state changed from BDR to Down
Nov 22 22:41:44 OSPF Interface fe-1/1/1.0 event NeighborChange
Nov 22 22:41:48 OSPF Interface fe-1/1/1.0 event Up
Nov 22 22:41:48 OSPF interface fe-1/1/1.0 state changed from Down to Waiting
Nov 22 22:41:49 OSPF Interface fe-1/1/1.0 event NeighborChange
Nov 22 22:41:49 OSPF Interface fe-1/1/1.0 event BackupSeen
Nov 22 22:41:49 OSPF interface fe-1/1/1.0 state changed from Waiting to BDR
Nov 22 22:42:28 OSPF Interface fe-1/1/1.0 event WaitTimer
```

Figure 4.36 JUNOS traceoptions log entries of state changes on an OSPF interface.

4.6.3 The IS-IS Interface Data Structure

As with OSPF, IS-IS maintains a database of its interface parameters. Figure 4.37 shows an example of the data structure associated with a single interface.

```
jeff@Juniper6> show isis interface fe-0/0/2.0 extensive
IS-IS interface database:
fe-0/0/2.0
  Index: 3, State: 0x6, Circuit id: 0x3, Circuit type: 3
  LSP interval: 100 ms, CSNP interval: 10 s
  Level 1
    Adjacencies: 0, Priority: 64, Metric: 10
    Hello Interval: 9 s, Hold Time: 27 s
  Level 2
    Adjacencies: 1, Priority: 64, Metric: 10
    Hello Interval: 9 s, Hold Time: 27 s
    Designated Router: Juniper7.02 (not us)
```

Figure 4.37 The data for an IS-IS interface from the interface database.

- **Index** is just a JUNOS kernel assignment for tracking the interface, and has nothing to do with open IS-IS implementation.

- Likewise, **State** also relates to the internal state machine of the Juniper Networks IS-IS implementation and is not part of the open standard. In fact, unlike OSPF, ISO 10589 does not specify any kind of state machine for IS-IS interfaces. The interface is either up or down, according to the underlying physical and data link protocols.

- **Circuit ID** is the identifier that IS-IS assigns to all interfaces on the router to differentiate one interface from another. It normally has only local significance, although it is included in the Local Circuit ID field of Point-to-Point Hellos.

- **Circuit Type** identifies the type value, as listed in Table 4.1 earlier in this chapter: 1 for level 1 only, 2 for level 2 only, and 3 for both. The interface in Figure 4.37 is type 3, supporting both level 1 and level 2.

- **LSP Interval** is the interval between the transmission of multiple LSPs. In Figure 4.37, the LSP interval is 100ms.

- **CSNP Interval** is the interval between periodic transmissions, if the router is the DIS on the attached interface, of CSNP PDUs (used for link state database synchronization, as described in Chapter 6). In Figure 4.37, the CSNP interval is 10 seconds, the default.

Because the circuit type is 3, indicating support for both level 1 and level 2 adjacencies, the remaining parameters are specified separately for level 1 and level 2, indicating that they can be configured separately for each level:

- **Adjacencies** specifies the number of existing adjacencies on the interface. You can see that the interface in Figure 4.37 has one level 2 adjacency and no level 1 adjacencies.

- **Priority** is the value added to the LAN Hellos transmitted out this interface to be used in the election of the DIS. In Figure 4.37, the priority is 64 for both levels.

- **Metric** is the outgoing cost of the interface. The interface in Figure 4.37 has a metric of 10 for both levels.

- **Hello Interval** is the interval, in seconds, between the periodic transmission of Hellos to the attached link. The Hello interval in Figure 4.37 is 9 seconds.

- **Hold Time** is the time, in seconds, advertised in Hellos sent on the attached network. It tells adjacent neighbors on the link the maximum time to wait for a Hello from this router before declaring the router dead. The hold time for both levels in Figure 4.37 is 27 seconds—three times the hello interval, which is the usual default.

You can also see in Figure 4.37 that the DIS for the single level 2 adjacency is identified.

Figure 4.38 shows the entries in a JUNOS traceoptions file made when, as was done in Figures 4.35 and 4.36, the Ethernet connector was disconnected and reconnected. You can readily see that the interface is either down or up, unlike the states associated with OSPF interfaces. There is state associated with the adjacency on the interface, but even that is a simple three-step state change.

```
jeff@Juniper6> show log isis_state
Nov 23 01:44:31 ISIS link layer change on interface fe-1/1/0.0
Nov 23 01:44:31 ISIS interface fe-1/1/0.0 down
Nov 23 01:44:31 Adjacency state change, Juniper5, state Up -> Down
Nov 23 01:44:31     interface fe-1/1/0.0, level 2
Nov 23 01:44:31 ISIS interface fe-1/1/0.0 down
Nov 23 01:44:34 ISIS link layer change on interface fe-1/1/0.0
Nov 23 01:44:34 ISIS interface fe-1/1/0.0 up
Nov 23 01:44:37 Adjacency state change, Juniper5, state Down -> New
Nov 23 01:44:37     interface fe-1/1/0.0, level 2
Nov 23 01:44:38 Adjacency state change, Juniper5, state New -> Initializing
Nov 23 01:44:38     interface fe-1/1/0.0, level 2
Nov 23 01:44:40 Adjacency state change, Juniper5, state Initializing -> Up
Nov 23 01:44:40     interface fe-1/1/0.0, level 2
```

Figure 4.38   JUNOS traceoptions log entries of state changes on an IS-IS interface.

Review Questions

1. What is the format of OSPF RIDs and AIDs?
2. What is the significance of OSPF AID 0.0.0.0?
3. How are IS-IS AIDs and SysIDs derived?
4. What is the format of an IS-IS NET?
5. What information is carried in OSPF Hellos?
6. What is the usual OSPF hello interval on LAN interfaces, as suggested by RFC 2328?
7. What is the usual OSPF RouterDeadInterval, as suggested by RFC 2328?
8. What information is carried in an IS-IS LAN Hello message?
9. What information is different in an IS-IS Point-to-Point Hello from a LAN Hello?
10. In what way is an IS-IS Holding Timer the same as an OSPF RouterDeadInterval, and in what way is it different? What is the normal value of this timer?
11. What TLVs are carried in IS-IS Hellos, and what is the purpose of each?
12. What is the purpose of the Dynamic Hostname Exchange extension to IS-IS?
13. What is meant by a "full" OSPF adjacency?
14. What is the function of the IS Neighbors TLV in forming an IS-IS adjacency?

15. In what way does a receiving router treat the Area Addresses TLV differently in an L1 LAN Hello and an L2 LAN Hello?

16. Where is a Three-Way Adjacency TLV used, and why?

17. What does it mean if the adjacency state of an IS-IS neighbor is Up but the three-way adjacency state of the same neighbor is Down?

18. What is a pseudonode, and what is its significance to an SPF tree?

19. What is a designated router (or designated IS), and what are its two basic duties?

20. How do the router priority and RID values effect the OSPF DR/BDR election process? Under what circumstances do these two values not effect a DR/BDR election?

21. In what five ways, related to designated routers, does IS-IS behave differently on a broadcast network than OSPF?

22. How do the priority and SNPA values effect the election of an IS-IS DIS?

23. What are the five OSPF network types?

24. What network types are supported by IS-IS?

25. What information is recorded in the OSPF interface database for each OSPF interface on a router?

26. When an OSPF interface is in the Waiting state, what is it doing? How long will it remain in this state?

27. What does the DROther interface state indicate?

28. What information is recorded in the IS-IS interface database for each IS-IS interface on a router?

CHAPTER 5

Flooding

When outlining the chapters and chapter sequence for this book, I encountered a dilemma: Should flooding or link state synchronization be covered first? Flooding happens whenever a link state router first starts up and forms an adjacency, as does database synchronization. But flooding also happens as an ongoing mechanism in a steady-state network to maintain the database. So does synchronization. I argued with myself over this for some time (which is one of many bits of evidence my wife cites for why I should be in a secure institution someplace).

My conclusion is that flooding can happen without synchronization, but synchronization cannot happen without flooding, so this chapter discusses flooding, and the following chapter discusses link state database synchronization. You might disagree, and want to know about synchronization first. If you do, go ahead and read Chapter 6 first and then come back and read this chapter. Just don't argue with yourself about it.

5.1 Flooding Components

Recall from Chapter 2 that flooding is the mechanism by which the topological information originated by an OSPF or IS-IS router is received by all other routers in an area, so that the routers can add the information to their link state databases. Also recall from Chapter 2 that for a link state protocol to operate correctly, the link state databases of every router in an area must be identical. Therefore, flooding requires not just a transport mechanism but also reliability features. Given these requirements, both OSPF and IS-IS flooding use the following components:

- A "container" packet or PDU for transporting information from one router to the next

- ▓ Reliability features:

  Aging

  Sequencing

  Checksums

- ▓ A means of acknowledging the receipt of flooded information

- ▓ A set of rules governing what information a router can flood, when the information can be flooded, under what conditions a router accepts flooded information, and the scope of the flooding

5.1.1 OSPF Flooding

You already know that OSPF's basic unit of topological information comprising its link state database is an LSA. OSPF uses an Update packet (Figure 5.1) to send LSAs from one router to another during the flooding process. Whereas LSAs are flooded throughout an area, Update packets are exchanged only between directly connected routers. That is, their scope is the local link. If an LSA received in an Update packet must be forwarded to another router, it is put into a new Update packet for the next hop. This is in keeping with the fact that none of the five OSPF message types are forwarded beyond the local link.

You can see from Figure 5.1 that the Update (OSPF message type 4) payload is one or more LSAs, preceded by a field specifying how many LSAs are contained in the packet. Any one of the following events causes a router to send an LSA to one or more neighbors:

- ▓ A new, previously unknown LSA is received from a neighbor.

- ▓ A more recent copy (determined by the LSA age and/or sequence number) of a known LSA is received from a neighbor.

- ▓ The refresh timer associated with a locally originated LSA expires.

- ▓ An adjacency or link changes state.

- ▓ The metric associated with a link or reachable address changes.

- ▓ The router's RID changes.

- ▓ The router is elected or removed as DR.

- ▓ The AID associated with one of the router's interfaces changes.

- ▓ A Link State Request message is received from a neighbor asking for a copy of a known LSA.

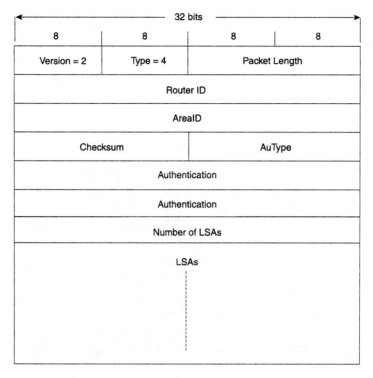

Figure 5.1   The OSPF Update message format.

The first three events are a part of routine maintenance of the link state database, and are discussed in this section. The fourth event is the normal routing protocol procedure of communicating network information. The last event, sending an LSA in response to a Link State Request message, is part of the database synchronization process and is discussed in Chapter 6.

The manner in which the Update is sent depends on the type of network link over which it is transmitted:

- If the OSPF network type is a point-to-point, point-to-multipoint, or virtual link, the Update packet is unicast to the neighbor.
- If the OSPF network type is broadcast, and the OSPF interface state is DROther or Backup, the Update is sent to the multicast destination address AllDRouters (224.0.0.6). If the OSPF interface state is DR, the Update is sent to the multicast destination address AllSPFRouters (224.0.0.5). Using these multicast addresses enforces the designated router mechanism by ensuring that only the DR and BDR receive all LSAs flooded on the link by a non-DR router, and that only the DR refloods the LSA to the other routers on the link.

- If the network type is NBMA, the designated router mechanism is still observed, but the nonbroadcast nature of the network means that non-DR routers must unicast their Updates to the DR. The DR then unicasts its own Updates to all non-DR routers to complete the flooding process on the NBMA network.

5.1.1.1   Acknowledgment of LSAs

Whenever an Update message is sent, the LSAs it contains must be acknowledged by the receiving neighbors to ensure reliable flooding. So when a router floods an LSA on a link, it adds the LSA to a *retransmit list* and sets a *retransmit timer*. Every time the retransmit timer expires, the router retransmits the LSA. When the LSA is acknowledged, it is removed from the retransmit list. The retransmit timer is configurable to between 1 and 65,535 seconds, with a typical default of 5 seconds. This is a long enough interval that on normal networks an LSA should almost always be acknowledged and removed from the retransmit list before the retransmit timer expires. A good OSPF implementation might also include a mechanism for "windowing" the retransmission rate so as not to overwhelm a slow neighbor, and a mechanism for handling a case where a neighbor never acknowledges an LSA, such as removing the LSA from the retransmit list and logging a flooding error message.

If an LSA is flooded on a broadcast link, and all the neighbors except one acknowledge the LSA, you do not want to retransmit the LSA to every neighbor. Rather, you want to retransmit only to the neighbor that did not acknowledge its receipt. Therefore Update messages carrying retransmitted LSAs are always unicast, regardless of the network type.

There are two things to know about the way OSPF acknowledges the receipt of an LSA:

- The acknowledgment can be explicit or implicit.
- The acknowledgment can be delayed or direct.

An *explicit* acknowledgment of an LSA is accomplished by sending an OSPF Acknowledgment message to the neighbor that sent the Update. The Acknowledgment message, shown in Figure 5.2, carries the headers of one or more LSAs. The LSA header contains all the information needed to acknowledge a specific LSA and a specific instance of that LSA.

An *implicit* acknowledgment occurs when a router that sent an LSA to a neighbor receives an Update from that same neighbor, containing the same instance of the same LSA. In this situation the router knows the neighbor has a copy of the LSA, and removes the LSA from its retransmit list just as it would if an explicit acknowledgment had been made. Implicit acknowledgments are most likely to occur during the database synchronization process when Update packets are being sent between neighbors simultaneously, or during flooding where two neighbors each receive a copy of the LSA from other neighbors and then send Updates to each other more or less simultaneously.

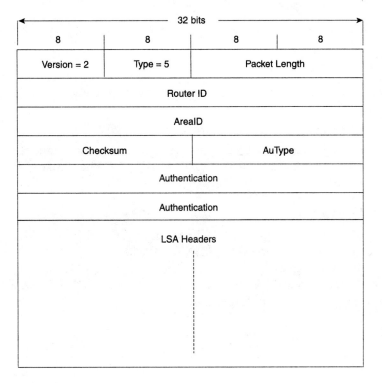

Figure 5.2 The OSPF Acknowledgment message format.

A *delayed* acknowledgment means that an OSPF router waits some specified amount of time before sending an Acknowledgment message. There are several benefits to delaying an acknowledgment:

■ It allows for more LSAs to be included in a single acknowledgment, reducing the amount of acknowledgment traffic on a link and protocol message processing on the routers.

■ On broadcast networks, a single Acknowledge message can acknowledge LSAs to multiple attached routers by multicasting the message.

■ On multi-access networks where several routers might be trying to send acknowledgments at the same time, delaying helps randomize the transmission of the messages.

If an acknowledgment is delayed too long, however, the neighbor's retransmit timer will expire and retransmits will occur unnecessarily. Therefore, the acknowledgment delay should be less than the typical retransmit period.

A *direct* acknowledgment means an LSA is acknowledged immediately upon receipt, and the Acknowledgment packet is unicast directly to the sender. Delayed acknowledgments are preferred, but there are two cases in which a direct acknowledgment must be sent as soon as an LSA is received:

- A duplicate LSA is received from a neighbor. Although there might be other causes for this happening, it must be assumed that the neighbor retransmitted the LSA because its retransmission timer expired.
- A router somewhere in the area wants to flush a self-originated LSA from the link state databases. It sends the LSA with its Age field set to the maximum value (3,600 seconds). Routers receiving such an "aged-out" LSA acknowledge it directly.

5.1.1.2   The LSA Header Format

An Acknowledgment message carries just the LSA header, rather than the entire LSA, because everything needed to completely identify an LSA is in the header. All OSPF LSAs use the same header format, shown in Figure 5.3. The Type, Link State ID, and Advertising Router fields together identify a specific LSA. The Age, Sequence Number, and Checksum fields together identify a specific instance of that LSA, so that when multiple instances exist in a network the most recent can be determined. The Length field specifies the length, including the header length, of the LSA.

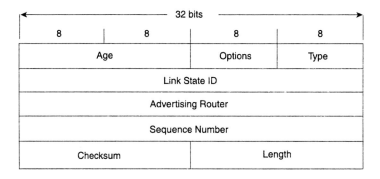

Figure 5.3   The OSPF LSA header format.

- **Options** is a set of flags indicating optional capabilities of the originating router. This is the same Options field carried in OSPF Hello messages, and is described in more detail in Section 6.1.2.
- **Type** specifies the type of LSA. Table 5.1 shows the most common types of OSPFv2 LSAs along with the associated type numbers. You are already familiar with the functions of the Router and Network LSAs. LSA types 1 through 5 in Table 5.1 are the most essential to the operation of OSPFv2, and they are described in detail later in this chapter. Other types, such as NSSA External, Group Membership, and

Opaque LSAs are used by OSPF to support optional capabilities and are detailed in the chapters relevant to those capabilities. There is also a separate set of LSAs for the IPv6-capable OSPFv3, discussed in Chapter 13.

Table 5.1   Common OSPFv2 LSA Types

Type Number	LSA
1	Router LSA
2	Network LSA
3	Network Summary LSA
4	ASBR Summary LSA
5	AS External LSA
6	Group Membership LSA
7	NSSA External LSA
8	External Attributes LSA
9	Opaque LSA (link-local scope)
10	Opaque LSA (area-local scope)
11	Opaque LSA (AS scope)

■ The **Link State ID** field of the LSA header is a 32-bit field that carries some IP address by which the LSA is identified. The derivation of this IP address varies from one LSA type to another, as shown in Table 5.2. More details about the Link State ID, as it relates to the individual LSA type, are given later in this chapter and other chapters where specific LSAs are detailed.

Table 5.2   Link State IDs for Individual OSPFv2 LSA Types

Type Number	LSA	Link State ID
1	Router LSA	Originating router's RID
2	Network LSA	IP interface address of the network's DR
3	Network Summary LSA	Destination network's IP address
4	ASBR Summary LSA	RID of the described AS boundary router
5	AS-External LSA	Destination network's IP address
6	Group Membership LSA	Destination multicast group address
7	NSSA External LSA	Destination network's IP address
8	External Attributes LSA	Encoded BGP path attributes
9	Opaque LSA (link-local scope)	8-bit opaque type + 24-bit opaque ID (see Chapter 10 for details)
10	Opaque LSA (area-local scope)	8-bit opaque type + 24-bit Opaque ID (see Chapter 10 for details)
11	Opaque LSA (AS scope)	8-bit opaque type + 24-bit Opaque ID (see Chapter 10 for details)

- **Advertising Router** is always the RID of the router that originated the LSA.

- **Sequence Number** is a signed 32-bit integer. OSPF uses a linear sequence number. When a router first originates an LSA, it sets the value of the Sequence Number field to 0x80000001, which is the OSPF constant InitialSequenceNumber. The router then increments the sequence number for each subsequent instance of the LSA it originates, up to a maximum value of 0x7fffffff. When a new instance of an LSA is to be originated, and the existing LSA has this maximum sequence number, the existing LSA must be flushed from the databases through premature aging. The new LSA can be flooded as soon as all adjacent neighbors have acknowledged the aged-out LSA.

  There is a situation in which the sequence number needs to be incremented by more than 1. After an OSPF router restarts, it might find that there are LSAs still in the area databases that it originated before the restart. If the router wants to keep a previously originated LSA in the databases, it sets the sequence number of the LSA to one more than the existing number and refloods the LSA.

- **Checksum** is a 16-bit IP-style checksum[1] calculated over the entire LSA except for the Age field, to ensure that the LSA is not corrupted during flooding. The age is not included, because if it were, the checksum would have to be recalculated every time the age changed. In addition to being checked by every receiving router before the LSA is placed into the link state database, the checksum is revalidated every five minutes as the LSA resides in the database.

- **Age** indicates the age of the LSA in seconds. It is an unsigned 16-bit integer, and can range from 0 to 3,600 seconds (1 hour). Every OSPF interface data structure has a parameter called InfTransDelay, which is configurable in most OSPF implementations but typically defaults to 1 second. When a router originates an LSA, it sets the value of the Age field to 0. Every time a router floods the LSA, it increments the age by the InfTransDelay value of the interface out which the LSA is flooded. The age is also incremented as the LSA resides in the link state database. The upper limit of 3,600, which is an OSPF constant called MaxAge, signifies that the LSA is expired and is no longer valid. What this tells you is that the router which originated the LSA must refresh it—that is, flood a new copy of the LSA—on some periodic basis less than 3,600 seconds. For OSPF, this refresh period (LSRefreshTime) is half of the MaxAge, or 1,800 seconds (30 minutes).

  The age is also used when a router wants to flush a self-originated LSA from the area databases. It does this by prematurely "aging out" the LSA—that is, setting the age of the LSA to MaxAge and then flooding the LSA. Receiving routers, seeing the MaxAge value, do a direct acknowledgment and immediately reflood the LSA.

5.1.1.3   Multiple Copies of an LSA

As a single instance of an LSA is flooded throughout an area, a router might receive multiple copies of the LSA with different age values. Figure 5.4 shows how this might happen. After

---

[1]   This is the same checksum algorithm used throughout TCP/IP.

an LSA is received by R1, it is replicated and flooded to two neighbors. The two copies of the LSA both reach R5; because there are a different number of router hops along the two paths, however, the age is incremented differently. As a result, the two copies of the LSA have the same sequence number but different ages. Assuming the router has already accepted one of the copies, it would be inefficient for it to assume incorrectly that the second copy is newer. To remedy such a situation, OSPF defines a constant called MaxAgeDiff, which is 15 minutes. If two copies of an LSA have ages that differ by less than MaxAgeDiff, but are otherwise identical, they are assumed to be the same instance.

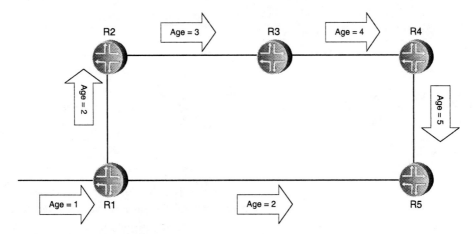

Figure 5.4 A router can receive multiple copies of the same LSA instance but with different ages.

Figure 5.5 shows a summary display of an OSPF link state database. As you can see, all the LSAs in the database are fully described by displaying the values of the header fields.

```
jeff@Juniper6> show ospf database

      OSPF link state database, area 0.0.0.0
Type      ID             Adv Rtr         Seq         Age   Opt  Cksum   Len
Router    192.168.254.5  192.168.254.5   0x80001802  1375  0x2  0xadd4  36
Router   *192.168.254.6  192.168.254.6   0x800000c1  2774  0x2  0x1205  84
Router    192.168.254.7  192.168.254.7   0x800014a3   173  0x2  0xee6d  48
Network  *192.168.3.1    192.168.254.6   0x8000000c  2774  0x2  0x8c0b  32
Network   192.168.4.2    192.168.254.7   0x800000d9    80  0x2  0xedd6  32
Summary   192.168.1.0    192.168.254.5   0x800001c0  1729  0x2  0x13b0  28
Summary   192.168.2.0    192.168.254.5   0x800001bf  1675  0x2  0xab9   28
Summary   192.168.254.5  192.168.254.5   0x800017e0   175  0x2  0x6a21  28
Summary   192.168.254.7  192.168.254.7   0x80001481   980  0x2  0x12d7  28
      OSPF external link state database
Type      ID             Adv Rtr         Seq         Age   Opt  Cksum   Len
Extern    192.168.100.0  192.168.254.7   0x80001480   773  0x2  0x768b  36
Extern    192.168.200.0  192.168.254.7   0x80001480   680  0x2  0x2677  36
```

Figure 5.5 An LSA can be completely identified by the contents of its header.

When multiple LSAs are received with identical Type, Link State ID, and Advertising Router values, the Age, Sequence Number, and Checksum fields of the LSAs are compared to determine which of the LSAs is the most recent—and hence, the one that should be accepted. The steps for comparing these three fields is as follows:

1. The LSA with the newer sequence number is more recent.
2. If the sequence numbers are the same, but the checksums differ, the LSA with the larger checksum is more recent.
3. If the sequence numbers and checksums are the same, and only one LSA has an age of MaxAge, that LSA is more recent.
4. If the sequence numbers and checksums are the same and neither age is MaxAge, and the ages differ by more than MaxAgeDiff, the LSA with the lower age is more recent.
5. If the sequence numbers and checksums are the same and neither age is MaxAge, and the ages differ by less than MaxAgeDiff, the LSAs are considered identical.

5.1.1.4   Limitations on OSPF Flooding

When an LSA is received, its checksum indicates that it is valid, and the LSA is either new or a more recent instance of a known LSA, the router must determine which interfaces the LSA must be flooded out. Essentially, the LSA is flooded out the same interface from which it was received only if the connected network is broadcast or NBMA and the router is the DR. Otherwise, the LSA is not sent on the same interface from which it was received. Another limitation on flooding is the area to which the interface belongs. If the scope of the LSA type is limited to a single area, it is not flooded out interfaces belonging to a different area from the area of the interface from which it was received. With these rules, the flooding of the LSA will, even in complex topologies, end when the LSA has reached all routers within the flooding scope.

5.1.2   IS-IS Flooding

A source of confusion for people trying to learn IS-IS is in trying to correlate IS-IS LSPs to an OSPF entity. Does the LSP serve an equivalent function to an OPSF Update message? Like Updates, it is the "package" by which information is sent from one router to another. But unlike Updates, LSPs are not limited in scope to a single link. They are flooded intact throughout an area. And also unlike Updates, the information contained in a single LSP pertains only to the router that originated it.

Perhaps we can say, then, that an LSP is more like an OSPF LSA. Just as LSAs are the basic data structures that the OSPF link state database is built from, LSPs are the basic data structures of the IS-IS link state database. But you saw in the previous section, and will see in greater detail later in this chapter, that there are a number of different LSA types providing a number of different kinds of information. There is, in contrast, only a single LSP for each adjacency type (L1 or L2). The kinds of information carried in different LSAs are carried in a single LSP, by different TLVs.

So, then, can we say that the real parallel is between IS-IS TLVs and OSPF LSAs? We cannot, because LSAs are more self-contained than TLVs. They have their own ages, checksums, and sequence numbers, whereas TLVs do not. LSAs also provide a complete set of functional information (about, for instance, a router, a pseudonode, or an external destination), whereas the information in a TLV (such as a list of addresses or neighbors, or authentication information) is intended to be used in conjunction with information in other TLVs.

The bottom line is that you cannot always draw a direct correlation between OSPF and IS-IS. The most you can say here is that LSPs, like OSPF LSAs, are the basic data units produced and flooded by individual routers for building link state databases. Because IS-IS runs over the data link level rather than the network level, LSPs are themselves packets and do not require a separate means of transport the way LSAs require Update packets.

Any of the following events causes an IS-IS router to generate and flood a new LSP:

- Router startup.
- The periodic refresh timer expires.
- A new adjacency is established.
- An adjacency or link changes state.
- The metric associated with a link or reachable address changes.
- The router's SysID changes.
- The router is elected or superseded as DIS.
- An area address associated with the router is added or removed.
- The overload status of the database changes. (Overloading is discussed in Chapter 8)

5.1.2.1   The LSP Format

A router generates separate LSPs for L1 and L2 adjacencies. On broadcast networks, L1 LSPs are sent to the multicast address AllL1IS (0180.c200.0014), and L2 LSPs are sent to multicast address AllL2IS (0180.c200.0015). Figure 5.6 shows the format of the IS-IS LSP.

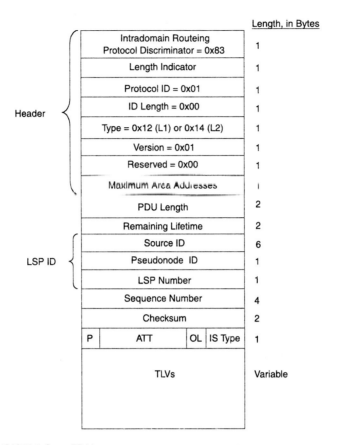

Figure 5.6   The IS-IS Link State PDU.

- A **Type** value of 18 (0x12) in the header indicates an L1 LSP, and a value of 20 (0x14) indicates and L2 LSP.

- **PDU Length** specifies the length of the entire LSP, including the header. This value helps in determining how many TLVs are included in the LSP.

- **Remaining Lifetime** is a 16-bit unsigned integer representing the number of seconds remaining before the LSP is "aged out." As such it serves the same purpose as the Age field in OSPF LSAs, but with one very significant difference: As the two names imply, age increases—starts at 0 and increments upward—whereas remaining lifetime decreases—starts at some value and decrements downward. The reason this is significant is that OSPF defines an architectural constant of MaxAge, which is 3,600 seconds, and a starting value of 1, which means the age of its LSAs is always constrained between these two constants. The IS-IS age has only one constant: 0, indicating an expired LSP. IS-IS also defines a MaxAge, which is the starting value of the Remaining Lifetime field, but the IS-IS MaxAge is configurable up to the

16-bit maximum of 65,535 seconds (18.2 hours), providing much more flexibility in managing the reflooding of LSPs and controlling the aging of its LSPs in the databases of other routers.

The typical default MaxAge is 1,200 seconds (20 minutes). As the LSP is flooded, the remaining lifetime is decremented at each router's outgoing interface, and it is also decremented once each second as the LSP resides in the link state database. So, like OSPF LSAs, the LSP must be refreshed by the originating router at some interval reliably less than the configured or default MaxAge. The refresh interval might be configurable, as it is with Cisco's IS-IS implementation, or it might be automatically determined from the MaxAge. Juniper Networks' IS-IS implementation, for example, automatically sets the refresh timer 317 seconds less than the MaxAge.

IS-IS can flush an LSP from all link state databases, just as OSPF can, by prematurely aging out the LSP and reflooding it. The difference, of course, is that setting the Remaining Lifetime to 0 ages out the LSP.

- **Checksum** is a 16-bit Fletcher checksum[2] for detecting corruption of the LSP when it is received. The checksum is also rechecked as the LSP resides in the database, typically every 30 seconds. The checksum is calculated over all of the LSP after the Remaining Lifetime field. That field is not included in the calculation because it does not remain constant.
- **Sequence Number** is a 32-bit integer. Unlike the OSPF sequence number, it is unsigned, meaning it starts at 1 and is incremented up to a maximum of SequenceModulus $- 1(2^{32} - 1)$. Although this maximum sequence number should never be reached in normal networks, it is important to understand what happens if and when it is. An IS-IS router that must refresh an LSP whose existing sequence number is SequenceModulus $- 1$ must wait MaxAge + 60 seconds, to ensure that the existing LSP is aged out of all databases. A new copy of the LSP can then be flooded with a sequence number of 1. This means that for the interval between the time MaxAge is reached and the time the flooding of the new LSP is completed, the originating router is considered unreachable.

Given the rule that sequence numbers must start at 1, the value of 0 becomes handy. Because it is always less than any normally incremented sequence number, a router that wants to receive the latest copy of a known LSP from a neighbor can set the sequence number of the LSP to 0 and flood it. The neighbor, having a copy of the LSP with a higher (and therefore newer) sequence number will send this LSP to the originator.

As with OSPF, IS-IS can increase an LSP's sequence number more than 1 in some situations. The most common case is a restarted router that discovers that an LSP it generated before the restart still exists in other routers' databases. The router will increment the LSP's sequence number one beyond the existing sequence number and reflood the LSP.

There is the remote possibility that a restarted router can flood an LSP while a previously generated LSP still exists in other routers' databases, and that the two LSPs contain different

---

[2] Defined in ISO 8473.

information but the same sequence numbers. In such a case, the routers receiving the flooded LSP and noting the differing checksums will install the new LSP in their databases but with a remaining lifetime value of 0 (expired) and reflood the LSP.

IS-IS uses the following procedure when comparing two copies of the same LSP to determine which is more recent:

1. If one of the LSPs has a remaining lifetime of 0, it is the most recent.
2. If the remaining lifetimes of both LSPs are non-zero, the PDU with the larger sequence number is the most recent.
3. If the remaining lifetimes of both LSPs are non-zero and the sequence numbers are equal, and no checksum error has occurred, the LSPs are considered identical.

The *LSP ID* consists of three fields which together identify a particular LSP:

- **Source ID** is the SysID of the originating router. ISO 10589 allows for much flexibility in the kind of address that can be included in this and other address-based fields, based on the value of the ID Length field of the header. An ID Length value of between 1 and 8 specifies the Source ID Length in octets. An ID Length value of 255 specifies that there is no Source ID field (zero length). And an ID Length of 0 specifies a Source ID Length of 6 octets. For IP routing the LSP always uses a 6-byte SysID as the Source ID, so the ID Length value is always 0, as you can see in Figure 5.6.

- The **Pseudonode ID** is non-zero only when the LSP is originated by a DIS to represent a pseudonode. When this is the case, the LSP corresponds loosely to an OSPF Network LSA. This 1-byte field is the same value as the Local Circuit ID assigned to the broadcast link by the DIS originating the LSP.

- The **LSP Number** is non-zero when a router must break its LSP into multiple parts. The maximum size of a single LSP, as specified by ISO 10589, is 1,492 bytes.[3] So if a router cannot fit all of its TLVs into this maximum length, it produces a multipart LSP: The first part will have an LSP number of 0x00, the second 0x01, the third 0x02, and so on. It is important to understand that even though each of these parts has its own sequence number, remaining lifetime, and checksum (as it must, because there is no guarantee that the parts will all follow the same paths during flooding), and is marked separately in LS database displays, the information the parts contain makes up a single LSP for the purpose of the SPF calculation. If parts of an LSP are in the database but there is no LSP number 0x00 for the LSP, the other parts are ignored by the SPF calculation.

Figure 5.7 shows five LSP IDs from an IS-IS LS database, along with their associated sequence numbers, checksums, and remaining lifetimes. The structure of the LSP ID is the Source ID followed by a period, then the Pseudonode ID followed by a dash, and then the

---

[3] More accurately, 1492 bytes is the LSP size all IS-IS routers must be capable of receiving.

LSP number. In the display the Source ID (SysID) is represented as the router's host name, thanks to the wonders of Dynamic Hostname Exchange.

```
jeff@Juniper6> show isis database
IS-IS level 1 link-state database:
  0 LSPs

IS-IS level 2 link-state database:
LSP ID                     Sequence Checksum Lifetime Attributes
Juniper5.00-00               0x3743   0x5ca6      769 L1 L2
Juniper5.04-00               0x3732   0xfd3d      769 L1 L2
Juniper6.00-00               0x380b   0x8526      984 L1 L2
Juniper7.00-00               0x37f4   0xee08      517 L1 L2
Juniper7.02-00               0x37cd   0x2576     1127 L1 L2
Juniper7.03-00               0x37d5   0xe84       520 L1 L2
  6 LSPs
```

Figure 5.7 An LSP can be completely identified by the contents of its header.

■ **P** in the LSP format of Figure 5.6 is the Partition Repair bit. When set, the bit indicates support for the partition repair function as described in ISO 10589. No commonly used commercial IS-IS implementation has ever supported this function, so the bit should normally be cleared.

■ **ATT**, the 4 bits following the P bit, are used in L1 areas to identify routers with L2 adjacencies. Section 7.4.3 describes these bits and their function.

■ **OL**, the single bit following the 4 ATT bits, is the Overload bit.[4] This bit signals an overload condition in the LS database, and Chapter 8 describes its use.

■ **IS Type**, the 2 bits following the OL bit, specifies whether the originating router is L1 (IS type = 1) or L2 (IS type = 3). The values 0 and 2 are not used in this field.

An internal flag, called the *Send Routing Message* (SRM) flag, is used in the transmission of LSPs. For each LSP in its LS database, IS-IS creates a set of SRMs—one per link. That is, if a router has 20 LSPs in its LS database and 5 interfaces, 5 SRMs will be associated with each of the LSPs for a total of 100 SRMs. When IS-IS determines that an LSP needs to be sent on a particular link, it sets the LSP's SRM flag for that interface. At a set interval, known as the *minimum LSP transmission interval*, the LS database is scanned. On point-to-point links, all LSPs that have the SRM for that link set are sent. On broadcast links, the behavior is more interesting: The LS database is scanned once every minimum LSP transmission interval, and out of the set of LSPs with their SRMs set for that interface, one[5] is randomly chosen and sent. The reason for this behavior on broadcast networks has to do with the way IS-IS LS databases are synchronized on such networks, and so is explained in detail in Section 6.2.2.

---

[4] The "official" name of this bit is LSPDBOL, for Link State PDU DataBase OverLoad, but that seems like a big mouthful for a single bit. OL is sufficient for our purposes.

[5] Some IS-IS implementations might randomly choose more than one LSP for transmission at each scan, but it must be a small number. ISO 10589 recommends no more than 10.

But in a nutshell, this randomization reduces the chance of multiple routers sending the same LSP to the DIS at the same time.

ISO 10589 recommends a minimum LSP transmission interval value of 5 seconds. This interval, like many IS-IS timers, has a random jitter of up to 25 percent added to prevent timer synchronization.

5.1.2.2   Acknowledgment of LSPs

The receipt of an LSP is acknowledged between adjacent neighbors to ensure reliable flooding. But there is no distinct acknowledgment message as there is with OSPF. Instead, IS-IS uses two PDUs called the Partial Sequence Number PDU (PSNP) and Complete Sequence Number PDU (CSNP). These PDUs, which are normally used for LS database synchronization, are detailed in Section 6.2.1. But for the purposes of discussing LSP acknowledgment, suffice it to say that both PDUs (collectively called Sequence Number PDUs) carry descriptions of one or more LSPs by listing their Remaining Lifetime, LSP ID, Sequence Number, and Checksum fields. The difference between the two is that CSNPs describe all LSPs in the originator's LS database, whereas PSNPs carry only a subset of the LSPs in the originator's LS database.

Explicit and implicit acknowledgments are used by IS-IS, but differently than the way they are used by OSPF. The receipt of an LSP on a point-to-point link is always explicitly acknowledged by sending a PSNP to the sender identifying the LSP. More than one LSP can be acknowledged in a single PSNP. If the receiver has a newer instance of the LSP in its LS database than the one it received, it sends a copy of the newer LSP back to the neighbor rather than sending a PSNP acknowledgment.

When an LSP is sent on a point-to-point link, the LSP's SRM for that link is not cleared until an acknowledgment is received, either in the form of a PSNP or a newer or same-aged LSP. This creates a behavior similar to the OSPF retransmission list. If the LSP is not acknowledged, it is sent again at the next minimum LSP transmission interval.

Receipt of an LSP on a broadcast link is always implicitly acknowledged. The mechanism for acknowledging LSPs is a part of the LS database synchronization and maintenance procedures, and so is described in Section 6.2.4. But in brief, the mechanism works as follows: The DIS periodically (every 10 seconds) multicasts a CSNP on the broadcast link, which describes the LSPs in its LS database. When a router sends an LSP on the broadcast link, the LSP should be included in subsequent CSNPs. If it is not, the originating router will resend the LSP.

Unlike point-to-point links, an LSP's SRM for a broadcast link is cleared as soon as the LSP is sent. This is because of the implicit acknowledgment via the CSNP. If the new instance of the LSP is not indicated in subsequent CSNPs, the sending router resets the SRM and retransmits the LSP at the appropriate time.

5.2 Areas and Router Types

Throughout this chapter, I have pointed out topics that are discussed in more detail in the context of LS database synchronization in Chapter 6. With the completion of the discussion of flooding, we are almost there. But there are still three basics you need to know about before tackling synchronization: metric types, and the details of the OSPF LSAs and IS-IS TLVs used in the synchronization process. These three topics depend on some knowledge of OSPF and IS-IS router types, which are best understood in the context of areas. Chapter 7 discusses areas in depth, but the very basic concepts (beyond what was introduced in Chapter 2) are covered here for the purpose of defining router types.

You already know the purpose of areas from Chapter 2: They allow link state domains to grow large by limiting the scope of flooding. The limitation of flooding in turn limits the size of LS databases, which in turn limits the computational complexity of the SPF calculations. The end result is a limitation on the amount of network resources needed for flooding, the amount of memory needed for the LS database, and the amount of CPU needed for SPF calculation. The bottom line is that rather than having a single shortest-path tree spanning the entire link state domain, we use areas to break the domain up into multiple shortest-path trees. An area boundary delineates the boundary of a single shortest-path tree.

Both OSPF and IS-IS employ a two-level area hierarchy that provides for multiple possible lower-level areas and a single upper-level area. All inter-area traffic between lower-level areas must pass through the upper-level area, to avoid looping.

5.2.1 OSPF Areas and Router Types

Figure 5.8 shows a basic OSPF area structure, with lower-level areas attached to a single upper-level area. OSPF calls the upper-level area the *backbone* area, and this area is always identified by the AID 0.0.0.0 (or just area 0). Nonbackbone areas can have any 32-bit identifier except 0.0.0.0. Architecturally, area borders are defined by the routers that connect areas—called, logically enough, *area border routers* (ABRs). A router becomes an ABR, and an area border is created, when at least one of its interfaces is connected to a different area than at least one other interface. That is, an OPSF router is *not* an ABR if all of its interfaces connect to the same area. At least one of the ABR interfaces must connect to the backbone area. This enforces the rule that traffic between two nonbackbone areas cannot transit a third nonbackbone area.

Figure 5.8 is a simplistic illustration of ABRs. In any network design, two general principles will always serve you well: (1) Always have a backup, and (2) get the most out of what you have. Figure 5.9 shows how ABRs can adhere to those principles: (1) An area can be connected to the backbone by more than one ABR, and (2) a single ABR can connect more than one area to the backbone. Chapter 7 says much more about ABRs and area design, but for now pointing out these two very basic capabilities of ABRs will suffice.

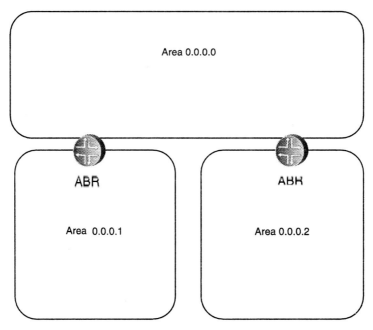

Figure 5.8   Area border routers connect the backbone area to all other areas.

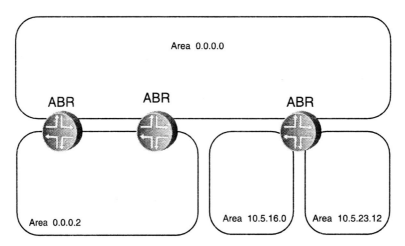

Figure 5.9   An area can have more than one ABR, and one ABR can connect more than one area to the backbone.

Some IP networks are completely self-contained and never speak to the "outside world." OSPF serves such a network just fine. But the great majority of networks need connectivity outside their own IGP domain—whether to the worldwide Internet or just to another private routing domain. When such connectivity is necessary, external routes—routes to destination prefixes outside of the local domain—must be advertised into the domain. This might be a single default route or it might be a subset of the global Internet routing table.[6] The route might be learned from another routing protocol, or it might be a statically configured route. The routers that advertise external prefixes into an OSPF domain are called *autonomous system boundary routers* (ASBRs). As Figure 5.10 shows, an ASBR can be located anywhere within an OSPF domain. An ASBR can be in the backbone area or in a nonbackbone area,[7] and an ABR can also be an ASBR.

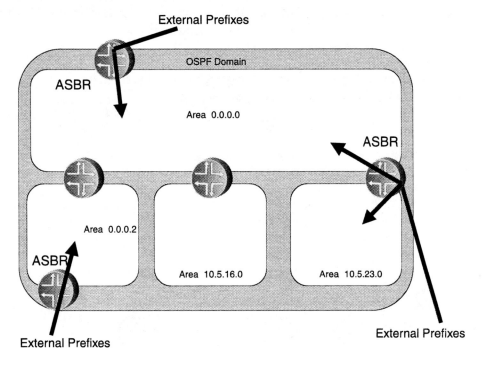

Figure 5.10 An autonomous system boundary router advertises the prefixes of destinations outside of the OSPF domain.

5.2.2 IS-IS Areas and Router Types

Areas are one of the few IS-IS concepts that are difficult to grasp at first. A big part of the reason, in my opinion, is that most people encountering IS-IS for the first time have at least some previous experience with OSPF. As a result, we want to force IS-IS to fit into our understanding of OSPF. You have already seen at least one example of where there is not a direct parallel between the two protocols (LSPs and LSAs). Although the basic function of areas is the same in the two protocols, their structure differs distinctly.

---

[6] Chapter 9 discusses the hazards of redistributing Internet routes into OSPF or IS-IS domains.

[7] In certain areas, called stub areas, an ASBR cannot appear. Stub areas are described in Chapter 7.

Like OSPF, IS-IS uses a two-level hierarchy, and all inter-area traffic must pass through the upper-level area to avoid loops. IS-IS terminology fits nicely here: The upper-level area is the *level 2* (L2) area, and the lower-level (nonbackbone) areas are *level 1* (L1) areas. However, there is no reserved AID for the L2 area the way there is for the OSPF backbone area. An IS-IS L2 area can be any legitimate AID.

You already know that the IS-IS AID is a part of the NET address, and the NET is assigned to the entire router, not to a specific interface. What this tells you is that unlike OSPF, where different interfaces can be assigned to different areas, an IS-IS router and all of its interfaces belong to a single area.[8] An IS-IS router in an L1 area that can form adjacencies only with routers having the same AID is an L1 router. Likewise, a router that is in the L2 area and can form adjacencies only with routers having the same AID is an L2 router. These capabilities are determined by configuring all interfaces on the router as L1-only or L2-only.

There must, of course, be a way to connect L1 areas to the L2 area. This is done by configuring certain interfaces on certain routers to accept an adjacency to a router with a different AID. These routers are called L1/L2 routers.

Here's where things get confusing. We want to "see" IS-IS areas depicted the same way we depict OSPF areas: as neat boundaries encompassing some set of routers, as in Figure 5.11. The problem is, IS-IS does not always fit this picture easily. In some cases, both an L1 and L2 adjacency can exist between the same two routers. And when multiple IS-IS routers are connected to a broadcast link, there can be a jumble of L1 and L2 adjacencies on the same link. Where do the area boundaries really lie?

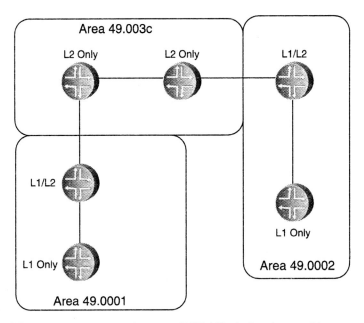

Figure 5.11   L1/L2 routers are roughly analogous to OSPF ABRs in that they provide connectivity
between areas.

---

[8] Like so many other things, there is an exception to this, which is discussed in Section 7.4.8.

You will be well served if, instead of thinking of IS-IS areas in terms of physical links and logical boundaries, you think in terms of adjacencies, as shown in Figure 5.12. The AID still describes a group of routers, but relates more to the individual routers than some sort of logical "real estate." An IS-IS area, then, is a contiguous set of adjacencies between routers with the same AID. Although this is a bit more difficult to visualize than OSPF areas, the approach permits a surprising amount of flexibility, as Section 7.4.1 will show.

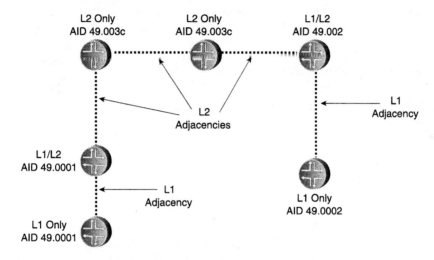

Figure 5.12 IS-IS areas are best understood as sets of adjacencies.

If we define IS-IS areas as a set of adjacencies, one of the most important factors in understanding the areas is understanding how and when adjacencies are formed. Table 5.3 is a summary of Table 4.2, showing the different possible relationships between two routers and the resulting adjacencies that result depending on whether their AIDs are the same or different. You will see the table again in Chapter 7 when area architectures and design are discussed in much greater detail.

IS-IS does not have a named router type for routers that advertise external prefixes into the domain, as does OSPF. But certain rules must be followed, and these are also discussed in Chapter 7.

Table 5.3   Summary of Different L1/L2 and Area ID Combinations, and the Resulting Adjacencies

R1 Type	R2 Type	AIDs	Adjacency
L1-only	L1-only	Same	L1
L1-only	L1-only	Different	None
L2-only	L2-only	Same	L2
L2-only	L2-only	Different	L2
L1-only	L2-only	Same	None
L1-only	L2-only	Different	None
L1-only	Both	Same	L1
L1-only	Both	Different	None
L2-only	Both	Same	L2
L2-only	Both	Different	L2
Both	Both	Same	L1 and L2
Both	Both	Different	L2

5.3   Metric Types

Both OSPF and IS-IS use a dimensionless metric that is best named *cost*. The metric is assigned to every interface on which the protocol runs, either administratively or by some default value, and is essential for determining the shortest path between any two nodes. When evaluating the route from some source A to some destination Z, the cost of the route is the sum of the costs of all outgoing router interfaces from A to Z.

5.3.1   OSPF Metrics

RFC 2328 and its predecessors do not specify or suggest a default interface cost for OSPF, other than that it must be greater than 0. That leaves the potential for implementations to vary widely in their default value. Fortunately, many vendors have copied Cisco Systems' method for determining default costs, thereby creating a reasonable consistency across vendors.

This method, rather than having a single default for all interfaces, calculates the cost by dividing 100Mbps by the interface bandwidth. So, for example, a 10Mbps Ethernet interface will have a cost of 100/10 = 10, and a 56kbps link will have a cost of 100000/56 = 1,785 (fractional values are ignored). This 100Mbps constant is called the *reference bandwidth*.

The problem with the costing algorithm is that it was invented in the days when 100Mbps was a very high-bandwidth link. Any interface bandwidth of 100Mbps yields a cost of 1, the lowest cost possible. When a bandwidth greater than 100Mbps is used, the result of this calculation is rounded up to 1. But modern large-scale networks routinely use links with greater bandwidth, and even in smaller networks it is not unusual to find 1G Ethernet links.

To compensate for the realities of modern networks, the reference bandwidth is configurable to a higher value.

You can set the interface manually rather than use the automatic costing algorithm. If your network is large, it is usually wise to develop a well thought-out costing plan that realistically reflects your ideas about traffic behavior, and use this plan to administratively assign interface costs. Manually assigned costs might be based, for example, on line-of-sight or wire/fiber distance between sites.

The metric assigned to prefixes within an area is 16 bits long. Prefixes that are outside of an area—either somewhere else within the OSPF domain or external to the OSPF domain—are given a 24-bit metric when they are advertised into the area. The rationale for this is that the path to an external destination is likely to be longer, and therefore of a higher cost, and can require a larger size metric.

When an external prefix is advertised into the OSPF domain, there can be no assumption that any metric externally assigned to it will be meaningful to OSPF. So the prefix is assigned a metric by the ASBR that advertises it into the domain. This metric assignment is specified as a part of the routing policy configuration on the ASBR that redistributes the prefix.

The metric assigned to external prefixes can be one of two types:

- Type 1 External (E1) metrics take into account both the cost assigned by the ASBR and the cost to the ASBR.
- Type 2 External (E2) metrics remain just the cost assigned by the ASBR, and do not change as the prefix is advertised through the OSPF domain.

Figure 5.13 illustrates how E1 and E2 metrics differ. ASBRs 1 and 2 both are advertising a route to external prefix 192.168.1/24, but ASBR1 assigns a cost of 10 to the prefix and ASBR2 assigns a cost of 5. The router on the left has paths to both ASBRs, but the cost of the path to ASBR1 is 20, whereas the cost to ASBR2 is 30. If the two ASBRs make the assigned cost of the external prefix E1, the cost of the route to the prefix through ASBR1 is 30 (20 + 10) whereas the cost of the route to the prefix through ASBR2 is 35 (30 + 5). The route through ASBR1 is chosen as the lower-cost route.

If the ASBRs make the assigned costs E2 metrics, the costs of the paths to the ASBRs is not taken into consideration when choosing the shortest route to the destination. As a result, the router on the left sees the cost of the route through ASBR1 as 10 and the cost of the route through ASBR2 as 5. The route through ASBR2 then has the lower cost and is chosen.

The availability of these two external metric types gives you flexibility in choosing how to reach external destinations. If you always want to choose the closest exit out of the OSPF domain, use E1. However, in most cases, choosing the ASBR that is "closest" to the external destination is more important, either for financial or performance reasons. In this case, E2 metrics are used.

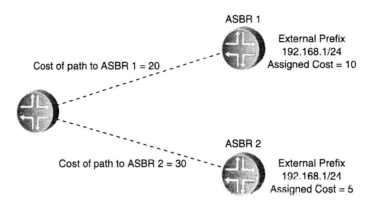

Figure 5.13   The choice of route to the external prefix 192.168.1/24 depends on whether the two ASBRs assign their costs as E1 or E2 metrics.

E1 and E2 metrics can both exist in an OSPF domain, and can even be assigned to the same prefix by different ASBRs. Therefore, there are two rules for managing conflicts:

- If one ASBR advertises a prefix with an E1 metric and another ASBR advertises the same prefix with an E2 metric, the E1 metric takes precedence.
- If two ASBRs advertise the same prefix with the same E2 cost, the cost of the internal paths to the ASBRs is considered and the route through the lowest-cost ASBR is chosen.

5.3.2   IS-IS Metrics

There is quite a bit of divergence between the IS-IS metrics prescribed by ISO 10589 and the IS-IS metrics used in real-life networks. ISO 10589 specifies four different 6-bit metric fields that can be assigned to an IS-IS interface:

- A **default** metric, which must be understood by every router in the IS-IS domain. The dimension of this metric is undefined, and can represent whatever you want it to represent. In practice it normally represents interface cost, the same as the OSPF metric.
- A **delay** metric, which represents the transit delay of the attached link.
- An **expense** metric, which represents the monetary cost of using the attached link.
- An **error** metric, which represents the probability of encountering errors on the network—in other words, a measure of the relative reliability of the link.

The use of the default metric is mandatory, and the other three metrics are optional. The idea behind these four metrics is to provide a rudimentary (by today's standards) QoS-based traffic engineering capability. A router performs separate SPF calculations for each of the supported metrics, to derive separate routes based on each of the metrics.

No commercial IS-IS implementation supports the three optional metrics. Aside from the potential impact on router performance and memory of running separate SPF calculations for each metric and recording the multiple resulting routes, no user demand for such a scheme has arisen to warrant vendor support. Only the default metric is used.

Both Juniper Networks and Cisco Systems routers set the IS-IS metric to a default value of 10 for all interfaces. You should have a good costing plan for your IS-IS network that reflects the realities of your link types and physical architecture. Leaving all metrics at the default values means that IS-IS will choose its routes based on the least number of router hops.

Associated with the 6-bit IS-IS metric is an *internal/external* (I/E) bit. This bit distinguishes whether the prefix is located internally to the IS-IS domain or external to the domain.

The 6-bit metric width means that the range of metric values that can be assigned to an interface is 0 through 63. Part of the original thinking behind this small metric value was that the SPF algorithm would be more efficient and require fewer processor cycles. But with modern routers, this concern is unfounded. And in larger networks, there is a concern that such a limited range does not provide enough metric granularity (64 possible values versus OSPF's 65,535 possible values). To alleviate this concern, an extension to IS-IS is now supported by many implementations that allows for a 32-bit metric field. To distinguish which metrics routers support, the original 6-bit metrics are called *narrow* metrics, and the 32-bit metrics are called *wide* metrics. The TLV that supports wide metrics, the Extended IP Reachability TLV, is described in Section 5.5.8.

Wide and Narrow IS-IS Metrics in Multi-Vendor Networks

Although several router vendors support wide metrics (primarily those that sell to carriers or that support traffic engineering), it seems that they all support them a bit differently. For example, Cisco Systems routers default to narrow only but can be configured to support wide only (`metric-style wide`) or both narrow and wide (`metric-style wide transition`). Juniper Networks, on the other hand, defaults to both narrow and wide metrics but can be configured for wide only (`wide-metrics-only`). A difference still exists, however, because when a Cisco router is configured for either narrow only or wide only, it is limited to generating and receiving only that metric type. When a Juniper router is configured for wide only, it generates only that type but still accepts both narrow and wide metrics.

Then there is Avici Systems, which can be configured to support narrow only (`use-metric-style narrow`), wide only (`use-metric-style wide`), support both but prefer narrow (`use-metric-style prefer-narrow`), or support both but prefer wide (`use-metric-style prefer-wide`). Avici's default is narrow only.

The point is that in a multivendor network, if you want to use wide metrics be sure you understand each of your vendors' procedures for both generating and receiving metrics. Manuals are not always clear, so talk to engineers from each of your vendors.

5.4   Essential LSAs

This section and Section 5.5, covering TLVs, examine the nuts and bolts of the essential data entities used by OSPF and IS-IS. This kind of information is admittedly dry as toast, so whether you read these two sections in depth or just skim them depends on your tolerance for such details. However, at least a passing familiarity with the LSAs and TLVs is necessary if you want to understand OSPF and IS-IS.

By "essential LSAs," I mean the five LSAs necessary for basic OSPF operation. If you are running traffic engineering, a not-so-stubby area, or a number of other extended features, other LSAs are essential to your network as well. They are introduced in the succeeding chapters covering the extensions they support.

The five essential LSAs are:

- Router LSAs
- Network LSAs
- Network Summary LSAs
- ASBR Summary LSAs
- AS-External LSAs

5.4.1   Router LSAs

Every router originates a Router LSA (Figure 5.14). The purpose of the LSA is to advertise the originating router, the router's attached links, the cost of those links, and its adjacent neighbors. The Router LSA has an area flooding scope: It is flooded throughout the area in which it is originated, but never to other areas.

- The Router LSA type is 1, and the Link State ID is the originating router's RID.
- V (Virtual Link), when set, indicates that the originating router is a virtual link endpoint. Virtual links are covered in Chapter 7.
- E (External), when set, indicates that the router is an ASBR.
- B (Border), when set, indicates that the router is an ABR.
- Number of Links specifies how many router links are listed in this LSA. The remaining fields in the LSA repeat the number of times specified here.

- **Type** indicates the type of link described by the fields to follow. Table 5.4 lists the possible values of this field and the link types the values represent.

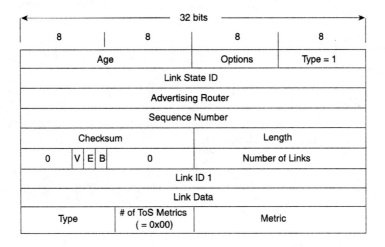

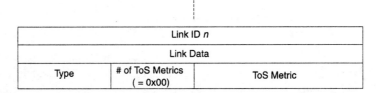

Figure 5.14   The Router LSA.

Table 5.4   Link Type Values and Their Meanings

Type	Description
1	Point-to-point connection to another router
2	Connection to a transit network
3	Connection to a stub network
4	Virtual link

- **Link ID** varies according to the link type. Table 5.5 shows what the Link ID field contains for various link types. If the link connects to another router (type 1, 2, or 4), the value shown is also the value of the neighbor's LSA Link State ID. This is how the two routers' LSAs are related during the SPF calculation.

Table 5.5   Information in the Link ID Field for the Four Link Types

Type	Link ID
1	Neighboring router's RID
2	IP address of DR
3	Network IP address
4	Neighboring router's RID

■ **Link Data** also varies according to the link type. This information is used to derive the next-hop address for routes passing over the link. Table 5.6 shows the contents of the Link Data field for each link type.

Table 5.6   Information in the Link Data Field for the Four Link Types

Type	Link Data
1	For numbered point-to-point links: the IP address of the originating router's interface to the link
	For unnumbered links: the MIB-II ifIndex value of the router's interface to the link
2	IP address of the originating router's interface to the link
3	Stub network's IP address mask (Note that host routes are type 3 links, and this field contains a mask of 255.255.255.255.)
4	The MIB-II ifIndex value of the originating router's interface to the virtual link

■ **Number of ToS Metrics** is included for backward compatibility with earlier OSPFv2 specifications (RFC 1583 and before). If this field is non-zero, a matching number of 32-bit fields containing various ToS metrics and their type numbers follow the metric field for this link. However, modern OSPF implementations do not utilize these ToS metrics, and so this field is always 0. The format in Figure 5.14 reflects this absence of ToS metric fields.

Figure 5.15 shows a display of a Router LSA from an OSPF database. After the LSA header information, you can see that none of the three flags are set (`bits 0x0`) and that the number of links is 5. The Link ID, Link Data, Type, Number of ToS Metrics, and Metric field values for each link are then listed. `TOS 0` refers to the metric in the context of the old ToS metrics; this metric is ToS metric type 0.

```
jeff@Juniper6> show ospf database router lsa-id 192.168.254.6 extensive

    OSPF link state database, area 0.0.0.0
 Type    ID              Adv Rtr         Seq          Age   Opt  Cksum Len
Router  *192.168.254.6  192.168.254.6   0x800001c8   1458  0x2  0x10e  84
  bits 0x0, link count 5
  id 172.16.1.0, data 255.255.255.0, type Stub (3)
  TOS count 0, TOS 0 metric 10
  id 192.168.3.1, data 192.168.3.1, type Transit (2)
  TOS count 0, TOS 0 metric 1
  id 192.168.4.2, data 192.168.4.1, type Transit (2)
  TOS count 0, TOS 0 metric 1
  id 192.168.5.0, data 255.255.255.0, type Stub (3)
  TOS count 0, TOS 0 metric 1
  id 192.168.254.6, data 255.255.255.255, type Stub (3)
  TOS count 0, TOS 0 metric 0
  Gen timer 00:25:42
  Aging timer 00:35:42
  Installed 00:24:18 ago, expires in 00:35:42, sent 00:24:18 ago
  Ours
```

Figure 5.15 An OSPF database display of a Router LSA.

5.4.2 Network LSAs

The Network LSA (Figure 5.16) is generated by the DR to represent a pseudonode. Like the Router LSA, it has an area flooding scope. The LSA type is 2, and the Link State ID is the IP address of the DR's interface attaching to the pseudonode (broadcast or NBMA network). Notice that there is no Metric field in the LSA. This is because, as you learned earlier, the cost from the pseudonode to all attached routers is 0.

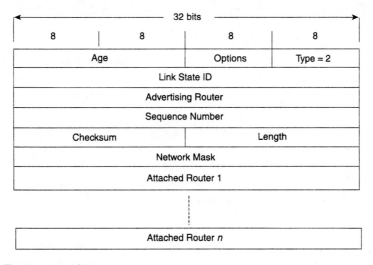

Figure 5.16 The Network LSA.

- **Network Mask** is the IP address mask for the network.
- **Attached Router** is the RID of one of the routers attached to the pseudonode network. This field repeats to include all attached routers that are fully adjacent to the DR, and the DR itself. The number of Attached Router fields in the LSA can be deduced from the value of the LSA's Length field.

Figure 5.17 shows a display of a Network LSA from an OSPF database. You can see from this display that the network has a 24-bit mask (255.255.255.0) and that there are two attached routers. Of these two, you can tell that the DR is 192.168.254.7, because that is the advertising router.

```
jeff@Juniper6> show ospf database network lsa-id 192.168.4.2 extensive

    OSPF link state database, area 0.0.0.0
 Type    ID            Adv Rtr        Seq         Age  Opt  Cksum  Len
Network  192.168.4.2   192.168.254.7  0x80000251  926  0x2  0xf852  32
  mask 255.255.255.0
  attached router 192.168.254.7
  attached router 192.168.254.6
  Aging timer 00:44:34
  Installed 00:15:25 ago, expires in 00:44:34, sent 00:15:25 ago
```

Figure 5.17   An OSPF database display of a Network LSA.

5.4.3 Network Summary LSAs

Network Summary LSAs are originated by ABRs and are flooded into an area to advertise prefixes that are in other areas. This LSA is the key to understanding why OSPF is "distance-vector-like" in its inter-area behavior. When an ABR learns a route to a prefix in another area—either because the prefix is in an attached area or because another ABR has advertised the prefix in its own Network Summary LSA—the ABR uses the Network Summary LSA to tell routers in an area, "I am a next hop to this prefix, at a cost of X." The routers within the area know from their shortest-path trees how to reach the ABR, but the trees to not reach outside of the area to the actual prefix. This is distance vector behavior.

Figure 5.18 illustrates the use of Network Summary LSAs. ABR1 knows, as a member of area 0.0.0.1, that prefix 172.16.6/24 exists in that area. It therefore originates a Network Summary LSA into its other attached area, area 0.0.0.0, to advertise that it can reach the prefix. Likewise, ABR2 knows that prefix 172.16.113/24 resides in area 0.0.0.2 and advertises the prefix into area 0.0.0.0. Both ABRs are attached to area 0.0.0.0, and so know about 172.16.25/24 in that area. They also receive each other's Network Summary LSAs, so ABR1 knows it can reach 172.16.113/24 via ABR2, and ABR2 knows it can reach 172.16.6/24 via ABR1. ABR1 originates Network Summary LSAs into area 0.0.0.1 and ABR2 originates Network Summary LSAs into area 0.0.0.2, each advertising the prefixes outside those areas.

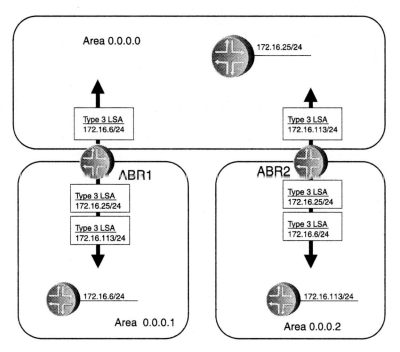

Figure 5.18 ABRs originate Network Summary LSAs to advertise destinations outside of the area in which the LSA is flooded.

Figure 5.19 shows the structure of the Network Summary LSA. Its type is 3, and it has area flooding scope. The inter-area prefix being advertised is carried in the Link State ID field. Because there is only one Link State ID field in an LSA, an ABR must originate a separate Network Summary LSA for each prefix it wants to advertise into an area. The ABR can also originate a Network Summary LSA to advertise a default route (0.0.0.0/0) into an area.

- **Network Mask** is the IP address mask of the prefix.
- **Metric** is the cost from the ABR to the destination. Notice that unlike the 16-bit intra-area metric, this one is 24 bits to accommodate presumably longer paths to the destination.
- **ToS** and **ToS Metric** are, as with the Router LSA, for backward compatibility with earlier OSPFv2 incarnations. ToS is not used in modern OSPFv2, and so the ToS type is always 0, and the ToS Metric is all 0s.

Figure 5.20 shows a Network Summary LSA from an OSPF database for a destination prefix 192.168.5.0/24.

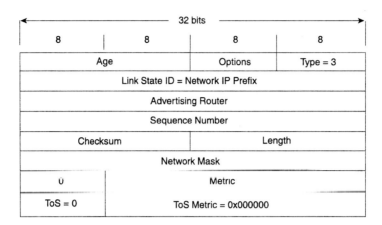

Figure 5.19   The Network Summary LSA.

```
jeff@Juniper4> show ospf database netsummary lsa-id 192.168.5.0
             extensive

   OSPF link state database, area 0.0.0.2
 Type    ID            Adv Rtr        Seq        Age   Opt  Cksum  Len
Summary  192.168.5.0   192.168.254.5  0x800001dd 1389  0x2  0xb6ea 28
  mask 255.255.255.0
  TOS 0x0, metric 2
  Aging timer 00:57:53
  Installed 00:02:06 ago, expires in 00:36:51, sent 00:02:06 ago
```

Figure 5.20   An OSPF database display of a Network Summary LSA.

5.4.4   ASBR Summary LSAs

The format of the ASBR Summary LSA (Figure 5.21) is identical to the Network Summary LSA, but it advertises an ASBR that is outside of the area rather than a prefix. When an ASBR floods an external prefix throughout an OSPF domain, the advertised prefix shows the ASBR as the next hop. This LSA is necessary for routers in different areas from the ASBR to learn how to reach the ASBR and hence the external destinations. Like the Network Summary LSA, the ASBR Summary LSA is originated by an ABR and flooded into an area, and has area flooding scope. The ABR learns about the advertised ASBR the same way it does inter-area prefixes: The ASBR is either in a connected area and thus learned from the ABR's shortest-path tree for the area, or it is learned from an ASBR Summary LSA originated by another ABR attached to another area.

The LSA type of the ASBR Summary LSA is 4, and the Link State ID is the ASBR's RID. An ABR must originate a separate ASBR Summary LSA for each ASBR it wants to advertise into an area.

- **Network Mask** has no meaning in ASBR Summary LSAs, and is set to all 0s.
- **Metric** is the cost of the path from the ABR to the ASBR.
- As with Network Summary LSAs, the **ToS** type and **ToS Metric** are for backward compatibility only and are set to 0.

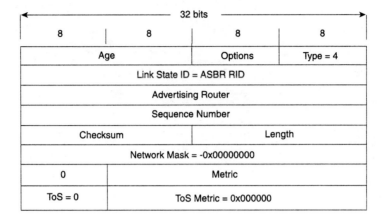

Figure 5.21 The ASBR Summary LSA.

Figure 5.22 shows an ASBR Summary LSA advertising a path to an ASBR 192.168.254.7.

```
jeff@Juniper4> show ospf database asbrsummary lsa-id 192.168.254.7
              extensive

    OSPF link state database, area 0.0.0.2
  Type    ID              Adv Rtr         Seq         Age  Opt  Cksum  Len
ASBRSum  192.168.254.7   192.168.254.5   0x800001df  1234 0x2  0xa0fc  28
  mask 0.0.0.0
  TOS 0x0, metric 2
  Aging timer 00:39:25
  Installed 00:20:31 ago, expires in 00:39:26, sent 00:20:31 ago
```

Figure 5.22 An OSPF database display of an ASBR Summary LSA.

5.4.5 AS-External LSAs

An ASBR originates a single AS-External LSA (Figure 5.23) for each external prefix it wants to advertise to the OSPF domain. Unlike the previous four LSAs examined, this LSA has autonomous system (domain) flooding scope. That is, it is flooded to all nonstub areas in the OSPF domain. (Stub areas, discussed Section 7.3.4, are defined by the fact that AS-External LSAs are not permitted into the area.) AS-External LSAs are also used to advertise a default route (0.0.0.0/0) out of the OSPF domain.

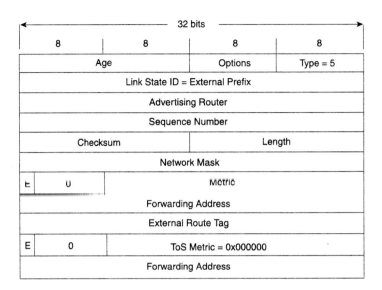

Figure 5.23   The AS-External LSA.

AS-External LSAs are type 5, and the Link State ID is the IP prefix of the external destination being advertised. An ASBR originates a separate AS-External LSA for every external prefix that it wants to advertise. In this lies a fundamental danger to OSPF. If a large number of prefixes is advertised into the domain, a corresponding large number of AS-External LSAs is flooded throughout the domain. The result can be undue stress on the OSPF routers trying to store and process all these LSAs. In some cases—such as the all-too-common mistake of redistributing all of the prefixes of the Internet routing table into OSPF—this stress can cause a domain-wide crash of routers. More is said about this vulnerability, and techniques for avoiding it, in Chapters 7 and 9.

- **Network Mask** is the IP address mask of the advertised prefix.
- **E** specifies whether the metric type of the advertised prefix is E1 (E = 0) or E2 (E = 1).
- **Metric** is the cost to the prefix from the ASBR, and is assigned by the ASBR based on an arbitrary configuration or on the value (as specified by a configured routing policy) of the metric of the protocol from which the prefix was learned. Like the metric in the Network Summary LSAs, this metric is 24 bits.
- **Forwarding Address** is the address that packets destined to the prefix should be forwarded to. Note that this field does not specify a next-hop address for the prefix, just an address that must be used to reach the prefix. When set to 0.0.0.0, packets to the prefix are forwarded to the originating ASBR. However, this field also gives the ASBR the capability of advertising a different forwarding address than itself. Notice that the format in Figure 5.23 shows two Forwarding Address fields.

The format of this LSA has changed somewhat from earlier (RFC 1583) specifications of OSPF, and the second field exists only for backward compatibility.

▪ **External Route Tag** allows information that has no relevance to OSPF to be carried across the OSPF domain. Typically, this information would be BGP route attributes but can be anything that an external routing protocol adds at one ASBR and extracts from another ASBR. The OSPF process itself ignores the contents of this field.

▪ **ToS Metric** and the related E flag are, as with the other LSAs discussed, for backward compatibility and are normally set to 0.

Figure 5.24 shows an AS-External LSA for a prefix 192.168.200.0/24. You can see that the metric type is E2 (`Type 2`), and the cost from the ASBR is 250. The forwarding address is 0.0.0.0, indicating packets to this prefix should be forwarded to the originating ASBR, which happens to be the same ASBR advertised in the ASBR Summary LSA of Figure 5.22.

```
jeff@Juniper4> show ospf database extern lsa-id 192.168.200.0 extensive
    OSPF external link state database
Type   ID              Adv Rtr         Seq         Age  Opt  Cksum  Len
Extern 192.168.200.0   192.168.254.7   0x8000160c  739  0x2  0xd43f 36
  mask 255.255.255.0
  Type 2, TOS 0x0, metric 250, fwd addr 0.0.0.0, tag 0.0.0.0
  Aging timer 00:47:41
  Installed 00:12:14 ago, expires in 00:47:41, sent 00:12:14 ago
```

Figure 5.24   An OSPF database display of an AS-External LSA.

Figure 5.25 shows another AS-External LSA, advertising a different prefix, but originated by the same ASBR. Notice that this prefix has a metric type of E1. Figure 5.26 shows the effect of the two metric types on the resulting routes. The route to the ASBR 192.168.254.7 is shown first, and you can see that the cost to the router is 3. The second display is the route to external prefix 192.168.200.0/24, which was advertised by the LSA in Figure 5.24. Because the metric type associated with that prefix is E2, the cost to the prefix is 250—the same cost shown in Figure 5.24. The third displayed route is to external prefix 192.168.100.0/24, which as Figure 2.25 shows has an E1 metric. The cost of the route is 253, which is the cost of the prefix from the ASBR (250) plus the cost of the route to the ASBR (3).

```
jeff@Juniper4> show ospf database extern lsa-id 192.168.100.0 extensive
    OSPF external link state database
Type    ID             Adv Rtr         Seq         Age  Opt  Cksum  Len
Extern  192.168.100.0  192.168.254.7   0x8000160e  484  0x2  0x9f58 36
  mask 255.255.255.0
  Type 1, TOS 0x0, metric 250, fwd addr 0.0.0.0, tag 0.0.0.0
  Aging timer 00:51:55
  Installed 00:08:00 ago, expires in 00:51:56, sent 00:08:00 ago
```

Figure 5.25   An OSPF database display of an AS-External LSA. The prefix advertised by this LSA has an E1 metric type.

```
jeff@Juniper4> show route 192.168.254.7

inet.0: 19 destinations, 20 routes (18 active, 0 holddown, 1 hidden)
+ = Active Route, - = Last Active, * = Both

192.168.254.7/32    *[OSPF/10] 02:34:38, metric 3
                    > to 192.168.2.2 via fxp1.0

jeff@Juniper4> show route 192.168.200.0

inet.0: 19 destinations, 20 routes (18 active, 0 holddown, 1 hidden)
+ = Active Route, - = Last Active, * = Both

192.168.200.0/24    *[OSPF/150] 00:13:21, metric 250, tag 0
                    > to 192.168.2.2 via fxp1.0

jeff@Juniper4> show route 192.168.100.0

inet.0: 19 destinations, 20 routes (18 active, 0 holddown, 1 hidden)
+ = Active Route, - = Last Active, * = Both

192.168.100.0/24    *[OSPF/150] 00:13:31, metric 253, tag 0
                    > to 192.168.2.2 via fxp1.0
```

Figure 5.26   The E2 and E1 metric types of the LSAs in the previous two figures cause different results in the routing table.

5.5   Essential TLVs

As with essential LSAs, by essential TLVs I mean those that are necessary for the basic functioning of IS-IS in an IP network. Certain TLVs would be essential to IS-IS in a CLNS network, but are not necessary—or relevant—to an IP network, and so are not covered in this book. Also covered here are the TLVs that enable the support of wide metrics. These are not essential to the operation of IS-IS, but are included because wide metrics are covered in this chapter. Many other TLVs are discussed in other chapters, in the context of the IS-IS features and extensions they support.

The essential TLVs are:

- Area Addresses TLV
- IS Neighbors TLV
- Protocols Supported TLV
- IP Interface Address TLV
- IP Internal Reachability Information TLV
- IP External Reachability Information TLV

The TLVs that enable wide metrics are:

- Extended IS Reachability TLV
- Extended IP Reachability TLV

5.5.1 Area Addresses TLV

The Area Addresses TLV carries a list of all AIDs assigned to the originating router. The number of AIDs listed in this TLV adheres to the constraints of the Maximum Area Addresses field in the PDU header:

- If Maximum Area Addresses = 0, up to three AIDs can appear in this TLV.
- If Maximum Area Addresses = 1 to 254, this TLV can carry that number of addresses.

Normally, an IS-IS router has only a single AID, and so this TLV would carry only a single AID. But IS-IS does allow for the assignment of multiple AIDs to a single router, which can be useful in network migrations. Section 7.4.8 discusses the use of multiple AIDs.

Figure 5.27 shows the format of the Area Addresses TLV. Its type value is 1, and both L1 and L2 LSPs carry it. It always appears before other TLVs in the LSP, which means it appears in LSPs whose LSP numbers is 0 (the first portion of a multipart LSP). It never appears in LSPs with non-0 LSP numbers. It also never appears in LSPs representing pseudonodes.

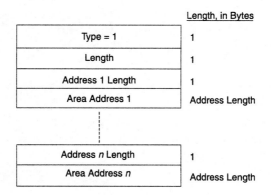

Figure 5.27 The Area Addresses TLV.

5.5.2 IS Neighbors TLV

The IS Neighbors TLV (Figure 5.28) lists the originator's adjacent neighbors. The TLV type is 2, and this TLV appears in both L1 and L2 LSPs.

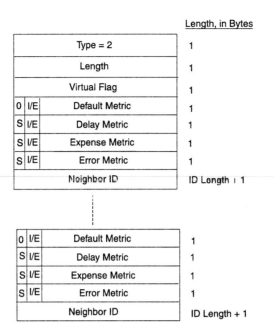

Figure 5.28   The IS Neighbors TLV.

- **Virtual Flag,** although 1 octet long, has only two values: 0 and 1. If 1, the flag indicates that the link is a virtual link. But because no commercial IS-IS implementations support virtual links, this flag is always 0.

- **I/E** is the Internal/External flag, to indicate whether the associated metric is internal (0) or external (1). Because neighbors are always within the IS-IS domain, this flag is always 0 for all metrics in the IS Neighbors TLV.

- **Default Metric** is the standard 6-bit IS-IS metric, indicating the cost of the link to the neighbor.

- **Delay Metric, Expense Metric,** and **Error Metric** are discussed in Section 5.3.2. To recap, they were intended to provide metric-based types of service but are never used in modern networks. The S bit preceding each of these metrics and their I/E bits indicates whether the metric is supported (0) or not supported (1). This bit is always set to 1.

- **Neighbor ID** is, if the neighbor is a router, the neighbor's System ID followed by an octet of 0s (0x00). If the neighbor is a pseudonode, the Neighbor ID is the L1 or L2 DIS's SysID followed by a non-zero octet assigned to the pseudonode by the DIS.

5.5.3 Protocols Supported TLV

Remember that IS-IS was originally just a CLNS routing protocol. The Protocols Supported TLV (Figure 5.29), specified in RFC 1195, is essential to the extension of IS-IS to route other protocols such as IP. This TLV is type 129, and can appear in both L1 and L2 LSPs. The TLV carries a list of Network Layer Protocol Identifiers (NLPIDs) that specify the protocols supported as assigned in ISO/TR 9577. IPv4, for example, is NLPID 204 (0xCC) and IPv6 is NLPID 142 (0x8E).

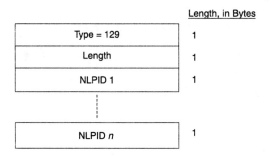

Figure 5.29 The Protocols Supported TLV.

5.5.4 IP Interface Addresses TLV

The IP Interface Address TLV (Figure 5.30) is specified in RFC 1195 to carry the IP addresses of the IS-IS interfaces on the originating router. These addresses are associated with the router's SNPAs. The TLV type is 132, and the TLV can appear in both L1 and L2 LSPs.

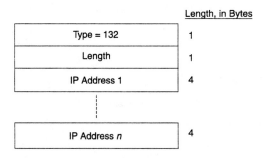

Figure 5.30 The IP Interface Addresses TLV.

5.5.5   IP Internal Reachability Information TLV

The IP Internal Reachability Information TLV (Figure 5-31), specified in RFC 1195, lists the IP prefixes directly connected to the originating router, and their associated metrics. The TLV also carries any summary prefixes advertised by the originating router. The TLV type is 128, and it can appear in both L1 and L2 LSPs. However, it never appears in a pseudonode LSP.

Length, in Bytes

		Type = 128	1
		Length	1
0	I/E	Default Metric	1
S	R	Delay Metric	1
S	R	Expense Metric	1
S	R	Error Metric	1
		IP Address 1	4
		Subnet Mask 1	4

0	I/E	Default Metric	1
S	R	Delay Metric	1
S	R	Expense Metric	1
S	R	Error Metric	1
		IP Address n	4
		Subnet Mask n	4

Figure 5.31   The IP Internal Reachability Information TLV.

- The **I/E** bit associated with the default metric is always 0 because the addresses carried by this TLV are always internal to the IS-IS domain.

- As with previous TLVs, the **Delay**, **Expense**, and **Error** metrics are unused, so the S bit associated with each is set to 1. The R bit associated with these metrics is reserved and is always 0.

- **IP Address** and **Subnet Mask** carry the advertised prefixes and their subnet masks. These fields and the associated metrics fields can repeat to advertise multiple prefixes.

5.5.6   IP External Reachability Information TLV

The IP External Reachability Information TLV, shown in Figure 5.32, looks exactly like the Internal Reachability Information TLV except for its type number of 130. Prefixes and their subnets external to the IS-IS domain are listed in this TLV. RFC 1195 specifies that this TLV is only carried in L2 LSPs, but with most IS-IS implementations you can configure L1 LSPs to carry the LSP.

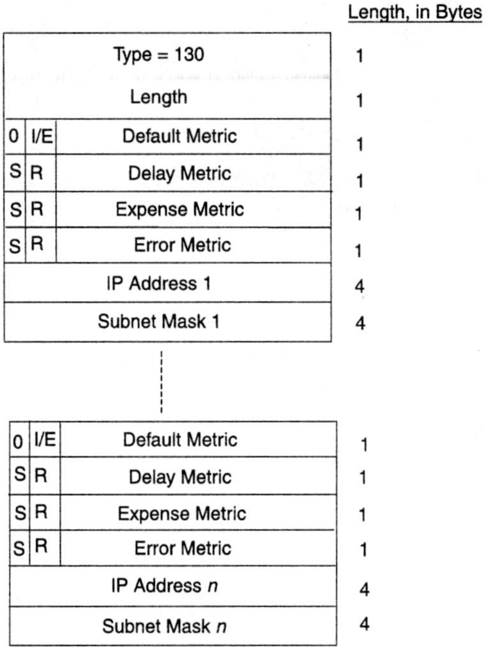

Figure 5.32   The IP External Reachability Information TLV.

You might expect, because the prefixes in the IP External Reachability Information TLV are external to the IS-IS domain, that the I/E bit associated with the metric would always be set to external (1). In fact, it can be set to either internal or external. The reason both for varying the I/E bit and for configuring L1 LSPs to carry this TLV is so that external prefixes can be advertised throughout the IS-IS domain, if you so desire. This issue, called *domain-wide prefix distribution*, is discussed in more depth in Sections 7.4.6 and 7.4.7.

5.5.7   Extended IS Reachability TLV

The Extended IS Reachability TLV, along with the Extended IP Reachability TLV, was proposed to support traffic engineering by carrying much more detailed information about a link. Accordingly, these TLVs are discussed in detail in Chapter 1. For now, our interest in them is that they allow a much larger metric to be assigned to a link.

The Extended IS Reachability TLV, shown in Figure 5.33, is analogous to the IS Neighbors TLV in that it describes the originating router's links to neighboring routers and the cost to those neighbors. But where that TLV wasted space with three octets of unused ToS metrics, the Extended IS Reachability TLV provides for a 24-bit default metric.

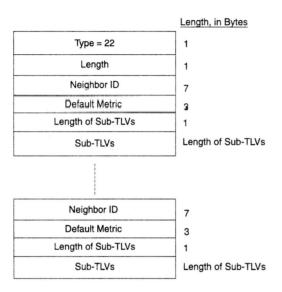

Figure 5.33   The Extended IS Reachability TLV.

- The TLV type is 22, and it can appear in both L1 and L2 LSPs of routers that support wide metrics.
- **Neighbor ID** is the 6-byte SysID of the neighbor and a 1-byte pseudonode number.

The sub-TLVs are not detailed here because they apply to traffic engineering. Chapter 11 explains these fields.

5.5.8   Extended IP Reachability TLV

The Extended IP Reachability TLV (Figure 5.34) can be used in place of both IP Internal Reachability Information and IP External Reachability Information TLVs to carry IP prefix information but with a 32-bit metric rather than a 6-bit metric. As with the Extended IS Reachability TLV, this TLV was proposed to support traffic engineering and so is detailed in Chapter 11.

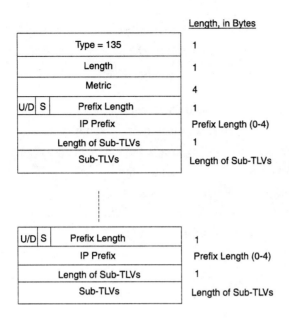

Length, in Bytes

Type = 135	1
Length	1
Metric	4
U/D	S	Prefix Length	1
IP Prefix	Prefix Length (0-4)
Length of Sub-TLVs	1
Sub-TLVs	Length of Sub-TLVs

U/D	S	Prefix Length	1
IP Prefix	Prefix Length (0-4)
Length of Sub-TLVs	1
Sub-TLVs	Length of Sub-TLVs

Figure 5.34   The Extended IP Reachability TLV.

- The TLV type is 135, and it can appear in both L1 and L2 LSPs.
- **U/D** is the Up/Down bit. This is a useful feature that allows route leaking from L2 to L1 without running the risk of looping—something not available in the original IS-IS specifications. Use of the Up/Down bit, in relation to domain-wide prefix distribution, is discussed in Section 7.4.6.
- S, when set, indicates the presence of sub-TLVs.
- **Prefix Length** indicates the number of significant bits in the prefix that follows.
- **IP Prefix** is the advertised prefix.

The sub-TLVs are not detailed here because they apply to traffic engineering. Chapter 11 explains these fields.

Review Questions

1. What four mechanisms are used by both OSPF and IS-IS to make flooding reliable?
2. What events cause an OSPF router to send an LSA to one or more of its neighbors?
3. Under what circumstances is the destination address of an OSPF Update packet unicast, and under what circumstances is it a multicast address?

4. What is the flooding scope of an OSPF Update message?

5. What is the difference between an explicit and implicit OSPF acknowledgment?

6. What are the advantages and disadvantages of direct and delayed acknowledgments?

7. Under what two circumstances is an LSA directly acknowledged?

8. What is the purpose of the OSPF retransmit list and retransmit timer?

9. Why are retransmitted LSAs always unicast, regardless of network type?

10. What are the initial and maximum OSPF sequence number values?

11. What is the OSPF IntTransDelay? What is the usual default value of this variable?

12. What are the minimum and maximum values of the OSPF Age variable?

13. What is the value of the OSPF constant LSRefreshTime?

14. How does a router flush an LSA that it previously originated?

15. What is the value of the OSPF constant MaxAgeDiff, and how is the constant used?

16. Which fields in an LSA header identify a particular LSA, and which fields identify a specific instance of a particular LSA?

17. If two LSAs are received with identical Type, LS ID, Advertising Router, and Sequence Number fields, but different Checksum fields, which is the newer LSA?

18. Does OSPF practice strict split horizon on LSAs during flooding, or is there any case in which an LSA is flooded back out the interface on which it was received?

19. What events cause IS-IS to originate and flood an LSP?

20. How is an IS-IS LSP like an OSPF Update message? How is it different?

21. How is an IS-IS LSP like an OSPF LSA? How is it different?

22. How does the IS-IS remaining lifetime differ from the OSPF age?

23. What are the maximum and minimum values of the IS-IS remaining lifetime? What is the typical default value?

24. How does an IS-IS router flush an LSP it has previously originated?

25. How does the linear IS-IS sequence number space differ from the linear OSPF sequence number space?

26. Why might an IS-IS router originate an LSP with a sequence number of 0?

27. If one LSP has a sequence number of 0 and one LSP has a sequence number of 10, and they are otherwise identical, which LSP is considered more recent?

28. What does an LSP number of 0x03 signify?

29. What is the IS-IS SRM flag?

30. What PDUs does IS-IS use for acknowledging the receipt of an LSP?

31. Is an LSP received on a point-to-point link implicitly or explicitly acknowledged? What about an LSP received on a broadcast link?

32. What is the difference between an ABR and an ASBR?

33. What is an L1/L2 router?

34. If two IS-IS neighbors are both L1-Only and their AIDs differ, can an adjacency be established?

35. Under what circumstances can both an L1 and an L2 adjacency be established between the same two IS-IS neighbors?

36. What is an OSPF reference bandwidth?

37. What is the difference between OSPF E1 and E2 metrics?

38. If an OSPF router receives two routes to the same prefix, one with an E1 metric and one with an E2 metric, which route is chosen?

39. What does the I/E bit associated with IS-IS metrics signify?

40. What are wide metrics? What TLV supports them?

41. What are the five "essential" LSAs, what are their type numbers, and what is the function of each?

42. What do the E and B bits signify in a type 1 LSA?

43. How many prefixes can be carried in a type 3 LSA? How prefixes can be carried in a type 5 LSA?

44. What is the flooding scope of a type 5 LSA?

45. What are the "essential" TLVs in an IP-only IS-IS network? How is each used?

CHAPTER 6

Link State Database Synchronization

I have said it many times already, and I will say it again: The key concept behind link state routing protocols is that each router in an area performs localized route calculations based on information in a common topological database. It is therefore essential that every router in an area have exactly the same topological database. This is the purpose of link state database synchronization. Whenever a router becomes active on an OSPF or IS-IS network, it must synchronize its database with its neighbors to guarantee that they are the same. If the router becomes active on a point-to-point link, it synchronizes with the neighbor at the other end of the link. If it becomes active on a multi-access network, it synchronizes with the DR or DIS. After the initial synchronization, the router must take steps to ensure that it remains synchronized with its neighbors.

Notice that routers do not synchronize with all other routers in an area, only with their neighbors. Those neighbors synchronize with their neighbors, and so on throughout the area, and this is good enough to ensure identical databases in every area router. An important assumption behind this procedure is that within an area there is a path from every router to every other router. If a path cannot be found from one or more routers to the other routers without leaving the area, there is no guarantee that all databases in the area are identical. This condition—called a *partitioned area*—is discussed in Chapter 7. For now, it is enough to understand that LS database consistency depends on an unbroken series of adjacencies connecting all routers within an area. At a minimum, the physical topology of an area should be such that no single link or interface failure can isolate some portion of the area from the rest of the area.

6.1 OSPF Database Synchronization

Everything you have seen about OSPF so far shows that it is a highly structured protocol. Knowing the importance of reliable and accurate database synchronization, it is no surprise that a rather complex state machine, called the *neighbor state machine*, manages the OSPF

179

synchronization procedure. In a nutshell, the neighbor state machine drives the following steps in the synchronization process:

1. When two neighbors decide to become adjacent, one of the neighbors becomes the master and the other the slave. The master controls the rest of the synchronization process, called *database exchange*.

2. Each neighbor describes all of the LSAs in its database to the other.

3. If a router finds, during the description process, that its neighbor has an LSA that it does not, or has a more recent copy of an LSA that it has, it requests a full copy of the LSA from the neighbor.

4. When all necessary LSAs have been exchanged and both neighbors are satisfied that their databases are identical, they end the exchange process and are fully adjacent. Only then can the link between them be used for forwarding packets.

This section first looks at the packets OSPF uses for database exchange, and then examines the neighbor state machine in detail.

6.1.1   OSPF Packets Used in Database Synchronization

Four of the five OSPF packet types are used for database exchange:

- Database Description (type 2) packets
- Link State Request (type 3) packets
- Link State Update (type 4) packets
- Link State Acknowledgment (type 5) packets

You already have seen, in Chapter 5, how Update packets are used to send complete LSAs from one neighbor to another, and how Acknowledgment packets carry LSA headers to explicitly acknowledge the receipt of LSAs for reliable flooding. Although the formats of these two packets were shown in Chapter 5, they are repeated in Figures 6.1 and 6.2 for your reference.

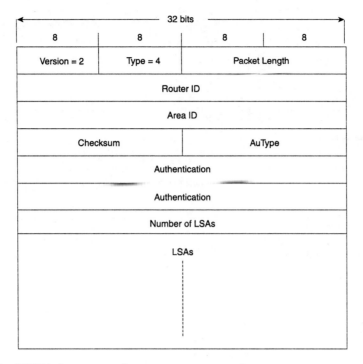

Figure 6.1   The OSPF Update message format.

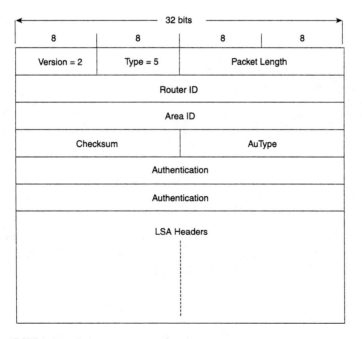

Figure 6.2   The OSPF Acknowledgment message format.

The Database Description packet (Figure 6.3), like the Acknowledgment packet, carries only the headers of the LSAs that completely describe both the LSA and the instance of the LSA. An OSPF router can describe all of the LSAs in its database by originating DD packets.

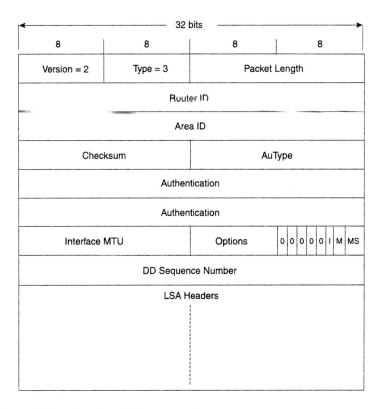

Figure 6.3   The OSPF Database Description message format.

- **Interface MTU** specifies the largest unfragmented packet that can be sent from the originating interface. If the MTUs do not match, the neighbors do not become adjacent. Otherwise, one neighbor might send messages larger than the other neighbor can receive.

- **Options** is the same Options field that is included in Hello packets and all LSAs to describe the originator's optional capabilities. This field has already been mentioned briefly in previous chapters; its format and use are described fully in the next section.

LS databases are often too large for all of their LSAs to be described by a single DD packet. Therefore, two bits indicate to the receiving neighbor whether the DD packet is one of a sequence:

- **I** (Init) indicates, when set to 1, that this DD packet is the first in a series.
- **M** (More) indicates, when set to 1, that there are more DD packets to follow.
  So the I and M bits are used as follows:
  If a single DD packet describes all LSAs, the two bit values are I=1, M=0.
  If there is a series of DD packets, the first in the series has I=1, M=1; the last DD packet has I=0, M=0; and any packets between the first and last have I=0, M=1.

- **MS** (Master/Slave) indicates whether the originating neighbor is the Master (MS = 1) or Slave (MS = 0) during the database exchange. The Master/Slave relationship is described in Section 6.1.5.
- **DD Sequence Number** is used, along with the I and M bits, when a series of DD packets describes a database. The use of the DD sequence number is also described in Section 6.1.5.

If during database exchange an OSPF router sees, in the received DD packets, that its neighbor has an unknown LSA or a more recent copy of a known LSA, the router sends a Link State Request packet (Figure 6.4) to ask for a full copy of the LSA. More than one LSA can be requested in a single LS Request packet, and more than one LS Request packet can be sent if a large number of LSAs are needed. The neighbor then sends an Update packet containing the requested LSAs.

Notice that the LS Request packet does not carry the full LSA header but just the LS Type, LS ID, and Advertising Router fields of the LSA. In other words, it requests the LSA but not the specific instance of the LSA. The receiving neighbor then sends the most recent copy of the LSA. This covers a situation in which a more recent LSA might have been received and installed in the database between the time the neighbor described the LSA in a DD packet and the time it received a LS Request packet for the LSA. The neighbor will send the more recent copy.

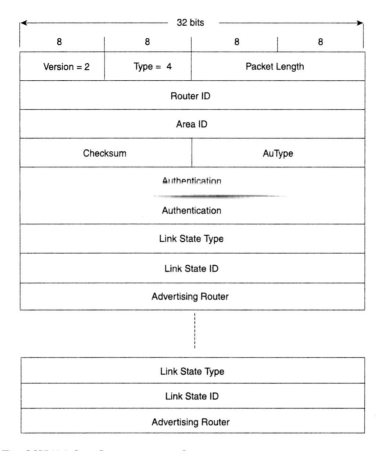

Figure 6.4   The OSPF Link State Request message format.

6.1.2   The Options Field

The OSPF Options field is an 8-bit collection of flags specifying optional capabilities of the originating router. With the introduction of the Database Description packet in the previous section, you have now encountered all of the OSPF entities in which the Options field appears:

- Hello packets
- Database Description packets
- The LSA header

Figure 6.5 shows the Options field. Seven of the bits are currently used as flags; the eighth bit, marked with an asterisk (*) in the illustration, is unused as of this writing. The originating router only sets bits representing capabilities it supports. Any bit representing an option that the router does not support is considered unknown by the router, and the router sets that bit to 0 in all Options fields it originates.

Figure 6.5   The OSPF Options field.

The bits of the Options field are briefly described here for general reference, but the descriptions might not be meaningful to you until you read the chapters describing the individual options:

- O indicates support for Opaque LSAs, described in Chapter 10. Briefly, Opaque LSAs allow OSPF to be extended for applications it was not originally intended for, such as traffic engineering, as described in Chapter 1. The O bit is only set in DD packets, and only by routers supporting Opaque LSAs. As a result, the capability is accounted for during the database exchange process. Opaque LSAs are then flooded only to Opaque-capable routers.

- DC indicates, when set, that the originating router supports the Demand Circuit capability and its associated DoNotAge LSAs, as described in Chapter 8. This capability is designed for use when a link between two neighbors incurs some usage-based cost. By configuring the OSPF interface to treat the link as a demand circuit, Hello packets and refreshed LSAs are suppressed across the link to avoid keeping the link up and incurring unnecessary charges. A router supporting DoNotAge LSAs sets the DC bit in all of the LSAs it originates. It also sets the DC bit in Hellos and DD packets sent across the link designated as a demand circuit. If the router receives Hellos or DD packets with the bit cleared, indicating that the neighbor either does not support the option or is not configured for it, the router reverts to normal Hello and refresh procedures. If a router that does not support Demand Circuit capability receives an Options field with the DC bit set, it ignores the bit.

- EA indicates support for the External Attributes (type 8) LSAs. This capability has never come into general use and is now considered obsolete.

- N/P is used to support Not-So-Stubby Areas, as described in Section 7.3.4. In Hello packets, this bit is the N bit and indicates, when set, support for NSSA (type 7) LSAs. If the N bit is set, the E bit (indicating support for type 5 LSAs) must be cleared. If neighbors do not agree on the setting of these bits, Hellos are dropped and no adjacency is formed. In NSSA LSA headers, the bit is the P bit and tells the NSSA ABR to translate the type 7 LSA into a type 5 LSA.

- MC indicates, when set, support for Multicast OSPF (MOSPF). An MOSPF router sets the MC bit in its Hello and DD packets and in all of its LSAs. However, the bit is only informational in the Hello packets. The capability is noted from the DD packets during database exchange, and MOSPF Group Membership (type 6) LSAs are flooded only to MOSPF-capable routers.

■ E indicates, when set, that the originating router supports external routing capability. When the bit is cleared, the originating router does not accept AS-External (type 5) LSAs. This capability is used in the configuration of stub areas, as described in Section 7.3.4. The bit is always set in AS-External LSAs, and is always set in DD packets and LSAs associated with area 0 and with nonstub areas. However, it is set in these LSAs and DD packets for informational purposes only. Where the flag has effect is in the Hello packet. If the value of the E bits conflict between neighbors— that is, one neighbor is sending Hellos with the bit set and the other neighbor sends Hellos with the bit cleared—the Hellos are not accepted and an adjacency is not formed.

■ T indicates, when set, support for ToS routing. This capability was never put into general use and is now obsolete.

6.1.3 The OSPF Neighbor Data Structure

When an OSPF router first discovers a neighbor on a link through receipt of a Hello, it initializes a neighbor data structure for this neighbor. The neighbor data structure, or neighbor table, contains all of the information the router needs to know about the neighbor. Some of the information is gleaned from the neighbor's received Hellos and DD packets, and some of the information comes from the router's own internal processes concerning the neighbor. The specific entries in the neighbor data table are as follows:

■ **State** records the router's view of the state of the neighbor, according to its own neighbor state machine, as described in Section 6.1.6. Note that this is not the same as the "state" entry of the interface data structure, which indicates only the interface state and its relation to other OSPF interfaces.

■ **Inactivity Timer** is a timer whose period is RouterDeadInterval, as defined for the interface connecting to the link on which the neighbor resides. Whenever a Hello is received from the neighbor, the timer is reset. Expiration of the timer triggers an event in the neighbor state machine that causes the neighbor state to be changed to Down.

■ **Master/Slave** specifies the results of the master/slave selection, as described in Section 6.1.5. This status is relevant to the database exchange process.

■ **DD Sequence Number** is the sequence number of the DD packet currently being sent to the neighbor, for database exchange.

■ **Last Received Database Description Packet** is used to determine, during database exchanges with the neighbor, whether a DD packet received from the neighbor is a duplicate. It records the values of the Sequence Number and Options fields and the settings of the I, M, and MS flags of the last DD packet received from the neighbor.

- **Neighbor ID** is the RID of the neighbor, learned from the neighbor's Hello packets or in some cases manually configured (such as with NBMA or virtual networks).

- **Neighbor Priority** is the value of the Router Priority field of Hellos received from the neighbor, and is used for DR/BDR election.

- **Neighbor IP Address** is the IP address of the neighbor's interface to the attached network, and is learned from the source IP address of Hellos received from the neighbor. This address is used when OSPF packets must be unicast to the neighbor. If the neighbor is the DR for the attached network, this address is used as the Link ID in Router LSAs for the attached network.

- **Neighbor Options** are the neighbor's optional capabilities, learned from its Hellos and from the DD packets during database exchange.

- **Neighbor's Designated Router** is the address of the DR (from the neighbor's perspective) carried in the neighbor's Hellos, and is only relevant on broadcast and NBMA networks.

- **Neighbor's Backup Designated Router** is the address of the BDR (from the neighbor's perspective) carried in the neighbor's Hellos. Again, this is only relevant to broadcast and NBMA links.

Figure 6.6 shows an example of a display of a neighbor table. You can readily see that it displays most—although not all—of the entries in the neighbor data structure.

```
jeff@Juniper6> show ospf neighbor 192.168.7.2 extensive
  Address     Interface        State    ID              Pri  Dead
192.168.7.2   fe-4/0/0.0        Full     192.168.254.8   1    35
  area 0.0.0.0, opt 0x42, DR 192.168.7.1, BDR 192.168.7.2
  Up 1w2d 00:47:03, adjacent 1w2d 00:47:03
```

Figure 6.6   A display of an OSPF neighbor table.

6.1.4   LSA Lists for Database Exchange and Flooding

In addition to the information described in the previous section, the neighbor data structure includes three lists. All three are lists of LSAs, and are populated only during the database exchange or flooding.

- **Link State Transmission List** is a list of LSAs that have been flooded but not yet acknowledged. The LSAs on this list are retransmitted every RxmtInterval, until they are acknowledged or until the adjacency is destroyed.

- **Database Summary List** is a list of all of the LSAs in the LS database pertinent to the area shared with the neighbor when the router begins the database exchange. This list comprises all of the LSAs that are to be described to the neighbor in DD packets.

- **Link State Request List** is a list of LSAs received in the neighbor's DD packets that are either unknown to this router or are more recent than this router's copy of the LSA. These are the LSAs that are requested from the neighbor in Link State Request packets. When a full copy of a requested LSA is received from the neighbor in an Update packet, the LSA is removed from the list.

6.1.5   Database Exchange Management: Masters and Slaves

The reliable exchange of database information is too important to be done haphazardly. So when two OSPF neighbors are comparing LSAs, one of the neighbors manages the exchange. It does not really matter which neighbor is the manager—or *master*—as long as both neighbors agree on which one is the master. The master is the neighbor with the higher RID, and the neighbor with the lower RID becomes the *slave*.

The responsibilities of the master are:

- To send the first DD packet
- To increment the sequence numbers of the DD packets. The Slave cannot increment the sequence numbers.
- To ensure that only one DD packet at a time is outstanding
- To retransmit a DD packet when necessary. A Slave cannot retransmit a DD packet.

To understand how the master is determined, imagine two neighboring routers, RA and RB. Immediately after establishing 2-way communication with RB and deciding to form an adjacency with it, RA sends an empty DD packet—a DD packet containing no LSA headers—to RB. RA sets the sequence number of the packet to some unique value; RFC 2328 suggests basing it on the time-of-day clock, but an OSPF implementation can use some other means to choose a beginning sequence number. The I, M, and MS bits are all set, indicating that this is the initial packet in a series, there are more to follow, and that RA claims to be the master.

When RB receives the empty DD packet, it examines RA's RID in the packet header. If RA's RID is higher than its own, RB knows that it is the master, and if lower, RB knows that it is the slave. One of two things then happens:

- If RB determines that it is the slave it responds by sending a DD packet listing its LSAs, beginning the database exchange process. The sequence number of the packet is the same as sequence number of the DD packet received from RA, and the MS bit is cleared, indicating that this router is the slave and RA is the master. The I bit is set if this is the first DD packet RB has sent, and the M bit is set or cleared depending on whether RB needs to send subsequent DD packets to describe all of its LSAs.

■ If RB determines that it is the master it sends an empty DD packet with its own beginning sequence number and the I, M, and MS bits set. RA then acknowledges that it is the slave by sending a DD packet with RA's initial sequence number and with the MS bit cleared. This acknowledging DD packet contains LSA headers from RA's database, beginning the database exchange process, and the M bit indicates whether RA needs to send more DD packets to complete the description of its database. In this case, the I bit is cleared, because this is not the first DD packet RA sent.

Both RA and RB could, after establishing 2-way communication, send empty DD packets more or less simultaneously, both claiming to be the master. In this case, both will know upon reception of the other's DD packet which of them is master and which is slave. It is up to the slave to begin the database exchange by sending a populated DD packet whose sequence number and MS bit acknowledge its neighbor as the master.

The complete database exchange is described in Section 6.1.6. For now, it is enough to understand that the master, once determined, manages the process. Only the master can increment the sequence number, so when it sends a DD packet with sequence number X, the slave implicitly acknowledges the receipt of the master's DD packet by sending its own DD packet, with sequence number X. Only when the master receives the slave's DD packet X can it send another DD packet with a sequence number of $X+1$. These rules make the database exchange a poll/response process in which the master polls and the slave responds.

Is the DR Always the Master?

Because the highest RID is used as a tiebreaker during DR election when the router priorities are equal, you might be lead to assume that the DR is always the master when a DROther must synchronize its database with the DR. And the responsibilities of the DR on broadcast and NBMA networks might reinforce this assumption. But in fact, it is quite possible for a DROther to be the master and the DR to be the slave when the two are exchanging databases. Remember that an OSPF DR cannot be preempted. So, for example, a router newly attaching to an Ethernet link can have a higher RID than the existing DR but cannot automatically replace the DR. But its higher RID does mean that it will be the master and the DR will be the slave.

6.1.6   The OSPF Neighbor State Machine

With all the necessary components that support the database exchange process described, we can now look at the various states an OSPF router can be in, the events that cause a change from one state to another, and the actions the router takes when a state change occurs. The full set of these states, events, and actions is the OSPF neighbor state machine, and is described in depth in Section 10.3 of RFC 2328.

Keep in mind that an OSPF router maintains separate state for each of its neighbors, and that the state describes the router's perception of its present relationship with that neighbor. Two neighbors might—particularly before full adjacency is established—show different states for each other. The OSPF neighbor states are:

- **Down** is the initial state of a neighbor conversation. This state indicates that no Hellos have been heard from the neighbor during the last RouterDeadInterval. Hellos are not sent to dead neighbors except on NBMA networks, where Hellos are sent to dead neighbors at some rate well below that of the Hello interval. This reduced rate, called PollInterval, is typically 2 minutes.

- **Attempt** is relevant only to NBMA networks where the neighbors have been manually configured and indicates that the router should be aggressive in attempting to get a response from the neighbor, by sending Hellos every HelloInterval rather than every PollInterval.

- **Init** indicates that the router has seen a Hello from the neighbor but has not yet seen its own RID in the neighbor's Hello. (Bidirectional communication is not yet established.) The router includes the RIDs of all neighbors in this state or higher in its own Hellos sent on the associated interface.

- **2-Way** indicates that bidirectional communication is established with the neighbor, by the router seeing its RID in the neighbor's Hellos. Routers must be in this state or higher to be eligible for DR/BDR election.

- **ExStart** indicates that the database exchange process has begun. When in this state the neighbors determine their master/slave relationship and the initial sequence number for DD packet exchange. Neighbors in this state or higher are considered adjacent, although they are not fully adjacent until synchronization is completed.

- **Exchange** indicates that the router is describing its database to the neighbor by sending DD packets, containing the headers of all LSAs in the Database Summary list. The router can also send link state Request packets, requesting copies of LSAs on the Link State Request list, while in this state. Neighbors in this state or higher are included when the router floods LSAs.

- **Loading** indicates that the router has finished describing its database to its neighbor but has not yet finished requesting LSAs from the neighbor or has not yet received all LSAs on its Link State Request list.

- **Full** indicates that the neighbor is fully adjacent and that the adjacency will appear in Router and Network LSAs.

Figure 6.7 shows a typical succession of state changes as two neighbors discover each other and then synchronize their databases to become fully adjacent.[1] The OSPF network type between the two neighbors in this example is broadcast.

---

[1]   This example is based on an example given in RFC 2328, Section 10.10 and expanded upon in the author's *CCIE Professional Development: Routing TCP/IP, Volume 1*, Cisco Press, 1998, pp. 445–447.

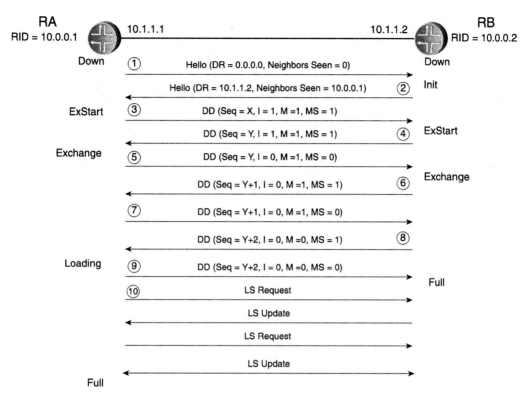

Figure 6.7   An example of neighbor discovery and database synchronization resulting in a full adjacency.

The following steps are shown in the example:

1. RA becomes active on the network and sends a Hello packet to announce its presence. The DR field is set to 0.0.0.0, and the Neighbor field is empty, indicating that RA is not yet aware of any neighbors.

2. When RB receives the Hello, it creates a neighbor data structure for RA. It sets RA's state to Init, because the Hello does not include RB's RID in its Neighbor field. When RB sends a Hello, it includes RA's RID (10.0.0.1) in the Neighbor field. In this example, RB is the DR for the network, so it includes its interface address (10.1.1.2) in the DR field.

3. When RA receives the Hello from RB, it creates a neighbor data structure for RB. Because it sees its own RID in the Neighbor field of the Hello, it knows that bidirectional communication is established. It could, at this point, set RB's state to 2-Way. But because RB is the DR RA must synchronize its database with it. So it sets

RB's state to ExStart, indicating that it is beginning the master/slave selection, and populates the Database Summary list with the LSAs to be described to RB. It sends an empty DD packet with its idea of an initial sequence number (X) and the MS bit set. As the first of multiple DD packets, the I and M bits are also set.

4. When RB receives RA's initial DD packet, it transitions RA's state to ExStart, populates its Database Summary list with LSAs to be described to RA, and sends its own empty DD packet. RB's RID is higher than RA's, so it knows it is the master and sets the MS bit accordingly and sends its initial sequence number (Y). The I and M bits are set to indicate that this is the first of multiple DD packets from this router.

5. When RA receives RB's initial DD packet, it sees that RB is the master. With master/slave selection complete, database exchange can begin, so RA changes RB's state to Exchange. It sends a DD packet to RB with RB's initial sequence number and the MS bit cleared, to indicate that RA is the slave. This DD packet is populated with as many LSA headers from the Database Summary list as it will hold. In this example, multiple DD packets are needed to describe RA's complete database, so the M bit is set to indicate more DD packets to follow. I is cleared, because this is no longer the initial packet.

6. When RB receives the DD packet from RA, it changes RA's state to Exchange. If the received DD packet describes any LSAs that RB needs, those LSAs are added to the Link State Request list. It then sends a DD packet to RA with LSAs from its Database Summary list. As the master, it is responsible for incrementing the sequence number to Y+1. And as with RA, RB cannot describe all of its LSAs in a single DD packet so the M bit is set. The LSAs that are described in this DD packet are added to the Link State Retransmission list and the Retransmit timer is started.

7. When RA receives RB's DD packet, it clears the LSAs it sent in its last DD packet from the Database Summary list. If RB describes any LSAs RA needs, the LSAs are added to the Link State Request list. RA then sends a new DD packet with the next set of LSAs from its Database Summary list. By setting the sequence number to Y+1, RA also acknowledges in this packet the receipt of RB's last DD packet and the LSAs it contained.

8. When RB receives RA's DD packet with sequence number Y=1, it clears the retransmit timer for the LSAs it described in its last DD packet and removes the LSAs from its Link State Retransmission list. RB then sends the next set of LSAs to be described in a new DD packet with sequence number Y+2. With this packet, all LSAs in RB's Database Summary list have been described, so the M bit of this packet is cleared to indicate the end of the sequence.

9. When RA receives RB's final DD packet with M = 0, it knows that RB has finished describing its database. But RA has LSAs on its Link State Request list that have not yet been requested from RB, so its sets the state of RB to Loading. RA then sends a DD packet with sequence number Y+2 to acknowledge receipt of the last packet from RB. This DD packet contains the last of the LSAs on RA's Database Summary list, so the M bit of this packet is cleared.

10. When RB receives RA's final DD packet, it clears the acknowledged LSAs from its Link State Retransmission list. There are no LSAs on its Link State Request list, so RB knows all of the LSAs in RA's database and changes RA's state to Full. But RA still has LSAs on its Link State Request list, so it sends link state Request packets to RB. RB responds by sending the complete LSAs in link state Update packets. When RA has received all of the LSAs it needs, indicated by an empty Link State Request list, it changes RB's state to Full.

In the example of Figure 6.7, state changes occur only after the receipt of a packet. The actual events causing the state changes are discoveries or changes of information included in the packets. Not all events causing state changes, however, are associated with the receipt of a packet. Events causing changes to a higher state are:

- **HelloReceived**—A Hello has been received from the neighbor.
- **Start**—Hellos should be sent to neighbors at the Hello interval. This event is only generated for neighbors on NBMA networks.
- **2-WayReceived**—The router sees its RID in the neighbor's Hello, indicating that bidirectional communication is established.
- **NegotiationDone**—The master/slave negotiation is done.
- **ExchangeDone**—Both routers have finished describing their databases in DD packets.
- **BadLSRequest**—A Link State Request packet has been received requesting an LSA that is not in the database, indicating an error in the database exchange process.
- **LoadingDone**—The Link State Request list is emptied after database exchange process.
- **AdjOK?** —This is a decision point for whether an adjacency should be established and maintained with the neighbor.

Figure 6.8 shows the relationship between states and these events that cause upward state changes.

Other events can cause a change to a lower state. These events are mostly caused by an error, a failure, or a timer expiration and can occur when the neighbor is in any number of states:

- **SeqNumberMismatch**—A DD packet has been received that either has an unexpected (nonsequential) sequence number, an improperly set I bit, or an Options field value that is different from the Options field in the last received DD packet. This event causes the database exchange process to be abandoned and restarted at the ExStart state.

- **1-Way**—Bidirectional communication with the neighbor is lost, as indicated by the reception of a Hello from the neighbor in which the receiving router's RID is not in the Neighbor list. If the neighbor state is 2-Way or greater, the neighbor state is changed to Init.

- **KillNbr**—Communication with the neighbor is impossible, and results in a change of the neighbor state to Down.

- **InactivityTimer**—No Hellos have been seen from the neighbor in the last Router-DeadInterval; the state of the neighbor is changed to Down.

- **LLDown**—A lower-level protocol indicates that the neighbor is unreachable, resulting in a change of the neighbor state to Down.

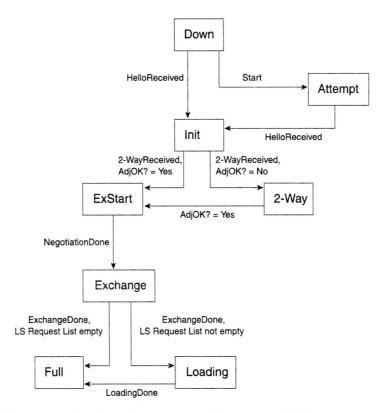

Figure 6.8   The events causing changes from a state to a higher state in OSPF.

6.1.7 *Troubleshooting: Reading OSPF Log Entries and Debug Output*

OSPF database synchronization is not always as clear-cut as it is described in the preceding section. For example, Link State Requests and Updates can be exchanged while DD packets are still being exchanged. And interface states can influence neighbor state transitions. But intimately understanding what is happening when routers are forming full adjacencies will greatly enhance your OSPF troubleshooting skills.

If an adjacency refuses to come up, the most likely culprits should be checked first:

- Are the interface addresses configured correctly?
- Can you ping the neighbor's interface?
- Are the interfaces configured in the same area?
- If authentication is used (Chapter 9), is it configured consistently on both sides? Do the passwords or keys match?
- Are OSPF options configured consistently?
- Are timers configured consistently?
- Is there an MTU mismatch?

If the answer to all of the above questions is "yes," and the adjacency still does not come up, it is time to dig deeper into what is happening between the neighbors. This means using whatever OSPF troubleshooting tools are available to you on the routers to record and decipher the conversation between the neighbors. Such tools can show exactly where the adjacency or database synchronization process failed, and will either tell you explicitly the cause of the failure or give you enough information for you to deduce the cause.

Figure 6.9 shows a log file resulting from tracing OSPF events, packets, and states on a Juniper router. The log file (and the debug output in the next example) has been edited to eliminate extraneous information, such as Hellos to and from other neighbors.

The log records the establishment of a full adjacency with a neighbor. At first glance, this pages-long log seems daunting. But with the knowledge you have gained concerning interface and neighbor states, events changing those states, and the packets and lists used for building an adjacency, you can follow what is going on. For that reason, the following text offers no explanation about what the log reveals, but instead challenges you to find your own answers. Here is the pertinent information:

- Router's RID: 192.168.254.6
- Router's interface address: 192.168.7.1
- Router's physical interface: fe-4/0/0.0
- Neighbor's RID: 192.168.254.8
- Neighbor's interface address: 192.168.7.2

As you read the log, pay attention to the timestamps, and be sure to differentiate between interface state changes and neighbor state changes. Consider the following:

- First break the log down by state changes.
- Beginning with the discovery of neighbor 192.168.254.8, how much time passes before the neighbor is fully adjacent?

- Notice that the neighbor state goes from Init to 2-Way and then to ExStart, rather than from Init to ExStart as in the example of the previous section. Examine the log entries for these state changes, and see whether you can find an explanation for this. (Hint: Pay attention to the interface state changes.)
- How long does the actual database exchange process take?
- Was there an existing DR or BDR on the network when synchronization began?

```
jeff@Juniper6> show log ospf_state
Dec 28 05:28:49 OSPF Interface fe-4/0/0.0 event Up
Dec 28 05:28:49 OSPF interface fe-4/0/0.0 state changed from Down to Waiting
Dec 28 05:28:49 OSPF trigger router LSA build for area 0.0.0.0
Dec 28 05:28:49 OSPF built router LSA, area 0.0.0.0
Dec 28 05:28:50 OSPF sent Hello 192.168.7.1 -> 224.0.0.5 (fe-4/0/0.0)
Dec 28 05:28:50   Version 2, length 44, ID 192.168.254.6, area 0.0.0.0
Dec 28 05:28:50   checksum 0x3d70, authtype 0
Dec 28 05:28:50   mask 255.255.255.0, hello_ivl 10, opts 0x2, prio 128
Dec 28 05:28:50   dead_ivl 40, DR 0.0.0.0, BDR 0.0.0.0
Dec 28 05:28:51 OSPF rcvd Hello 192.168.7.2 -> 224.0.0.5 (fe-4/0/0.0)
Dec 28 05:28:51   Version 2, length 44, ID 192.168.254.8, area 0.0.0.0
Dec 28 05:28:51   checksum 0x3ded, authtype 0
Dec 28 05:28:51   mask 255.255.255.0, hello_ivl 10, opts 0x2, prio 1
Dec 28 05:28:51   dead_ivl 40, DR 0.0.0.0, BDR 0.0.0.0
Dec 28 05:28:51 OSPF neighbor 192.168.7.2 (fe-4/0/0.0) state changed from Down
     to Init
Dec 28 05:28:51 OSPF neighbor 192.168.7.2 (fe-4/0/0.0) state changed by event
     HelloRcvd
Dec 28 05:28:52 OSPF neighbor 192.168.7.2 (fe-4/0/0.0) state changed from Init to
     2Way
Dec 28  05:28:52 RPD_OSPF_NBRUP: OSPF neighbor 192.168.7.2 (fe-4/0/0.0) state changed
     from Init to 2Way due to Two way communication established
Dec 28 05:28:52 OSPF neighbor 192.168.7.2 (fe-4/0/0.0) state changed by event
     2WayRcvd
Dec 28 05:28:52 OSPF Interface fe-4/0/0.0 event NeighborChange
Dec 28 05:29:29 OSPF Interface fe-4/0/0.0 event WaitTimer
Dec 28 05:29:29 OSPF interface fe-4/0/0.0 state changed from Waiting to DR
Dec 28 05:29:29 OSPF trigger router LSA build for area 0.0.0.0
Dec 28 05:29:29 OSPF trigger network LSA build for fe-4/0/0.0
Dec 28 05:29:29 OSPF DR is 192.168.254.6, BDR is 192.168.254.8
Dec 28 05:29:29 OSPF neighbor 192.168.7.2 (fe-4/0/0.0) state changed from 2Way to
     ExStart
Dec 28 05:29:29 OSPF neighbor 192.168.7.2 (fe-4/0/0.0) state changed by event AdjOK?
Dec 28 05:29:29 OSPF trigger router LSA build for area 0.0.0.0
Dec 28 05:29:29 OSPF sent DbD 192.168.7.1 -> 192.168.7.2 (fe-4/0/0.0)
Dec 28 05:29:29   Version 2, length 32, ID 192.168.254.6, area 0.0.0.0
Dec 28 05:29:29   checksum 0x881b, authtype 0
Dec 28 05:29:29   options 0x42, i 1, m 1, ms 1, seq 0xc0a0ae8e, mtu 1500
Dec 28 05:29:29 OSPF built router LSA, area 0.0.0.0
Dec 28 05:29:30 OSPF sent Hello 192.168.7.1 -> 224.0.0.5 (fe-4/0/0.0)
Dec 28 05:29:30   Version 2, length 48, ID 192.168.254.6, area 0.0.0.0
Dec 28 05:29:30   checksum 0xef65, authtype 0
Dec 28 05:29:30   mask 255.255.255.0, hello_ivl 10, opts 0x2, prio 128
Dec 28 05:29:30   dead_ivl 40, DR 192.168.7.1, BDR 192.168.7.2
Dec 28 05:29:31 OSPF rcvd DbD 192.168.7.2 -> 192.168.7.1 (fe-4/0/0.0)
Dec 28 05:29:31   Version 2, length 32, ID 192.168.254.8, area 0.0.0.0
Dec 28 05:29:31   checksum 0xdc16, authtype 0
```

```
Dec 28 05:29:31    options 0x42, i 1, m 1, ms 1, seq 0x1b32, mtu 1500
Dec 28 05:29:31 OSPF now slave for nbr 192.168.7.2
Dec 28 05:29:31 OSPF neighbor 192.168.7.2 (fe-4/0/0.0) state changed from ExStart to
    Exchange
Dec 28 05:29:31 OSPF neighbor 192.168.7.2 (fe-4/0/0.0) state changed by event
    NegotiationDone
Dec 28 05:29:31    In sequence
Dec 28 05:29:31 OSPF sent DbD 192.168.7.1 -> 192.168.7.2 (fe-4/0/0.0)
Dec 28 05:29:31    Version 2, length 192, ID 192.168.254.6, area 0.0.0.0
Dec 28 05:29:31    checksum 0x3a37, authtype 0
Dec 28 05:29:31    options 0x42, i 0, m 0, ms 0, seq 0x1b32, mtu 1500
Dec 28 05:29:31 OSPF rcvd DbD 192.168.7.2 -> 192.168.7.1 (fe-4/0/0.0)
Dec 28 05:29:31    Version 2, length 212, ID 192.168.254.8, area 0.0.0.0
Dec 28 05:29:31    checksum 0x34fe, authtype 0
Dec 28 05:29:31    options 0x42, i 0, m 1, ms 1, seq 0x1b33, mtu 1500
Dec 28 05:29:31    In sequence
Dec 28 05:29:31    Database copy is older
Dec 28 05:29:31    Database copy is older
Dec 28 05:29:31 OSPF rcvd LSReq 192.168.7.2 -> 192.168.7.1 (fe-4/0/0.0)
Dec 28 05:29:31    Version 2, length 84, ID 192.168.254.8, area 0.0.0.0
Dec 28 05:29:31    checksum 0xb70b, authtype 0
Dec 28 05:29:31 OSPF sent LSReq 192.168.7.1 -> 192.168.7.2 (fe-4/0/0.0)
Dec 28 05:29:31    Version 2, length 48, ID 192.168.254.6, area 0.0.0.0
Dec 28 05:29:31    checksum 0x3b5d, authtype 0
Dec 28 05:29:31 OSPF rcvd LSUpdate 192.168.7.2 -> 192.168.7.1 (fe-4/0/0.0)
Dec 28 05:29:31    Version 2, length 96, ID 192.168.254.8, area 0.0.0.0
Dec 28 05:29:31    checksum 0x9970, authtype 0
Dec 28 05:29:31    adv count 2
Dec 28 05:29:31 OSPF LSA Router 192.168.254.8 192.168.254.8 from 192.168.7.2 newer
    than db
Dec 28 05:29:31 OSPF LSA Router 192.168.254.8 192.168.254.8 newer, delayed ack
Dec 28 05:29:31 OSPF LSA Network 192.168.7.1 192.168.254.6 from 192.168.7.2 newer
    than db
Dec 28 05:29:31    Our LSA
Dec 28 05:29:31    Removed from LSREQ list
Dec 28 05:29:31    Removed from LSREQ list
Dec 28 05:29:31 OSPF sent DbD 192.168.7.1 -> 192.168.7.2 (fe-4/0/0.0)
Dec 28 05:29:31    Version 2, length 32, ID 192.168.254.6, area 0.0.0.0
Dec 28 05:29:31    checksum 0xdc1e, authtype 0
Dec 28 05:29:31    options 0x42, i 0, m 0, ms 0, seq 0x1b33, mtu 1500
Dec 28 05:29:31 OSPF sent LSUpdate 192.168.7.1 -> 192.168.7.2 (fe-4/0/0.0)
Dec 28 05:29:31    Version 2, length 200, ID 192.168.254.6, area 0.0.0.0
Dec 28 05:29:31    checksum 0xd628, authtype 0
Dec 28 05:29:31    adv count 5
Dec 28 05:29:31 OSPF rcvd DbD 192.168.7.2 -> 192.168.7.1 (fe-4/0/0.0)
Dec 28 05:29:31    Version 2, length 32, ID 192.168.254.8, area 0.0.0.0
Dec 28 05:29:31    checksum 0xdc1a, authtype 0
Dec 28 05:29:31    options 0x42, i 0, m 0, ms 1, seq 0x1b34, mtu 1500
Dec 28 05:29:31    In sequence
Dec 28 05:29:31 OSPF neighbor 192.168.7.2 (fe-4/0/0.0) state changed from Exchange
    to Full
Dec 28 05:29:31 RPD_OSPF_NBRUP: OSPF neighbor 192.168.7.2 (fe-4/0/0.0) state changed
    from Exchange to Full due to DBD exchange complete
Dec 28 05:29:31 OSPF trigger router LSA build for area 0.0.0.0
Dec 28 05:29:31 OSPF trigger network LSA build for fe-4/0/0.0
Dec 28 05:29:31 OSPF neighbor 192.168.7.2 (fe-4/0/0.0) state changed by event
    ExchangeDone
Dec 28 05:29:31 OSPF sent LSUpdate 192.168.7.1 -> 224.0.0.5 (fe-4/0/0.0)
Dec 28 05:29:31    Version 2, length 60, ID 192.168.254.6, area 0.0.0.0
```

```
Dec 28 05:29:31   checksum 0xb25, authtype 0
Dec 28 05:29:31   adv count 1
Dec 28 05:29:31 OSPF rcvd LSUpdate 192.168.7.2 -> 224.0.0.5 (fe-4/0/0.0)
Dec 28 05:29:31   Version 2, length 140, ID 192.168.254.8, area 0.0.0.0
Dec 28 05:29:31   checksum 0x9f55, authtype 0
Dec 28 05:29:31   adv count 4
Dec 28 05:29:31 OSPF LSA Summary 192.168.254.9 192.168.254.8 from 192.168.7.2
       newer than db
Dec 28 05:29:31 OSPF LSA Summary 192.168.254.9 192.168.254.8 newer, delayed ack
Dec 28 05:29:31 OSPF LSA Summary 192.168.9.0 192.168.254.8 from 192.168.7.2
       newer than db
Dec 28 05:29:31 OSPF LSA Summary 192.168.9.0 192.168.254.8 newer, delayed ack
Dec 28 05:29:31 OSPF LSA Summary 192.168.8.0 192.168.254.8 from 192.168.7.2
       newer than db
Dec 28 05:29:31 OSPF LSA Summary 192.168.8.0 192.168.254.8 newer, delayed ack
Dec 28 05:29:31 OSPF LSA ASBRSum 192.168.254.9 192.168.254.8 from 192.168.7.2
       newer than db
Dec 28 05:29:31 OSPF LSA ASBRSum 192.168.254.9 192.168.254.8 newer, delayed ack
Dec 28 05:29:31 OSPF sent DbD 192.168.7.1 -> 192.168.7.2 (fe-4/0/0.0)
Dec 28 05:29:31   Version 2, length 32, ID 192.168.254.6, area 0.0.0.0
Dec 28 05:29:31   checksum 0xdc1d, authtype 0
Dec 28 05:29:31   options 0x42, i 0, m 0, ms 0, seq 0x1b34, mtu 1500
Dec 28 05:29:32 OSPF rcvd LSUpdate 192.168.7.2 -> 224.0.0.5 (fe-4/0/0.0)
Dec 28 05:29:32   Version 2, length 64, ID 192.168.254.8, area 0.0.0.0
Dec 28 05:29:32   checksum 0x60e6, authtype 0
Dec 28 05:29:32   adv count 1
Dec 28 05:29:32 OSPF LSA Router 192.168.254.8 192.168.254.8 from 192.168.7.2
       newer than db
Dec 28 05:29:32 OSPF LSA Router 192.168.254.8 192.168.254.8 newer, delayed ack
Dec 28 05:29:32 OSPF sent LSAck 192.168.7.1 -> 224.0.0.5 (fe-4/0/0.0)
Dec 28 05:29:32   Version 2, length 124, ID 192.168.254.6, area 0.0.0.0
Dec 28 05:29:32   checksum 0x51dc, authtype 0
Dec 28 05:29:32 OSPF rcvd Hello 192.168.7.2 -> 224.0.0.5 (fe-4/0/0.0)
Dec 28 05:29:32   Version 2, length 48, ID 192.168.254.8, area 0.0.0.0
Dec 28 05:29:32   checksum 0xefe4, authtype 0
Dec 28 05:29:32   mask 255.255.255.0, hello_ivl 10, opts 0x2, prio 1
Dec 28 05:29:32   dead_ivl 40, DR 192.168.7.1, BDR 192.168.7.2
Dec 28 05:29:32 OSPF Interface fe-4/0/0.0 event NeighborChange
Dec 28 05:29:32 OSPF interface fe-4/0/0.0 state changed from DR to DR
Dec 28 05:29:32 OSPF DR is 192.168.254.6, BDR is 192.168.254.8
Dec 28 05:29:33 OSPF sent Hello 192.168.7.1 -> 224.0.0.5 (fe-4/0/0.0)
Dec 28 05:29:33   Version 2, length 48, ID 192.168.254.6, area 0.0.0.0
Dec 28 05:29:33   checksum 0xef65, authtype 0
Dec 28 05:29:33   mask 255.255.255.0, hello_ivl 10, opts 0x2, prio 128
Dec 28 05:29:33   dead_ivl 40, DR 192.168.7.1, BDR 192.168.7.2
```

Figure 6.9   A traceoptions log (JUNOS) of a full OSPF adjacency being established.

All router vendors have their own way of providing troubleshooting information, and the formats can vary widely. But if you understand the underlying protocol and its mechanisms, you should be able to adapt to any record of a protocol event with little effort.

The neighboring router of the Juniper router in Figure 6.9 is a Cisco Systems router, and its physical interface connecting to the network is E0. Figure 6.10 shows the output from an IOS debug of OSPF adjacency, event, and packet over roughly the same time period covered in Figure 6.9.

- Again, segment the entries by state changes.

- Match events in this debug output with the log entries in Figure 6.9.

- The clocks of the two routers are not synchronized, and might vary by a second or two. But identify matching events between the two router outputs. Do the time periods match?

- Try drawing a graph of exchanges and state changes between the two routers, similar to the graph in Figure 6.7, using the information in Figures 6.9 and 6.10.

```
Dec 28 05:28:50: OSPF: rcv. v:2 t:1 l:44 rid:192.168.254.6
        aid:0.0.0.0 chk:3D70 aut:0 auk: from Ethernet0
Dec 28 05:28:50: OSPF: Rcv hello from 192.168.254.6 area 0 from Ethernet0 192.168.7.1
00:42:40: %LINEPROTO-5-UPDOWN: Line protocol on Interface Ethernet0, changed
        state to up
Dec 28 05:28:51: OSPF: Interface Ethernet0 going Up
Dec 28 05:28:51: OSPF: Build router LSA for area 0, router ID 192.168.254.8, seq
        0x800001D9
Dec 28 05:28:51: OSPF: Build router LSA for area 20, router ID 192.168.254.8, seq
        0x800001D4
Dec 28 05:28:52: OSPF: 2 Way Communication to 192.168.254.6 on Ethernet0, state 2WAY
Dec 28 05:28:52: OSPF: End of hello processing
Dec 28 05:29:01: OSPF: rcv. v:2 t:1 l:48 rid:192.168.254.6
        aid:0.0.0.0 chk:7EBA aut:0 auk: from Ethernet0
Dec 28 05:29:29: OSPF: rcv. v:2 t:2 l:32 rid:192.168.254.6
        aid:0.0.0.0 chk:881B aut:0 auk: from Ethernet0
Dec 28 05:29:29: OSPF: Rcv DBD from 192.168.254.6 on Ethernet0 seq 0xC0A0AE8E opt
0x42 flag 0x7 len 32  mtu 1500 state 2WAY
Dec 28 05:29:29: OSPF: Nbr state is 2WAY
Dec 28 05:29:30: OSPF: rcv. v:2 t:1 l:48 rid:192.168.254.6
        aid:0.0.0.0 chk:EF65 aut:0 auk: from Ethernet0
Dec 28 05:29:30: OSPF: Rcv hello from 192.168.254.6 area 0 from Ethernet0 192.168.7.1
Dec 28 05:29:30: OSPF: End of hello processing
Dec 28 05:29:31: OSPF: end of Wait on interface Ethernet0
Dec 28 05:29:31: OSPF: DR/BDR election on Ethernet0
Dec 28 05:29:31: OSPF: Elect BDR 192.168.254.8
Dec 28 05:29:31: OSPF: Elect DR 192.168.254.6
Dec 28 05:29:31: OSPF: Elect BDR 192.168.254.8
Dec 28 05:29:31: OSPF: Elect DR 192.168.254.6
Dec 28 05:29:31:           DR: 192.168.254.6 (Id)   BDR: 192.168.254.8 (Id)
Dec 28 05:29:31: OSPF: Send DBD to 192.168.254.6 on Ethernet0 seq 0x1B32 opt 0x42
        flag 0x7 len 32
Dec 28 05:29:31: OSPF: rcv. v:2 t:2 l:192 rid:192.168.254.6
        aid:0.0.0.0 chk:3A37 aut:0 auk: from Ethernet0
Dec 28 05:29:31: OSPF: Rcv DBD from 192.168.254.6 on Ethernet0 seq 0x1B32 opt 0x42
        flag 0x0 len 192  mtu 1500 state EXSTART
Dec 28 05:29:31: OSPF: NBR Negotiation Done. We are the MASTER
Dec 28 05:29:31: OSPF: Send DBD to 192.168.254.6 on Ethernet0 seq 0x1B33 opt 0x42
        flag 0x3 len 212
Dec 28 05:29:31: OSPF: Database request to 192.168.254.6
Dec 28 05:29:31: OSPF: sent LS REQ packet to 192.168.7.1, length 60
Dec 28 05:29:31: OSPF: rcv. v:2 t:3 l:48 rid:192.168.254.6
        aid:0.0.0.0 chk:3B5D aut:0 auk: from Ethernet0
Dec 28 05:29:31: OSPF: rcv. v:2 t:2 l:32 rid:192.168.254.6
        aid:0.0.0.0 chk:DC1E aut:0 auk: from Ethernet0
```

```
Dec 28 05:29:31: OSPF: Rcv DBD from 192.168.254.6 on Ethernet0 seq 0x1B33 opt 0x42
     flag 0x0 len 32  mtu 1500 state EXCHANGE
Dec 28 05:29:31: OSPF: Send DBD to 192.168.254.6 on Ethernet0 seq 0x1B34 opt 0x42
     flag 0x1 len 32
Dec 28 05:29:31: OSPF: rcv. v:2 t:4 l:200 rid:192.168.254.6
     aid:0.0.0.0 chk:D628 aut:0 auk: from Ethernet0
Dec 28 05:29:31: OSPF: rcv. v:2 t:4 l:60 rid:192.168.254.6
     aid:0.0.0.0 chk:B25 aut:0 auk: from Ethernet0
Dec 28 05:29:31: OSPF: rcv. v:2 t:2 l:32 rid:192.168.254.6
     aid:0.0.0.0 chk:DC1D aut:0 auk: from Ethernet0
Dec 28 05:29:31: OSPF: Rcv DBD from 192.168.254.6 on Ethernet0 seq 0x1B34 opt 0x42
flag 0x0 len 32  mtu 1500 state EXCHANGE
Dec 28 05:29:31: OSPF: Exchange Done with 192.168.254.6 on Ethernet0
Dec 28 05:29:31: OSPF: Synchronized with 192.168.254.6 on Ethernet0, state FULL
Dec 28 05:29:32: OSPF: Build router LSA for area 0, router ID 192.168.254.8, seq
     0x800001DA
Dec 28 05:29:32: OSPF: rcv. v:2 t:5 l:124 rid:192.168.254.6
     aid:0.0.0.0 chk:51DC aut:0 auk: from Ethernet0
Dec 28 05:29:33: OSPF: rcv. v:2 t:1 l:48 rid:192.168.254.6
     aid:0.0.0.0 chk:EF65 aut:0 auk: from Ethernet0
Dec 28 05:29:33: OSPF: Rcv hello from 192.168.254.6 area 0 from Ethernet0 192.168.7.1
Dec 28 05:29:33: OSPF: Neighbor change Event on interface Ethernet0
Dec 28 05:29:33: OSPF: DR/BDR election on Ethernet0
Dec 28 05:29:33: OSPF: Elect BDR 192.168.254.8
Dec 28 05:29:33: OSPF: Elect DR 192.168.254.6
Dec 28 05:29:33:         DR: 192.168.254.6 (Id)   BDR: 192.168.254.8 (Id)
Dec 28 05:29:33: OSPF: End of hello processing
Dec 28 05:29:34: OSPF: rcv. v:2 t:4 l:120 rid:192.168.254.6
     aid:0.0.0.0 chk:B658 aut:0 auk: from Ethernet0
```

Figure 6.10   A debug output (IOS) of the same adjacency establishment, from the viewpoint of the other neighbor.

6.1.8   Troubleshooting: Comparing OSPF LS Databases

Routing problems—incorrect forwarding of packets—in modern OSPF or IS-IS networks almost always have a mundane cause such as a link failure or a router misconfiguration. The source of the problem can usually be discovered by analysis of the information in the routing and forwarding tables. Rarely is a routing problem the result of inconsistent LS databases in an area, because an unresolved inconsistency during database synchronization should cause an adjacency failure and the path between the routers involved is not considered in routing decisions.

However, unsynchronized LS databases do occur. They likely are the result of a bad or buggy OSPF implementation. This section demonstrates how to compare databases, for those rare occasions when no more obvious cause for your routing problems can be found.

You should start by comparing summaries of the databases, to ensure that they both have the same number of each type of LSA. As with the examples in the previous section, outputs will vary from router vendor to router vendor, but the information is the same as long as you know what you are looking for. Figures 6.11 and 6.12 show database summaries from a Juniper and Cisco router, respectively (the same neighbors that that were used in the example in the previous section). Comparing the two summaries, you can see that the databases for area 0 match:

- 4 Router LSAs
- 4 Network LSAs
- 10 Network Summary LSAs
- 1 ASBR Summary LSA
- 2 AS-External LSAs (shown in the IOS display under the Process 1 summary)

```
jeff@Juniper6> show ospf database summary
Area 0.0.0.0:
    4 Router LSAs
    4 Network LSAs
   10 Summary LSAs
    1 ASBRSum LSAs
Externals:
    2 Extern LSAs
```

Figure 6.11 A JUNOS summary of a link state database.

```
Cisco8#show ip ospf database database-summary

            OSPF Router with ID (192.168.254.8) (Process ID 1)

Area 0 database summary
  LSA Type       Count    Delete     Maxage
  Router         4        0          0
  Network        4        0          0
  Summary Net    10       0          0
  Summary ASBR   1        0          0
  Type-7 Ext     0        0          0
  Opaque Link    0        0          0
  Opaque Area    0        0          0
  Subtotal       19       0          0

Area 20 database summary
  LSA Type       Count    Delete     Maxage
  Router         2        0          0
  Network        1        0          0
  Summary Net    13       0          0
  Summary ASBR   0        0          0
  Type-7 Ext     0        0          0
  Opaque Link    0        0          0
  Opaque Area    0        0          0
  Subtotal       16       0          0

Process 1 database summary
  LSA Type       Count    Delete     Maxage
  Router         6        0          0
  Network        5        0          0
```

```
          Summary Net    23        0         0
          Summary ASBR   1         0         0
          Type-7 Ext     0         0         0
          Opaque Link    0         0         0
          Opaque Area    0         0         0
          Type-5 Ext     2         0         0
          Opaque AS      0         0         0
          Total          37        0         0
       Cisco8#
```

Figure 6.12   An IOS summary of a link state database.

The router in Figure 6.12 also has a LS database for area 20, because it is an ABR. But the information in that portion of the summary is irrelevant to us; the interfaces connecting the two neighbors are in area 0.

Even if the number of each type of LSA matches between the databases, an instance of one or more LSAs in the two databases may be inconsistent. You can check this by adding the checksums of all LSAs in each database: If the LSA instances are all the same, the sum of checksums will be equal. If the checksums are not equal, a one-by-one comparison of the checksums of each LSA will reveal the culprit.

Figures 6.13 and 6.14 show the LSA headers of the two neighbors in the previous example. Adding the checksums of the LSAs specific to area 0, both databases produce a sum of 0x6C0D:

- Router LSA checksum total = 0x2938A.
- Network LSA checksum total = 0x24718.
- Network Summary checksum total = 0x5F5AE.
- ASBR Summary checksum = 0x7BBD.

```
jeff@Juniper6> show ospf database

      OSPF link state database, area 0.0.0.0
 Type    ID           Adv Rtr        Seq          Age   Opt  Cksum    Len
 Router  192.168.254.5 192.168.254.5 0x80001d0b   2082  0x2  0x96dc   36
 Router *192.168.254.6 192.168.254.6 0x80000772   932   0x2  0x826f   96
 Router  192.168.254.7 192.168.254.7 0x80001945   1193  0x2  0x7acb   48
 Router  192.168.254.8 192.168.254.8 0x800001ef   867   0x22 0xff74   36
 Network 192.168.3.2   192.168.254.5 0x80000004   126   0x2  0x9c03   32
 Network 192.168.4.2   192.168.254.7 0x80000004   1651  0x2  0x9901   32
 Network 192.168.5.2   192.168.254.7 0x80000003   1335  0x2  0x900a   32
 Network *192.168.7.1  192.168.254.6 0x80000010   846   0x2  0x820a   32
 Summary 192.168.1.0   192.168.254.5 0x800006c9   1168  0x2  0xf1c3   28
 Summary 192.168.2.0   192.168.254.5 0x800006c9   1025  0x2  0xe6cd   28
 Summary 192.168.6.0   192.168.254.5 0x8000033f   883   0x2  0xe25a   28
 Summary 192.168.8.0   192.168.254.8 0x8000001a   867   0x22 0x7cbb   28
 Summary 192.168.9.0   192.168.254.8 0x80000018   867   0x22 0xd955   28
 Summary 192.168.254.2 192.168.254.5 0x8000033b   1183  0x2  0x1a2d   28
```

```
Summary   192.168.254.4 192.168.254.5  0x8000033a   868  0x2  0x83e   28
Summary   192.168.254.5 192.168.254.5  0x80001ce3   725  0x2  0x552e  28
Summary   192.168.254.7 192.168.254.7  0x80001916  1351  0x2  0xd976  28
Summary   192.168.254.9 192.168.254.8  0x80000018   867  0x22 0x93a5  28
ASBRSum   192.168.254.9 192.168.254.8  0x80000018   867  0x22 0x7bbd  28
     OSPF external link state database
Type    ID            Adv Rtr         Seq          Age  Opt  Cksum  Len
Extern  192.168.120.0 192.168.254.9  0x800001d0    14   0x20 0x3a8d  36
Extern  192.168.220.0 192.168.254.9  0x800001d0    14   0x20 0xe979  36


jeff@Juniper6>
```

Figure 6.13   A JUNOS display of the LSA headers in a LS database.

```
Cisco8# show ip ospf database

        OSPF Router with ID (192.168.254.8) (Process ID 1)


                Router Link States (Area 0)

Link ID          ADV Router       Age       Seq#        Checksum Link count
192.168.254.5    192.168.254.5    1969      0x80001D0B 0x96DC    1
192.168.254.6    192.168.254.6    819       0x80000772 0x826F    6
192.168.254.7    192.168.254.7    1079      0x80001945 0x7ACB    2
192.168.254.8    192.168.254.8    752       0x800001EF 0xFF74    1

                Net Link States (Area 0)

Link ID          ADV Router       Age       Seq#        Checksum
192.168.3.2      192.168.254.5    12        0x80000004 0x9C03
192.168.4.2      192.168.254.7    1537      0x80000004 0x9901
192.168.5.2      192.168.254.7    1222      0x80000003 0x900A
192.168.7.1      192.168.254.6    733       0x80000010 0x820A

                Summary Net Link States (Area 0)

Link ID          ADV Router       Age       Seq#        Checksum
192.168.1.0      192.168.254.5    1055      0x800006C9 0xF1C3
192.168.2.0      192.168.254.5    914       0x800006C9 0xE6CD
192.168.6.0      192.168.254.5    772       0x8000033F 0xE25A
192.168.8.0      192.168.254.8    754       0x8000001A 0x7CBB
192.168.9.0      192.168.254.8    754       0x80000018 0xD955
192.168.254.2    192.168.254.5    1072      0x8000033B 0x1A2D
192.168.254.4    192.168.254.5    756       0x8000033A 0x83E
192.168.254.5    192.168.254.5    614       0x80001CE3 0x552E
192.168.254.7    192.168.254.7    1240      0x80001916 0xD976
192.168.254.9    192.168.254.8    755       0x80000018 0x93A5

                Summary ASB Link States (Area 0)

Link ID          ADV Router       Age       Seq#        Checksum
192.168.254.9    192.168.254.8    755       0x80000018 0x7BBD
```

```
                    Router Link States (Area 20)

Link ID            ADV Router        Age      Seq#        Checksum Link count
192.168.254.8      192.168.254.8     755      0x800001E9  0x2256      1
192.168.254.9      192.168.254.9     1173     0x800001D5  0xD4A6      3

                    Net Link States (Area 20)

Link ID            ADV Router        Age      Seq#        Checksum
192.168.8.1        192.168.254.9     1173     0x80000017  0x93CA

                    Summary Net Link States (Area 20)

Link ID            ADV Router        Age          Seq#        Checksum
172.16.1.0         192.168.254.8     756          0x00000016  0x6283
192.168.1.0        192.168.254.8     1004         0x80000003  0xC48
192.168.2.0        192.168.254.8     1004         0x80000003  0x152
192.168.3.0        192.168.254.8     1004         0x80000005  0xE769
192.168.4.0        192.168.254.8     237          0x8000000A  0xD278
192.168.5.0        192.168.254.8     1996         0x80000012  0xB78A
192.168.6.0        192.168.254.8     1004         0x80000003  0xDE6F
192.168.7.0        192.168.254.8     756          0x80000018  0x8BAF
192.168.254.2      192.168.254.8     1004         0x80000003  0xE46
192.168.254.4      192.168.254.8     1004         0x80000003  0xF958
192.168.254.5      192.168.254.8     1004         0x80000003  0xE56C
192.168.254.6      192.168.254.8     756          0x80000016  0xAB93
192.168.254.7      192.168.254.8     237          0x80000003  0xD17E

                    Type-5 AS External Link States

Link ID            ADV Router        Age      Seq#        Checksum Tag
192.168.120.0      192.168.254.9     1948     0x800001D0  0x3C8C    0
192.168.220.0      192.168.254.9     1949     0x800001D0  0xEB78    0
Cisco8#
```

Figure 6.14   An IOS display of the LSA headers in a LS database.

The sum of the two AS-External checksums is 0x12406. Of course, with just two LSAs comparing the individual checksums is easier than comparing their sums. In fact, it is debatable whether it is easier to compare sums of checksums or just compare checksums one by one even in larger databases. The problem is that in large-scale networks, the link state databases are likely to be very much longer than these examples and either method of comparing checksums is going to be tedious and error-prone. Adding to the difficulties, if a database refresh takes place between the time you capture the first database display and the time you capture the second, the checksums will change and your sums will not match—even though there is no real inconsistency between the databases.

Fortunately, there is a solution. If you are managing a large OSPF network, you are likely using some SNMP-based management software. Some OSPF MIBs return the sums of checksums, saving you the tedium of hand calculating them:

- ospfAreaLsaCksumSum returns the sum of checksums for an area, not including AS-External LSAs.
- ospfExternLsaCksumSum returns the sum of AS-external (type 5) LSA checksums.

Unfortunately, mismatched sums of checksums only indicate a synchronization problem. This information does not show the cause or reveal which LSAs do not match. But you probably do not need to know more than that the databases are out of sync. If you've confirmed that much, try manually breaking and then restarting the adjacency, allowing the neighbors to resynchronize. If the problem does not go away (and stay away), a call to your vendor's support team is needed for in-depth analysis of what is probably an implementation problem.

6.2   IS-IS Database Synchronization

Whereas OSPF requires neighbors to explicitly agree to begin a database-exchange process and relies on a strict state machine to manage the process, IS-IS relies on a simple process in which a router periodically describes its complete database to its neighbors.[2]

On point-to-point links, neighbors exchange CSNPs to describe the contents of their databases. If a router sees in a received CSNP an unknown LSP or more recent copy of a known LSP, it sends a PSNP to its neighbor requesting a copy of the LSP. Likewise, if the router sees in the received CSNP that the neighbor does not know about an LSP in the router's database or that the neighbor has an older copy of an LSP, the router sends the neighbor a copy of the LSP.

On broadcast networks, the DIS periodically multicasts CSNPs; all other routers compare the contents of the CSNPs with the contents of their databases and, as with point-to-point links, sends LSPs or sends a PSNP to request an LSP as necessary. Multicasting helps the entire process, too. When a router multicasts an LSP, everyone on the link sees it and can keep a copy if necessary.

This section details CSNPs and PSNPs, and shows how these messages are used to describe, request, and implicitly acknowledge LSPs.

6.2.1   IS-IS PDUs Used in Synchronization

Three of the four basic IS-IS PDU types are used for database synchronization:

- Link State PDUs (type 18 for L1, type 20 for L2)
- Complete Sequence Numbers PDUs (type 24 for L1, type 25 for L2)
- Partial Sequence Numbers PDUs (type 26 for L1, type 27 for L2)

You saw in Chapter 5 how LSPs are flooded between neighbors and how Sequence Number PDUs are used to acknowledge the receipt of LSPs. However, the Sequence Numbers PDUs were not detailed in Chapter 5. They are essential to database synchronization, and are detailed here.

---

[2]   In reality, ISO 10589 does not require periodic database descriptions on point-to-point links, although some implementations do it as an optimization.

Figure 6.15 shows the format of a Complete Sequence Numbers PDU (CSNP), which is used to advertise the complete contents of a router's LS database to L1 or L2 neighbors. The L1 CSNP is type 24 (0x18) and the L2 CSNP is type 25 (0x19).

	Length, in Bytes
Intradomain Routeing Protocol Discriminator = 0x83	1
Length Indicator	1
Protocol ID = 0x01	1
ID Length = 0x00	1
Type = 0x18 (L1) or 0x19 (L2)	1
Version = 0x01	1
Reserved = 0x00	1
Maximum Area Addresses	1
PDU Length	2
Source ID	7
Start LSP ID	8
End LSP ID	8
TLVs	Variable

Figure 6.15   The format of the IS-IS Complete Sequence Numbers PDU.

- **Source ID** is the 6-byte SysID of the originating router plus the 1-byte Circuit ID. The Circuit ID is set to 0x00.

- **Start LSP ID** and **End LSP ID** together describe the contiguous range of possible LSP IDs that can be described in this CSNP. They do not necessarily describe actual LSP IDs. For example, if all the LSPs in a database can be described by a single CSNP, the Start LSP ID is 0000.0000.0000.00.00 and the End LSP ID is ffff.ffff.ffff.ff.ff: the range of all possible LSP IDs. If multiple CSNPs are necessary, the range described by these two fields is the range included in this CSNP. For example, suppose two CSNPs are required to describe the complete database. The first might have a Start LSP ID of 0000.0000.0000.00.00 and an End LSP ID of 0000.abcd.1234.00.00, whereas the second CSNP has a Start LSP ID of 0000.abcd.1234.00.01 and an End LSP ID of ffff.ffff.ffff.ff.ff. Thus, a receiving router can recognize the beginning and end of a series of CSNPs, and detect whether one or more in a series of CSNPs are missing, by observing these two fields.

Two TLVs can be carried in the CSNP:

■   LSP Entries TLVs
■   Authentication Information TLVs

Authentication Information TLVs are for secure authentication of the packet and are discussed in Chapter 9. LSP Entries TLVs are the essential TLVs for CSNP, and uniquely identify the LSP and the specific instance of the LSP by listing the Remaining Lifetime, LSP ID, LSP Sequence Number, and Checksum fields from the LSP header. The LSP Entries TLV, shown in Figure 6.16, is identified as TLV type 9 (0x09).

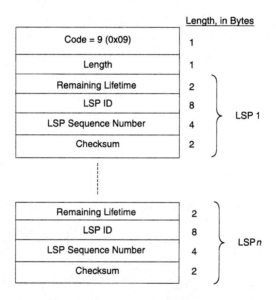

Figure 6.16   The format of the LSP Entries TLV.

The Partial Sequence Numbers PDU (PSNP), shown in Figure 6.17, carries—as the name implies—a description of only some of the LSPs in a router's LS database. It is used both to acknowledge explicitly the receipt of LSPs (on point-to-point links) and to request needed LSPs from an L1 or L2 neighbor. Its PDU type is 26 (0x1A) for L1 and 27 (0x1B) for L2.

■   **Source ID** is the 6-byte SysID of the originating router plus the 1-byte Circuit ID. The Circuit ID is set to 0x00.

Like the CSNP, a PSNP can carry Authentication Information TLVs and LSP Entries TLVs, with LSP Entries TLVs being the essential TLV for describing LSPs.

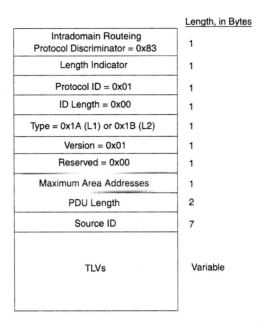

Figure 6.17   The format of the IS-IS Partial Sequence Numbers PDU.

6.2.2   Send Routing Message and Send Sequence Number Flags

You read briefly about Send Routing Message (SRM) flags in Chapter 5, as they apply to flooding. To recap that discussion:

The SRM is an internal flag. For each LSP in its LS database, IS-IS creates a set of SRMs—one per link. That is, if a router has 20 LSPs in its LS database and 5 interfaces, 5 SRMs will be associated with each of the LSPs for a total of 100 SRMs. When IS-IS determines that an LSP needs to be sent on a particular link, it sets the LSP's SRM flag for that interface. At a set interval, known as the *minimum LSP transmission interval*, the LS database is scanned. On point-to-point links, all LSPs that have the SRM for that link set are sent. On broadcast links, the behavior is more interesting: The LS database is scanned once every minimum LSP transmission interval and out of the set of LSPs with their SRMs set for that interface, one[3] is randomly chosen and sent. This randomization prevents multiple routers from sending the same LSP to the DIS at the same time.

SRM flags are used not only as a part of the flooding procedure but also as a part of the database synchronization procedure. The flag is set when the associated LSP is to be sent on the associated interface. On broadcast circuits the flag is cleared as soon as the LSP is sent, and on point-to-point circuits the flag is cleared only when the sent LSP is acknowledged. In this, SRM flags perform a function similar to the OSPF Link State Transmission list. A key

---

[3] Some IS-IS implementations might randomly choose more than one LSP for transmission at each scan, but it must be a small number. ISO 10589 recommends no more than 10.

difference, however, is that where the OSPF Transmission list is associated with a neighbor (as a part of the OSPF neighbor data structure), the SRM is associated with an interface.

Another internal flag used in the LS database synchronization procedure is the Send Sequence Number (SSN) flag. Like the SRM flag, each LSP has one SSN flag for each of the router's IS-IS interfaces. When an SSN flag is set, it indicates that the LSP is to be described in a PSNP sent on the associated interface. The SSN flag is cleared when the PSNP describing the LSP is sent. The SSN flag, then, performs a function similar to the OSPF Link State Request list during database synchronization. But again, the difference is that the SSN flag is associated with an interface rather than a specific neighbor.

The use of these flags and the synchronization procedure itself are different on point-to-point and broadcast networks. The next two sections discuss the synchronization procedure for these two network types.

6.2.3   *Synchronization on Point-to-Point Networks*

When an adjacency is newly established on a point-to-point link, the neighbors set the SRM flags of all LSPs for the interface attached to the link and then describe their complete databases to each other using CSNPs. L1 CSNPs are sent for L1 adjacencies, and L2 CSNPs are sent for L2 adjacencies. Each neighbor compares each LSP described in the received CSNPs with the LSPs in its own database. The comparison is sequential between the LSP IDs in the CSNP and the LSP IDs in the database, through the range of LSP IDs specified in the CSNP's Start LSP ID and End LSP ID fields. At each comparison, one of the following actions is taken:

- If the LSP is the same as an existing LSP in the database, clear the LSP's SRM flag associated with that interface.
- If the LSP is unknown (no equivalent LSP ID exists in the database), create an entry for the LSP in the database with a sequence number of 0, indicating that no information yet exists for the LSP. LSPs with sequence number 0 cannot have a SRM flag set, so they cannot be flooded. Set the entry's SSN flag for the interface, so that a PSNP describing this LSP will be sent to the neighbor.
- If the database contains a newer copy of the LSP, clear the LSP's SSN flag and set the SRM flag for this interface so that the LSP will be unicast to the neighbor.
- If the database contains an older copy of the LSP, clear the LSP's SRM flag and set the SSN flag for this interface so that the existing LSP will not be flooded to the neighbor and a PSNP describing this LSP will be unicast to the neighbor.
- If an LSP exists in the database whose LSP ID is in the range specified by the CSNP's Start and End LSP ID fields but is not described in the LSP Entries TLV (and the LSP has a non-zero sequence number and remaining lifetime), set the LSP's SRM flag for the interface so that it is sent to the neighbor.

On point-to-point links, PSNPs serve as acknowledgments of received LSPs. When a router sends an LSP to its neighbor, the SRM flag remains set for that interface. Every *minimumLSPTransmissionInterval*—5 seconds—LSPs that have had their SRM flags for the interface set and have not been transmitted on the interface in the past 5 seconds are retransmitted. When the neighbor acknowledges the receipt of the LSP in a PSNP, the router clears the SRM flag so the LSP is no longer retransmitted.

When a router receives an LSP, it takes one of the following actions:

- If the LSP is newer than a copy in the database (or contains an entry with a sequence number of 0), replace the existing LSP with the new one. Set the SRM flag for all interfaces other than the one the LSA was received on, and clear the flag on this interface, so the new LSP is flooded to all neighbors except the one that sent it. Set the SSN flag for this receiving interface so that a PSNP will be sent acknowledging the LSP.

- If the database does not contain an LSP whose ID matches the received LSP, install the LSP in the database. Then, as with newer LSPs as described in the preceding bullet, set the SRM flag for all interfaces other than the one it was received on, and clear the flag on this interface so that the new LSP is flooded to neighbors except the one that sent it. Set the SSN flag for this receiving interface so that a PSNP will be sent acknowledging the LSP.

- If the database contains a copy of the LSP that is newer than the received LSP, set the LSP's SRM flag for the interface so that the newer copy will be sent to the neighbor. Clear the LSP's SSN flag for the interface.

- If the database contains the same instance of the received LSP, clear the LSP's SRM flag for the interface and set the SSN flag, so that a PSNP is sent acknowledging receipt of the LSP.

Note that when an adjacency first comes up, as described in the first paragraph of this section, the router sets the SRM flag for this interface in all of the LSPs in its database. This way even if the LSP is not requested by the neighbor in a PSNP, the LSP will be sent after the minimumLSPTransmissionInterval of 5 seconds and every 5 seconds afterward, until the LSP is acknowledged or a newer copy is received.

Interestingly, this means that because the SRM mechanism triggers flooding, database synchronization would take place even without the CSNPs. The CSNPs provide an optimization so that only the LSPs required by each of the neighbors are exchanged.

6.2.4 Synchronization on Broadcast Networks

Just as all OSPF routers on a broadcast network synchronize their databases with the DR, all IS-IS routers on a broadcast network synchronize their databases with the DIS. But the similarity ends there.

One significant difference is that rather than have separate multicast addresses for the DIS and all other routers, as OSPF does for DR/BDRs and DROthers, IS-IS multicast addresses on broadcast networks distinguish only between L1 and L2 adjacencies. CSNPs, PSNPs, and LSPs are all multicast, and all routers on the broadcast network receive them equally. So, for example, if a router sends a PSNP to request an LSP, other routers that might also need the LSP can see that the LSP has been requested. And when any router sends an LSP, all routers see it and can keep a copy if needed.

A DIS describes its complete database in CSNPs every *CompleteSNPInterval*, which typically is 10 seconds but is configurable between 0 and 65,535 seconds.[4] But rather than unicast, the CSNPs are multicast so that all attached routers see them. When a router receives a CSNP, it performs the same sequential comparison to its database, as described in Section 6.2.3 for point-to-point synchronization.

But when an LSP is multicast, the SRM flag for the interface is cleared rather than remaining set as with point-to-point links. The reason for this is that the periodic CSNPs act as an indirect acknowledgment. If a non-DIS router sends an LSP that is not received by the DIS, the router will know it when the subsequent CSNP does not describe the LSP. The LSP can then be re-sent. Likewise, if a router on the broadcast network does not receive an LSP, the router will re-request the LSP in a new PSNP when the CSNP is again sent.

Receipt of LSPs also is handled as described in Section 6.2.3, with the exception that if the LSP is newer than or equal to an LSP in the database, the SSN flag is not set. As a result, PSNPs are not sent to acknowledge receipt of these LSPs. This approach avoids a situation in which many routers on the network might try to acknowledge an LSP at the same time, and is accomplished without reducing reliability by the periodic transmission of CSNPs.

As mentioned briefly in Section 5.1.2, the LS database is scanned once every minimum LSP transmission interval, and out of the set of LSPs with their SRMs set for that interface, one[5] is randomly chosen and sent. This procedure spreads the burden of updating LSPs across as many routers as possible. Because all of the IS-IS packets on the broadcast network are multicast, all routers see what is going on during the synchronization process. So, if one router sends a PSNP requesting a set of LSPs, all routers see it. If the requesting router is new, all routers likely have a copy of the requested LSPs; but only the DIS will send an LSP in response to a PSNP, to avoid multiple copies of the LSP being sent on the link. Where OSPF routers are strictly synchronized to the DR, the IS-IS DIS acts more as a reference point by sending CSNPs. Likewise, an LSP multicast on a broadcast network at the request of one router can be received by multiple routers needing the LSP.

---

[4] Although the configurable range of the CompleteSNPInterval is large, there is seldom if ever any reason to change the default period. Recall from Chapter 5 that unlike OSPF, IS-IS does not have an acknowledgment message. Instead, LSPs are implicitly acknowledged on broadcast networks by CSNPs. A long CompleteSNPInterval will inhibit these acknowledgments, and a period lower than the default does not significantly improve them.

[5] Some IS-IS implementations might randomly choose more than one LSP for transmission at each scan, but it must be a small number. ISO 10589 recommends no more than 10.

6.2.5 Troubleshooting: Reading IS-IS Log Entries and Debug Output

Just as you need to be able to read log entries tracking database synchronization for OSPF when a check of all the more obvious potential problem sources does not reveal why two neighbors will not synchronize, the same holds true for IS-IS. Figures 6.18 and 6.19 show two routers synchronizing their databases.

The two routers are a Juniper (Juniper6) and a Cisco (Cisco8). As you read through the two routers' accounts of the synchronization, ask yourself the following questions:

- What are the MAC addresses of the two interfaces?
- What are the IP addresses of the two interfaces?
- For each router, is the interface L1 only, L2 only, or L1/L2?
- Is this an L1 or L2 adjacency?
- What are the LSP IDs of the LSPs sent by each router?
- From the perspective of each router, when is bidirectional communication first established?

```
jeff@Juniper6> show log isis_sync
Dec 28 22:01:48 ISIS link layer change on interface fe-4/0/0.0
Dec 28 22:01:48 ISIS interface fe-4/0/0.0 up
Dec 28 22:01:48 ISIS interface fe-4/0/0.0 up
Dec 28 22:01:50 Received L2 LAN IIH, source id Cisco8 on fe-4/0/0.0
Dec 28 22:01:50     intf index 5 addr 0.e0.1e.60.a.3e, snpa 0:e0:1e:60:a:3e
Dec 28 22:01:50     max area 0, circuit type 1112, packet length 1497
Dec 28 22:01:50     hold time 10, priority 64, circuit id Cisco8.01
Dec 28 22:01:50     speaks IP
Dec 28 22:01:50     area address 47.0020 (3)
Dec 28 22:01:50     IP address 192.168.7.2
Dec 28 22:01:50     1443 bytes of total padding
Dec 28 22:01:50 new neighbor for Cisco8
Dec 28 22:01:50 new adjacency for Cisco8 on fe-4/0/0.0, level 2
Dec 28 22:01:50 Adjacency state change, Cisco8, state New -> Initializing
Dec 28 22:01:50     interface fe-4/0/0.0, level 2
Dec 28 22:01:51 Sending L2 LAN IIH on fe-4/0/0.0
Dec 28 22:01:51     max area 0, circuit type l2
Dec 28 22:01:51     neighbor 0:e0:1e:60:a:3e
Dec 28 22:01:51     No candidates for DR
Dec 28 22:01:51     hold time 27, priority 64, circuit id Juniper6.05
Dec 28 22:01:51     speaks IP
Dec 28 22:01:51     speaks IPv6
Dec 28 22:01:51     IP address 192.168.7.1
Dec 28 22:01:51     area address 47.0103 (3)
Dec 28 22:01:51     1429 bytes of total padding
Dec 28 22:01:51 Received L2 LAN IIH, source id Cisco8 on fe-4/0/0.0
Dec 28 22:01:51     intf index 5 addr 0.e0.1e.60.a.3e, snpa 0:e0:1e:60:a:3e
Dec 28 22:01:51     max area 0, circuit type 1112, packet length 1497
Dec 28 22:01:51     hold time 10, priority 64, circuit id Cisco8.01
Dec 28 22:01:51     speaks IP
Dec 28 22:01:51     area address 47.0020 (3)
Dec 28 22:01:51     IP address 192.168.7.2
```

```
Dec 28 22:01:51     neighbor 0:d0:b7:7f:d:5 (ourselves)
Dec 28 22:01:51     1435 bytes of total padding
Dec 28 22:01:51     updating neighbor Cisco8
Dec 28 22:01:51 Adjacency state change, Cisco8, state Initializing -> Up
Dec 28 22:01:51     interface fe-4/0/0.0, level 2
Dec 28 22:01:51     Updating LSP
Dec 28 22:01:51     Scheduling L2 LSP Juniper6.00-00 sequence 0x8a on interface
    fe-4/0/0.0
Dec 28 22:01:51 Sending L2 LSP Juniper6.00-00 on interface fe-4/0/0.0
Dec 28 22:01:51     sequence 0x8a, checksum 0x3d2a, lifetime 1200
Dec 28 22:01:52 Received L2 LSP Cisco8.00-00, interface fe-4/0/0.0
Dec 28 22:01:52     from Cisco8
Dec 28 22:01:52     sequence 0x9, checksum 0xce83, lifetime 1199
Dec 28 22:01:52     max area 0, length 78
Dec 28 22:01:52     no partition repair, no database overload
Dec 28 22:01:52     IS type 3, metric type 0
Dec 28 22:01:52     area address 47.0020 (3)
Dec 28 22:01:52     speaks IP
Dec 28 22:01:52     dyn hostname Cisco8
Dec 28 22:01:52     IP address 192.168.7.2
Dec 28 22:01:52     IS neighbors:
Dec 28 22:01:52     IS neighbor Cisco8.01
Dec 28 22:01:52     internal, metrics: default 10
Dec 28 22:01:52     IP prefix 192.168.7.0 255.255.255.0
Dec 28 22:01:52     internal, metrics: default 10
Dec 28 22:01:52     Updating LSP
Dec 28 22:01:52 Received L2 LSP Cisco8.01-00, interface fe-4/0/0.0
Dec 28 22:01:52     from Cisco8
Dec 28 22:01:52     sequence 0x7, checksum 0xdcee, lifetime 1199
Dec 28 22:01:52     max area 0, length 52
Dec 28 22:01:52     no partition repair, no database overload
Dec 28 22:01:52     IS type 3, metric type 0
Dec 28 22:01:52     IS neighbors:
Dec 28 22:01:52     IS neighbor Cisco8.00
Dec 28 22:01:52     internal, metrics: default 0
Dec 28 22:01:52     IS neighbor Juniper6.00
Dec 28 22:01:52     internal, metrics: default 0
Dec 28 22:01:52     Updating LSP
Dec 28 22:01:52 Adding a half link from Cisco8.01 to Juniper6.00
Dec 28 22:01:52 Adding a half link from Cisco8.01 to Cisco8.00
Dec 28 22:01:55 Received L2 CSN, source Cisco8, interface fe-4/0/0.0
Dec 28 22:01:55     LSP range 0000.0000.0000.00-00 to ffff.ffff.ffff.ff-ff
Dec 28 22:01:55     packet length 163
Dec 28 22:01:55     LSP Juniper5.00-00 lifetime 672
Dec 28 22:01:55     sequence 0x4567 checksum 0x646c
Dec 28 22:01:55     Matched database, matching sequence numbers
Dec 28 22:01:55     LSP Juniper5.04-00 lifetime 752
Dec 28 22:01:55     sequence 0x1c checksum 0xcfb8
Dec 28 22:01:55     Matched database, matching sequence numbers
Dec 28 22:01:55     LSP Juniper6.00-00 lifetime 973
Dec 28 22:01:55     sequence 0x84 checksum 0xbbcc
Dec 28 22:01:55     Matched database, neighbor is out of date, sending LSP
Dec 28 22:01:55     LSP Juniper7.00-00 lifetime 474
Dec 28 22:01:55     sequence 0x466c checksum 0x415a
Dec 28 22:01:55     Matched database, matching sequence numbers
Dec 28 22:01:55     LSP Juniper7.02-00 lifetime 705
Dec 28 22:01:55     sequence 0x26 checksum 0x1a60
Dec 28 22:01:55     Matched database, matching sequence numbers
Dec 28 22:01:55     LSP Juniper7.03-00 lifetime 416
```

```
Dec 28 22:01:55      sequence 0x1f checksum 0x215f
Dec 28 22:01:55      Matched database, matching sequence numbers
Dec 28 22:01:55      LSP Cisco8.00-00 lifetime 1196
Dec 28 22:01:55      sequence 0x9 checksum 0xce83
Dec 28 22:01:55      Matched database, matching sequence numbers
Dec 28 22:01:55      LSP Cisco8.01-00 lifetime 1196
Dec 28 22:01:55      sequence 0x7 checksum 0xdcee
Dec 28 22:01:55      Matched database, matching sequence numbers
Dec 28 22:01:55 Sending L2 LSP Juniper6.00-00 on interface fe-4/0/0.0
Dec 28 22:01:55      sequence 0x8a, checksum 0x3d2a, lifetime 1198
Dec 28 22:02:00 Analyzing subtlv's for Cisco8.01
Dec 28 22:02:00      IP address: 192.168.7.1
Dec 28 22:02:00 Analysis complete
Dec 28 22:02:00      Scheduling L2 LSP Juniper6.00-00 sequence 0x8b on interface
     fe-4/0/0.0
Dec 28 22:02:00 Sending L2 LSP Juniper6.00-00 on interface fe-4/0/0.0
Dec 28 22:02:00      sequence 0x8b, checksum 0x26e7, lifetime 1200

jeff@Juniper6>
```

Figure 6.18   A traceoptions log (JUNOS) of an IS-IS database synchronization.

```
Cisco8#
17:15:39: %LINEPROTO-5-UPDOWN: Line protocol on Interface Ethernet0, changed state to
up
Dec 28 22:01:50: ISIS-Adj: Sending L1 LAN IIH on Ethernet0, length 1497
Dec 28 22:01:50: ISIS-Adj: Sending L2 LAN IIH on Ethernet0, length 1497
Dec 28 22:01:51: ISIS-Adj: Rec L2 IIH from 00d0.b77f.0d05 (Ethernet0), cir type L2,
cir id 0192.0168.0006.05, length 1492
Dec 28 22:01:51: ISIS-Adj: New adjacency, level 2 for 00d0.b77f.0d05
Dec 28 22:01:51: ISIS-Adj: Sending L2 LAN IIH on Ethernet0, length 1497
Dec 28 22:01:51: ISIS-Upd: Received LSP from SNPA 00d0.b77f.0d05 (Ethernet0) without
     adjacency
Dec 28 22:01:52: ISIS-Upd: Building L1 LSP
Dec 28 22:01:52: ISIS-Upd: Full SPF required
Dec 28 22:01:52: ISIS-Upd: Building L2 LSP
Dec 28 22:01:52: ISIS-Upd: Full SPF required
Dec 28 22:01:52: ISIS-Adj: Adjacency state goes to Up
Dec 28 22:01:52: ISIS-Adj: Run level-2 DR election for Ethernet0
Dec 28 22:01:52: ISIS-Adj: No change (it's us)
Dec 28 22:01:52: ISIS-Upd: Building L2 pseudonode LSP for Ethernet0
Dec 28 22:01:52: ISIS-Upd: Full SPF required
Dec 28 22:01:52: ISIS-Upd: Sending L2 LSP 0192.0168.0008.00-00, seq 9, ht 1199 on
     Ethernet0
Dec 28 22:01:52: ISIS-Upd: Sending L2 LSP 0192.0168.0008.01-00, seq 7, ht 1199 on
     Ethernet0
Dec 28 22:01:53: ISIS-Adj: Sending L1 LAN IIH on Ethernet0, length 1497
Dec 28 22:01:53: ISIS-Upd: Building L2 LSP
Dec 28 22:01:53: ISIS-Upd: No change, suppress L2 LSP 0192.0168.0008.00-00, seq A
Dec 28 22:01:55: ISIS-Snp: Sending L2 CSNP on Ethernet0
Dec 28 22:01:55: ISIS-Upd: Rec L2 LSP 0192.0168.0006.00-00, seq 8A, ht 1194,
Dec 28 22:01:55: ISIS-Upd: from SNPA 00d0.b77f.0d05 (Ethernet0)
Dec 28 22:01:55: ISIS-Upd: LSP newer than database copy
Dec 28 22:01:55: ISIS-Upd: Full SPF required
Dec 28 22:02:00: ISIS-Adj: Run level-2 DR election for Ethernet0
Dec 28 22:02:00: ISIS-Adj: No change (it's us)
```

```
Dec 28 22:02:00: ISIS-Upd: Rec L2 LSP 0192.0168.0006.00-00, seq 8B, ht 1198,
Dec 28 22:02:00: ISIS-Upd: from SNPA 00d0.b77f.0d05 (Ethernet0)
Dec 28 22:02:00: ISIS-Upd: LSP newer than database copy
Dec 28 22:02:00: ISIS-Upd: Full SPF required
Dec 28 22:02:03: ISIS-Upd: Building L1 LSP
Dec 28 22:02:03: ISIS-Upd: Important fields changed
Dec 28 22:02:03: ISIS-Upd: Full SPF required
Dec 28 22:02:03: ISIS-Snp: Sending L2 CSNP on Ethernet0
```

Figure 6.19 A debug output (IOS) of the same database synchronization, from the viewpoint of the other neighbor.

6.2.6 Troubleshooting: Comparing IS-IS LS Databases

On the rare occasion that an IS-IS LS database does not match the others in the area, you need to be able to compare databases. The same strategies you saw with OSPF apply to IS-IS: A sum of the checksums tells you quickly whether the contents match.

Figures 6.20 and 6.21 show the LS databases from the two routers that synchronized in the previous example. Notice that the Juniper router in this example is L2 only, whereas the Cisco is L1/L2, because it has both L1 and L2 entries in its database. Compare the databases and match the LSPs.

```
jeff@Juniper6> show isis database
IS-IS level 1 link-state database:
  0 LSPs

IS-IS level 2 link-state database:
LSP ID                    Sequence Checksum Lifetime Attributes
Juniper5.00-00             0x456b   0x5c70      528 L1 L2
Juniper5.04-00              0x1f    0xc9bb      528 L1 L2
Juniper6.00-00              0x9d    0x89e5     1134 L1 L2
Juniper7.00-00             0x4676   0x190       605 L1 L2
Juniper7.02-00              0x29    0x1463      480 L1 L2
Juniper7.03-00              0x23    0x1963      400 L1 L2
Cisco8.00-00                0xf     0x5f6f     1156 L1 L2
Cisco8.01-00                0xb     0xd4f2     1127 L1 L2
Cisco8.02-00                0x3     0x29a2     1150 L1 L2
Cisco9.00-00                0x6     0x49fc     1149 L1 L2
  10 LSPs

jeff@Juniper6>
```

Figure 6.20 A JUNOS display of the LSP headers in an IS-IS LS database.

```
Cisco8#show isis database

IS-IS Level-1 Link State Database:
LSPID            LSP Seq Num    LSP Checksum  LSP Holdtime    ATT/P/OL
Cisco8.00-00     * 0x00000003   0x3E07        1104            1/0/0
Cisco8.02-00     * 0x00000001   0x9DA7        1104            0/0/0
Cisco9.00-00       0x00000003   0x537F        1117            1/0/0
IS-IS Level-2 Link State Database:
LSPID            LSP Seq Num    LSP Checksum  LSP Holdtime    ATT/P/OL
Juniper5.00-00     0x0000456B   0x5C70        478             0/0/0
Juniper5.04-00     0x0000001F   0xC9BB        478             0/0/0
Juniper6.00-00     0x0000009D   0x89E5        1084            0/0/0
Juniper7.00-00     0x00004676   0x0190        555             0/0/0
Juniper7.02-00     0x00000029   0x1463        430             0/0/0
Juniper7.03-00     0x00000024   0x1764        1147            0/0/0
Cisco8.00-00     * 0x0000000F   0x5F6F        1110            0/0/0
Cisco8.01-00     * 0x0000000B   0xD4F2        1080            0/0/0
Cisco8.02-00     * 0x00000003   0x29A2        1104            0/0/0
Cisco9.00-00       0x00000006   0x49FC        1102            0/0/0
Cisco8#
```

Figure 6.21   An IOS display of the LSP headers in an IS-IS LS database.

Review Questions

1. What messages (by name and type number) does OSPF use for database synchronization?

2. What is the purpose of the I and M flags in the OSPF Database Description message?

3. In what OSPF entities is the Options field found?

4. What does the E bit of the OSPF Options field signify?

5. What is the purpose of the OSPF neighbor data structure? What information is stored there?

6. What is the purpose of the OSPF Link State Transmission list?

7. What is the purpose of the Link State Request list?

8. Before a database exchange, how does OSPF determine the Master and the Slave?

9. What functions does the Master control during the database exchange?

10. What are the eight OSPF neighbor states, and what does each indicate?

11. On a broadcast link, what state normally exists between two DROthers?

12. In Figure 6.9, does the router from which the log entries were taken become the DR or the BDR?

13. Referring to the information in Figures 6.9 and 6.10, which router is the master and which is the slave for the database synchronization?

14. What PDUs does IS-IS use for database synchronization?

15. How is the receipt of an LSP acknowledged on a point-to-point link?

16. How is the receipt of an LSP acknowledged on a broadcast link?

17. How does a router on a broadcast link know that it needs a copy of an LSP? How does it request that LSP?

18. In Figure 6.18, what is the AID of the router from which the log entries are taken? What is the AID of its neighbor?

19. Are the routers in Figures 6.18 and 6.19 L1 Only, L2 Only, or Both?

CHAPTER 7

Area Design

Areas, as discussed in Chapter 2, are used to control the size of the link state database and the negative impact of flooding and SPF calculations on network bandwidth and router resources. They accomplish this control by breaking up the network into individual SPF domains. That is, rather than having a network in which every router has an identical link state database and in which the SPF process computes a single shortest-path tree spanning the entire routing domain, the routing domain is broken up into multiple SPF domains. The link state databases must be identical only within these individual areas, and the area borders are defined by the scope of the individual SPF trees calculated from these area databases.

In order to communicate routing information between two areas, at least one router must be connected to both of the areas, have a copy of the link state database for each the two areas, and run separate SPF calculations for each area. OSPF calls this router the Area Border Router (ABR). The IS-IS L1/L2 router is analogous to the OSPF ABR, but area boundaries are a bit trickier in IS-IS, as you will see later in this chapter.

The ABR sends the routing information it learns from one connected area into the other connected area. And in this behavior is a significant but often misunderstood characteristic of OSPF and IS-IS: The two protocols are always called link state protocols, but in fact they are link state *only within an area*.

Because shortest-path trees do not cross area borders, the inter-area routing information sent into the area by the ABR basically says, "I can reach prefix X at a cost (or distance) of Y." The routers within the area have no visibility beyond the ABR, and must trust the ABR to accurately advertise the prefixes it can reach. This behavior is distance vector, not link state.

You learned in Chapter 2 that the nature of distance vector protocols (a sequence of routers telling their neighbors, "You can get there from here. Trust me.") makes them susceptible to information corruption, possibly leading to routing loops. Distance vector protocols use several strategies and mechanisms to avoid routing loops, such as split horizon and route poisoning. OSPF and IS-IS must also take steps to prevent potential loops from being created due to the distance vector behavior at area borders.

The most basic way to avoid loops is to impose a loop-free inter-area architecture, as depicted in Figure 7.1(b). In this architecture, inter-area routing information can only be exchanged through the backbone area; nonbackbone areas are not allowed to exchange routing information directly. Understanding this concept is key to designing multi-area OSPF and IS-IS networks. But beyond this concept are a number of factors—both general and protocol specific—to consider when designing area topologies. This chapter focuses on these factors.

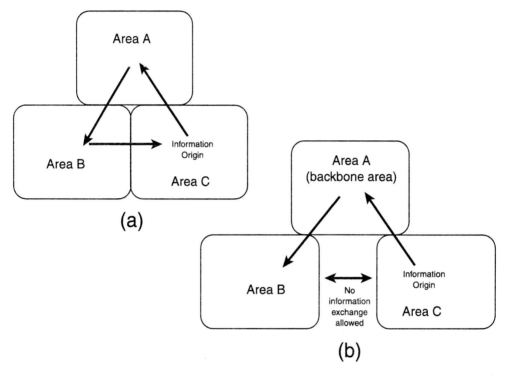

Figure 7.1 Allowing routing information to be freely distributed among areas (a) can lead to routing loops. You can remedy this by requiring routing information to be exchanged over loop-free paths (b).

7.1 Area Scalability

A logical question to ask when first learning OSPF or IS-IS is "What is the maximum number of routers I can put within a single area?" You will find no shortage of engineers answering with their own "rule of thumb." But the more people you ask, the wider variation of opinions you will encounter, typically stating somewhere between 10 and 100 routers as a maximum. About the only thing these rules of thumb have in common is that they are wrong.

The maximum number of routers you can put into an area depends on a number of variables, and so is itself a variable. One of these variables is the number of links in the area. Each link is represented by a subnet address, which must be recorded in the link state database. If the link connects two routers, the link represents an inter-node path to be considered by the SPF calculations. Another factor is the number of external prefixes known within an area: both prefixes external to the area and prefixes external to the routing domain. The number of subnet addresses and the number of external prefixes contribute to the size of the link state database.

The maximum size of the link state database is also a variable, bounded by the amount of memory in the router storing the database. Because all routers in an area must have the same LS database, the router with the lowest amount of memory dictates the maximum size of the area database and hence the size of the area (keeping in mind that a router's memory is used for much more than just storing link state databases).

The stability of the links in an area is another factor influencing the maximum number of routers in an area. A link flap causes an LSA or LSP flood and can trigger a new SPF calculation. If a network is built over unreliable links and flapping is expected to be a regular event, areas must be kept small to limit the adverse effects of the flapping.

Just as the router with the smallest memory is a weak link in an area, the router with the slowest CPU is also a weak link (the lowest memory and the slowest CPU are likely to belong to the same router). So a network built with high-performance routers is more tolerant of link instabilities than a network built with low-performance routers. But, network operators that can afford high-performance routers can also afford more reliable link technologies, and so are even less likely to have instability problems.

Low-bandwidth links are often cited as a limiting factor in area size. However, the cases in which a low-speed link must carry a high enough volume of LSA or LSP packets for the packets to significantly impact available bandwidth are rare. This chapter covers more on OSPF and IS-IS bandwidth considerations in the sections relevant to each protocol.

Less-tangible factors to consider when determining area size are future growth and network manageability. Five years between network reengineering projects is generally a good assumption. (Network components such as routers can be assumed to have a useful service life of three to six years before obsolescence sets in.) So as you are designing your network, consider how much larger the network is likely to grow from its initial size over the next five years. Some segments of the network are likely to grow faster, and so initially might be bounded by a small area that can accommodate the growth. Other areas, such as the backbone, might have a low growth rate and so can start out as a larger area.

Manageability is the most nebulous and therefore difficult area design factor to anticipate. At one extreme, take a large network in which the IGP is a single area encompassing the entire routing domain. The very simplicity of the architecture—no area borders and no ABRs—makes the network easy to understand. But traffic patterns in such a network might be complicated and very difficult to predict. At the other extreme, take a large network broken up into many, many areas. As the network grows, consideration must be given to whether expansion takes place within existing areas or whether new areas are added, and how such additions affect traffic patterns. If IP addressing is designed in such a way that prefixes are assigned per area and then summarized at area boundaries, the network is easy to troubleshoot from an addressing viewpoint. But at the same time, address summarization might complicate traffic patterns by obscuring network details within a summarized area when multiple ABRs are used. And if areas are too small, they might be limited to a single ABR, which becomes a single point of failure that can isolate the area.

The remainder of this chapter examines the mechanisms and strategies available to you when designing OSPF and IS-IS areas to scale correctly to specific network requirements. Chapter 8 continues the discussion of scalability as it applies not just to areas but also to the entire routing domain.

7.2   Area Reliability

A reliable area is one that can sustain the failure of one or more of its components without isolating a large segment of the network. The more failures the area can tolerate, the more robust the area.

Large network segments can be isolated in one of two ways:

- The failure of a router connecting two areas isolates an area from the rest of the network (Figure 7.2).
- The failure of a router or link partitions an area (Figure 7.3).

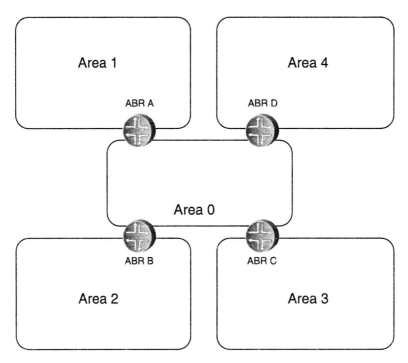

Figure 7.2   A failure of one of the ABRs will isolate its attached nonbackbone area from the rest of the network.

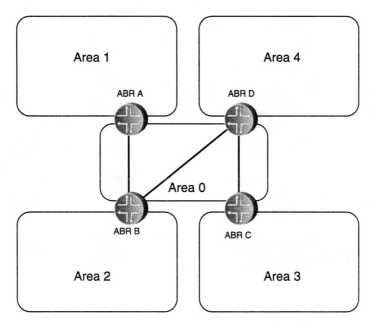

Figure 7.3 A failure of any one of the three links connecting the ABRs across area 0 will partition area 0, resulting in the isolation of one or more areas from the rest of the network.

The obvious way to avoid the isolation of an area from a failed ABR is to provide multiple ABRs and multiple paths to each ABR, as shown in Figure 7.4. In this network, area 2 cannot be isolated from area 0 by the failure of a single ABR or ABR interface. Likewise, no router in the area can be isolated from the rest of the network by the failure of a single, or even any two, links or interfaces.

Similarly, robust connectivity in the backbone area depicted in area 2 of Figure 7.4 ensures that the backbone cannot be easily partitioned. This area is important enough that at the least it should be designed so that no two link or router failures can partition the area. Additionally, every router connecting a nonbackbone area to the backbone should have connections to at least two other routers in the backbone. This further reduces the chance of isolating a nonbackbone area.

Just because you can divide your network into areas does not mean you must. Many networks can avoid the potential pitfalls of poor multi-area designs by simply using a single area for their entire IGP domain. When designing your network, consider all the factors influencing the scale of the network, the primary purpose of the network and its IGP, and the future growth of the network. Then consider what advantage multiple areas provide, and weigh them against the potential advantages of a single area. As you will see in the remainder of this chapter and the next chapter, such factors can influence not only how you design your network, but also what IGP you choose.

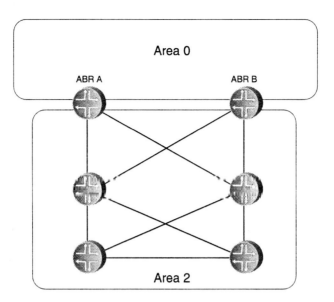

Figure 7.4   A robustly connected nonbackbone area.

7.3   OSPF Areas

OSPF is almost always the preferred IGP for multi-area topologies. Multi-area OSPF networks are easier to design, configure, and administer than multi-area IS-IS networks. Although you can implement almost all the same intra- and inter-area behaviors in IS-IS as you can in OSPF, doing so often involves the use of routing policies that are not as easy to understand as the more straightforward OSPF mechanisms.

7.3.1   Backbone and Non-Backbone Areas

Normal OSPF design uses a loop-free inter-area topology, as discussed in the introduction to this chapter, by ensuring that all inter-area traffic originates in, terminates in, or passes through the backbone area. OSPF identifies the backbone area with an all-zero AID (0.0.0.0), commonly called area 0.

But saying that all inter-area OSPF traffic *should* touch area 0 is not the same thing as saying all inter-area OSPF traffic *must* touch area 0. Nothing in the OSPF protocol forces you to follow the recommended design procedure.[1] Take for example the topology in Figure 7.5, in which an ABR is configured between two nonzero areas: area 1 and area 2. Figure 7.6 shows that subnet 10.1.3.0/24 is installed in the routing table of router R3, demonstrating

---

[1]   Although nothing in the protocol forces you to follow recommended design procedure, some implementations do. The Cisco Systems OSPF implementation, for example, does not generate a type 3 LSA into a connected nonzero area for prefixes it learns from another connected nonzero area.

that ABR R2 has advertised the prefix from area 1 into area 2. Figure 7.7 shows the type 3 LSA advertised by the ABR (10.10.10.2), and you can see that there is no information in the LSA indicating what area the prefix is in or what inter-area path the route takes to reach the destination. In keeping with the distance vector nature of inter-area OSPF, knowledge of network details ends at the area boundary.

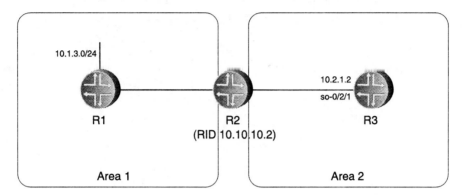

Figure 7.5 An example multi-area OSPF network with no area 0.

```
jeff@R3> show route 10.1.3.0 extensive

inet.0: 12 destinations, 14 routes (12 active, 0 holddown, 0 hidden)
10.1.3.0/24 (1 entry, 1 announced)
TSI:
KRT in-kernel 10.1.3.0/24 -> {so-0/2/1.0}
         *OSPF    Preference: 10
                  Next hop: via so-0/2/1.0, selected
                  State: <Active Int>
                  Age: 8  Metric: 3
                  Area: 0.0.0.2
                  Task: OSPF
                  Announcement bits (1): 0-KRT
                  AS path: I
```

Figure 7.6 R3, in area 2, knows about the prefix 10.1.3.0/24 in area 1.

```
jeff@R3> show ospf database netsummary lsa-id 10.1.3.0 extensive

    OSPF link state database, area 0.0.0.2
Type      ID            Adv Rtr       Seq          Age  Opt  Cksum  Len
Summary  10.1.3.0      10.10.10.2     0x80000001   43   0x2  0xc069 28
  mask 255.255.255.0
  TOS 0x0, metric 2
  Aging timer 00:59:17
  Installed 00:00:41 ago, expires in 00:59:17, sent 00:30:24 ago
```

Figure 7.7 The Network Summary (type 3) LSA originated by the ABR (10.10.10.2) does not contain any information about the actual inter-area path to the destination.

In Figure 7.8, an area 0 has been added to the topology. In Figure 7.9 you can see that
R3 now has two type 3 LSAs in its database advertising prefix 10.1.3.0/24: one originated by
R2, and one originated by R4 (10.10.10.4), which is the ABR to area 0. Other than the RIDs
of the originating ABRs, the LSAs appear identical.

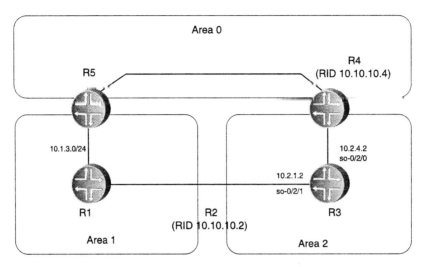

Figure 7.8   A path through area 0 is added to the topology of Figure 7.5.

```
jeff@R3> show ospf database netsummary lsa-id 10.1.3.0 extensive

    OSPF link state database, area 0.0.0.2
Type     ID            Adv Rtr       Seq            Age  Opt  Cksum   Len
Summary  10.1.3.0      10.10.10.2    0x80000001     660  0x2  0xc069  28
  mask 255.255.255.0
  TOS 0x0, metric 2
  Aging timer 00:49:00
  Installed 00:10:58 ago, expires in 00:49:00, sent 00:04:27 ago
Summary  10.1.3.0      10.10.10.4    0x80000001     208  0x2  0xa282  28
  mask 255.255.255.0
  TOS 0x0, metric 2
  Aging timer 00:56:32
  Installed 00:03:25 ago, expires in 00:56:32, sent 00:03:25 ago
```

Figure 7.9   R3 has two type 3 LSAs in its database, one originated by ABR R2 and one originated by ABR R4.

Figure 7.10 shows the resulting routing table entry in R3 for 10.1.3.0/24. As you might
expect, the identical information in the two LSAs pertains to the prefix results in two route
entries. A close look shows that R3 has selected the route through ABR R4—reachable
from SONET interface so-0/2/0—over the path through ABR R2 reachable from interface
so-0/2/2.

```
jeff@R3> show route 10.1.3.0 extensive

inet.0: 15 destinations, 17 routes (15 active, 0 holddown, 0 hidden)
10.1.3.0/24 (1 entry, 1 announced)
TSI:
KRT in-kernel 10.1.3.0/24 -> {so-0/2/2.0}
        *OSPF   Preference: 10
                Next hop: via so-0/2/1.0
                Next hop: via so-0/2/2.0, selected
                State: <Active Int>
                Age: 2:54       Metric: 3
                Area: 0.0.0.2
                Task: OSPF
                Announcement bits (1): 0-KRT
                AS path: I
```

Figure 7.10 R3 has selected the path through area 0, via R4, as the route to 10.1.3.0/24.

But the information in the two LSAs indicates that the metric of both paths is 2. So has R2 somehow detected that one of the paths passes through the backbone area while the other does not, or is it a coincidence of randomly selecting between two equal-cost paths? The question is easily answered by changing the cost of one of the paths. In Figure 7.11, another router is added in area 0 so that the cost of that path from ABR R4 is now 3, while the cost from R2 remains 2, as reflected by the LSAs shown in Figure 7.12. This means that R3 now sees the cost of the path to the destination prefix through R4 as 4, while the cost of the path through R2 is 3. Because the costs of the two paths are no longer equal, only the shortest path—through R2—is entered into the routing table (Figure 7.13).

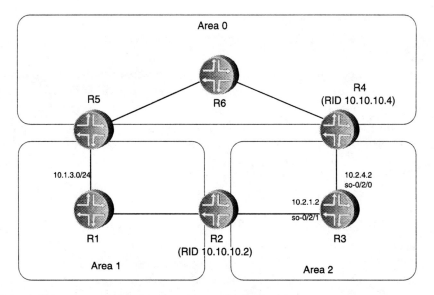

Figure 7.11 An extra router hop is added to the area 0 path.

```
jeff@R3> show ospf database netsummary lsa-id 10.1.3.0 extensive

    OSPF link state database, area 0.0.0.2
Type     ID          Adv Rtr       Seq         Age  Opt  Cksum  Len
Summary 10.1.3.0    10.10.10.2    0x80000002  821  0x2  0xbe6a  28
  mask 255.255.255.0
  TOS 0x0, metric 2
  Aging timer 00:46:18
  Installed 00:13:38 ago, expires in 00:46:19, sent 00:04:08 ago
Summary 10.1.3.0    10.10.10.4    0x80000001  252  0x2  0xbe68  28
  mask 255.255.255.0
  TOS 0x0, metric 3
  Aging timer 00:55:47
  Installed 00:04:08 ago, expires in 00:55:48, sent 00:04:08 ago
```

Figure 7.12   The increased path cost of 3 is shown in the LSA originated by R4.

```
jeff@R3> show route 10.1.3.2 extensive

inet.0: 17 destinations, 19 routes (17 active, 0 holddown, 0 hidden)
10.1.3.0/24 (1 entry, 1 announced)
TSI:
KRT in-kernel 10.1.3.0/24 -> {so-0/2/1.0}
        *OSPF   Preference: 10
                Next hop: via so-0/2/1.0, selected
                State: <Active Int>
                Age: 6:20        Metric: 3
                Area: 0.0.0.2
                Task: OSPF
                Announcement bits (1): 0-KRT
                AS path: I
```

Figure 7.13   R3 enters only the lowest-cost path, through R2, into its routing table.

The point of this demonstration is that while all inter-area OSPF traffic should touch area 0, enforcing this rule through area topology design is up to you. Nothing in the protocol will enforce the rule for you.

And although a two-area topology is inherently loop-free, you should never assign non-zero AIDs to both areas as in Figure 7.5. Even if you are sure you will never need to add a third area, it makes no sense, and gains you nothing, to purposely exclude the possibility of ever doing so.

7.3.2   Factors for Scaling OSPF Areas

A useful guideline when designing a network is that network control traffic should never exceed 5 percent of the available bandwidth of any link in the network, and in normal circumstances should not exceed 1 percent. OSPF Hello packets are 44 bytes of fixed-length fields plus an additional 4 bytes for each neighbor on the subnet and are typically sent every 10 seconds by each neighbor. This means that on a point-to-point link, OSPF Hellos use 76.8

bits per second. Even on a low-speed 56kbps link, this amounts to only 0.14 percent of the total bandwidth.

More significant is the amount of bandwidth used by the LSAs as they are flooded across the links during database synchronization and periodic database refreshes. Although many LSA types are likely to be present in your network, you can normally get a reasonably accurate idea of the bandwidth requirements to support flooding, and the memory requirements to support the database, by accounting for just LSA types 1, 3, and 5.

First, consider type 1 LSAs. Each has 24 bytes of fixed fields (the 20-byte header plus another 4 bytes) and 12 bytes for each prefix advertised. Each router generates a type 1 LSA, so add 24 bytes for each router in the area and 12 bytes for each connected prefix in the area.

Next, consider type 3 LSAs. These LSAs are 32 bytes in length, and an ABR originates one for each prefix it advertises into an area. So simply multiply all prefixes outside the area but internal to the OSPF domain by 32.

Last, consider type 5 LSAs. These LSAs are 44 bytes in length, and an ASBR originates one for every external prefix it advertises into the OSPF domain. So multiply the number of AS-external prefixes by 44.

Of course, these LSAs are carried between routers in Update packets, which have a 28-byte header. But like Hello packets, this is a small amount of the overall bandwidth requirement and can be reasonably disregarded.

As an example of calculating the impact LSAs will have on link bandwidth, take an area with 50 routers, each with 20 connected prefixes. The amount of space taken up in the link state database by type 1 LSAs is then:

$$24(50) + 12[(50)(20)] = 13,200 \text{ bytes}$$

Recall that each router refreshes its LSAs every 1800 seconds (30 minutes). So in a 30-minute period, 13,200 bytes are flooded in the area. This means that each link in the area must carry an average of 105,600 bits every 1800 seconds, or 58.7 bits per second.

Next, suppose a total of 2000 prefixes are outside of the area but inside the OSPF domain, and that the example area has two ABRs to area 0. Assuming that both of the ABRs advertise all 2000 prefixes into the area, type 3 LSAs take up the following amount of space in the link state database:

$$32(2000) = 64,000 \text{ bytes}$$

These 64,000 bytes, or 512,000 bits, refreshed every 1800 seconds, require an average of 284.5 bits per second for flooding.

Last, suppose 5000 prefixes are advertised into the OSPF domain. Type 5 LSAs will account for:

$$44(5000) = 220,000 \text{ bytes}$$

With the ASBRs refreshing these 5000 type 5 LSAs every 1800 seconds, flooding them requires an average of 977.8 bits per second.

Therefore, the total average flooding load on each link in the area is:

$$58.7 + 284.5 + 977.8 = 1321 \text{bps}$$

Presumably, an area of such size would be unlikely to have links smaller than T1, and 1321bps accounts for only 0.08 percent of the bandwidth of a T1 link. Even a small 56kbps link in this area will use an average of only 2.4 percent of its bandwidth carrying OSPF flooding traffic; this is outside of the recommended 1 percent range, but still not too bad.

Of course, these averages assume that the expiration times of the refresh timers throughout the network are distributed evenly across a 30-minute period. In reality, refresh timers expire in a bursty pattern: many within some short periods of time, few within other short periods of time. But you can safely expect that over the 1800-second period the flooding load will be low enough at any one period to stay safely within 5 percent of the bandwidth of a T1 link.

From these calculations you can see that as long as sufficient bandwidth is available to support the size of the network, flooding should not be an issue. Usually, the larger issue is router memory for storing the database and router CPU for processing the LSAs. The LSA calculations demonstrated in this section are also useful for determining with reasonable accuracy the size of the database and so the amount of router memory the database will require. CPU requirements are much more difficult to determine.

Yet another factor when considering the number of LSAs in a network is the time two neighbors will take to synchronize their databases. Section 7.3.3 presents an example of how an abnormally large number of LSAs can effect synchronization time.

Passive Interfaces Versus Redistributing Connected Interfaces

It is often desirable to have external links—links that connect the OSPF domain to other routing domains—known to OSPF, usually for management purposes such as being able to ping the interfaces. But you do not want OSPF running on the links, risking the possibility of forming an unwanted adjacency with an OSPF router in the neighboring routing domain. The two most common approaches for making external links known within OSPF are running OSPF in passive mode on the links and redistributing connected links into OSPF.

A router includes the prefixes of any links running in passive mode in OSPF, but does not send Hellos on the link or respond to Hellos received on the link. Redistributing connected interfaces uses a policy to import the prefixes of all connected interfaces into OSPF. And although the functional objective of these two approaches is the same, their effects are quite different. Prefixes on passive interfaces are considered "internal" to OSPF, and so are included in the router's type 1 LSAs. Prefixes learned from redistributing connected interfaces are external prefixes, and so are advertised in type 5 LSAs.

So which is better? Passive interfaces are more economical, but redistributing connected interfaces can have less performance impact.

Consider a router with 25 external links that must be known by OSPF. If OSPF is run in passive mode on the interfaces, the size of the router's type 1 LSA is increased by 300 bytes. But if a policy is used to redistribute the prefixes of the 25 links into OSPF, the router becomes an ASBR and originates 25 type 5 LSAs with a total size of 1100 bytes.

On the other hand, if passive mode is used the router must flood a new type 1 LSA every time an external link is added or removed or the link state changes. In addition to the inefficiency of re-advertising all links just to notify area routers of the change in one link, the new type 1 LSA causes an SPF calculation in all routers in the area. Type 5 LSAs do not cause an SPF calculation when they are flooded, and the addition, removal, or change of an external prefix can be advertised with the origination of a single type 5 LSA.

In smaller networks, the approach you choose probably does not matter. As the network grows large, however, the tradeoff between database size and network stability becomes yet another factor to consider in your network design.

7.3.3   External Prefixes and OSPF Scaling

A limiting factor for both the scalability of an area and its robustness is the size of the area's link state database. Figure 7.14 shows the consequence of a very large OSPF database. These OSPF log entries, taken from an actual network,[2] show an OSPF adjacency being established. Notice that the database synchronization, from the time the neighbor state changes to Exchange to the time it changes to Full, is 95 seconds. This is an unacceptably long time for the databases to synchronize, and is the primary cause of the reliability and performance issues this network operator is experiencing.

---

[2] In this and any example taken from a real network, the IP addresses, router names, and any other detail by which the operator can be identified have been changed.

```
jdoyle@RT1> show log ospf-log
May 20 18:57:04 OSPF interface fe-0/3/11.0 (172.16.119.145) state changed from Down
      to Waiting
May 20 18:57:08 OSPF neighbor 172.16.119.146 (fe-0/3/11.0) state changed from Down to
      Init
May 20 18:57:08 OSPF neighbor 172.16.119.146 (fe-0/3/11.0) state changed from Init to
      2Way
May 20 18:57:08 OSPF interface fe-0/3/11.0 (172.16.119.145) state changed from
      Waiting to BDR
May 20 18:57:08 OSPF neighbor 172.16.119.146 (fe-0/3/11.0) state changed from 2Way to
      ExStart
May 20 18:57:08 OSPF neighbor 172.16.119.146 (fe-0/3/11.0) state changed from ExStart
      to Exchange
May 20 18:58:41 OSPF neighbor 172.16.119.146 (fe-0/3/11.0) state changed from
      Exchange to Loading
May 20 18:58:43 OSPF neighbor 172.16.119.146 (fe-0/3/11.0) state changed from Loading
      to Full
May 20 18:58:43 RPD_OSPF_NBRUP: OSPF neighbor 172.16.119.146 (fe-0/3/11.0) state
      changed from Loading to Full due to OSPF loading done
```

Figure 7.14   This router takes more than 1.5 minutes to synchronize its database with its neighbor.

A look at a summary of the route entries in the router shows that there are 24,068 entries learned from OSPF (Figure 7.15). Obviously, this many route entries requires a very large database. But where are most of these entries coming from? The answer is easily seen in the database summary of Figure 7.16. There are 23,349 type 5 LSAs in the database, representing an extraordinarily large number of external prefixes redistributed into the OSPF domain.

```
jdoyle@RT1> show route summary
Router ID: 172.16.121.41

inet.0: 24073 destinations, 24075 routes (24072 active, 0 holddown, 1 hidden)
            Direct:     4 routes,      3 active
            Local:      2 routes,      2 active
             OSPF: 24068 routes,  24066 active
            Static:     1 routes,      1 active
```

Figure 7.15   OSPF has created 24,068 entries in the routing table.

```
jdoyle@RT1> show ospf database summary
Area 0.0.0.5:
    12 Router LSAs
    2 Network LSAs
    2387 Summary LSAs
    153 ASBRSum LSAs
Externals:
    23349 Extern LSAs
```

Figure 7.16   The major source of the 24,068 route entries in Figure 7.15 are the 23,349 external prefixes redistributed into the OSPF domain.

Examining the OSPF statistics in Figure 7.17 gives some further insight into what happened during the synchronization process. First, notice that the router sent only 176 LSAs to its neighbor, indicating that the great majority of the LSAs are coming from the neighbor's database. But notice that 58,596 LSAs were requested from the neighbor, and 86,685 LSAs were acknowledged—far more than the already large number of LSAs summarized in Figure 7.16. The conclusion from these statistics is that the router struggled to process all the LSAs and that multiple requests, timeouts, and retransmissions of the same LSAs occurred.

```
jdoyle@RT1> show ospf statistics

Packet type             Total                 Last 5 seconds
                   Sent      Received       Sent      Received
    Hello           27           11          0            0
      DbD         1259         1212          0            0
    LSReq          523           12          0            0
  LSUpdate         114         4533          0            2
    LSAck         2121           16          0            0

DBDs retransmited      :       60, last 5 seconds :              0
LSAs flooded           :        5, last 5 seconds :              0
LSAs flooded high-prio :        3, last 5 seconds :              0
LSAs retransmited      :        0, last 5 seconds :              0
LSAs transmited to nbr :      176, last 5 seconds :              0
LSAs requested         :    58596, last 5 seconds :              0
LSAs acknowledged      :    86685, last 5 seconds :              0

Flood queue depth      :           0
Total rexmit entries   :           0
db summaries           :           0
lsreq entries          :           0

Receive errors:
  None
```

Figure 7.17   The OSPF statistics show that the number of LSAs requested from the neighbor and acknowledged to the neighbor are far greater than the number of LSAs in the database, implying that many retransmits took place, further lengthening the synchronization time.

The point of this example is that when the size of an OSPF (or IS-IS) database gets out of hand, external prefixes are usually the reason. In even the largest link state networks, if intelligently designed, type 1 and 2 LSAs should number in the low hundreds, and type 3 LSAs should number in the low thousands. A large OSPF network using a single-area topology might have type 1 and 2 LSAs numbering in the mid to high hundreds, but will have no type 3 LSAs. The number of type 4 LSAs, of course, depends on the number of routers in the OSPF domain redistributing external prefixes, but in the most extreme case will not exceed the number of routers in the domain.

The most common causes of excessive type 5 LSAs in an OSPF domain are:

- A faulty routing policy that redistributes prefixes from BGP into the IGP
- Redistribution of very large numbers of static routes into the IGP
- Redistribution of very large numbers of directly connected link prefixes into the IGP

Results of redistribution from BGP vary from poor performance, if partial routes are redistributed, to catastrophic network failure, if full Internet routes are redistributed. The only realistic remedy for this situation is to locate the faulty routing policy and correct it.

Redistribution of static and directly connected prefixes is most likely to occur in service provider networks where there are external links to thousands or tens of thousands of customers and the customer prefixes are statically routed. Such is the case in the example network shown in this section.

The best approach to relieving the external prefix problem is to redistribute customer prefixes and external link prefixes into BGP, which is much better suited for handling large numbers of routes, instead of OSPF. In some situations, however, stub areas can help you cope with external prefixes in your OSPF domain. The next three sections introduce stub areas and two variants of it, and discuss the circumstances in which they can be useful.

7.3.4 Stub Areas

If an OSPF area does not have an ASBR in it, all packets to and from external destinations are going to pass through the area's ABR. For example, the network in Figure 7.18 has two ASBRs: one in area 0 and one in area 1. Any packets that the router in area 2 sends to or receives from the external destinations must pass through area 2's ABR. In this case, a default route[3] with the ABR as the next hop serves just as well as multiple route entries for any packets being sent from an area 2 router to an external destination. You have the option of making this area a stub area.

OSPF defines a stub area as one in which type 5 LSAs are illegal. The area's ABR does not flood any type 5 LSAs into the area, and instead uses a type 3 LSA to advertise a default route into the area with itself as the next hop. If routers within a stub area have no specific information about external prefixes other than a default route to the ABR, they have no need for information about the ASBRs that advertise the external prefixes. Therefore, in addition to type 5 LSAs, an ABR blocks type 4 LSAs from entering a stub area.

---

[3] A default route is a route to an all-zeroes prefix with a prefix length of 0 (variously written as 0.0.0.0/0, 0/0, or 0.0.0.0 0.0.0.0), which is matched if the route lookup finds no more-specific route to a destination.

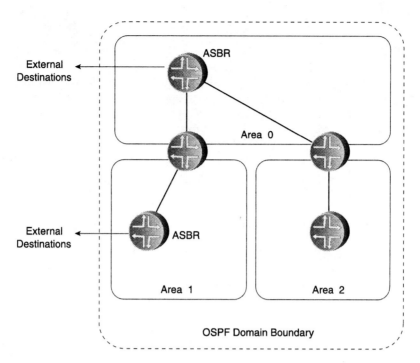

Figure 7.18 Packets sent from the router in area 2 to any external destination must send the packet through the ABR. A single default route to the ABR will work just as well for the routers in this area as individual route entries to each external destination.

To make stub areas work as expected, a few rules are defined:

- Because no type 5 LSAs are allowed in a stub area, it follows that no ASBRs can appear in the area.

- The ABR must know that its attached area is a stub area so that it knows to block type 5 LSAs and advertise a default route.

- All routers in the area must know that they are in a stub area so that they will reject any type 5 LSAs that might be injected in the area by mistake. Otherwise, if some routers accepted the type 5 LSAs, the area databases would not be identical across the area, violating a basic tenet of link state routing.

- Area 0 cannot be a stub area, because at a minimum the backbone area and the connected ABRs must know the specific external routes. Any or all other areas in the OSPF domain can be stub areas.

- Virtual links (described later in this chapter) cannot be configured across a stub area.

The second and third rules say that all routers in the area, including the ABR, must know that they are in a stub area. Figure 7.19 shows Juniper Networks JUNOS and Cisco Systems IOS configurations for setting up a stub area. As you can see, both configurations clearly and simply designate area 2 as a stub area: IOS with the statement **area 2 stub** and JUNOS with the statement **stub** under the area 2 configuration.

```
IOS Configuration:
router ospf 1
 area 2 stub
 network 10.2.1.2 0.0.0.0 area 2
 network 10.2.2.1 0.0.0.0 area 2
!

JUNOS Configuration:
[edit]
jeff@Juniper4# show protocols ospf
area 0.0.0.2 {
    stub;
    interface fe-0/1/1.0;
    interface so-0/0/0.0;
}
```

Figure 7.19   Cisco Systems and Juniper Networks stub area configurations.

When a router is configured with a stub area, the OSPF Hellos it sends out all interfaces in that area have the E bit cleared (E = 0) in the Options field (Figure 7.20) to indicate that it does not support an external routing capability—that is, it does not accept or originate type 5 LSAs. If the router receives a Hello from a neighbor with the E bit set (E = 1), indicating that the neighbor does support external routing capability, the router drops the Hello. As a result new adjacencies do not form between neighbors whose E bits do not agree, and an existing adjacency is broken if the value of the E bit is changed in one neighbor but not the other.[4]

Stub areas prove useful when you want to minimize the size of an area's link state database, either to control performance problems (such as when you need to protect a few underpowered routers) or to simplify management and troubleshooting. But there can be a tradeoff when the stub area has multiple ABRs. A router in the area does not have specific metric information on the external destinations, but only default routes from each of the ABRs. As a result the router will choose the ABR whose default route is the lowest cost, and send all packets to external destinations it. Although that ABR is metrically closest to the router, the path from the ABR to the ASBR at which the packet exits the OSPF domain might not be the optimal path. Whether this reduction in routing accuracy within the domain is significant is something you must consider when deciding whether to make an area stubby.

---

[4] Note that the E bit is always set in the Options field of type 5 LSAs, and it is set or cleared as appropriate in the options field of Database Description packets. But the value of the flag in the DD packet is informational only.

Figure 7.20   The E bit in the Options field of the OSPF Hello messages is set to indicate support of external
routing capability (a nonstub area) and is cleared to indicate nonsupport of external routing
capability (a stub area).

7.3.5   Totally Stubby Areas

If a default route to the ABR is being used in a stub area to reach all destinations external to
the OSPF domain to reduce the size of the area database, why not use the same default route
to reach all destinations external to the area? This is the logic behind making an area totally
stubby, so that the ABR blocks not only type 5 and type 4 LSAs, but also all type 3 LSAs with
the exception of the type 3 LSA carrying the default route.

Figure 7.21 shows the IOS and JUNOS stub configurations similar to the previous example, but with an optional keyword that tells the ABR to block all Summary LSAs. Note that
unlike the simple stub configuration, only the ABR has to be configured with the **no-summaries**
option to create a totally stubby area, because only the ABR creates type 3 LSAs.

```
IOS Configuration:
router ospf 1
 area 2 stub no-summary
 network 10.0.0.5 0.0.0.0 area 0
 network 10.0.0.15 0.0.0.0 area 0
 network 10.2.1.2 0.0.0.0 area 2
 network 10.2.2.1 0.0.0.0 area 2
!

JUNOS Configuration:
[edit]
jeff@Juniper4# show protocols ospf
area 0.0.0.0 {
     interface so-0/0/1.0;
     interface so-0/1/0.0;
}
area 0.0.0.2 {
     stub no-summaries;
     interface fe-0/1/1.0;
     interface so-0/0/0.0;
}
```

Figure 7.21   The addition of the **no-summary** (IOS) or **no-summaries** (JUNOS) keyword at the ABR
makes an area totally stubby.

Looking back to the very large database in Figure 7.16, you can see that in addition to
the 23,349 external LSAs and 153 type 4 LSAs there are 2387 type 3 LSAs. By making this
area totally stubby, you can reduce the area database from 25,903 LSAs to a mere 15 LSAs.

If you choose to make an area with a single ABR stub, there is little reason to not make it totally stubby. But if there are multiple ABRs, you must again consider the price of reduced routing accuracy—with totally stubby areas routing accuracy is reduced not only to destinations external to the domain, but also to destinations internal to the OSPF domain.

7.3.6 Not-So-Stubby Areas

Imagine a case in which an ASBR is originating a large number of type 5 LSAs into your OSPF domain, and you want to keep these LSAs out of a certain area by making it stubby. But you also need to place an ASBR in that same area to reach other external destinations. Stub areas are an all-or-nothing solution. If you want to keep some type 5 LSAs out of the area, you must keep all type 5 LSAs out of the area. Not-so-stubby areas (NSSAs)[5] allow you to be more selective, preventing an ABR from flooding type 5 LSAs into an area while at the same time permitting an ASBR to reside in the area. Continuing to make type 5 LSAs illegal in the area, as with regular stub areas, and carrying any external prefixes advertised by an ASBR within the area in a different LSA type accomplishes that objective.

The LSA that makes NSSAs possible is a type 7 LSA, unsurprisingly called an NSSA LSA. Figure 7.22 shows the LSA's format. You can readily see that the format is exactly the same as the format of the type 5 LSA (Figure 5.23), except that the value of the type field in the header is 7.

The rules for using the forwarding address field in the type 7 LSA differ somewhat from the rules for using the forwarding address field in the type 5 LSA. Type 5 LSAs can have the forwarding address set to 0.0.0.0, indicating that packets to the advertised prefix should be sent to the originating ASBR, or to the address of its external neighbor's interface if the connecting link is advertised into OSPF as an internal route,[6] or some other internal address for a "route server" function. The forwarding address of type 7 LSAs must be either the address of the external peer's interface address or, if the connecting link is not advertised as an OSPF internal route, one of the ASBR's interface addresses (normally the ASBR's RID).

NSSAs use the fifth bit in the Options field to indicate functional support. Notice in Figure 7.20 that this bit is labeled as the N/P bit. This is because the same bit serves different purposes in an NSSA depending upon whether the Options field is in a Hello message or in a type 7 LSA.

In a Hello, the fifth bit of the Options field is the N bit and indicates support (N = 1) or nonsupport (N = 0) of type 7 LSAs. As with the E bit, if the N bit in the Hellos exchanged between two neighbors does not match the Hellos are dropped and an OSPF adjacency is not formed. This ensures that all routers in an area agree on whether they are in an NSSA.

---

[5] Rob Coltun and Vince Fuller, "The OSPF NSSA Option," RFC 1587, March 1994.

[6] Where this might happen is when the external prefix is learned from an External BGP (EBGP) session, which sets the next hop of the route to the interface address of the router in the adjacent AS that is advertising the prefix.

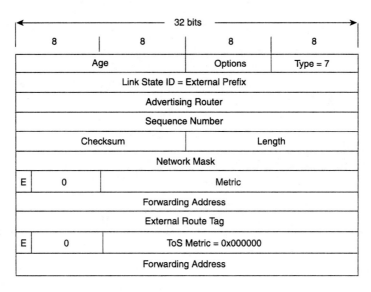

Figure 7.22 The NSSA LSA format.

In a type 7 LSA, the fifth bit of the Options field is the P (Propagate) bit. This bit enables flexibility in the NSSA by telling the ABR how it should handle the type 7 LSA. Type 7 LSAs have an area flooding scope—that is, they are not permitted outside of the area in which they are originated—because there is no assurance that they will be understood in other areas. So, if you want an external prefix advertised by an NSSA ASBR to be known throughout the OSPF domain, the P bit of the type 7 LSA carrying the prefix is set to 1. When the ABR receives this LSA, it translates the LSA into a type 5 LSA and floods it to all its connected nonstub areas. The type 5 LSA, having AS flooding scope, makes the prefix known throughout the OSPF domain.

But you might want a prefix advertised by the NSSA ASBR to be known only within the NSSA. In this case, the P bit of the prefix's type 7 LSA is cleared, telling the ABR to not translate the LSA into a type 5 LSA. Because the type 7 LSA is not permitted outside its area, the prefix is not known outside the area.

An interesting application of an NSSA is one in which you want all routers in one area to send all packets with external destinations to an ASBR in the area. At the same time, you want routers elsewhere in the OSPF domain to be more selective in how they forward packets to external destinations by selecting the best route from prefixes advertised by multiple ASBRs. In this case the NSSA ASBR can originate a single type 7 LSA advertising a default route. Packets with destination addresses not matching any of the internal prefixes advertised in type 3 LSAs by the ABR are then routed out of the domain at the NSSA ASBR. As with other type 7 LSAs, you have the option of setting the P bit in a type 7 LSA carrying a default route, causing the ABR to translate it into a type 5 LSA and advertising the default route into the rest of the domain. There are a few special rules for ABRs attached to an NSSA. First, unlike with totally stubby areas the ABR should always advertise all prefixes internal to the OSPF domain into the NSSA in type 3 LSAs. Otherwise, you run the risk of incorrectly matching an external route to the NSSA ASBR and sending a packet out of the domain when it should be routed through the ABR to an internal destination.

Conversely, if the ABR advertises a default route into the NSSA it should be sent in a type 7 LSA rather than a type 3. This is because prefixes advertised in type 3 LSAs are always considered internal, and prefixes advertised in type 7 LSAs are always considered external. Internal prefixes are always preferred over external prefixes, so a default prefix advertised in a type 3 LSA would always be chosen over any more-specific external route or default route advertised in a type 7 LSA, again resulting in incorrect routing.

Then there is the case in which an ABR attached to an NSSA is also an ASBR. In this situation, the ABR/ASBR will advertise its external prefixes into the NSSA using type 7 LSAs, and the same prefixes into the backbone and any attached non-NSSAs using type 5 LSAs. However, an ABR never sets the P bit of any type 7 LSA it originates. Otherwise, the risk is run that another ABR attached to the same NSSA will translate the LSA into a type 5 and flood it, possibly causing inaccurate routing.

7.3.7 Address Summarization

The advantage of stub areas is that some set of prefixes, whether all prefixes external to the OSPF domain or all prefixes external to the area, are represented in the area with a default route, thereby reducing the LS database size. The default route is nothing more than a prefix that summarizes all possible IP addresses.

A summary address[7] represents an aggregation of all prefixes that are longer than the summary address but whose beginning bits match the summary address. For example, consider the following prefixes:

- 192.168.1.0/25
- 192.168.1.128/25

These two prefixes can be represented with the single summary address 192.168.1.0/24.

The 24-bit summary matches the first 24 bits of all the longer prefixes it represents. When performing an IP route lookup, a router always chooses the prefix with the longest number of bits matching the destination address of the IP packet. For example, if a router does a route lookup for a destination address 192.168.1.135 and 192.168.1.0/24 is the longest matching prefix in the routing table, that route is selected for forwarding the packet. But if both 192.168.1.0/24 and 192.168.1.128/25 exist in the routing table the latter, longer route prefix is selected.

From this example, you can see that a summary route always has a shorter prefix length than the prefixes it summarizes. That is why a default route is a summary of all possible IP prefixes: Any IP prefix has a longer prefix length than the 0 length of the default.

---

[7] Summary addresses are also called *address aggregates*.

Summary routes can be used to help with OSPF area scalability in two ways:

■ An ABR can summarize a set of prefixes in a nonbackbone area into the backbone area.
■ An ASBR can summarize external prefixes into the OSPF domain.

Note that because all routers in an area must have identical LS databases, address summaries can be generated only at an area border or at the domain boundary. A router internal to an area cannot summarize a set of prefixes in the same area, or inconsistent databases within the area would result.

The backbone area cannot be a stub area because by definition it is the transit area for all inter-area traffic. But by summarizing all nonbackbone area prefixes into the backbone, you can significantly reduce the size of the backbone database. How significant that reduction is depends on how many prefixes you can represent with a single summary route. The ideal case is one in which all prefixes in an area can be represented with a single summary route. For example, if you are assigning all prefixes in your OSPF domain from the aggregate address block 172.16.0.0/16, you might assign all backbone prefixes from 172.16.0.0/24, and then all other area prefixes subsequently from blocks 172.16.1.0/24, 172.16.2.0/24, 172.16.3.0/24, and so on. By having each ABR advertise only its area summary address into the backbone, and blocking all more-specific area prefixes, the backbone database will contain only as many type 3 LSAs as there are ABRs in the network.

When this approach is used, it is common to see the aggregate assigned to an area also used as the AID. If the prefixes in an area are assigned from the aggregate 172.16.5.0/24, for example, the AID of that area is 172.16.5.0. This can prove handy for operational understanding of the network. An ASBR can also summarize external prefixes into an area—either using one or more address aggregates to represent some subsets of external IP addresses, or using a default address to represent all external prefixes. With good summarization from ABRs and defaults from the ASBRs, you can make the backbone database almost as small as that of a stub area.

The price you pay for summarization is the same as you pay for stub areas with multiple ABRs: a possible loss of routing accuracy. If multiple ABRs into an area are summarizing the area prefixes, there is no way to choose the best ABR to a particular destination in the area. Instead, a router in the backbone just selects the closest ABR. Similarly, if multiple ASBRs advertise a summary or default, a router just selects the closest ASBR, which might not necessarily be the best ASBR for a given destination.

7.3.8 Virtual Links

OSPF offers a tool called a virtual link that enables you to logically connect an ABR to a backbone area when a physical connection is not available. Virtual links have two applications:

- To connect to the backbone an area that has no direct physical link to the backbone
- To prevent or repair partitions of the backbone area

Figure 7.23 illustrates the first application. Area 2 has been added to the OSPF domain, but a physical link from that area's ABR to the backbone is not available. An example of where such a situation might arise is when two OSPF domains are being merged into one. Area 2 is connected to the backbone by creating a virtual link through area 1 between ABR A and ABR B. Although the packets crossing the virtual link actually pass through routers RTC and RTD in area 1, OSPF interprets the virtual link as a direct link to a backbone router.

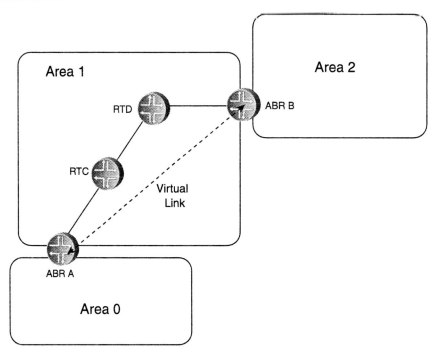

Figure 7.23 A virtual link can be used to connect an ABR to the backbone when there is no direct physical link to the backbone area.

Figure 7.24 illustrates the second application. Here, the backbone area is vulnerable to partitioning if either the link between ABR A and RTE or the link between ABR B and RTE fails, or if RTE itself fails. If any of those failures occur, areas 1 and 2 would still have connectivity to area 3 but they would not have connectivity to each other because ABRs A and B cannot "see" each other through area 3. A virtual link between ABRs C and D in area 3 is treated as a link in the backbone area, making a more robust backbone. Although the virtual link actually passes through RTF, OSPF again sees it as a direct connection between the two ABRs.

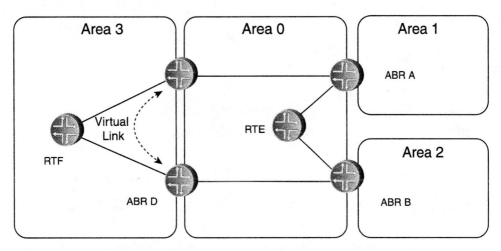

Figure 7.24 A virtual link can be used to reduce the partitioning vulnerability in a poorly designed backbone.

When a virtual link is configured between ABRs, the ABRs attempt to form a virtual adjacency. When that adjacency is established, OSPF treats the link as an unnumbered point-to-point backbone link. OSPF packets flow over the link, and the link is included in backbone type 1 LSAs.

Keep in mind a few rules when using virtual links:

- The virtual link must be configured through a single area—that is, ABRs at each end of the link must have an attachment to a common area.
- Although the virtual link is considered by OSPF as a backbone link, it must be configured through a nonbackbone area.
- The cost of a virtual link is not configurable. Instead, it is always the cost of the intra-area path between the two ABR endpoints.
- Virtual links cannot be configured in stub areas.
- An ABR describes the neighboring ABR at the other end of a virtual link in its neighbor table by the neighbor's RID.
- An ABR that has at least one fully adjacent virtual link sets the V bit in its type 1 LSAs.
- An ABR gives the virtual link a Link Type of 4 in its type 1 LSAs.
- The Link ID field in a type 1 LSA describing a virtual link is set to the RID of the neighboring ABR.
- The Data Link field in a type 1 LSA describing a virtual link is set to the IP address of the originating router's interface associated with the virtual link.

- OSPF packets sent over the virtual link are routed within the link's transit area as intra-area packets. This is the only time OSPF packets are not limited to directly connected neighbors.
- The AID of packets sent over the virtual link is 0. This is the only situation in which a router's interface can be attached to a nonzero area and receive an OSPF packet with an AID other than that area's AID.
- Hellos on virtual links are unicast to neighboring ABRs, as would be expected of point-to-point links.
- No network address mask is associated with a virtual link, so the Address Mask field in the Hellos sent on the link is set to 0.0.0.0.
- The Interface MTU field in Database Description packets sent over virtual links is set to 0.
- Type 5 LSAs are never flooded over virtual links because they appear in all areas anyway (except for stub areas, where virtual links are not permitted).

Figure 7.25 shows an application of a virtual link. Area 1 is connected to two different areas with AIDs of 0. Such a situation might have arisen from two OSPF domains being merged in such a way that the only connection point between them is through area 1.

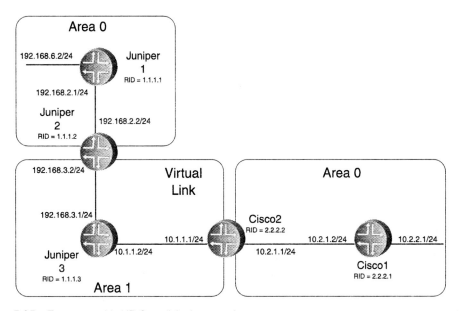

Figure 7.25   Two areas with AID 0 are linked to area 1.

No problem is apparent in the neighbor tables in Juniper2 and Cisco2 in Figure 7.26: Both ABRs show full adjacencies to both of their neighbors. But examining the OSPF entries in the routing tables of Juniper1 and Cisco1, you can see that both routers have learned the prefixes in area 1 but neither of them have learned the prefixes in the opposing area 0: Juniper1 does not have entries for 10.2.1.0/24 or 10.2.2.0/24, and Cisco1 does not have entries for 192.168.2.0/24 or 192.168.6.0/24.

```
jeff@Juniper2> show ospf neighbor
Address          Interface      State      ID            Pri         Dead
192.168.2.1      fxp2.0         Full       1.1.1.1       128         32
192.168.3.1      fxp3.0         Full       1.1.1.3       128         30


-------------------------------------------------------------------

Cisco2#show ip ospf neighbor

Neighbor ID    Pri    State      Dead Time    Address      Interface
1.1.1.3        128    FULL/DR    00:00:38     10.1.1.2     Ethernet0
2.2.2.1          1    FULL/DR    00:00:38     10.2.1.2     Ethernet1
```

Figure 7.26 The neighbor tables of both Juniper2 and Cisco2 in Figure 7.25 show the expected adjacencies.

```
jeff@Juniper1> show route protocol ospf

inet.0: 16 destinations, 17 routes (15 active, 0 holddown, 1 hidden)
+ = Active Route, - = Last Active, * = Both

10.1.1.0/24        *[OSPF/10] 00:15:28, metric 12
                   > to 192.168.2.2 via fxp1.0
192.168.3.0/24     *[OSPF/10] 02:44:11, metric 2
                   > to 192.168.2.2 via fxp1.0


-------------------------------------------------------------------

Cisco1#show ip route ospf
     10.0.0.0/24 is subnetted, 3 subnets
O IA    10.1.1.0 [110/20] via 10.2.1.1, 00:18:38, Ethernet0
O IA 192.168.3.0/24 [110/21] via 10.2.1.1, 00:18:38, Ethernet0
```

Figure 7.27 Juniper1 and Cisco1 in Figure 7.25 have both learned the prefixes in area 1, but neither has learned the prefixes in the opposing area 0.

Adding a virtual link between the two ABRs, Juniper2 and Cisco2, as depicted in Figure 7.28, solves the problem. Figure 7.29 shows the configurations of these ABRs. Although the syntax differs, the information supplied to the router is the same: The RID of the neighbor at the other end of the link and the transit area are specified.

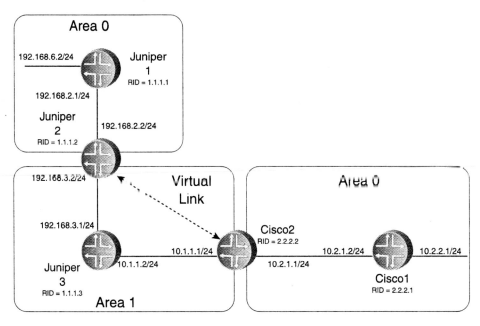

Figure 7.28   A virtual link connecting the two ABRs through area 1 allows the full exchange of prefixes.

```
Juniper2:

[edit]
jeff@Juniper2# show protocols ospf
area 0.0.0.0 {
     virtual-link neighbor-id 2.2.2.2 transit-area 0.0.0.1;
     interface fxp2.0;
}
area 0.0.0.1 {
     interface fxp3.0;
}

----------------------------------------------------------------------

Cisco2:

router ospf 1
 router-id 2.2.2.2
 area 1 virtual-link 1.1.1.2
 network 10.1.1.1 0.0.0.0 area 1
 network 10.2.1.1 0.0.0.0 area 0
 !
```

Figure 7.29   A virtual link is configured between Juniper2 and Cisco2.

The OSPF entries in the routing tables of Juniper1 and Cisco1 are again displayed in Figure 7.30. You can see that the two routers have now learned the prefixes in the other area 0.

```
jeff@Juniper1> show route protocol ospf

inet.0: 18 destinations, 19 routes (17 active, 0 holddown, 1 hidden)
+ = Active Route, - = Last Active, * = Both

10.1.1.0/24          *[OSPF/10] 00:38:28, metric 12
                      > to 192.168.2.2 via fxp1.0
10.2.1.0/24          *[OSPF/10] 00:26:15, metric 22
                      > to 192.168.2.2 via fxp1.0
10.2.2.0/24          *[OSPF/10] 00:26:15, metric 32
                      > to 192.168.2.2 via fxp1.0
192.168.3.0/24       *[OSPF/10] 00:38:42, metric 2
                      > to 192.168.2.2 via fxp1.0


------------------------------------------------------------------------

Cisco1#show ip route ospf
      10.0.0.0/24 is subnetted, 3 subnets
O IA    10.1.1.0 [110/20] via 10.2.1.1, 00:29:16, Ethernet0
O IA    192.168.6.0/24 [110/23] via 10.2.1.1, 00:29:16, Ethernet0
O IA    192.168.2.0/24 [110/22] via 10.2.1.1, 00:29:16, Ethernet0
O IA    192.168.3.0/24 [110/21] via 10.2.1.1, 00:29:16, Ethernet0
```

Figure 7.30   Juniper1 and Cisco1 in Figure 7.28 have learned the prefixes in the opposing area 0.

Figure 7.31 shows the entries in the interface databases of Juniper2 and Cisco2 for the virtual link between them. You can observe in these entries that the default Hello interval, router dead interval, retransmit interval, and transmit (transit) delay for a point-to-point link are used. All of these parameters are configurable, as is authentication between the neighbors.

```
jeff@Juniper2> show ospf interface vl-2.2.2.2 extensive
Interface      State     Area       DR ID         BDR ID        Nbrs
vl-2.2.2.2     PtToPt    0.0.0.0    0.0.0.0       0.0.0.0          1
Type Virtual, address 192.168.3.2, mask 0.0.0.0, MTU 0, cost 11
  adj count 1
Hello 10, Dead 40, ReXmit 5, Not Stub


------------------------------------------------------------------

Cisco2# show ip ospf virtual-links
Virtual Link OSPF_VL2 to router 1.1.1.2 is up
  Run as demand circuit
  DoNotAge LSA not allowed (Number of DCbitless LSA is 24).
  Transit area 1, via interface Ethernet0, Cost of using 11
  Transmit Delay is 1 sec, State POINT_TO_POINT,
  Timer intervals configured, Hello 10, Dead 40, Wait 40, Retransmit 5
  Hello due in 00:00:05
  Adjacency State FULL
  Index 2/1, retransmission queue length 0, number of retransmission 0
  First 0x0(0)/0x0(0) Next 0x0(0)/0x0(0)
  Last retransmission scan length is 0, maximum is 0
  Last retransmission scan time is 0 msec, maximum is 0 msec
```

Figure 7.31   The virtual link appears as an entry in the interface database of Juniper2 and Cisco2.

Although virtual links are easy to configure, they nonetheless add complexity, making the network harder to understand and troubleshoot. You should therefore consider them a tool of last resort. In the hypothetical domain merge depicted in Figure 7.25, for example, you should consider the following alternatives:

- Can a physical link from Cisco2 to the existing backbone area be established?
- Can area 1 be reconfigured as area 0 to make a contiguous backbone topology?
- Can the merging domain be reconfigured as area 1?
- Rather than merge the OSPF domains, can BGP or static routes be used to connect them?

As for backbone topologies, a robust backbone with enough physical links to withstand at least two simultaneous link failures is the foundation of a good OSPF design. Virtual links are a poor substitute for doing the design right in the first place. When virtual links must be used—either for merging domains or for reducing backbone vulnerabilities—they should be considered a temporary feature of your network, put in place only until a better alternative is implemented.

7.4   IS-IS Areas

In the introduction to Section 7.3, I stated that OSPF areas are easier to design, configure, and administer than IS-IS areas because the tools for creating different kinds of network behaviors are inherent in the protocol, whereas similar behaviors in IS-IS must be created using routing policies. While this is true, here is a factor in favor of IS-IS: Those same routing policies, although more difficult to configure and administer, might make IS-IS easier to troubleshoot. Whether you are dealing with automobiles, home appliances, or routing protocols, ease of use on the surface often means complexity "under the hood," and you have to get into those greasy parts under the hood to do troubleshooting. In the case of OSPF, the easy configuration of different area types is made possible by optional flags and LSAs being exchanged in the background. When things go wrong, particularly when the problem is not your own configuration but a bug in the OSPF code, you might have to dive into the various RFCs to gain a deeper understanding of how to find the source of the problem. But the routing policies creating various IS-IS area behaviors are right in the configuration, readily available for you to read and debug.

7.4.1   Backbone and Non-Backbone Areas

You have already gotten some hints that area concepts are somewhat different in IS-IS than they are with OSPF. For one thing, the AID, found as a part of the IS-IS Network Entity Title, applies to the entire router rather than to an interface as it does in OSPF. Then there are the adjacencies, which are either L1 for adjacencies between routers with the same AID, or L2, which can be between routers with the same or different AIDs.

But it gets more complicated. The default behavior of most IS-IS implementations is to accept both L1 and L2 Hellos on an interface. You learned in Chapter 4 that if the AIDs match between neighbors and the neighbors are not set to either L1-only or L2-only, both an L1 and an L2 adjacency will be established between the neighbors. Table 7.1 repeats the table of adjacency rules that you first saw in that chapter.

Table 7.1 Summary of Different L1/L2 and Area ID Combinations, and the Resulting Adjacencies

R1 Type	R2 Type	AIDs	Adjacency
L1-only	L1-only	Same	L1
L1-only	L1-only	Different	None
L2-only	L2-only	Same	L2
L2-only	L2-only	Different	L2
L1-only	L2-only	Same	None
L1-only	L2-only	Different	None
L1-only	Both	Same	L1
L1-only	Both	Different	None
L2-only	Both	Same	L2
L2-only	Both	Different	L2
Both	Both	Same	L1 and L2
Both	Both	Different	L2

Figure 7.32 shows what effect the IS-IS adjacency rules can have. The adjacencies between RTR2 and RTR3, and between RTR4 and RTR5, are L2 adjacencies because the AID portions of their NETs are different. But wherever the AIDs are the same, both L1 and L2 adjacencies are created by default. How, then, do you differentiate the backbone and nonbackbone areas in this topology?

Figure 7.32 illustrates that it is not always easy to draw nice neat circles, with ABRs interconnecting them, to illustrate IS-IS areas. It is therefore best to think of IS-IS areas not topologically, as with OSPF areas, but to think of them as a set of contiguous adjacencies. So, an IS-IS backbone area is a contiguous[8] set of L2 adjacencies. An IS-IS nonbackbone area is a contiguous set of L1 adjacencies. As with OSPF, all inter-area traffic must pass through the backbone, and therefore the backbone interconnects all nonbackbone areas. ISO 10589, in fact, does not speak of a backbone area at all; instead, it calls the backbone area an *L2 subdomain*, a descriptive and useful term. You can and usually should make the area topologies more distinct that that shown in Figure 7.32 by manipulating the adjacency type a router will accept. If a router is in an L1 area and does not have connections to any other area, it should be configured as an L1-only router. If a router is in the L2 subdomain, it should be

---

[8] That is, not partitioned.

configured as an L2-only router. If the router is in an L1 area but has a connection to an L2 router (which has a different AID), the router is configured to accept both L1 and L2 adjacencies. Depending on the specific implementation, you can accomplish this either by setting the entire router to accept both adjacency types, knowing that its neighbors in its area will send only L1 Hellos and the routers in the L2 subdomain will send only L2 Hellos, or by configuring per interface the adjacency types that are accepted.

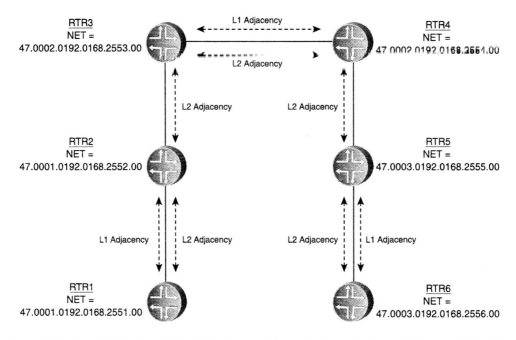

Figure 7.32   By default, both and L1 and L2 adjacency is formed between routers with the same AIDs. If the AIDs differ, only an L2 adjacency is formed.

Figure 7.33 shows the effect of setting the accepted adjacency types. The area topology is more distinct, and circles can be drawn to indicate a bit more clearly where the areas appear. Note that the circles still do not indicate clear boundaries like they do in OSPF; they only serve to show what groups of routers belong to the same area.

An L2 subdomain does not need to contain any L2-only routers. Take the network in Figure 7.34. Here, the L1 areas are completely and reliably interconnected among their L1/L2 routers. The connections within the areas are L1, and the connections between the L1/L2 routers are L2. This network again illustrates why it is best to think of the L2 subdomain as a contiguous set of L2 adjacencies rather than as a distinct topological area.

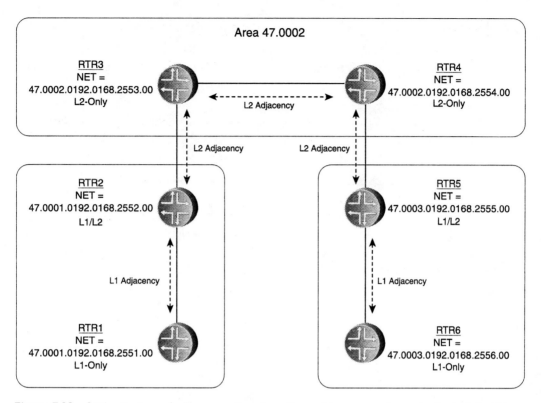

Figure 7.33   Setting the type of adjacency each router will accept is necessary to create clearly distinct L1 and L2 areas.

One final note should be made about L1/L2 routers. Because the L1 area address is assigned to the entire router rather than to an interface, an IS-IS router with one AID can only connect a single L1 area to the L2 subdomain. This differs from OSPF ABRs, which can connect multiple nonbackbone areas to area 0. However, as Section 7.4.8 discusses, an IS-IS router can have more than one AID. In addition to AID migrations, multiple AIDs can be used to attach multiple L1 areas to an L1/L2 router.

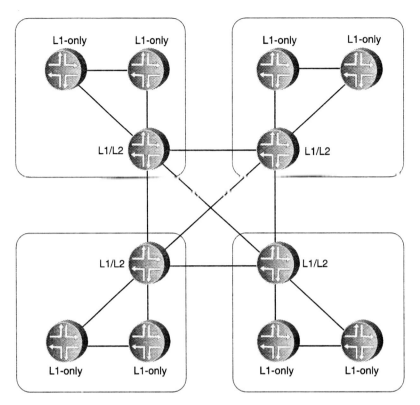

Figure 7.34   An L2 subdomain can consist entirely of the connections between L1/L2 routers, with no L2-only routers in it.

7.4.2   Factors for Scaling IS-IS Areas

One reason you might want to consider setting the adjacency types on an L1/L2 router by interface rather than on the entire router is that if the entire router is set to accept both, it will originate both L1 and L2 Hellos on all interfaces. Its L1-only neighbors will reject the L2 Hellos, and its L2-only neighbors will reject the L1 Hellos, ensuring that the right adjacency types are established. But the L1/L2 router is originating twice as many Hellos on its links than it needs to, unnecessarily using up some portion of the link bandwidth. And as stated in Section 7.3.2, network control traffic should normally consume less than 1 percent of a link's bandwidth and should never exceed 5 percent.

As you learned from Chapter 4, IS-IS messages have a standard 8-byte header. To that, LAN Hellos add 19 bytes of header and Point-to-Point Hellos add 12 bytes of header. The remainder of the Hellos is TLVs, which can be one or more of the following types:[9]

---

[9]   Hellos can actually carry more TLV types than the ones listed here; they are discussed in later chapters in the context of the extensions the TLVs support.

- Area Addresses TLV (type 1)
- Intermediate System Neighbors TLV (type 6)
- Protocols Supported TLV (type 129)
- IP Interface Address TLV (type 132)
- Authentication Information TLV (type 10)
- Padding TLV (type 8)

For simplicity, assume a Hello on a point-to-point link in which the originating router has only one AID, one interface IP address, supports only IPv4, and does not use authentication. The size of the Hello message adds up to:

- IS-IS header = 8 bytes
- Point-to-Point Hello header = 12 bytes
- 1 Area Addresses TLV = 6 bytes
- 1 Protocols Supported TLV = 3 bytes
- 1 IP Interface Address TLV = 6 bytes

The total size of the Hello, then, is 35 bytes. That compares favorably with an OSPF Hello, which under similar conditions would be 48 bytes. Whereas the OSPF Hello is sent every 10 seconds, the IS-IS Hello varies according to implementation, but is typically 9 or 10 seconds. Still a favorable comparison. And you saw in Section 7.3.2 that the OSPF Hello does not use a significant amount of bandwidth even on lower-speed links such as 56kbps, so you know that IS-IS Hellos on point-to-point links also will not add significant load.

An IS-IS LAN Hello would compare less favorably to an OSPF Hello on a LAN link. Not only are there another 7 bytes of Hello header, there is an IS Neighbors TLV that adds 2 bytes plus 6 bytes for each neighbor on the link. And in some implementations such as that of Juniper Networks, the DIS sends this LAN Hello every 3 seconds. However, these days a LAN link almost always means Ethernet, and 10M Ethernet is quickly being replaced with 100M and 1000M Ethernet. So again, Hellos are an insignificant part of the link load.

As is the case with OSPF and its LSAs, IS-IS LSPs are the entities that most impact flooding, processing, and memory loads. Again, there is the 8-byte IS-IS header. This is followed by 19 bytes of LSP header information, and the rest of the LSP is a set of TLVs:

- **Area Addresses TLV (type 1)**—Add 3 bytes plus the total number of bytes of all area addresses configured on the router.
- **IS Neighbors TLV (type 2)**—Add 3 bytes plus 11 bytes for each neighbor.
- **Protocols Supported TLV (type 129)**—Add 2 bytes plus 1 byte for each protocol supported.
- **IP Interface Address TLV (type 132)**—Add 2 bytes plus 4 bytes for every IP address configured on an interface from which the LSP is transmitted.

- **Authentication Information TLV (type 10)**—Add 3 bytes plus the number of bytes of the authentication value. This is normally the number of bytes of the ASCII representation of the password configured on the router.

- **IP Internal Reachability Information TLV (type 128)**—Add 2 bytes plus 12 bytes for each IP address directly connected to the originating router that the router is advertising to IS-IS as reachable. Also include, if the router is L1/L2, 12 bytes for every summary prefix the router advertises.

- **IP External Reachability Information TLV (type 130)**—Add 2 bytes plus 12 bytes for every external prefix the router is advertising into the IS-IS domain.

- **Extended IS Reachability TLV (type 22)**—If wide metrics are configured, add 2 bytes plus, for each neighbor, 11 bytes plus the total length of all sub-TLVs. The use of this TVL and its sub-TLVs is detailed in Chapter 11.

- **Extended IP Reachability TLV (type 135)**—If wide metrics are used, add 6 bytes plus, for each internal prefix (directly connected or summary) or external prefix the router is advertising into IS-IS, 6 bytes plus the total length of all sub-TLVs. The use of this TLV and its sub-TLVs is detailed in Chapter 11.

Using the same parameters as the OSPF example in Section 7.3.2, we will assume an IS-IS area with:

- 50 routers
- 20 connected prefixes per router
- 2000 prefixes internal to the IS-IS domain but outside of the area
- 5000 external prefixes advertised into the IS-IS domain

For simplicity, we will assume only one AID per router, one IP address per interface, only IPv4 support, all routers connected by point-to-point links, and no wide metrics.

The total header space is:

$$50(8 + 19) = 1350 \text{ bytes}$$

The 8-byte IS-IS PDU header is, of course, not stored in the database and only influences flooding calculations, but the overall number is small enough that you can keep it in your calculations for both flooding and database size.

Assuming a 3-byte AID, the total size of the Area Addresses TLVs is:

$$50(3 + 3) = 300 \text{ bytes}$$

The total size of the IS Neighbors TLVs is harder to estimate accurately without summing the number of neighbors each router has. For simplicity, we will use an average of 3 neighbors per router:

$$50[3 + 3(11)] = 1800 \text{ bytes}$$

Protocols Supported TLVs are:

$$50(2 + 1) = 150 \text{ bytes}$$

IP Interface Address TLVs are:

$$50(2 + 4) = 300 \text{ bytes}$$

If a six-character password is used throughout the area, the Authentication Information TLVs are:

$$50(3 + 6) = 450 \text{ bytes}$$

The IP Internal Reachability Information TLVs carrying the prefixes internal to the area are:

$$50[20(2 + 12)] = 14,000 \text{ bytes}$$

If the area is an L1 area, you can disregard the 2000 prefixes internal to the domain but external to the area. The reason for this is explained in the next section. If the area is an L2 area, the IP Internal Reachability Information TLVs are:

$$2000(2 + 12) = 28,000 \text{ bytes}$$

If the area is an L2 area, the 5000 external prefixes must be accounted for. If the area is L1, these prefixes might or might not need to be accounted for, depending on the inter-area policies you implement as described in Chapters 8 and 9. We will assume that the 5000 prefixes are advertised in the area, so the IP External Reachability Information TLVs are:

$$5000(2 + 12) = 70,000 \text{ bytes}$$

A fair estimate of the size of the IS-IS LS database for this area, and the load that must be carried during flooding, is then:

$$1350 + 300 + 1800 + 150 + 300 + 450 + 14,000 + 28, 000 + 70,000 = 116,350 \text{ bytes}$$

This compares quite favorably with an OSPF area of the same size, where the OSPF LS database was estimated in Section 7.3.2 to be 220,000 bytes. Even with this smaller database size, however, notice that the great majority of the 116,350 bytes is to account for the prefixes external to the area. The following section shows that these external prefixes might not be advertised into an L1 area at all.

7.4.3   Default IS-IS L1 Area Behavior

You have seen in previous sections how you can use special configurations to block all prefixes external to an OSPF domain from an OSPF area (stub areas) or to block all prefixes external to the area, both external to and internal to the OSPF domain (totally stubby areas). By default, however, all prefixes external to an OSPF area are advertised into the area.

IS-IS works from the opposite direction. By default, an IS-IS L1 area is "totally stubby"—that is, no prefixes are advertised from an L2 area into an L1 area. Take the network in Figure 7.35. Looking at the route tables of the three routers with L2 adjacencies in Figure 7.36—Juniper3, Juniper2, and Cisco2—you can see that they have full knowledge of all prefixes in all areas.

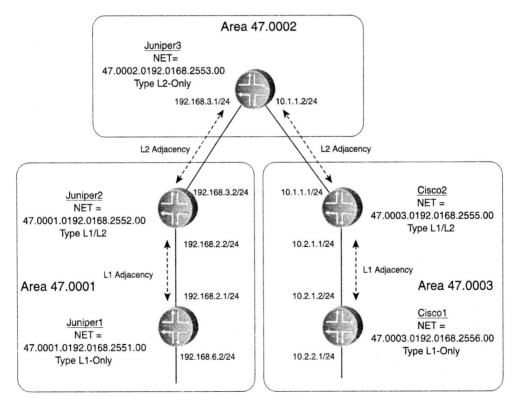

Figure 7.35   The L1/L2 routers (Juniper2 and Cisco2) do not advertise prefixes learned from their L2 neighbor to their L1 neighbor.

```
jeff@Juniper3> show route

inet.0: 21 destinations, 21 routes (20 active, 0 holddown, 1 hidden)
+ = Active Route, - = Last Active, * = Both

10.1.1.0/24        *[Direct/0] 1w0d 08:32:02
                    > via fxp4.0
10.1.1.2/32        *[Local/0] 1w0d 08:32:02
                     Local via fxp4.0
10.2.1.0/24        *[IS-IS/18] 23:33:41, metric 20, tag 2
                    > to 10.1.1.1 via fxp4.0
10.2.2.0/24        *[IS-IS/18] 00:35:34, metric 30, tag 2
                    > to 10.1.1.1 via fxp4.0
192.168.2.0/24     *[IS-IS/18] 23:26:55, metric 20, tag 2
                    > to 192.168.3.2 via fxp1.0
192.168.3.0/24     *[Direct/0] 12w5d 10:58:31
                    > via fxp1.0
192.168.3.1/32     *[Local/0] 16w2d 13:18:43
                     Local via fxp1.0
192.168.6.0/24     *[IS-IS/18] 23:26:31, metric 30, tag 2
                    > to 192.168.3.2 via fxp1.0




jeff@Juniper2> show route

inet.0: 18 destinations, 18 routes (17 active, 0 holddown, 1 hidden)
+ = Active Route, - = Last Active, * = Both

10.1.1.0/24        *[IS-IS/18] 23:30:04, metric 20
                    > to 192.168.3.1 via fxp3.0
10.2.1.0/24        *[IS-IS/18] 23:30:04, metric 30
                    > to 192.168.3.1 via fxp3.0
10.2.2.0/24        *[IS-IS/18] 00:38:21, metric 40
                    > to 192.168.3.1 via fxp3.0
192.168.2.0/24     *[Direct/0] 12w5d 11:22:42
                    > via fxp2.0
192.168.2.2/32     *[Local/0] 16w2d 13:48:54
                     Local via fxp2.0
192.168.3.0/24     *[Direct/0] 12w5d 11:22:42
                    > via fxp3.0
192.168.3.2/32     *[Local/0] 16w2d 13:48:54
                     Local via fxp3.0
192.168.6.0/24     *[IS-IS/15] 23:29:32, metric 20
                    > to 192.168.2.1 via fxp2.0


Cisco2#show ip route
Codes: C - connected, S - static, I - IGRP, R - RIP, M - mobile, B - BGP
       D - EIGRP, EX - EIGRP external, O - OSPF, IA - OSPF inter area
       N1 - OSPF NSSA external type 1, N2 - OSPF NSSA external type 2
       E1 - OSPF external type 1, E2 - OSPF external type 2, E - EGP
       i - IS-IS, L1 - IS-IS level-1, L2 - IS-IS level-2, ia - IS-IS inter area
       * - candidate default, U - per-user static route, o - ODR
       P - periodic downloaded static route

Gateway of last resort is not set

     10.0.0.0/24 is subnetted, 3 subnets
```

```
C        10.2.1.0 is directly connected, Ethernet1
i L1     10.2.2.0 [115/20] via 10.2.1.2, Ethernet1
C        10.1.1.0 is directly connected, Ethernet0
i L2 192.168.6.0/24 [115/40] via 10.1.1.2, Ethernet0
i L2 192.168.2.0/24 [115/30] via 10.1.1.2, Ethernet0
i L2 192.168.3.0/24 [115/20] via 10.1.1.2, Ethernet0
```

Figure 7.36   The route tables of all routers with L2 adjacencies have entries for all of the prefixes in the network of Figure 7.35.

But when you examine the route tables of the L1-only routers Juniper1 and Cisco1 (Figure 7.37), you find that the tables do not have entries for any prefixes outside of the routers' own areas. Instead, a default route points to the L1/L2 router in that area. The default routes provide the connectivity out of the area (Figure 7.38).

```
jeff@Juniper1> show route

inet.0: 10 destinations, 10 routes (9 active, 0 holddown, 1 hidden)
+ = Active Route, - = Last Active, * = Both

0.0.0.0/0          *[IS-IS/15] 00:51:52, metric 10, tag 1
                    > to 192.168.2.2 via fxp1.0
192.168.2.0/24     *[Direct/0] 12w5d 11:34:09
                    > via fxp1.0
192.168.2.1/32     *[Local/0] 16w2d 14:01:19
                      Local via fxp1.0
192.168.6.0/24     *[Direct/0] 12w5d 11:34:09
                    > via fxp2.0
192.168.6.2/32     *[Local/0] 16w2d 14:01:19
                      Local via fxp2.0


Cisco1#show ip route
Codes: C - connected, S - static, I - IGRP, R - RIP, M - mobile, B - BGP
       D - EIGRP, EX - EIGRP external, O - OSPF, IA - OSPF inter area
       N1 - OSPF NSSA external type 1, N2 - OSPF NSSA external type 2
       E1 - OSPF external type 1, E2 - OSPF external type 2, E - EGP
       i - IS-IS, L1 - IS-IS level-1, L2 - IS-IS level-2, ia - IS-IS inter area
       * - candidate default, U - per-user static route, o - ODR
       P - periodic downloaded static route

Gateway of last resort is 10.2.1.1 to network 0.0.0.0

10.0.0.0/24 is subnetted, 3 subnets
C        10.2.1.0 is directly connected, Ethernet0
C        10.2.2.0 is directly connected, Ethernet1
i*L1 0.0.0.0/0 [115/10] via 10.2.1.1, Ethernet0
```

Figure 7.37   The route tables of the L1-only routers in the network of Figure 7.35 have entries for only the prefixes in their own areas, plus a default route to the local L1/L2 router.

```
jeff@Juniper1> ping 10.2.2.1
PING 10.2.2.1 (10.2.2.1): 56 data bytes
64 bytes from 10.2.2.1: icmp_seq=0 ttl=252 time=7.801 ms
64 bytes from 10.2.2.1: icmp_seq=1 ttl=252 time=3.170 ms
64 bytes from 10.2.2.1: icmp_seq=2 ttl=252 time=3.308 ms
^C
--- 10.2.2.1 ping statistics ---
3 packets transmitted, 3 packets received, 0% packet loss
round-trip min/avg/max/stddev = 3.170/4.760/7.801/2.151 ms

Cisco1# ping 192.168.6.2

Type escape sequence to abort.
Sending 5, 100-byte ICMP Echos to 192.168.6.2, timeout is 2 seconds:
!!!!!
Success rate is 100 percent (5/5), round-trip min/avg/max = 4/4/8 ms
```

Figure 7.38   The default routes provide connectivity to destinations outside of the local area, as shown by these pings from the two L1-only routers in Figure 7.35 to prefixes attached to the other L1-only router.

What all of this means is that an L1/L2 router advertises the prefixes in its attached L1 areas to its L2 neighbors. However, it does not advertise prefixes in its attached L2 area, or that are learned from its L2 neighbors, into its attached L1 areas.

Interestingly, the L1/L2 routers also do not advertise the default routes you see in the route tables of Figure 7.37. Instead, an L1/L2 router sets the attached bit (ATT) in its L1 LSP to indicate that it has connectivity to the L2 subdomain.[10] When an L1 router receives an LSP with the ATT bit set, it installs a default route pointing to the LSP's originator—the L1/L2 router. A detailed display of the LSP from Juniper2 in Juniper1's IS-IS LS database indicates this set ATT bit (Figure 7.39). Figure 7.40 shows the L1 LSP originated by Cisco2. Although the display format differs, you can again see that the ATT bit has been set.

```
jeff@Juniper1> show isis database Juniper2.00-00 extensive
IS-IS level 1 link-state database:

Juniper2.00-00  Sequence: 0x75, Checksum: 0x8d18, Lifetime: 574 secs
   IS neighbor:               Juniper2.03  Metric:       10
   IP prefix:                 192.168.2.0/24 Metric:     10 Internal

  Header: LSP id: Juniper2.00-00, Length: 137 bytes
    Allocated length: 157 bytes, Router ID: 1.1.1.2
    Remaining lifetime: 574 secs, Level: 1,Interface: 2
    Estimated free bytes: 0, Actual free bytes: 20
    Aging timer expires in: 574 secs
    Protocols: IP

  Packet: LSP id: Juniper2.00-00, Length: 137 bytes, Lifetime : 1198 secs
    Checksum: 0x8d18, Sequence: 0x75, Attributes: 0xb <L1 L2 Attached>
```

---

[10] There are actually 4 ATT bits, one associated with each of the four IS-IS metric fields defined by IS-IS. But because the default metric is the only metric used in dual IS-IS implementations, the ATT bit associated with that metric is also the only one used.

```
      NLPID: 0x83, Fixed length: 27 bytes, Version: 1, Sysid length: 0 bytes
      Packet type: 18, Packet version: 1, Max area: 0

   TLVs:
     Area address: 47.0001 (3)
     Speaks: IP
     Speaks: IPv6
     IP router id: 1.1.1.2
     IP address: 1.1.1.2
     Hostname: Juniper2
     IS neighbor: Juniper2.03, Internal, Metric: default 10
     IS neighbor: Juniper2.03, Metric: default 10
       IP address: 192.168.2.2
     IP prefix: 192.168.2.0/24, Internal, Metric: default 10
     IP prefix: 192.168.2.0/24 metric 10 up
   No queued transmissions
```

Figure 7.39   The L1 LSP originated by Juniper2 indicates that the attached bit (shown in bold) is set.

```
Cisco1#show isis database detail

IS-IS Level-1 Link State Database:
LSPID          LSP Seq Num     LSP Checksum  LSP Holdtime     ATT/P/OL
[…]
Cisco2.00-00   0x00000077      0xCF46        910              1/0/0
   Area Address: 47.0002
   NLPID:        0x81 0xCC
   Hostname: Cisco2
   IP Address:   192.168.254.2
   Metric: 10         IP 10.1.1.0 255.255.255.0
   Metric: 10         IP 10.2.1.0 255.255.255.0
   Metric: 10         IS Cisco2.03
   Metric: 10         IS Cisco2.02
   Metric: 10         IS Cisco2.01
   Metric: 0          ES Cisco2
[…]
```

Figure 7.40   The L1 LSP originated by Cisco2 indicates that the attached bit (shown in bold) is set.

7.4.4   Redundant L1/L2 Routers

As with OSPF ABRs, it is always good design practice to have more than one L1/L2 router in an L1 area so that if one fails, the area is not isolated. If an L1/L2 router receives an LSP with the ATT bit set, it does not install a default route to the originator. Consider the network in Figure 7.41. In this network, the link from RTR1 to its L2 neighbor has failed. This does not present a problem for the L1-only routers because they have installed default routes to both of the L1/L2 routers.

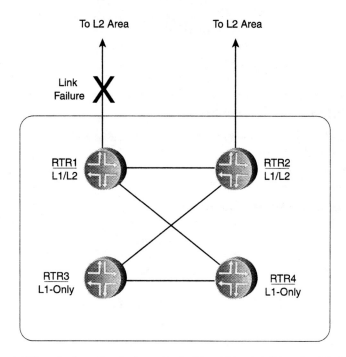

Figure 7.41   If an L1/L2 router loses its attachment to its L2 neighbor, it will install a default route to the
other L1/L2 router in its area.

This situation might seem to be a problem for any packets with area-external destinations that reach RTR1. Because it is an L1/L2 router, RTR1 does not normally install a default route to any other L1/L2 router. But when its L2 adjacency fails, it ceases to be an "attached" router. Seeing a set ATT bit from RTR2, it then installs a default route pointing to RTR2. It clears the ATT bit in its LSP and refloods. The L1-only routers then remove the default route to RTR1.

When the link is restored, RTR1 again becomes an attached router, removes its default route to RTR2, and refloods its LSP with the ATT bit set.

7.4.5   Address Summarization, Again

As with OSPF, you can summarize the prefixes within an IS-IS L1 area to reduce the size of the L2 LS database. How effective the summarization is depends on your address design: The more prefixes you can summarize with a single aggregate address, the more effective the summarization.

Also as with OSPF, an L1-only router cannot summarize local prefixes because doing so would lead to inconsistent databases within the L1 area. Only an L1/L2 router can summarize to its L2 neighbors.

Finally, external prefixes can be summarized into the IS-IS domain either as aggregates of prefix sets or as a default route. The advertisement of external prefixes into IS-IS, either as they are or as aggregates, is discussed in Section 7.4.7.

Address Summarization and BGP

In addition to the possible problems of loss of route accuracy discussed in this section and in Section 7.3.7, summarization might pose two problems to networks that speak BGP to external autonomous systems.

The first problem involves the advertisement of BGP routes into the local AS. When BGP advertises a route to an external destination into the local AS, it associates a next-hop address with the route that is either (depending on how you set up your BGP policies) the interface of the external BGP peer from which the route is learned or the loopback address of the local BGP router speaking to that external peer. When a router internal to the AS receives the BGP route advertisement from the local BGP router, it looks up the IGP route to the next-hop address. If a route to the next-hop address cannot be found, the BGP route is declared invalid and is not entered into the routing table.

If, on the other hand, the internal router finds multiple IGP routes to the next-hop address, it selects what it perceives as the shortest path to the next hop and installs that as part of the BGP route. But if address summarization is used within the AS, along with its associated loss of route information, the route selected to the next-hop address might not be the actual shortest path to the AS exit point.

The other problem involves the BGP Multi-Exit Discriminator (MED) route attribute. When there are multiple peering points from your AS to a neighboring AS, MEDs are sometimes attached to routes advertised to that neighbor to indicate the best entry point into your AS—either the shortest path to a local destination or the shortest transit path across your AS to another exit point. The MED value that is advertised to a neighboring AS is normally based on the value of the IGP metric to the local destination or next-hop address of the transit route. But again, because of the loss of routing accuracy, summarization within your AS can cause inaccurate MEDs to be advertised, resulting in the neighboring AS forwarding packets to your AS through a suboptimal entry point.

If you are running BGP, you must consider these factors along with the general loss of routing information internal to the routing domain when weighing the benefits of summarization against its possible costs.

7.4.6   L2 to L1 Route Leaking

The problem of routing information loss with summary routes can also apply within an IS-IS L1 area, where only a default route exists. If there is only one L1/L2 router through which to exit the area, there is no problem. If there are multiple L1/L2 routers, however, the information available to the L1-only routers limits them to choosing the closest L1/L2 router. For a given route, this router might or might not be the best exit point from the area. The L1-only routers have no way to know.

So, to expand your area design choices, it is good to be able to "leak" more specific routes from the L2 area into an L1 area when better routing information is desired. The problem is that RFC 1195 prohibits the advertisement of prefixes from L2 to L1. Figure 7.42 illustrates the reason for this prohibition. In this network, prefix X, which resides somewhere outside of the L1 area, is advertised from some L2 peer to RTR1. RTR1 advertises the prefix into the L1 area in an L1 IP Internal Reachability Information TLV within its L1 LSP. RTR2 receives that L1 LSP and, assuming the prefix to be internal to the L1 area advertises it back into the L2 area in an IP Internal Reachability TLV within its L2 LSP, creating a potential routing loop.

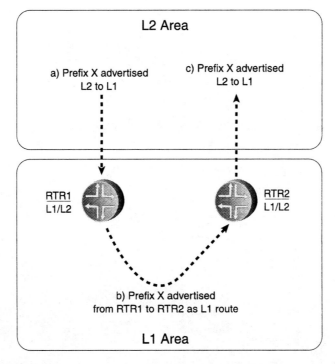

Figure 7.42   RFC 1195 prohibits advertising prefixes from L2 to L1 to prevent potential routing loops such as depicted here.

OSPF does not have this problem, because routes are advertised from area 0 into backbone areas in type 3 LSAs. ABRs receiving a type 3 LSA within a nonbackbone area do not advertise the LSA's prefixes into area 0. However, the IP Internal Reachability and IP External Reachability Information TLVs, as originally specified in RFC 1195, contained no facility for distinguishing the inter-area status of their prefixes.

As IS-IS has come into general use as an IP routing protocol, designers have recognized a need to sometimes inject more detailed route information into an L1 area and that a workaround to the limitations of RFC 1195 is needed. That workaround is offered in RFC 2966.[11]

Notice in the format of the IP Internal and External Reachability Information TLVs in Figures 5.31 and 5.32 that the default metric field is a 6-bit metric value and an Internal/External (I/E) type flag. The eighth bit is unused, and normally ignored. RFC 2966 redefines this bit as the Up/Down (U/D) bit (Figure 7.43). When an L1/L2 router advertises a prefix from L2 to L1, it sets the Up/Down bit associated with the prefix. An L1/L2 router receiving a prefix from an L1 area with the U/D bit set does not advertise that prefix to its L2 peer. Older IS-IS implementations that do not understand the RFC 2699 extension ignore the eighth bit of the default metric field, and so pose no compatibility problem. However, be sure when advertising prefixes L2 to L1 that all L1/L2 routers do understand the extension.

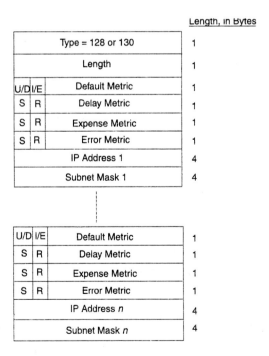

Figure 7.43   RFC 2966 defines the eighth bit of the default metric field as the UP/Down bit, and uses the bit to identify prefixes that have been advertised into an L1 area from an L2 adjacency.

[11] Tony Li, Tony Przygienda, and Henk Smit, "Domain-Wide Prefix Distribution with Two-Level IS-IS," RFC 2966, October 2000.

L2 to L1 route leaking is accomplished by configuring a routing policy on the L1/L2 router. The term *leaking* is commonly used because with a routing policy you can be very specific about what prefixes you want to have advertised into the L1 area—you can allow all prefixes learned from an L2 neighbor, or you might limit the allowed prefixes by such attributes as internal or external type, or you can even allow only one specific prefix. Routing policies give you quite a bit of flexibility.

Figure 7.44 shows a simple policy configuration applied at Juniper2 in Figure 7.35. A policy named L2_Leaking has been created that identifies and accepts IS-IS L2 prefixes. The policy is then applied as an export policy to the IS-IS configuration so that L2 prefixes are advertised into L1. Comparing Juniper1's route table in Figure 7.45 with its previous table in Figure 7.37, you can see that there are now entries for the prefixes in area 47.0003.

```
[edit]
jeff@Juniper2# show policy-options
policy-statement L2_Leaking {
    term 1 {
        from {
            protocol isis;
            level 2;
        }
        then accept;
    }
}

[edit]
jeff@Juniper2# show protocols isis
export L2_Leaking;
interface fxp2.0 {
    level 2 disable;
}
interface fxp3.0 {
    level 1 disable;
}
```

Figure 7.44   A simple JUNOS policy for advertising all prefixes from L2 to L1.

```
\jeff@Juniper1> show route

inet.0: 16 destinations, 16 routes (15 active, 0 holddown, 1 hidden)
+ = Active Route, - = Last Active, * = Both

0.0.0.0/0          *[IS-IS/15] 22:22:57, metric 10, tag 1
                    > to 192.168.2.2 via fxp1.0
10.1.1.0/24        *[IS-IS/18] 05:19:16, metric 30, tag 1
                    > to 192.168.2.2 via fxp1.0
10.2.1.0/24        *[IS-IS/18] 05:19:16, metric 40, tag 1
                    > to 192.168.2.2 via fxp1.0
10.2.2.0/24        *[IS-IS/18] 05:19:16, metric 50, tag 1
                    > to 192.168.2.2 via fxp1.0
192.168.2.0/24     *[Direct/0] 12w6d 09:05:14
                    > via fxp1.0
```

```
192.168.2.1/32      *[Local/0] 16w3d 11:32:24
                       Local via fxp1.0
192.168.6.0/24      *[Direct/0] 12w6d 09:05:14
                     > via fxp2.0
192.168.6.2/32      *[Local/0] 16w3d 11:32:24
                       Local via fxp2.0
```

Figure 7.45   The route table in Juniper1 of Figure 7.35 now shows entries for all prefixes learned via L2.

The one prefix in Figure 7.35 that is conspicuously missing in Juniper1's route table is 192.168.3.0/24. The reason is quite simple: That prefix is directly attached to Juniper2, not learned from a L2 adjacency. An additional term in the routing policy (Figure 7.46) gives the results at Juniper1 that we want (Figure 7.47).

```
jeff@Juniper2# show policy-options
policy-statement L2_Leaking {
    term 1 {
        from {
            protocol isis;
            level 2;
        }
        then accept;
    }
    term 2 {
        from protocol direct;
        then accept;
    }
}
```

Figure 7.46   The policy of Figure 7.44 is modified to include redistributing prefixes directly connected to Juniper2 into the L1 area.

IOS routing policy syntax is very different from JUNOS, but the result are the same if the configuration is done correctly. Figure 7.48 shows an example of an IOS configuration at Cisco2 that again leaks routes into an L1 area. But this time we are being a bit more specific, allowing only prefix 192.168.6.0/24 into the L1 area. The distribute-list 100 that is referred to in the redistribute statement accomplishes this by specifying the prefix we are interested in and denying all others. The route table in Cisco1, displayed in Figure 7.49, shows that the policy is working as expected.

```
jeff@Juniper1> show route

inet.0: 18 destinations, 19 routes (17 active, 0 holddown, 1 hidden)
+ = Active Route, - = Last Active, * = Both

0.0.0.0/0            *[IS-IS/15] 1d 00:08:06, metric 10, tag 1
                      > to 192.168.2.2 via fxp1.0
10.1.1.0/24          *[IS-IS/18] 07:04:25, metric 30, tag 1
                      > to 192.168.2.2 via fxp1.0
10.2.1.0/24          *[IS-IS/18] 07:04:25, metric 40, tag 1
                      > to 192.168.2.2 via fxp1.0
10.2.2.0/24          *[IS-IS/18] 07:04:25, metric 50, tag 1
                      > to 192.168.2.2 via fxp1.0
192.168.2.0/24       *[Direct/0] 12w6d 10:50:23
                      > via fxp1.0
192.168.2.1/32       *[Local/0] 16w3d 13:17:33
                        Local via fxp1.0
192.168.3.0/24       *[IS-IS/15] 00:00:30, metric 20, tag 1
                      > to 192.168.2.2 via fxp1.0
192.168.6.0/24       *[Direct/0] 12w6d 10:50:23
                      > via fxp2.0
192.168.6.2/32       *[Local/0] 16w3d 13:17:33
                        Local via fxp2.0
```

Figure 7.47   Juniper1's route table now shows subnet 192.168.3.0/24.

```
router isis
 redistribute isis ip level-2 into level-1 distribute-list 100
 net 47.0002.0192.0168.2558.00
 !
access-list 100 permit ip 192.168.6.0 0.0.0.255 any
```

Figure 7.48   This policy permits only the prefix 192.168.6.0/24 learned from the L2 area to be leaked into the L1 area.

```
Cisco1#show ip route
Codes: C - connected, S - static, I - IGRP, R - RIP, M - mobile, B - BGP
       D - EIGRP, EX - EIGRP external, O - OSPF, IA - OSPF inter area
       N1 - OSPF NSSA external type 1, N2 - OSPF NSSA external type 2
       E1 - OSPF external type 1, E2 - OSPF external type 2, E - EGP
       i - IS-IS, L1 - IS-IS level-1, L2 - IS-IS level-2, ia - IS-IS inter area
       * - candidate default, U - per-user static route, o - ODR
       P - periodic downloaded static route

Gateway of last resort is 10.2.1.1 to network 0.0.0.0

10.0.0.0/24 is subnetted, 3 subnets
C       10.2.1.0 is directly connected, Ethernet0
i L1    10.1.1.0 [115/20] via 10.2.1.1, Ethernet0
C       10.2.2.0 is directly connected, Ethernet1
i ia 192.168.6.0/24 [115/178] via 10 2.1.1, Ethernet0
i*L1 0.0.0.0/0 [115/10] via 10.2.1.1, Ethernet0
```

Figure 7.49   Prefix 192.168.6.0/24 is the only prefix external to Cisco1's area that is added to its route table.

7.4.7 Redistributing External Prefixes into IS-IS

External prefixes are carried within the IP External Reachability Information TLVs. They can have either internal or external metric types, as indicated by the I/E bit in the default metric field.[12] The usual definition of these metric types is the internal metric type points to destinations within the IS-IS domain and the external metric type points to destinations outside of the IS-IS domain. But in fact when you redistribute prefixes into IS-IS, you can set the metric type to internal. The only real difference is that IS-IS gives a higher preference to external routes with a metric type of internal than to external routes with a metric type of external. The metric type therefore gives you some flexibility in manipulating how IS-IS selects external routes, somewhat similarly to OSPF E1 and E2 metric types.

RFC 1195 specifies that IP External Reachability Information TLVs are carried only in L2 LSPs. This rule restricts you to locating externally connected routers only in the L2 area. Fortunately, RFC 2966 again comes to our rescue. By observing that there is no reason why IP External Reachability TLVs cannot also be carried in L1 LSPs (which IS-IS implementations have been doing for a number of years anyway), it standardizes the ability to redistribute external prefixes into an L1 area.

Figure 7.50 shows a simple redistribution policy configured on Cisco1 of the network in Figure 7.35. In this configuration, two static routes are defined and are redistributed into IS-IS with a metric of 30 and a metric type of internal. The prefixes are learned by Cisco2, which advertises them into the L2 area as it would any other prefixes learned in its L1 area. Because the route leaking policy of Figure 7.44 still exists at Juniper2, the prefixes are leaked into that router's L1 area (Figure 7.51).

```
router isis
 redistribute static ip metric 30 level-1 metric-type internal
 net 47.0002.0192.0168.2557.00
 is-type level-1
 !
ip route 192.168.120.0 255.255.255.0 Null0
ip route 192.168.220.0 255.255.255.0 Null0
```

Figure 7.50 A simple policy for redistributing static routes into an IS-IS L1 area.

```
eff@Juniper4> show route

inet.0: 20 destinations, 21 routes (19 active, 0 holddown, 1 hidden)
+ = Active Route, - = Last Active, * = Both

0.0.0.0/0          *[IS-IS/15] 1d 01:39:57, metric 10, tag 1
                    > to 192.168.2.2 via fxp1.0
10.1.1.0/24        *[IS-IS/18] 08:36:16, metric 30, tag 1
                    > to 192.168.2.2 via fxp1.0
10.2.1.0/24        *[IS-IS/18] 08:36:16, metric 40, tag 1
                    > to 192.168.2.2 via fxp1.0
```

---

[12] Although there is an I/E bit in the default metric field of the IP Internal Reachability Information TLV, it always indicates a metric type of internal.

```
10.2.2.0/24           *[IS-IS/18] 08:36:16, metric 50, tag 1
                       > to 192.168.2.2 via fxp1.0
192.168.2.0/24        *[Direct/0] 12w6d 12:22:14
                       > via fxp1.0
192.168.2.1/32        *[Local/0] 16w3d 14:49:24
                         Local via fxp1.0
192.168.3.0/24        *[IS-IS/15] 01:32:21, metric 20, tag 1
                       > to 192.168.2.2 via fxp1.0
192.168.6.0/24        *[Direct/0] 12w6d 12:22:14
                       > via fxp2.0
192.168.6.2/32        *[Local/0] 16w3d 14:49:24
                         Local via fxp2.0
192.168.120.0/24      *[IS-IS/18] 00:07:52, metric 70, tag 1
                       > to 192.168.2.2 via fxp1.0
192.168.220.0/24      *[IS-IS/18] 00:07:52, metric 70, tag 1
                       > to 192.168.2.2 via fxp1.0
```

Figure 7.51   The redistributed routes can be seen in Juniper1's route table.

The point of this and the previous section is that you can create, using route policies, the same kinds of inter-area behaviors in IS-IS as you can for OSPF. The difference is that whereas OSPF begins by leaking everything into nonbackbone areas and enables you to optionally configure restrictions to that behavior, IS-IS begins by leaking nothing into an L1 area and enables you to configure exceptions to that behavior.

7.4.8   Multiple Area IDs

Chapter 5 mentioned briefly that the Area Addresses TLV can carry up to 255 AIDs. Although a router would likely never need anywhere near 255 AIDs, in some cases 2 can be handy.

Suppose two IS-IS neighbors are each configured with AIDs 47.0001 and 47.0002. The routers still form at most one L1 adjacency and one L2 adjacency, but they recognize that they have two AIDs in common. If one of the AIDs is changed or disabled, the adjacency remains up because of the other AID. This proves useful because you can now perform area changes while the area is in operation. For example:

■ You can change the area's AID by bringing up adjacencies on the new AID before removing the old AID.

■ You can merge two areas by adding the AID of the first area to all routers on the second area, allowing the new adjacencies to form, and then removing the IAD of the second area.

■ You can split a single area by adding a new AID to the portion of the existing area that is to become the new area, waiting for adjacencies to form on the new AID, and then removing the old AID from the routers in the new area.

The use of this capability is not common, and so support for it varies from one router vendor to another depending usually on their customer demand for it.

7.4.9   IS-IS Virtual Links

ISO 10589 specifies the use of virtual links, also called virtual adjacencies, for repairing partitioned L1 areas. Briefly, this function works by electing two *L2 Partition Designated Intermediate Systems* in a partitioned L1 area, one in each partition. These L2 ISs then create an L1 repair path through the L2 subdomain (Figure 7.52) between *Virtual Network Entity Titles*. The L2 ISs then forward packets between the two partitions by encapsulating them in ISO 8473 NPDUs and forwarding them over the virtual link with the ISs' Virtual Network Entity Titles used as the source and destination addresses.

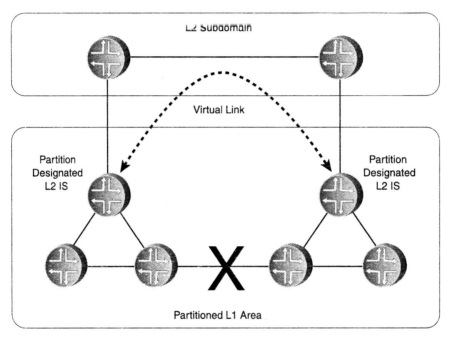

Figure 7.52   ISO 10589 specifies a procedure for creating a virtual link to repair a partitioned L1 area.

Interestingly, the application of virtual links in OSPF is to repair a partitioned backbone by creating a virtual link through a nonbackbone area. You cannot create an OSPF virtual link through the backbone area. IS-IS, conversely, uses virtual links to repair partitioned L1 areas by creating a virtual link through the L2 subdomain. No provision is made to use virtual links to repair L2 areas.

For the purposes of this book, the discussion of IS-IS virtual links is moot. No major router vendor implementing IS-IS for IP has provided the virtual link capability. The reason for this is that IS-IS is primarily found in carrier and ISP networks where there are usually either no L1 areas or where areas are so well designed that no need for a partition repair function is seen. Because no customers ask for it, router vendors find no reason to expend engineering resources developing it.

7.5   BGP and Area Design

You probably have heard that IS-IS—at least when used in support of IP—is seldom found outside carrier and Internet service provider networks. The IGP is the foundation of all but a few very large enterprise networks, and so the many features OSPF offers for multi-area topologies are attractive: The network is likely to have many low-powered, low-memory routers and low-bandwidth links, calling for area designs that can protect these routers and links from being overloaded.

However, the mission of carrier and ISP networks is not routing between points internal to the network but transit routing: receiving packets from outside the network and forwarding them as efficiently as possible to destinations also outside of the network. The fundamental protocol for these networks is BGP, which is designed to manage very large numbers of prefixes and complex routing policies.

The role of the IGP in such networks is much simpler than it is in enterprise networks. The IGP must provide the means for internal BGP to find the endpoints for the TCP sessions it operates over and the next-hop addresses of the BGP routes being advertised through the network (almost always, in both cases, the loopback interfaces of the internal routers). The IGP design should therefore be kept as simple as possible in keeping with the role it plays.

One way to keep the IGP design simple is to put the entire network in a single area. Carrier and ISP networks are, because of their mission, built with high-end routers and high-speed links.[13] The designers of carrier and ISP networks often choose IS-IS over OSPF both because of its relative simplicity and because of the characteristics of the protocol that make it scalable and stable within large areas. So although this chapter examines the details of multi-area IS-IS, the reality is that IS-IS-based IP networks are usually single area.

When designing single-area networks, whether with OSPF or IS-IS, one key piece of advice is offered: Build the single area with L2 adjacencies or as area 0. Then if you ever need to attach another area, adding it as an L1 area or a nonbackbone area is straightforward.

Review Questions

1. Why is a loop-free inter-area architecture required in OSPF and IS-IS networks?
2. What technological factors limit the size of an area?
3. What are some of the less-tangible factors to consider when determining the size of an area?
4. What is a stub area? Why are ASBRs illegal in a stub area?
5. How do routers indicate to each other that they are in a stub area?
6. Can area 0 be a stub area?

[13] Core links in carrier networks are seldom below DS-3 or OC-3, and range up to OC-192. As of this writing, the high end of core links is moving toward OC-768.

7. What is the difference between a stub area and a totally stubby area?

8. How many type 3 LSAs are in the database of a totally stubby area?

9. What is an NSSA? What LSA type is unique to an NSSA, and what does it do?

10. When is the N/P bit in the Options field used as an N bit, and when is it used as a P bit?

11. What does the N bit indicate?

12. What does the P bit indicate?

13. Why should an ABR use a type 7 LSA rather than a type 3 LSA to advertise a default route into an NSSA?

14. Why can summary routes be originated by only ABRs and ASBRs?

15. What is a virtual link? What are its applications?

16. Can a virtual link transit multiple areas?

17. Can a virtual link transit area 0?

18. How does a router indicate that it has one or more fully adjacent virtual links?

19. Is it possible to have an L2 adjacency between the same two IS-IS routers when their AIDs match?

20. Is it possible to have both an L1 adjacency between the same two IS-IS routers when their AIDs differ?

21. Is it possible to have both an L1 and an L2 adjacency between the same two IS-IS routers, on the same link?

22. Why is an IS-IS L1 area considered "totally stubby" by default?

23. What is the purpose of the ATT bit?

24. What is the primary advantage of prefix summarization? What is its primary disadvantage?

25. What is the purpose of the I/E bit associated with the IS-IS metric field?

26. What is the purpose of the U/D bit?

27. Why might a prefix redistributed into an IS-IS domain be given an "internal" metric?

CHAPTER 8

Scaling

Scalable may well be one of the most overused words in the network designer's lexicon. It applies to protocols, to software, to operating systems, to hardware architecture, and to networks. Scalable means, simply enough, the ability of the relevant entity (select one from the list just given) to get much bigger than it presently is without reducing performance, stability, or accuracy; making your customers angry; or getting you fired.

You have already encountered in this book a number of features that make OSPF and IS-IS scalable from the smallest to the largest networks. The most prominent feature for both protocols is areas. By dividing a network into multiple areas, you can control in each area the scope of flooding, the size of the link state database, and the complexity of the SPF calculations. By bounding these three fundamental link state functions, you constrain the demand OSPF and IS-IS put on router memory, router processing cycles, and link bandwidth, respectively.

You have also encountered features or extensions that can increase scalability, such as configurable refresh timers and increased metric sizes. This chapter delves further into features and extensions that can increase the scalability of the protocols.

8.1 SPF Enhancements

Chapter 2 gave you an idea of how an SPF algorithm works. And while that overview is enough to give you an understanding of the SPF algorithm, it is too simplistic for a practical link state protocol implementation. In fact, even if you follow the OSPF and IS-IS standards, you will get an implementation that is workable (if naïve) for small networks, but that lacks the stability, scalability, and accuracy necessary to survive in large-scale networks. For router vendors wanting to market to the largest network operators, sophisticated OSPF and IS-IS implementations are essential. Demonstrably robust implementations are a competitive advantage, and as a result, many of the enhancements to the SPF algorithm—and in fact the

SPF algorithm itself—can be closely guarded corporate secrets. Therefore, it is impossible to detail many vendor-specific enhancements, but the general areas of enhancement can be examined.

8.1.1   Equal-Cost Multipath

The basic Dijkstra calculation described in Chapter 2 uses the following steps:

1. The router adds itself to the tree database as the root of the tree. It shows itself as its own neighbor, with a cost of 0.

2. All entries in the link state database describing links from the root to its neighbors are added to the candidate database.

3. The cost from the root to each node in the candidate database is calculated. The link in the candidate database with the lowest cost is moved to the tree database, along with the cost from the root. If two or more links are an equally low cost from the root, choose one. If any entries are left in the candidate database with a link to the neighbor just moved to the tree, those entries are deleted from the candidate database.

4. The router ID of the neighbor on the link just added to the tree is examined. Entries originated by that neighbor are added to the candidate database, except for entries in which the ID of the neighbor is already in the tree database.

5. If entries remain in the candidate database, return to Step 3. If the candidate database is empty, terminate the calculation. At this time, every router in the network should be represented as a neighbor on one of the links in the tree database, and every router should be represented just once.

However, there is an inefficiency in Step 3. Namely, "If two or more links are an equally low cost from the root, choose one. *If any entries are left in the candidate database with a link to the neighbor just moved to the tree, those entries are deleted from the candidate database.*" An example is needed to understand why this is an inefficiency. Figure 8.1 shows a small network and its link state database. What is important about this network is that unlike the network in Figure 2.15 that was used for the SPF example in that chapter, all of the links in this network have the same cost. This example will show the SPF calculation at R1.

Steps 1 and 2 are shown in Figure 8.2. R1 adds itself to the tree database, the links to its neighbors are added to the candidate database, and the costs from the root to the destination nodes are calculated.

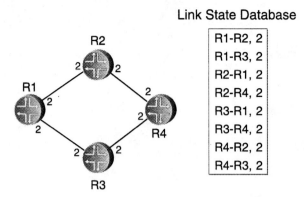

Figure 8.1   All links in this network have a cost of 2.

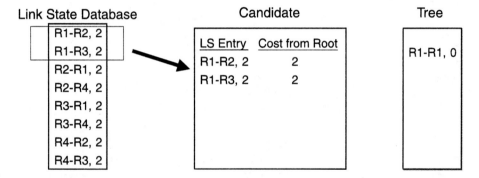

Figure 8.2   The links from R1 to its neighbors are added to the candidate database.

Step 3 is performed in Figure 8.3. The costs to the root are equal, so one of the entries is randomly chosen and moved from the candidate database to the tree database. The inefficiency in Step 3 will not be apparent until the end of the SPF calculation.

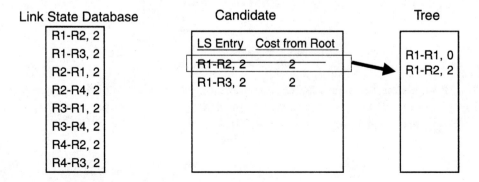

Figure 8.3   The link from R1 to R2 is moved to the tree database.

Step 4 is performed in Figure 8.4. R2 was added to the tree database, so all the links from R2 to its neighbors are examined in the link state database. R1 is already in the tree database, so only the link from R2 to R4 is added to the candidate database. The cost from the root to R4 is 4.

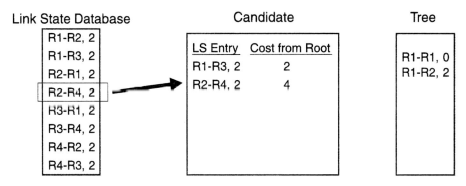

Figure 8.4   The link from R2 to R4 is added to the candidate database.

There are entries remaining in the candidate database, so, as Step 5 prescribes, Figure 8.5 shows a return to Step 3. The cost to root associated with the R1-R3 link is the lowest, so that link is moved from the candidate database to the tree database.

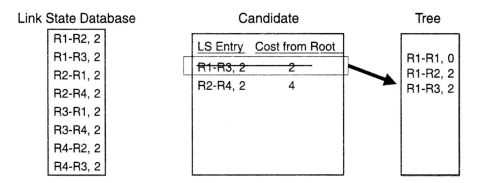

Figure 8.5   The R1-R3 link is moved to the tree database.

With R3 added to the database, the links to its neighbors are examined in the link state database. R1 is already in the tree database, so only the R3-R4 link is added to the candidate database in Figure 8.6. The cost from the root to R4 is 4.

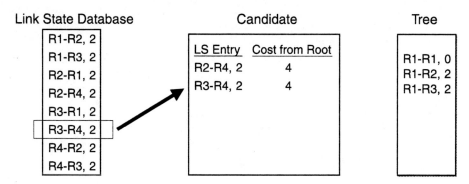

Figure 8.6 The R3-R4 link is added to the candidate database.

In Figure 8.7, the cost from the root of both entries in the candidate database is 4, so one (R2-R4) is randomly chosen and moved to the tree database.

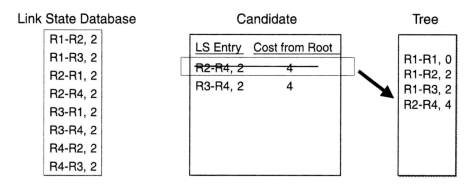

Figure 8.7 The R2-R4 link is moved to the tree database.

In Figure 8.8, the link state database is examined for R4's links to its neighbors: There are two, R4-R2 and R4-R3. However, both R2 and R3 are already in the tree database, so there are no new entries to add to the candidate database. But there is still an entry in the candidate database, and Step 5 says the SPF calculation stops only when the candidate database is empty. This is the reason for the part of Step 3 that says, "If any entries are left in the candidate database with a link to the neighbor just moved to the tree, those entries are deleted from the candidate database." If the "leftover" entries in the candidate database are not removed, the SPF calculation cannot end.

But the inefficiency of this rule also reveals itself at this point. If multiple equal-cost paths exist, choosing only one of the paths means all traffic will be routed on that path, possibly congesting it, while other equally good paths are ignored. We can modify Step 3 so that if there are multiple links in the candidate database to the same node and equally low cost, all the links can be moved from the candidate database to the tree database. In Figure 8.9, moving the R3-R4 link to the tree database empties the candidate database so that the SPF can stop. An enhancement to the router's forwarding processes can then be made that takes advantage of these multiple equal-cost paths by spreading traffic across all of them. This is *equal-cost multipath* (ECMP), or *load balancing*.[1]

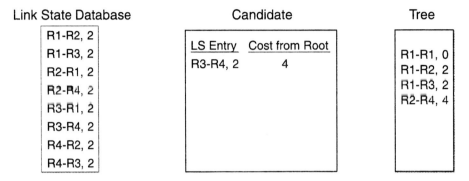

Figure 8.8 The R3-R4 link remains on the candidate database and must be removed before the SPF calculation can end.

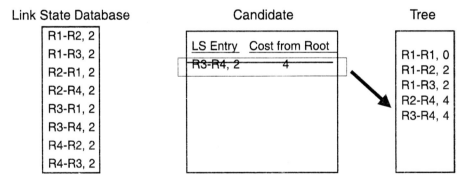

Figure 8.9 By moving the R3-R4 link to the tree database rather than just deleting it from the candidate database, an SPF tree is created in which two equal-cost paths from R1 to R4 exist.

Figure 8.10 shows one situation in which ECMP can apply. In this topology, the next hop from Router A to subnet 10.1.1.0 is Router B. But there are three links to Router B, each with a cost of 50. Router A can balance the traffic going to 10.1.1.0—and any other destination for which Router B is the next hop—across the three links.

---

[1] *Load balancing* is a more generic term that can also refer to data processing, such as spreading traffic across multiple Web servers. ECMP is more specific to the forwarding of network traffic.

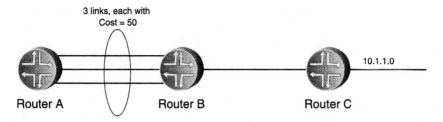

Figure 8.10 ECMP allows Router A to utilize all three links to Router B for traffic going to subnet 10.1.1.0.

Figure 8.11 shows another application of ECMP. Here, Router A has two next hops—Router B and Router C—to subnet 10.2.2.0. Routes to the destination through either next hop have the same cost because all four of the links shown have the same cost. So in this case, Router A can select both next hops and balance the traffic to 10.2.2.0—and any other traffic to destinations that pass through Router D—between Routers B and C.

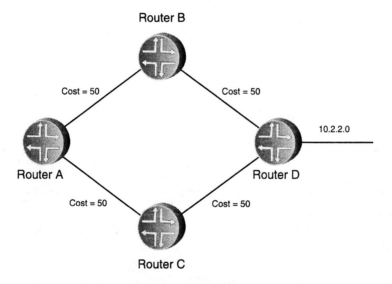

Figure 8.11 ECMP allows Router A to use two equal-cost routes to subnet 10.2.2.0.

Given multiple equal-cost paths—either to the same next-hop router as in Figure 8.10 or through separate next-hop routers as in Figure 8.11—a router can balance traffic across them in several ways. One approach is *per-packet* load balancing, in which the router forwards packets round-robin or randomly over each path as shown in Figure 8.12. The problem with this approach is that different links, although of equal cost, might not be of equal delay. Link propagation, router latency and buffering, and link MTUs requiring fragmentation might differ from one path to another. As a result, packets can become reordered at the receiving end. This can cause problems for TCP, which when it sees out-of-sequence packets can request retransmits. The result is reduced performance and wasted bandwidth.

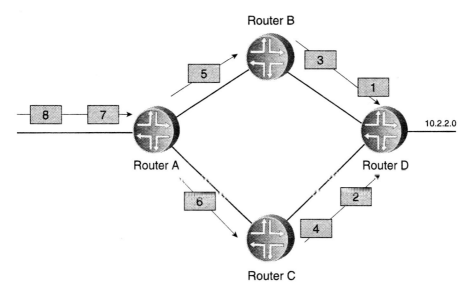

Figure 8.12   Per-packet load balancing distributes packets individually over equal-cost paths.

A better approach is *per-destination* load balancing, in which packets are distributed across multiple paths by destination, as shown in Figure 8.13. In this example, Router A knows it has two equal-cost paths to the destinations 10.1.1.0 and 10.2.2.0. It chooses Router B as the next hop for the route to 10.1.1.0, and Router C for the route to 10.2.2.0. As Router A discovers more routes to destinations reachable through Router D, it continues to alternately assign Router B and Router C as next hops. The functional difference is that per-packet load balancing assigns all ECMP next hops to each route, whereas per-destination load balancing selects, either round-robin or randomly, one next hop from the set of ECMP next hops for each route.

Although per-destination load balancing is an improvement over per-packet, it is still not very good. If substantially more packets are sent to one destination than to another, the overall bandwidth utilization will be uneven. For example, suppose Router E in Figure 8.14 is providing Internet access. When it advertises BGP routes to the other routers in the figure, the routes are given a next-hop address of 10.255.0.1, Router E's loopback address. This is common practice; Router E is advertising that it is the next hop for any Internet destinations. When Router A receives these BGP advertisements, it does a lookup of 10.255.0.1 in its IGP routes to find out how to reach the BGP next hop. If the router is performing per-destination load balancing, it selects either Router B or Router C as the "next hop to the next hop"—that is, the IGP next hop to the BGP next hop. The potential problem is that if traffic passing through Router A to the Internet is relatively heavy compared to other traffic passing through Router A to Router D, the loading across the equal cost paths can be severely unbalanced.

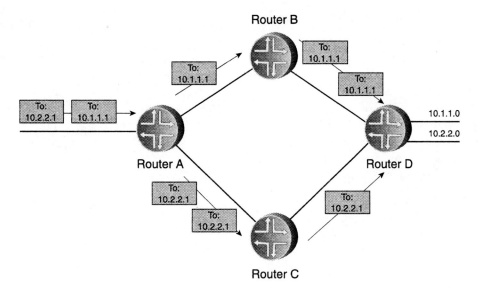

Figure 8.13   Per-destination load balancing distributes next hops or outgoing interfaces among multiple equal-cost routes.

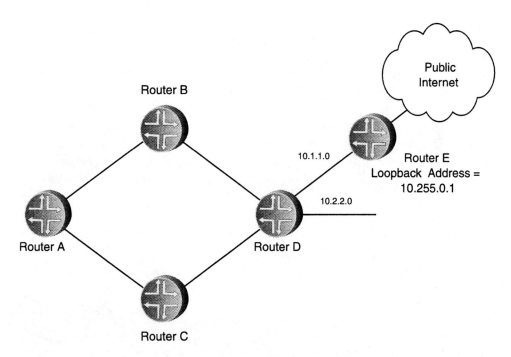

Figure 8.14   Per-destination load balancing might be inefficient in this topology.

Per-flow load balancing improves the traffic distribution by identifying individual traffic flows and forwarding all packets belonging to the flow to the same next hop or out the same interface. At a minimum, a flow might be defined as all packets with the same source and destination addresses. However, flows can be made more granular by defining a flow not only by source and destination address but also by protocol number, source and destination port,[2] and perhaps ToS or DSCP (differentiated services code point) values. When a packet is to be forwarded, the values of these fields become the input to a hashing algorithm. (Router vendors define their own hashing algorithms.) The packet is then associated with a flow based on the resulting hash value, and all packets belonging to the same flow are forwarded to the same next hop.

8.1.2   Pseudonodes and ECMP

If some but not all of the links in an ECMP group are broadcast links, a subtle problem can arise from simplistic SPF implementations. Another example SPF run will help you understand the problem.

The physical topology in Figure 8.15 shows two routers, R1 and R2, interconnected with both a point-to-point link and an Ethernet link. The outgoing cost on both of R1's interfaces is 2, so the two links comprise equal cost paths, and load balancing can be performed between R1 and R2. The logical topology shows that the Ethernet link is represented as a pseudonode, which is labeled in this example as P3. Recall from the discussion of pseudonode basics in Section 4.4 that the cost from a pseudonode to any of its attached routers is 0, so that the pseudonode does not affect the transit cost of the broadcast link. Figure 8.16 shows the start of the SPF calculation at R1 for this small network, in which R1 installs itself in the tree database as the root and then adds all links to its neighbors to the candidate database.

The two links added to the candidate database are of equal cost (2) to the root, so as in previous examples, one is chosen at random and added to the tree database (Figure 8.17). In this case, the chosen link is R1-R2. Although not yet apparent, this random choice will cause a problem with ECMP.

---

[2] When source and destination ports are included in the flow identification, the flow is called a *microflow*. Implementations that load balance by microflow are more challenging to create because they require the router to look further into the packet than just the IP header.

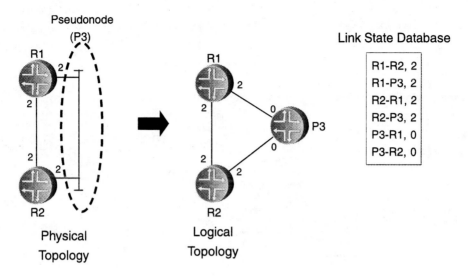

Figure 8.15   There are two equal-cost paths between R1 and R2, one of which is point-to-point and one of which is broadcast.

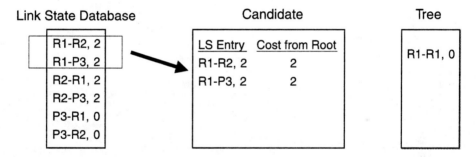

Figure 8.16   R1 installs itself as root and adds the links to its neighbors to the candidate database.

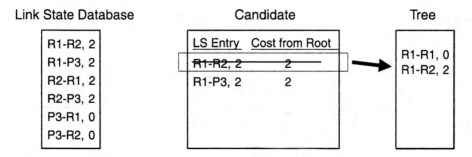

Figure 8.17   The R1-R2 and R1-P3 links are of equal cost from the root, so one is randomly chosen to move to the tree database.

Because a link to R2 was added to the tree, the links to R2's neighbors are examined in the link state database (Figure 8.18). There are two, R2-R1 and R2-P3. R1 is already in the tree database, so only the R2-P3 link is added to the candidate database.

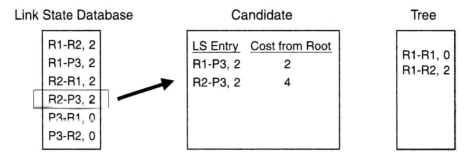

Figure 8.18   A link to R2 was added to the tree database in the last step, so the R2-P3 link is added to the candidate database.

In Figure 8.19, R1-P3 has the lowest cost from the root and so is moved to the tree database. Because there is now a path to P3 in the tree database, the higher-cost R2-P3 link is deleted from the candidate database.

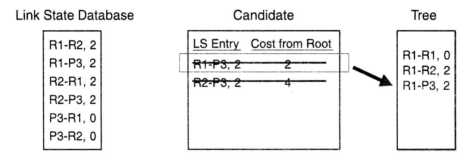

Figure 8.19   The lower-cost R1-P3 link is moved to the tree database and the higher-cost R2-P3 link is deleted from the candidate database.

With P3 added to the tree, its links to its neighbors are examined in the link state database. There are two, P3-R1 and P3-R2. But both R1 and R2 are already on the tree, so neither of these links is moved to the candidate database. At this point, the candidate database is empty, so the SPF calculation stops. And now, in Figure 8.20, we can look at the resulting tree and see the ECMP problem. R1 has branches to R2 and to P3, each at cost of 2, but the tree does not include a branch from P3 to R2. Therefore, R1 forwards all traffic to R2 across the point-to-point link and none across the Ethernet link. No load balancing can take place.

As mentioned, the problem actually arose with the random selection in Figure 8.17 of the R1-R2 link from the candidate database. So let's back up to that step and select the other link instead. Figure 8.21 shows the candidate database in the same state as in Figure 8.17, but now R1-P3 is selected and moved to the tree database instead of R1-R2.

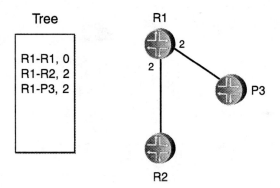

Figure 8.20   The resulting tree does not allow load balancing across the two equal-cost paths because it does not include a branch from P3 to R2.

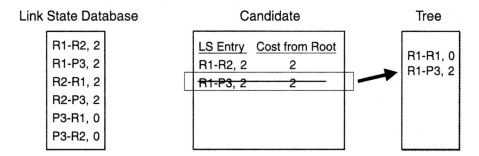

Figure 8.21   Returning to the point in the SPF calculation where either R1-R2 or R1-P3 is randomly selected for the tree database, R1-P3 is now chosen instead of R1-R2 as in Figure 8.17.

Continuing on with the SPF calculation, because a link to P3 was added to the tree, the links to P3's neighbors are examined in the link state database. R1 is already on the tree, so only P3-R2 is added to the candidate database (Figure 8.22).

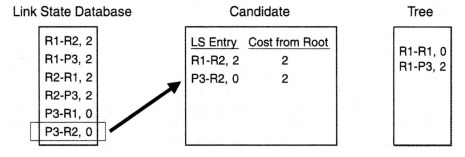

Figure 8.22   The P3-R2 link is added to the candidate database.

Now, in Figure 8.23, the candidate database contains two equal-cost entries for links to R2. Using the modification to the SPF algorithm described in Section 8.1.1 to accommodate ECMP, rather than randomly selecting one and discarding the other, both are moved to the tree database. No links remain in the link state database to nodes that are not already on the tree, and the candidate database is now empty, so SPF stops.

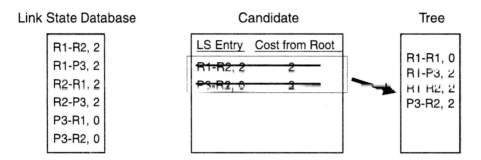

Figure 8.23   R1-R2 and P3-R2 are equal-cost links to the same node, so they are both moved to the tree database.

Figure 8.24 shows the resulting tree. Both equal-cost paths are now represented, and R1 can load balance traffic to R2. The significant step that prevented disruption of ECMP is that in Figure 8.21 the link to the pseudonode was selected for the tree database *before* the link to R2. Therefore, to ensure that ECMP works correctly when the ECMP group consists of a mixture of point-to-point and broadcast links, the following simple rule is added to the SPF procedure:

> If there are multiple entries in the candidate database with equally low cost, and if at least one link is to a pseudonode and at least one link is to a router, always select the link to the pseudonode first rather than randomly selecting among the links.

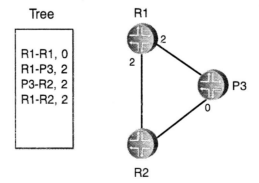

Figure 8.24   The resulting tree correctly accounts for the two equal-cost paths, and so allows load balancing.

Specific OSPF or IS-IS implementations might or might not include this modification. So if load balancing is a part of your network design, be sure to verify with your vendor that their SPF routine includes this rule.

8.1.3   *Incremental SPF Calculations*

It is not difficult to find network engineers and operators who think distance vector protocols are preferable over link state for all but the largest networks. Ask them why, and their answer is "because the SPF calculations are complex and CPU intensive, and they will hurt my routers' performance." These folks are stuck in the nineties. Concern over the price in router resources needed to pay for SPF was partially justified a decade or so ago, but there is no longer reason to fear SPF (in relation to distance vector protocols, at least). Several factors contribute to this change in attitude:

- Increased router performance and memory capacity
- Increased sophistication of physical and logical router architectures
- Increased base of experience designing and operating large, complex networks
- Increased base of vendor experience designing sophisticated SPF processes

One of the improvements several router vendors have incorporated into their SPF procedures is Incremental SPF (iSPF). To understand iSPF, consider the network shown in Figure 8.25. Using the link costs given in the illustration, you can determine with little trouble that R1 will calculate the shortest-path tree shown in Figure 8.26.

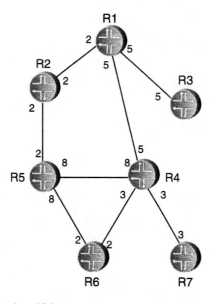

Figure 8.25   *An example network and link costs.*

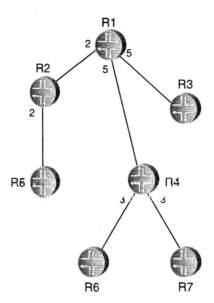

Figure 8.26   The shortest-path tree calculated by R1.

Now consider a change to the network topology. Figure 8.27 shows the addition of a new node, R8. The change to the tree to account for the new node is shown in Figure 8.28. With the SPF procedures as you have seen them so far, the addition of the new node requires the reflooding of LSAs or LSPs and a recalculation of SPF by all routers in the area. But a cursory look at the new topology shows that most of the tree has not changed; the addition of R8 involves the simple addition of a branch from R5.

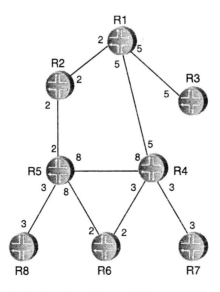

Figure 8.27   Node R8 is added to the topology of Figure 8.25.

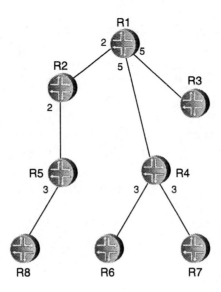

Figure 8.28   The new shortest-path tree from R1 shows the added router R8.

Consider another topological change, shown in Figure 8.29. Here, the link between R4 and R5 has failed or been disabled. Again, our understanding of SPF so far requires that this information be flooded throughout the area and that all nodes rerun SPF. But this link is not a part of the shortest-path tree shown in Figure 8.26, so rerunning SPF results in a tree that looks exactly the same as it did before the link failure.

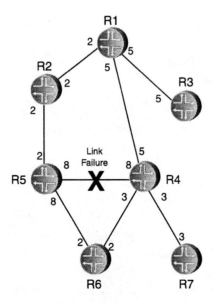

Figure 8.29   Failure of the R4-R5 link does not change the shortest-path tree, because it was not a branch of the tree to begin with.

These two topological changes are the basis for iSPF. In the first example, in which a router with a single link to the network was added (that is, a *stub router*), there are no alternative links to consider and so no need to attempt to calculate a shortest path. There is only one path to the new node. Therefore, a full SPF run is unnecessary for the routers that were already on the tree; they only need to add the new branch from R5 to R8.

In the second example, the failure of the link has no affect whatsoever on the shortest-path tree and so again there is no need for the nodes in the area to rerun SPF. Only a reduction in the metrics associated with the R4-R5 link would necessitate a full SPF run.

iSPF takes into consideration topological changes, such as the two shown in this section, and performs SPF only to the extent necessary to allow for the changes. In the first case, a simple distance vector–like addition to the tree is required; in the second case, no action at all is required. Experience has shown that iSPF provides the greatest benefit in cases of the first example, when stub routers are added to or removed from the topology.

8.1.4   *Partial Route Calculations*

The topology changes described in the previous section are by no means unusual in an IGP-routed topology, so it is easy to understand how the changes to the basic SPF procedure incorporated by iSPF can improve efficiency. Another network change, as common as those of the previous section, is the addition, deletion, or metric change of IP addresses. Reviewing the basic SPF procedure, you can see that the only addresses used in the computation of the shortest-path tree are the RIDs. Although recording the distance and direction of IP prefixes from each router is the ultimate goal of any routing protocol, the prefixes themselves have no bearing on an SPF calculation; after the location and cost of each node on the shortest-path tree are determined, it should be a simple matter to record what prefixes are attached to or advertised by what node.

This is the basis of *Partial Route Calculations* (PRC). When a node advertises the addition, deletion, or metric change of an IP prefix, rather than unnecessarily rerunning the SPF calculation the other nodes on the tree simply record the change. Although a full SPF run in even large networks is very fast—a high-performance router should be able to process 500 to 1000 nodes in 50 to 100ms—PRC is substantially faster, ranging from 0.5 to 10ms depending on the number of prefixes to be scanned.

PRC's increased efficiency is more substantial in IS-IS than in OSPFv2 because of the way each protocol advertises IP prefixes. IS-IS advertises all IP prefixes in IP Reachability TLVs, whereas node information necessary for SPF calculations is advertised in IS Neighbors or IS Reachability TLVs. This clear separation of prefix information from topology information makes PRC easily applicable to any IP address change.

OSPFv2, on the other hand, incorporates IP address semantics into type 1 and type 2 LSAs. That is, routers or pseudonodes advertise both topological information and their attached IP addresses in the same LSAs. So for example, if an IP address attached to an OSPFv2 router changes, the router must originate a type 1 LSA to advertise the change. However, because node information is also carried in type 1 LSAs, flooding the LSA triggers a full SPF calculation in all routers in an area—even though the address change is irrelevant to the node topology. As a result, only type 3, 4, 5, and 7 LSAs—whose only purpose is to advertise prefix information—trigger a PRC in OSPFv2.

The applicability of PRC to all IP prefixes in an IS-IS domain, not just prefixes external to an area as in OSPFv2, is a significant contributing factor to the better scaling properties of IS-IS in a single area. You will see in Chapter 12 that OSPFv3 improves its scaling by removing addressing semantics from its Router and Network LSAs and using a new type of LSA to advertise attached prefixes.

8.1.5 SPF Delay

Although the kinds of network events that trigger iSPF and PRC are common, they are not necessarily frequent. In large networks, the kinds of address changes that trigger PRC happen only a few times a day, and the kinds of topological changes that trigger iSPF might happen only a few times a week. Moreover, a full SPF run in even a very large network takes only tens of milliseconds. Given these facts, the value of iSPF and PRC becomes evident mainly when abnormal things happen. But in a large area, LSAs or LSPs will flood regularly because of the random expiration of refresh timers around the network, requiring regular SPF runs. And when bad things happen, routers can become inundated with changing LSA/LSPs. If each LSA/LSP triggers a full or incremental SPF run, and if they are arriving fast and furious, SPF can begin eating up the majority of CPU cycles. Scheduler slips result, important tasks become delayed or completely missed, and the router can become seriously destabilized.

The challenge in large-scale networks, then, is to quickly react to network changes while at the same time not allowing SPF calculations to dominate the route processors. This is the goal of *SPF delay*, also called *SPF holddown* or *SPF throttling*. Rather than kick off an SPF calculation every time a new LSA/LSP arrives, SPF delay forces the router to wait a bit between SPF runs. If a large number of LSA/LSPs are being flooded, a delay between SPF runs means that more LSA/LSPs are added to the link state database during the holddown period. Efficiency is then increased because when the holddown period expires and SPF is run, more network changes are included in a single calculation.

SPF delay arguably adds another small efficiency. When an SPF calculation is being run, it is necessary to "freeze" the link state database so that new LSA/LSPs are not added.[3] The reason for this is obvious: Changing the link state database in the middle of an SPF calculation could corrupt the results. So, all LSA/LSPs that arrive during a running SPF calculation must be buffered until the calculation ends, and only then added to the link state database (likely triggering another SPF run). SPF delay, by reducing the overall frequency of SPF runs, reduces the frequency that LSA/LSPs must be buffered.

Of course, the price you pay for delaying an SPF calculation is an increased network convergence time. So, the challenge when determining a delay interval is to make it long enough that a heavy surge of LSA/LSPs does not destabilize the router while still keeping it short enough that convergence is not hurt significantly. Even better would be to have normal "fast" SPF calculations when conditions in the network are normal, and delayed SPF calculations when the network is unstable. Several vendors do offer such adaptive SPF timers.

---

[3] A more elegant approach than freezing the database is to lock just the LSPs that are being processed.

Juniper Networks uses a delay scheme in which the normal period between SPF runs is short. This period is 200ms by default, meaning an SPF run cannot take place any sooner than 200ms after the last run. The period is configurable with the **spf-delay** command to between 50 and 1000ms; the command can be used with both OSPF and IS-IS, and applies to both full and partial SPF calculations. If three SPF runs are triggered in quick succession, indicating instability in the network, the delay period is automatically changed to 5 seconds. This "slow mode" period is not configurable. The routers remain in this "slow mode" until 20 seconds have passed since the last SPF run—indicating that the network has stabilized— and then switches back to "fast mode."

Cisco Systems originally had a similar linear fast/slow algorithm (configured for OSPF with the command **timers spf**). But more recently, Cisco has taken a different approach to adaptive SPF delays by using an *exponential backoff* algorithm. *Initial delay*, *delay increment*, and *maximum delay* periods[4] are configured. The router waits the initial delay period before first running SPF. After the first run, the delay is increased by doubling the delay increment every time SPF runs. So for example, if the initial delay is 100ms and the delay increment is 1000ms, the router delays the first SPF run by 100ms, the second by 1000ms, the third by 2000ms, the fourth by 4000ms, and so on. The maximum delay value specifies in seconds the largest value to which the delay can be incremented—an obvious necessity to prevent an unstable network from causing the SPF delay to increase so much that SPF does not run at all. When SPF has not run for twice the time specified by the maximum delay period, the router switches back to "fast" mode in which the initial delay period is used.

These three timers are specified for OSPF with the IOS command **timers throttle spf** and for full IS-IS SPF with the command **spf-interval**. Partial SPF for IS-IS is configured separately with the IOS command **prc-interval**.

8.2   Flooding Enhancements

Section 8.1.5 refers several times to network instabilities causing a flood of LSA/LSPs, but the focus is on enhancing SPF so that the router's processor is not overwhelmed during unusually busy periods. In other words, the focus is on the router protecting itself. But as in any community, self-protection becomes less of an issue if all the members of the community behave themselves and watch out for their neighbors. In the case of link state protocols, enhancing the flooding mechanism to reduce the chance that a router will overwhelm a neighbor or an area with LSA/LSPs makes a router a better neighbor.

As with SPF enhancements, most flooding enhancements are not a part of the open protocol specifications. (IS-IS mesh groups are the exception.) They have been developed by vendors in an effort to make their OSPF and IS-IS implementations scalable to large networks. What enhancements are developed by a given vendor likely depend on the specific kinds of networks the vendor's routers must accommodate and the features requested by the vendor's customers.

---

[4] The actual IOS command terms for these three values varies depending on whether you are configuring exponential backoff for OSPF or IS-IS, but their function is the same.

8.2.1   Transmit Pacing

Increasing the interval between subsequent LSA/LSP transmissions is variously called delay, pacing, or throttling. Whatever you want to call it, delaying the transmission of LSA/LSPs prevents a router from dominating a link or overwhelming a neighbor. There are two aspects to delaying LSA/LSP transmission: delaying self-originated LSA/LSPs, and delaying LSA/LSPs forwarded through the router during the flooding process.

To understand how delaying can help make flooding more efficient, consider first a naïve implementation that refreshes at some set interval (every 30 minutes for OSPF, every 20 minutes for IS-IS). Whenever the refresh timer expires, the link state database is scanned and all of its self-originated LSAs or LSPs are flooded. This single-timer refresh interval results in a periodic, heavy flooding interspersed by equal periods of complete quiet, as illustrated in Figure 8.30(a). Implementing individual refresh timers for each LSA/LSP spreads the refresh load out randomly, as shown in Figure 8.30(b), so that neighbors are not hit with a large number of LSA/LSPs all at once.

However, individualizing the refresh timers is not as efficient as it could be, especially for OSPF where Update packets might carry a single or a very few LSAs. If, instead of immediately transmitting an LSA when its refresh timer expires, the transmission is delayed for some period, additional refresh timers are more likely to expire during the waiting period and more LSAs can be carried in a single Update. The "grouping" effect of this delay is shown in Figure 8.30(c).

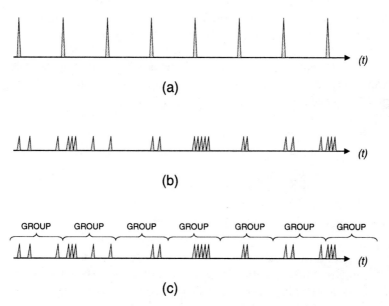

Figure 8.30   A single refresh timer for the entire link state database results in possibly heavy floods every refresh interval (a), whereas separate refresh timers for each database entity results in smaller, more random floods (b). Adding a delay to the individual refresh timers improves efficiency by grouping several entities into one flood (c).

Cisco's IOS uses a default LSA pacing timer of 4 minutes; the timer can be changed to between 10 seconds and 1800 seconds (30 minutes) with the command **timers pacing lsa-group**[5] This pacing applies not only to LSA refreshing but also to aging and checksumming. If the link state database is very large, on the order of thousands of LSAs, the default pacing delay might cause spikes in the flooding similar to those in Figure 8.30(a); reducing the pacing delay can smooth out the flooding pattern.

Delaying the transmission of self-originated LSA/LSPs has its greatest benefit when there is instability local to the router—most usually the flapping of a connected link. Rather than flooding a new LSA/LSP every time the link changes state, a delay period might span several state changes, thereby dampening the impact the flapping has on flooding activity. Both OSPF and IS-IS standards do specify delays that help in this regard. OSPF specifies two architectural constants: New instances of a given LSA cannot be generated more frequently than 5 seconds (MinLSInterval), and new instances of a given LSA cannot be received more frequently than 1 second (MinLSArrival). IS-IS specifies similar delays, although ISO 10589 suggests values for the delays rather than making them constants: 30 seconds between the generation of new LSPs (minimumLSPGenerationInterval), and 5 seconds between transmissions of LSPs from the same originator (minimumLSPTransmissionInterval). Vendor implementations often enhance these basic delays to scale to different network sizes.

Cisco's IOS uses the same exponential backoff mechanism described in Section 8.1.5 to throttle the transmission of self-originated LSPs: Using the command **lsp-gen-interval**, you can specify initial delay, delay increment, and maximum delay periods. As described, the initial delay specifies the time to wait, in milliseconds, after the first generation of a new LSP before transmitting it. The delay increment is the multiplier used to exponentially increase the delay between subsequent transmissions, in milliseconds. The interval between the first and second transmission is the delay increment value, and then the interval between subsequent transmissions is twice the interval of the previous transmission: IncrementValue, 2*IncrementValue, 4*IncrementValue, 8*IncrementValue, and so on, until the maximum delay value, specified in seconds, is reached. The delay between subsequent transmissions then remains at the maximum delay. If no new LSPs are generated for twice the maximum delay value, at that point the exponential backoff mechanism is reset.

Juniper's JUNOS does not use an exponential backoff, nor does it provide configurable options for the LSP delay. Instead, it uses a "fast mode" and "slow mode" scheme similar to that described for its SPF delay in Section 8.1.5. The normal "fast mode" transmission delay of self-originated LSPs is 20ms. If three LSPs are generated in quick succession, IS-IS switches to "slow mode" and delays each transmission by 10 seconds until the network stabilizes.

The other aspect of transmission pacing is the control of flooding of LSA/LSPs originated by other routers. In times of instability, hundreds or thousands of LSA/LSPs can be flooded within an area; a router must be able to pace the transmission of OSPF Updates or IS-IS LSPs to limit the rate its neighbors receive these messages.

IOS uses the command **timers pacing flood** to configure the minimum interval, in milliseconds, between transmitted OSPF Update packets. The default interval is 33ms and can

---

[5] Older versions of IOS use the command **timers lsa-group-pacing**.

be changed in the range of 5 to 100ms. JUNOS uses a hard-coded delay interval that cannot be changed.

For IS-IS, IOS uses the command **isis lsp-interval** to specify the pacing of LSP transmissions. The default is again 33ms. JUNOS uses the very similar command, **lsp-interval**, to change its default interval of 100ms.

Simple arithmetic shows that an interval of 100ms, for example, means that Updates or LSPs cannot be transmitted any faster than one every .1 seconds, or a maximum transmission rate of 10 packets per second; 50ms means a maximum rate of 20 packets per second, and so on.

In all cases, these commands are configured per interface so that the change from the default is applied to specific neighbors. It must be noted that in the great majority of cases, the default (or hard-coded) transmission interval is sufficient. There are better ways to protect a low-powered neighbor from the impact of large-scale flooding, such as good OSPF area design and well-designed packet queues.

8.2.2 Retransmit Pacing

Yet another aspect of controlling flooding is the pacing of LSA/LSP retransmits. Recall from the discussion in Chapter 5 that flooding must be reliable, and so LSA/LSPs that are not acknowledged either implicitly or explicitly within a specified time are retransmitted. OSPF does this by placing a copy of a transmitted LSA on a Retransmit List and setting a retransmit timer (normally 5 seconds). If the LSA is acknowledged, it is removed from the Retransmit List. If the retransmit timer expires, a copy of the LSA is retransmitted and the retransmit timer is restarted.

The IS-IS retransmission process for point-to-point and broadcast links is different. On point-to-point links, the Send Routing Message (SRM) flag of a transmitted LSP is not cleared until the LSP is explicitly acknowledged with a PSNP. So if the SRM for that link is still set the next time the LS database is scanned (which happens every 5 seconds or minimumLSP-TransmissionInterval), the LSP is retransmitted. On broadcast links, transmitted LSPs are always implicitly acknowledged by CSNPs, transmitted by the DIS every 10 seconds. If a router does not see the instance of an LSP that it transmitted in the next received CSNP, it retransmits the LSP.

The problem here is that if flooding is heavy, a low-powered router might be so busy processing received LSA/LSPs that it does not acknowledge their receipt promptly, causing its neighbors to retransmit. If the router is already busy, the retransmissions can just make matters worse. You can use the IOS command **ip ospf retransmit-interval** or the JUNOS command **retransmit-interval** to change the default OSPF retransmission interval from 5 seconds to an interval in the range of 1 to 65,535 seconds; both commands are applied per interface.

IOS can also change the default IS-IS retransmission interval of 5 seconds on point-to-point links using the command **isis retransmit-interval**. The interval you can set with this command ranges from 0 to 65,535 seconds. Although this command changes the interval between scans of the database for any SRM flags set for the interface, there is another command—**isis retransmit-throttle-interval**—that actually controls the rate, in milliseconds, at which retransmitted LSPs are sent. JUNOS does not allow the default IS-IS retransmission interval to be changed.

8.2.3   Mesh Groups

Flooding load is a particular problem in heavily meshed networks—such as those built on ATM or Frame Relay infrastructures. Recall from the basics of flooding that when a router receives a flooded LSA/LSP, it forwards it to all neighbors except the one from which it received the data unit. This is simple split-horizon forwarding. With heavily meshed networks, however, each router has many paths to other routers; in a fully meshed network such as the one in Figure 8.31, each router has a connection to *every* other router. This meshing means that there are numerous ways for an LSA/LSP to be replicated so that one router is likely to receive many copies of the same LSA/LSP. In Figure 8.32, for example, a router originates and floods an LSA or LSP. The direct connections mean that the information is communicated to all other routers with this initial flood. But the other routers have no way of knowing that all of their neighbors have received the information, so they flood the LSA/LSPs to all neighbors except the one they received the information from as shown in Figure 8.33. This second phase of flooding is entirely unnecessary.

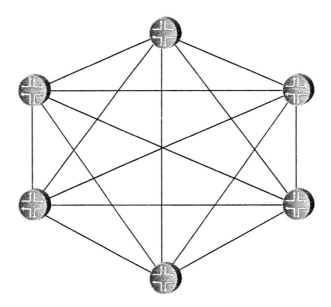

Figure 8.31   In a fully meshed network, every router has a connection to every other router.

In a fully meshed network, every router except the originator will flood $(n - 2)$ unnecessary LSA/LSPs, where n is the number of routers in the network. This works out to $(n - 1)(n - 2)$ or $(n^2 - 3n + 2)$ unnecessary LSA/LSPs. The example network shown here is small enough that the extra flooding load—20 extra LSA/LSPs—does not significantly impact network resources. As the network grows larger, however, the waste of resources also becomes larger. One flooded LSA/LSP in a fully meshed network of 50 routers, for example, results in 2352 unnecessary replications; in a network of 100 routers, 9702 unnecessary LSA/LSPs are flooded.

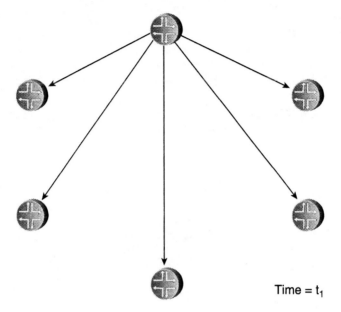

Figure 8.32   When a router floods an LSA or LSP in a fully meshed network, the information is immediately received by all other routers.

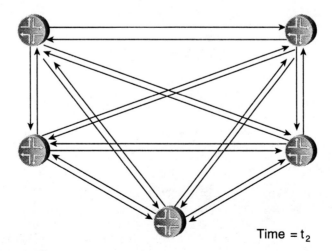

Figure 8.33   Because the other routers in the meshed network have no way to know that their neighbors have received the flooded information, they unnecessarily flood to their neighbors.

IS-IS provides a technique for limiting the scope of unnecessary flooding called *mesh groups*.[6] Mesh groups apply to point-to-point interfaces, and when mesh groups is enabled an interface can be in one of three modes:

- Inactive
- Blocked
- Set

Inactive mode means the mesh group is inactive for that interface, and LSPs are flooded normally. In blocked mode, no LSPs are flooded out that interface. Figure 8.34 shows how blocked mode might be applied to the network in Figure 8.31. Here, all links depicted with a dashed line are in blocked mode and do not flood LSPs. Each router has two unblocked links, so flooding can still take place if any one link fails. However, some redundancy is exchanged for scalability. If both of the unblocked links to one of the routers fail, the router cannot flood LSPs even though it still has three perfectly good—but blocked—links to the rest of the network.

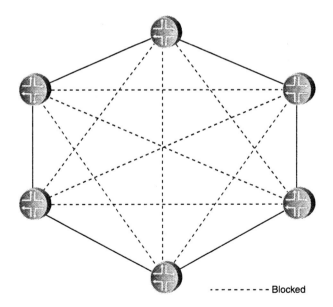

Figure 8.34   Interfaces in blocked mode do not flood any LSPs.

⁶ Rajesh Balay, Dave Katz, and Jeff Parker, "IS-IS Mesh Groups," RFC 2973, October 2000.

Some convergence time might also be sacrificed. In Figure 8.35, for example, an LSP flooded from one router must pass through a few other routers before the LSP reaches all routers, even though the originator has direct links to every router.

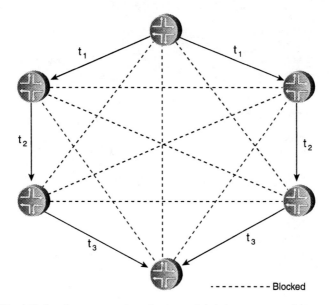

Figure 8.35 Blocking LSP flooding on some interfaces can slightly increase overall network convergence time.

Set mode offers a compromise between the sharply reduced flooding load but reduced redundancy and increased convergence time of blocked mode. Rather than grouping all interfaces into either blocked or unblocked, set mode groups interfaces into numbered groups. For example, in Figure 8.36 all interfaces belong to either group 1 or group 2. The rule for set mode is then very simple: A received LSP is not flooded out any interface belonging to the same group as the interface on which it was received.

Suppose a router in the network of Figure 8.36 originates an LSP, as shown in Figure 8.37. As the originator, it floods the LSP to all neighbors. Comparing this illustration with the numbered mesh groups in Figure 8.36, you can see that some neighbors receive the LSP on an interface belonging to mesh group 1 and some neighbors receive the LSP on interfaces belonging to mesh group 2.

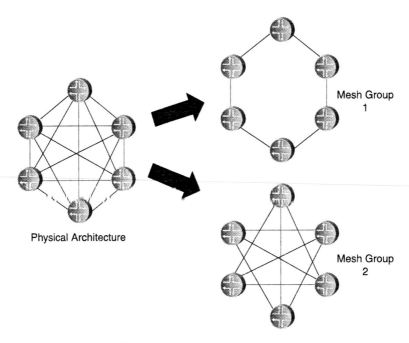

Figure 8.36   Set mode assigns interfaces to a numbered group.

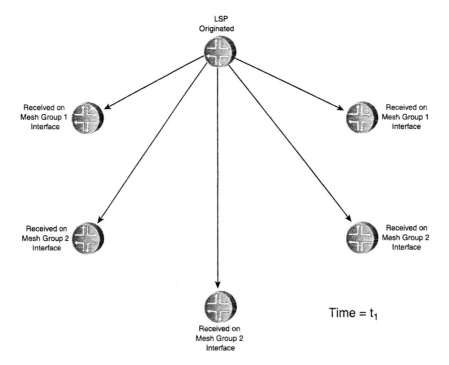

Figure 8.37   When an LSP is initially flooded, it is received by some neighbors on group 1 interfaces and by some neighbors on group 2 interfaces.

In Figure 8.38, the neighbors flood the LSP. Comparing the illustration to the groups in Figure 8.36, you can see that if the LSP was received on a group 1 interface, it is not flooded on any group 1 interface; and if the LSP was received on a group 2 interface, it is not flooded on any group 2 interface. You can also see that although there is less unnecessary flooding than in the fully meshed network in Figure 8.33, there is more than with the blocked mode in Figure 8.35. However, the reduced convergence seen with the blocked mode architecture is eliminated in this set mode architecture.

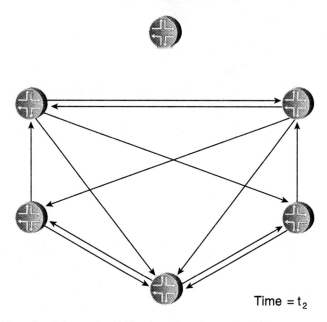

Time = t_2

Figure 8.38   Neighbors flood the received LSP only on interfaces belonging to groups other than the receiving interface's group.

In more complex topologies than shown here, you can use a combination of inactive, blocked, and set mode interfaces to manage the flooding patterns in the network. However, any time you use mesh groups, you trade some redundancy or convergence time or both for improved scalability, so you should consider carefully whether mesh groups are right for your network and, if so, design them carefully for the best balance between reduced flooding and reduced reliability.

OSPF does not have a comparable feature to IS-IS mesh groups. But some implementations do provide an LSA filtering function that enables you to create an effect similar to mesh groups. The Cisco IOS **database-filter** command, for instance, can be applied to block the flooding of LSAs on a given interface. However, OSPF networks typically consist of multiple areas that help scale flooding, whereas IS-IS is often used in very large, single-area networks where flooding load is more of a problem. Therefore, mesh groups are not as important for OSPF as they can be for IS-IS.

8.2.4 Demand Circuits and Flood Reduction

Although IS-IS is usually found only in relatively large IP networks, OSPF is found in networks of all sizes. And in small networks, you are more likely to find *demand circuits*—links that should be used only when there is a demand for them, and should otherwise be silent. The most common modern examples of demand circuits are links that treat data exchanges as a "call," such as dial-up and low-bandwidth ISDN. You do not want such connections to stay up permanently. Demand circuits also include any circuit for which you are billed based on the amount of packets traversing it.

Running OSPF over demand circuits is problematic because the Hellos will either keep the circuit up permanently or cause the circuit to connect and disconnect every 10 seconds just to transport the Hello packets. Additionally, periodically refreshing LSAs across a demand circuit when nothing has changed can cause unwanted connections or billing. An extension to OSPF makes the following modifications to accommodate demand circuits:[7]

- Hellos are sent only to bring up the circuit for the initial database synchronization of the neighbors on each side of the link. After synchronization, no Hellos are sent.
- LSAs are flooded across the demand circuit during synchronization, but are not periodically refreshed; LSAs are sent across the link only if there is a change in the LSA warranting a new instance.

If an LSA is not going to be periodically refreshed across a demand circuit, it must not "age out" of the link state databases in which it resides. That is, the age should not reach MaxAge. To accomplish this, the highest-order bit in the 16-bit Age field of the LSA header is designated as the *DoNotAge* bit. When this bit is set in an LSA, the age is incremented as usual during flooding, but is not incremented after the LSA has been installed in the link state database.

Of course, for this scheme to work all routers must understand and support the DoNotAge bit. If one router in the area does not, and increments the age to MaxAge, it will delete the LSA and the databases in the area will no longer be identical. Therefore, for OSPF over demand circuits to be reliable, all routers in an area must indicate their support for the extension by setting the Demand Circuit (DC) bit in the Options field of all LSAs it originates (Figure 8.39). If any LSA appears in any link state database in the area with the DC bit cleared, the router flushes all DoNotAge LSAs from its database.[8] The originators of these LSAs must then flood new instances, with the DoNotAge bit cleared. The DC bit is also set in the Options field of Hello and Database Description packets sent across demand circuits during synchronization, to negotiate an agreement to stop sending Hellos after the neighbors are synchronized.

---

[7] John Moy, "Extending OSPF to Support Demand Circuits," RFC 1793, April 1995.

[8] Note that this is an exception to the rule that no router can flush an LSA from its database that it did not originate.

Figure 8.39 The DC bit in the Options field indicates support for DoNotAge LSAs.

Because all LSAs in an area in which OSPF is running over a demand circuit must have their DC bits set, it is best to put demand circuits in stub, totally stubby, or NSSA areas. Doing so eliminates the necessity of an ABR or ASBR having to set the DC bits in all type 3, 4, and 5 LSAs.

Obviously, if LSAs are not being refreshed periodically, some of the robustness inherent to OSPF is lost. This should be a factor when considering whether to run OSPF over a demand circuit.

Another consideration is that with no Hellos exchanged across a demand circuit, there is no keepalive function. If a router on one end of the circuit becomes unreachable, the neighbor on the other end will not detect it. A solution to the detection of a failed neighbor, called neighbor probing, is proposed in RFC 3883.[9] With neighbor probing, any time the link is connected for the transmission of application packets OSPF can send Updates and look for Acknowledgments. However, probing only takes place when the link is up for packet transmission; the link is not brought up just for probing.

There is also a potential situation in which the neighbor is available but the link is not. Again, the lack of Hellos means this condition cannot be detected. So, there must be a *presumption of reachability*, meaning that the circuit is presumed to be available when needed. If for some reason a connection cannot be established, OSPF does not report the link as down. Instead, the link is considered oversubscribed and packets destined to transit the link are dropped.

Yet another consideration has to do with network management software. The routers at each end of a demand circuit still refresh their LSAs out all other interfaces; periodic refreshes are suppressed only across the demand circuit. This means that the sequence number of the same LSA might not match in databases on each side of the circuit, which can lead some network management applications to falsely conclude that the databases in an area are not synchronized.

All in all, running OSPF over demand circuits in a modern network is probably a bad idea. The extension was developed in the mid-1990s, when such links were more common than they are today. But when a dial-up or low-bandwidth ISDN link is used in current networks, presumably it connects a stub router to the network rather than serving as a transit link in the middle of an area. Therefore, a better and simpler solution is likely to be static routes at each end of the link.

Although OSPF over demand circuits might not be a good idea, the demand circuit extensions can be exploited for limiting overall flooding.[10] A router performing this *flood*

---

[9] Sira Panduranga Rao, Alex Zinin, and Abhay Roy, "Detecting Inactive Neighbors over OSPF Demand Circuits (DC)," RFC 3883, October 2004.

[10] Padma Pillay-Esnault, "OSPF Refresh and Flooding Reduction in Stable Technologies," draft-pillay-esnault-ospf-flooding-07.txt, June 2003.

reduction continues to send Hellos to its neighbors but sets the DoNotAge bit in its LSAs as they are flooded so that they are not aged in other databases. The Cisco IOS command **ip ospf flood-reduction** is an example of a command enabling flood reduction. As with the demand circuit extensions, existing LSAs are then reflooded only when a change occurs warranting a new instance. Specifically, a new instance of an LSA is flooded only if

- The LSA's Options field changes.
- A new instance of an LSA is received which has an age of MaxAge or DoNotAge+MaxAge.
- The Length field in the LSA header changes
- The contents of the LSA have changed, excluding the 20-octet header (because the sequence number and checksum are expected to change and do not indicate a topology change).

As with OSPF over demand circuits, the price you pay for this OSPF flood reduction is diminished robustness of the link state database maintenance. Therefore, you should use this option only in topologies that are normally stable and reliable.

8.3   Fragmentation

Sections 7.3.2 and 7.4.2 discuss the issue of large LSAs and LSPs and the effect they have on the scalability of an area in terms of bandwidth usage during flooding and memory usage as they are stored in the link state databases. Another issue with the scaling of LSAs and LSPs concerns the ability of link MTUs to accommodate them. That issue is the question of how to handle an LSA or LSP that is larger than the MTU of a link it is supposed to traverse. When there is a low-MTU link along the flooding path, an OSPF or IS-IS implementation can do one of three things:

- It can limit the information units it generates to a very small size to ensure that they never exceed the lowest possible MTU of any link. This is not a very practical approach.
- It can perform path MTU discovery and adjust the transmitted unit sizes accordingly. This adds a layer of complexity to the flooding mechanism.
- It can use fragmentation as necessary.

Fragmentation is a common and well-understood part of IP networks, so using fragmentation makes sense in situations where an OSPF or IS-IS protocol data unit is larger than the MTU of a link it must traverse.

Fragmentation is less of an issue for OSPF than for IS-IS for two reasons. First, because a single originator can generate many different LSAs of several different types to convey information, no one LSA is likely to grow extremely large. Types 3, 4, 5, and 7 LSAs carry only a single prefix, so they are always small. Type 2 LSAs might grow large, but it is rare to find a pseudonode with a great number of neighbors. Of all the LSA types, only type 1 is likely to grow large and even then only if the router has a large number of neighbors or stub links (an access router is a good example of a router with a very large number of stub links). The maximum size of an LSA is 64KB. Given 24 bytes of fixed fields and 12 bytes to represent each link, a type 1 LSA can advertise a maximum of 5331 links. In any reasonable network design, this LSA capacity should more than suffice.

The second reason that fragmentation is less of an issue for OSPF is that the LSAs, whatever their size, are encapsulated in Update messages for transmission to neighbors. The Update message is in turn encapsulated in an IP packet, and IP packet headers are formatted to accommodate fragmentation. In other words, the standard IP fragmentation procedures serve OSPF just fine.

IS-IS is a little more problematic: Unlike OSPF's many LSAs, IS-IS generates one LSP per level, per router. As a result, this one LSP can become quite large. And because the LSP is not an IP packet, it cannot take advantage of IP's fragmentation mechanism. Therefore, IS-IS must have its own fragmentation mechanism.

Prerequisite to IS-IS fragmentation, IS-IS must be able to assume that every link on which it floods LSPs can handle PDUs up to at least a certain size. That is, there must be a minimum guaranteed MTU such that IS-IS knows it can send PDUs up to that size without them exceeding the link MTU. Recall from the discussion of IS-IS Hello protocol basics in Section 4.2.2 that when Hellos are initially exchanged between IS-IS neighbors the Padding TLV is used to pad the Hello up to the ReceiveLSPBufferSize of 1492 bytes.[11] If a neighboring interface has an MTU lower than 1492 bytes, it cannot receive the padded Hellos and drops them, so that an adjacency is not formed. Therefore, if an adjacency exists with a neighbor, an IS-IS router knows that so long as its PDUs do not exceed 1492 bytes they will not exceed the MTU of any of its links.

If the number of TLVs a router originates would result in an LSP larger than 1492 bytes IS-IS breaks the LSP into fragments, none of which are larger than 1492 bytes (including the header). The 8-bit LSP Number field in the LSP header (Figure 8.40) is used to track these "LSP fragments." The first LSP, whether it is fragmented or not, has an LSP number of 0x00. Subsequent fragments are numbered 0x01, 0x02, and so on. Figure 8.41 shows a database display with 17 fragments of the same LSP.

---

[11] The 1492-byte limitation in the standards is to accommodate SNAP encapsulation. But in practice, vendors use LLC encapsulation, which increases the maximum LSP size to 1497 bytes. Therefore, you will commonly find IS-IS Hellos padded to 1497 bytes.

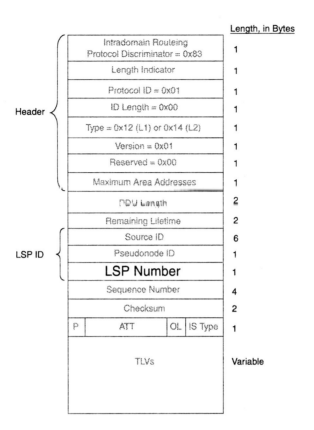

Length, in Bytes

Intradomain Routeing Protocol Discriminator = 0x83	1
Length Indicator	1
Protocol ID = 0x01	1
ID Length = 0x00	1
Type = 0x12 (L1) or 0x14 (L2)	1
Version = 0x01	1
Reserved = 0x00	1
Maximum Area Addresses	1
PDU Length	2
Remaining Lifetime	2
Source ID	6
Pseudonode ID	1
LSP Number	1
Sequence Number	4
Checksum	2
P ATT OL IS Type	1
TLVs	Variable

Header
LSP ID

Figure 8.40   The LSP Number in the LSP header is used for tracking a fragmented LSP.

```
jeff@Juniper2> show isis database RTR1-SFO
IS-IS level 1 link-state database:
LSP ID                      Sequence Checksum Lifetime Attributes
RTR1-SFO.00-00               0x4298   0x8144    47193 L1 L2 Attached
RTR1-SFO.00-01               0x2c84   0x73c2    41078 L1 L2
RTR1-SFO.00-02               0x2919   0x72f4    41078 L1 L2
RTR1-SFO.00-03               0x21b2   0x1974    65420 L1 L2
RTR1-SFO.00-04               0x2213   0xdbc2    46671 L1 L2
RTR1-SFO.00-05               0x1e07   0x5036    65429 L1 L2
RTR1-SFO.00-06               0x1b63   0xe8e2    41078 L1 L2
RTR1-SFO.00-07               0x1624   0x7676    41078 L1 L2
RTR1-SFO.00-08               0x1598   0x4b2d    41078 L1 L2
RTR1-SFO.00-09               0x18c6   0xc7d7    41078 L1 L2
RTR1-SFO.00-0a               0x19a4   0x595d    65429 L1 L2
RTR1-SFO.00-0b               0x246b   0x3f98    65429 L1 L2
RTR1-SFO.00-0c               0xfe6    0x1a34    65429 L1 L2
RTR1-SFO.00-0d               0x1369   0x35e5    51739 L1 L2
RTR1-SFO.00-0e               0x81e    0xb82     41078 L1 L2
RTR1-SFO.00-0f               0x1211   0x8e7c    57266 L1 L2
RTR1-SFO.00-10               0x165a   0xca63    49398 L1 L2
   17 LSPs
```

Figure 8.41   The last octet of the LSP ID is the LSP Number, used for relating fragments of the same LSP.

A note about semantics is in order here. If you deal mostly with IETF terminology, using the term *fragments* when discussing a multipart LSP such as the one shown in Figure 8.41 might make the most sense to you. However, you might also say that the router RTR1-SFO has originated 17 LSPs. That is, instead of saying a router fragments its LSPs when they are large, you can say that a router produces multiple LSPs when necessary, and that the LSP number is used to differentiate the multiple LSPs from the same source. In fact, the language of ISO 10589 is oriented to multiple LSPs rather than fragments. Looking at the entries in Figure 8.41, you can see that each of the fragments have their own sequence numbers, checksums, and remaining lifetimes. And they are stored in the database as separate LSPs. But although they are flooded and stored separately, during the SPF calculations all the fragments from a single originating router are considered as a single LSP. So, you can consider these entities as fragments of the same LSP or as multiple LSPs originated from the same router. Either term is acceptable; use the one that makes more sense to you.

Also note that IS-IS does not do any sort of summation or other checking of the LSP numbers to ensure that all fragments are in the database; if there is a gap in the LSP number sequence, the SPF calculation still takes place. The one exception to this is LSP number 0. If that first fragment is missing, the other fragments are discarded. The reason for this is that only LSP number 0 contains information that is vital to the correct inclusion of the originating node in the SPF calculation, such as the ATT bit and the Overload bit (discussed in the next section).

Yet another scaling issue with IS-IS fragmentation has to do with the size of the LSP Number field. Because it is 8 bits, a single originator can generate a maximum of 256 fragments. Considering that every LSP can carry up to 1470 bytes of TLV space (after the 8 byte IS-IS header and a 19 byte LSP header, as discussed in Section 7.4.2), 256 fragments constitutes 256 * 1470 = 376,320 bytes of payload space for TLVs. If every TLV is 12 bytes long (a conservative assumption—many TLVs are much shorter), 256 LSP fragments can carry over 31,000 TLVs. This would seem to be more than sufficient for an intelligent network design. Nevertheless, the 256-fragment maximum has been the cause for some concern that IS-IS might not scale into the future, given the evolution of large-scale networks. Among the contributing factors to larger and larger LSPs are:

- The ongoing extension of the protocol, requiring new TLVs, for support of things like traffic engineering and IPv6
- The injection of more and more prefixes into the domain for increased routing precision
- The advent of multi-chassis routing platforms for very large core networks, which can easily support thousands or tens of thousands of links and adjacencies

Whether the 256-fragment limitation turns out to be imagined or real, an extension now permits IS-IS to exceed that limit.[12] Looking once more at the fragments in Figure 8.41, you can see that the identical LSP ID identifies the fragments as belonging to the same

---

[12] Amir Hermelin, Stefano Previdi, and Mike Shand, "Extending the Number of Intermediate System to Intermediate System (IS-IS) Link State PDU (LSP) Fragments Beyond the 256 Limit," RFC 3786, May 2004.

originator; the LSP number differentiates the fragments from one another. And of course, the LSP ID is based on the system ID assigned to the originator. So, overcoming the 256-fragment limitation becomes a simple matter of assigning more than one SysID to the same router. This additional SysID is then viewed as identifying a *virtual system* attached to the originating router. For every additional SysID given to it, an originator can generate an additional 256 LSP fragments.

The SPF calculation ordinarily would view the virtual system as a separate node from the originating system. To circumvent this potential problem, the virtual system is instead viewed as leaf node from the originator and is calculated as a cost of 0 from the originator. In this, the concept is similar to that of a pseudonode.

The additional SysIDs for the virtual systems are advertised in type 24 TLVs (Figure 8.42), called the IS Alias ID TLV. This TLV must always be included, if it exists, in fragment 0 of the originator's LSP, and notifies other routers that the specified additional SysIDs are a part of the originator's LSPs.

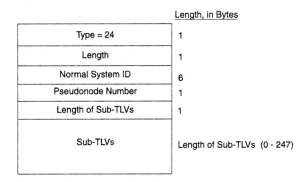

Figure 8.42   Type 24 TLVs enable the use of additional SysIDs to overcome the IS-IS 256-fragment limitation.

- **Normal System ID** is the SysID of the originating router.
- **Pseudonode Number** acts to relate the additional SysIDs with the normal SysID.
- **Sub-TLVs** include the additional SysIDs (also called IS-Alias-IDs).

8.4   Overloading

The previous section dealt with the issue of adjusting the size of LSAs and LSPs to existing link bandwidth—the assumption being that in large networks OSPF Updates and IS-IS can become very large. There is a "flip side" to this issue: What happens when a router's memory is not large enough to store all of the LSA/LSPs being flooded in an area? We know that all link state databases in an area must be identical. If the memory allocated to storing the link state database becomes full so that not all information can be recorded, the SPF calculation at that router will likely be incorrect. The router then cannot be trusted to route correctly on the shortest-path tree and should not be included as a transit node.

IS-IS has a facility for coping with this situation. If the database memory fills up—that is, if the memory becomes overloaded—the router notifies the other routers in the area by setting the *Overload* (OL) bit in its LSAs (Figure 8.43). The other routers in the area treat an overloaded router as a leaf router on the shortest-path tree: It is included for reachability of its directly connected links, but not as a transit path to other routers.

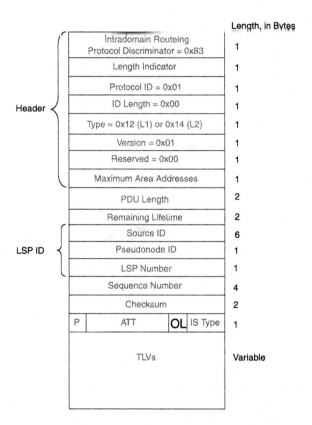

Figure 8.43   The Overload (OL) bit, when set, signals to other routers in the area that the originator's database memory is overloaded.

Like several other features of OSPF and IS-IS, both of which were created in the days when routers were sharply limited in CPU power, memory capacity, and throughput time, the original intention of the overload mechanism is now mostly irrelevant. Modern core routers have enormous memory capacity that will not be overloaded by IS-IS in any intelligently designed network.[13]

---

[13] A not-so-bright design is one in which a low-powered, low-memory router is exposed to a large core network. Such routers, if they are used at all, must be protected behind static routes or in totally stubby areas.

However, unlike other now-obsolete features of OSPF and IS-IS, the OL bit is tremendously useful in modern networks for a reason that has nothing to do with memory depletion: helping to prevent unintentional blackholing of packets in BGP transit networks. To understand this function, you must understand some basics of BGP. Figure 8.44 shows a very simple BGP transit network, AS 65502. BGP is used for routing through the AS between AS 65501 and AS 65503. BGP is a point-to-point protocol, running over TCP sessions. The sessions running between the autonomous systems are External BGP (EBGP), and the sessions running internal to an autonomous system are Internal BGP (IBGP). Whereas EBGP sessions are usually[14] between directly connected neighbors, IBGP sessions often pass through several routers internal to the AS. In Figure 8.44, the IBGP session between RTR A and RTR E passes through three internal routers. When RTR A and RTR E exchange routes learned from their EBGP neighbors, they show their RIDs (normally loopback addresses) as the next-hop address of the routes.[15] IBGP depends on the AS's IGP for two things:

- Finding the route through the AS to its IBGP peers for establishing its point-to-point TCP sessions
- Finding the routes to the next-hop addresses of the external routes advertised by its IBGP peers

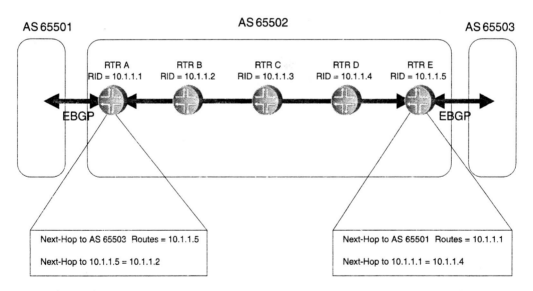

Figure 8.44   IBGP relies on the autonomous system's IGP to find its IBGP peers and the next-hop addresses of the external routes advertised by its IGP peers.

---

[14] EBGP sessions are occasionally multihop for some specialized applications, but that is irrelevant to this discussion.

[15] The default BGP behavior is to use the interface address of the external peer as the next-hop address of IBGP routes, but current best practice is to use a policy to change that next hop to the loopback address of the edge router advertising the prefixes to its IBGP peers.

If RTR A in Figure 8.44 needs to route a packet to a destination in AS 65503, it performs a route lookup and finds that the next hop for the route is RTR E, at 10.1.1.5. It then performs a second lookup for 10.1.1.5 and finds that the next hop for that destination is RTR B. The packet is then forwarded to RTR B. If the IBGP session shown in Figure 8.44 were the only IBGP session in the AS, there would now be a problem. Because RTR B has no IBGP session with RTR E, it cannot learn the external routes RTR E is advertising. So when RTR B receives the packet, it has no route entry for the destination in AS 65503 and drops the packet.

Therefore, in a transit AS, it is necessary to create a full mesh of IBGP sessions as shown in Figure 8.45.[16] Each internal router learns the external routes via IBGP. Now, when the packet in our example is forwarded from RTR A to RTR B, RTR B and subsequent routers along the path to RTR E can perform the correct lookups to get the packet to RTR E.

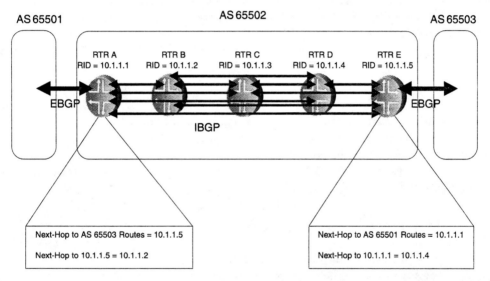

Figure 8.45   A full mesh of IBGP sessions is necessary for the non-EBGP routers to know how to forward packets transiting the AS.

But a potential problem lurks in the network, stemming from the nature of IGPs and BGP: OSPF and IS-IS converge very quickly, whereas BGP, which must first establish TCP sessions and then exchange tens or hundreds of thousands of routes, converges quite slowly. A BGP session carrying a full Internet routing table can take several minutes to converge. Suppose RTR C in Figure 8.45 is restarted intentionally or otherwise. The IGP routes will become known quickly, so that RTR A and RTR B again learn the route to RTR E through RTR C. If a packet to an AS 65503 destination is forwarded on the route after the IGP has converged but before IBGP has finished converging at RTR C, RTR C will not recognize the destination and will drop the packet.

---

[16] There are techniques—route reflectors and confederations—for avoiding a full IBGP mesh, which are again irrelevant to this discussion.

This is where the OL bit comes in handy. When a new IBGP router is added to the network, or a router is restarted, the IS-IS OL bit can be manually set. Because directly connected addresses on an overloaded router—including the loopback address that serves as an endpoint for IBGP sessions—are considered reachable by the other routers in the AS, IBGP can be brought up and can begin exchanging routes. However, the other routers will not include the overloaded router for transit traffic, and so will route packets transiting the AS on an alternate path. (In a correctly designed transit AS, unlike the simple example AS of Figure 8.45, there is always at least one alternate path.) When BGP has converged, the OL bit can be cleared and the router can then begin forwarding AS-transit packets.

In some special cases, you might want to leave the OL bit permanently set, so that the router has full network knowledge and other routers know its stub links, but the router is never used for transit traffic. Examples include routers that are connected for analysis purposes but should not be considered part of the production network, such as lab or network management routers, and IBGP route reflectors that you want to perform only as BGP route servers and not as transit nodes.

The OL bit is manually set in IOS with the command **set-overload-bit** and in JUNOS with the command **overload**. Removing the command from the configuration clears the OL bit. But remembering to set and then clear the OL bit whenever you add or restart a router is a hassle, and unplanned restarts give you no chance to use the OL bit. Both IOS and JUNOS have a very useful option—**set-overload-bit on-startup** in IOS and **overload timeout** in JUNOS—that allows you to specify a number of seconds that the OL bit is set automatically during startup. When the specified seconds expire—200 to 400 seconds is usually a reasonable period for allowing BGP to converge—the OL bit is automatically cleared. The option is highly recommended in any IBGP network.

OSPF has no comparable feature to the OL bit in its LSAs. However, some vendor implementations include a mechanism by which you can create the same kind of behavior in an OSPF area by setting the metric of all transit links on an "overloaded" router to 0xFFFF in its type 1 LSAs. This metric indicates that the links are unreachable, so that the router is not included as a transit node on the SPF tree. Stub links connected to the router are advertised with their normal metrics, so that they are still reachable when the router is in overload. OSPF overloading is supported in JUNOS, for example, using the same **overload** command, and allowing the same optional automatic overload timeout at startup, as with IS-IS.

Review Questions

1. Describe the modification to the simplistic SPF algorithm of Chapter 2 that allows ECMP.
2. Why is per-destination load balancing better than per-packet load balancing?
3. Why is per-flow load balancing better than per-destination load balancing?

4. What modification to the basic SPF algorithm is required, when there are equal costs involving both point-to-point links and broadcast links, to avoid disruption of ECMP?

5. What is Incremental SPF, and in what two general cases can it improve the efficiency of SPF in an area?

6. What is partial route calculation, and how does it improve the efficiency of SPF calculations?

7. How does SPF delay improve the efficiency of SPF calculations?

8. How can an excessive SPF delay reduce the performance of a network?

9. What is adaptive SPF delay, and what is its advantage over a set delay period?

10. Why are individual refresh timers for each self-originated LSA or LSP in a database better than a single monolithic timer?

11. How does adding a delay period to the refresh timers of self-originated LSAs or LSPs reduce problems associated with heavy flooding?

12. Under what circumstances can increasing the time a router waits for an acknowledgement of a transmitted LSA or LSP before retransmitting improve flooding efficiency?

13. What is a mesh group?

14. What are the advantages and disadvantages of using blocked mode in a mesh group?

15. What are the advantages and disadvantages of using set mode in a mesh group?

16. Can the three mesh group modes (inactive, blocked, and set) be used in the same network?

17. What is a demand circuit?

18. What is the OSPF DoNotAge bit?

19. What two changes are made to OSPF procedures in the extensions for support of demand circuits?

20. What is the purpose of the DC bit in the Options field of LSAs?

21. What is the purpose of the DC bit in the Options field of OSPF Hello and Database Description packets?

22. What does the presumption of reachability mean in regard to OSPF over demand circuits?

23. In what way can OSPF over demand circuits effect the consistency of LSA sequence numbers, and in what way can this be a problem?

24. What is OSPF flood reduction?

25. Why is fragmentation less of an issue with OSPF than with IS-IS?

26. What is the IS-IS ReceiveLSPBufferSize, and why are Hellos padded to this size during when attempting to form an adjacency?

27. What is the purpose of the LSP Number in the LSP header?

28. What happens if LSP Number 0 of a fragmented LSP is missing in a link state database?

29. What is the purpose of the IS-Alias-ID (type 24) TLV?

30. What does it mean when an IS-IS router is overloaded?

31. How is the OL bit useful in BGP transit networks?

32. What is the advantage of enabling an overload timeout option in BGP transit networks?

33. How can "overloading" behavior be created in an OSPF area?

CHAPTER 9

Security and Reliability

Security and reliability are two sides of the same coin. In the context of networking, they are the two qualities that determine the overall trustworthiness of a system to not stray outside of expected operational parameters, such as performance, stability, accuracy, and privacy. A system's security concerns its resistance to intentional harm, and reliability concerns a system's resistance to unintentional harm.

As an example of how security and reliability are intertwined, consider an authentication, authorization, and accounting (AAA) process on a server or router. This is primarily considered a security process, regulating who can log in to the machine, what tasks an authorized user can perform on it, and keeping a record of what each user does. However, AAA also contributes to reliability by preventing the wrong people from logging in, ensuring that authorized users do not inadvertently issue dangerous commands they are not qualified to use, and tracking what happened when mistakes do happen so that policies can be improved.

This chapter not only examines specific features of OSPF and IS-IS that can make the protocols more secure and reliable, but also shows how good design and good operational practice is essential for keeping your network up and running.

9.1 Routing Protocol Vulnerabilities

As you are sure to know, routing protocols can be classified as either interior or exterior gateway protocols (IGPs or EGPs). For routing IP, Border Gateway Protocol (BGP) is the only EGP currently in widespread use; all other commonly used IP routing protocols—including OSPF and IS-IS—are IGPs. Although the mission of both types of routing protocols is to exchange route information, how they go about the information exchange differs significantly. Like any device outside of your administrative domain, external routers must be considered untrusted. BGP is designed to work in conjunction with complex routing policies so that you have detailed control over what information is shared and accepted from external peers. IGPs on the other hand, because they are intended to run inside of your administrative domain, assume that all routers within the routing domain can be trusted. So, IGPs are designed to make peering and information sharing as easy and as open as possible.

Most attacks launched against routing protocols target BGP because it is the "public-facing" protocol and therefore most accessible from the outside. But you should never assume that your IGP is safe just because it is internal to your network. Malicious assaults against IGPs can and do occur, but the very nature of an IGP, to make information exchange as transparent as possible, can open the protocol to a number of accidental problems, too.

9.1.1   Malicious Threats

An attack against a routing protocol attempts to alter the normal behavior of the protocol in one of four ways:[1]

- **Disclosure**—The target protocol divulges network information to the attacker. This information can then be studied to further exploit weaknesses in the network.
- **Deception**—The target protocol is tricked into accepting routing messages from the attacker, believing the messages to come from a legitimate peer.
- **Disruption**—The target protocol is prevented from functioning correctly. This might be the result of a denial-of-service attack in which messages are flooded to a router, overwhelming its resources, or it might be the result of simply disconnecting or breaking something.
- **Usurpation**—The attacker gains control over the routing protocol process in one or more network routers. Disclosure, deception, or disruption can then be accomplished by causing packets to be routed to an illegitimate device or just blackholed.

A routing protocol might be compromised by an attacker gaining physical access to a link or a router. Such access can result in simple damage, or in the insertion of an illegitimate device into the protocol domain. Physical access almost always is the result of an "inside" attacker.

A routing protocol can also be compromised logically, for example by an attacker sending faked or malformed protocol messages, or by gaining logical access (such as Telnet or SNMP) to a router. Logical attacks can be launched either from inside or from outside of the protocol domain.

An attack can be aimed at one or more functional components of OSPF or IS-IS:

- **The Hello protocol**—A bogus Hello message with one or more intentionally incorrect fields can be used to break or hijack an adjacency to a legitimate peer.

---

[1] Abbie Barbir, Sandy Murphy, and Yi Yang, "Generic Threats to Routing Protocols," draft-ietf-rpsec-routing-threats-06.txt, April 2004.

- **The flooding process**—Sending spoofed LSAs or LSPs, which claim to be from existing routers in the domain, can trigger heavy flooding and SPF calculations as routers resend legitimate LSAs or LSPs.

- **The link state database**—Sending spoofed LSAs or LSPs from "phantom" routers can cause the LSAs or LSPs to be accepted into the LS database, causing incorrect routing. Or, the database can simply be filled up with spoofed LSAs or LSPs, causing memory overflow.

- **Aging**—Sending spoofed LSAs or LSPs that claim to be from legitimate peers and that have been "aged out" can cause legitimate LSAs or LSPs to be temporarily flushed from the LS database.

- **Sequence numbers**—Spoofed LSAs or LSPs that claim to be from legitimate peers can contain a maximum sequence number value, causing sequence number rollover.

- **DR or DIS process**—A bogus Hello with a null or illegitimate DR/BDR or DIS field, or with a high priority value, can trigger reelection or even cause other routers to accept a nonexistent DR or DIS, making the associated broadcast or NBMA link unavailable.

- **Options flags**—Spoofed options flags can cause broken adjacencies or acceptance of illegitimate information. For example, a "phantom" OSPF router sending Hellos with the E bit set causes the router to be accepted as an ASBR, which in turn allows it to inject illegitimate external routing information.

A "phantom" router—an illegitimate router or logical entity that establishes an adjacency with one or more legitimate routers in the network—can also mount attacks on OSPF and IS-IS. Creating a phantom router normally requires access to one of the network links.

Software for probing and attacking routing protocols is readily available for download. One well-known example is the Internetwork Routing Protocol Attack Suite (IRPAS), which provides a set of applications for active and passive scanning of protocol activity and for custom-building routing protocol packets.

9.1.2 Non-Malicious Threats

Non-malicious threats to routing protocols are the result of either misconfiguration or an implementation problem. When a non-malicious problem alters protocol behavior, the result is almost always disruption of some sort. However, the result might also be to open the protocol to a malicious attack.

In many cases, the result of a configuration mistake is harmless. For example, when bringing a new router into the network an incorrect configuration might prevent all the expected adjacencies from coming up. The missing neighbors are apparent, and the problem can be quickly identified and corrected. Other problems might be more subtle. An incorrect interface metric might result in suboptimal routing; incorrect timers might not have any effect at all until the protocol becomes unable to correctly respond to a network problem.

On the other hand, a configuration mistake can be disastrous. Failure to enable authentication or filtering might leave a door open for an attacker. Policy mistakes can bring the protocol down. The most glaring example of a policy problem, and one that still occurs with surprising frequency, is redistributing full Internet routes from BGP into OSPF or IS-IS. Such a mistake might happen on only one router, but the result is usually a system-wide meltdown as tens of thousands of external prefixes are flooded throughout the domain. Correcting the problem is not a matter of just eliminating the misconfigured policy or "pulling the plug" at the Internet-peering interface. In a large network, where clearing the prefixes from LS databases across the domain requires a systematic shutdown and reactivation of the protocol on many routers, recovery means hours of hard work—all while the network is down and all under a barrage of calls from angry customers and executives. It's not pretty.

Implementation problems are the fault of the coder or vendor of routing software. The problem might be a generally poor implementation or a bug in an otherwise stable protocol implementation. The result can be poor performance or a high failure rate. And attackers are quick to identify and exploit poor or buggy implementations.

9.2   Security and Reliability Features

OSPF and IS-IS have a number of features—some of them part of the protocol specifications, some of them extensions of the protocol, and some of them inherent characteristics of the protocol—that increase both the security and the reliability of the protocol.

9.2.1   *Inherent Security*

IS-IS has one significant security advantage over OSPF, which is that the protocol messages themselves are not carried in IP packets. Because of this, IS-IS cannot be attacked by sending faked protocol messages from an external source. Attacks on IS-IS require physical access to a link or router, or logical access such as Telnet or SNMP to a router running IS-IS.

In cases where OSPF accepts only IP packets addressed to the multicast AllSPFRouters address (224.0.0.5), the protocol is safe from faked packets sent from outside the network because the address has a link-local scope, and routers do not forward packets with such a destination address. Unfortunately, RFC 2328 requires only OSPF point-to-point interfaces to be limited to accepting this destination address. Interfaces to all other OSPF network types can accept unicast packets and so can be reached from external sources if not protected by other means.

An inherent security feature normally mentioned in association with OSPF but that also applies to IS-IS is "fightback."[2] Fightback is the result of normal protocol behavior in which a router, seeing an LSA or LSP that it supposedly originated but which does not match its own LS database information, will originate a new LSA or LSP or will attempt to flush the bogus LSA or LSP. So if an attacker tries to send a spoofed LSA or LSP that pretends to be

[2] Feiyi Wang and S. Felix Wu, "On the Vulnerabilities and Protection of OSPF Routing Protocols," In IEEE 7th International Conference on Computer Communication and Network (IC3N), October 1998.

from a legitimate router on the network, the effects of the bogus PDU is limited because the legitimate router will eventually see it and take measures to remove it. Attacks against sequence numbers or age values and attacks that attempt to inject false link state information should all trigger a fightback.

Because of the fightback behavior, an attack that lobs just a few bogus LSAs or LSPs into a network will not be very effective. The attacker must send persistent PDUs to defeat the fightback behavior, but this in turn increases the exposure of the attacker. If the attacker is willing to accept the exposure, or can otherwise hide himself, the persistent PDUs will overcome the fightback and create sufficient thrashing of SPF processes and routing information to effectively disrupt the domain, resulting in a successful denial of service.

The fightback behavior also can be circumvented by PDUs originated by a "phantom" router or if the target router can be fooled into thinking the bogus PDUs come from a legitimate but partitioned router.[3] So you should not rely too much on fightback to make your network safe.

9.2.2 Authentication

Enabling authentication is one of the two most important measures you can take to secure any routing protocol (the other is good filtering practice). Authentication, which is supported by both OSPF and IS-IS, is simply a mechanism by which two neighbors prove their identity to each other by using a shared secret. No protocol message is accepted from a neighbor unless the message is correctly authenticated. As a result, no logical attack involving sending spoofed messages can be launched unless the attacker can learn the shared secret.

Authentication is also useful in preventing certain non-malicious errors. Specifically, it can prevent routers from mistakenly joining an OSPF domain. For example, a service provider might accidentally enable OSPF on a customer-facing external link. At the same time, the customer might through accident or ignorance have OSPF running on his external link to the service provider. If both interfaces on the link happen to have the same AID, OSPF can create an adjacency, and the two domains can merge. If the provider and customer are lucky, nothing more than an undesirable situation will arise. If they are unlucky, address conflicts, incorrect routing, security breaches, and network outages will result. Although such a scenario might seem far-fetched, these mistakes can and do occur.

9.2.2.1 Authentication Types

Authentication is accomplished by means of either a simple password shared between neighbors or an MD5 (Message Digest version 5)[4] cryptographic checksum. When simple password authentication is used, two neighbors share a password, and all messages exchanged between them must contain the password. Any message that does not include the correct password is dropped. Although it is better than no authentication at all, this mechanism is

---

[3] Emanuele Jones and Olivier Le Moigne, "OSPF Security Vulnerabilities Analysis," draft-ietf-rpsec-ospf-vuln-00.txt, May 2004.

[4] Ronald L. Rivest, "The MD5 Message-Digest Algorithm," RFC 1321, April 1992.

not secure. The password is carried in the messages in clear text, so if an attacker can gain access to a link and "sniff" a protocol message, he can easily read the password. Figures 9.1 and 9.2 show protocol analyzer captures of OSPF and IS-IS Hellos, respectively, that are using simple password authentication. The password in both is easily read.

```
Frame 10 (82 bytes on wire, 82 bytes captured)
Ethernet II, Src: 00:90:27:9d:f1:33, Dst: 01:00:5e:00:00:05
Internet Protocol, Src Addr: 172.16.1.102 (172.16.1.102), Dst Addr: 224.0.0.5
    (224.0.0.5)
Open Shortest Path First
    OSPF Header
        OSPF Version: 2
        Message Type: Hello Packet (1)
        Packet Length: 44
        Source OSPF Router: 192.168.254.2 (192.168.254.2)
        Area ID: 0.0.0.0 (Backbone)
        Packet Checksum: 0x8ffc (correct)
        Auth Type: Simple password
        Auth Data: stan
    OSPF Hello Packet
        Network Mask: 255.255.255.0
        Hello Interval: 10 seconds
        Options: 0x2 (E)
        Router Priority: 128
        Router Dead Interval: 40 seconds
        Designated Router: 172.16.1.102
        Backup Designated Router: 0.0.0.0
```

Figure 9.1   This Ethereal capture of an OSPF Hello message using simple password authentication clearly reveals the password (stan).

When MD5 authentication is used, neighbors share a password—called a *key*—but the key is never exchanged between the neighbors. Instead, the neighbor originating a packet computes a 128-bit digital fingerprint called a *hash* or *message digest* by running a mathematical algorithm using a combination of the packet contents and the key. The hash is then added to the packet, and the packet is transmitted. The receiving neighbor, knowing the same secret key, runs the same computation against the packet contents and the key. If the resulting hash is identical to the hash contained in the packet, the packet is accepted. If the authentication fails, the packet is dropped.[5]

Note that MD5, as described in RFC 1321, is an algorithm only for encrypting some data string. The adaptation of this algorithm to hash together a combination of a key and a message for authentication is called *Hashed Message Authentication Code* (HMAC-MD5).[6] Although IS-IS documentation correctly references HMAC-MD5, OSPF documentation

[5]   An excellent technical discussion of the use of MD5 in message authentication is Mihir Bellare, Ran Canetti, and Hugo Krawczyk, "Keying Hash Functions for Message Authentication," Advances in Cryptology – Crypto 96 Proceedings, Lecture Notes in Computer Science Vol. 1109, N. Koblitz, ed., Springer-Verlag, 1996, pp 1–15. Also available at www.research.ibm.com/security/keyed-md5.html.

[6]   Hugo Krawczyk, Mihir Bellare, and Ran Canetti, "HMAC: Keyed-Hashing for Message Authentication," RFC 2104, February 1997.

consistently refers to just MD5 authentication (undoubtedly a legacy of having supported message/key hashing authentication years earlier than IS-IS did). The cryptographic authentication used by both OSPF and IS-IS is HMAC-MD5, so do not let the documentation mislead you into thinking they differ.

```
Frame 2 (72 bytes on wire, 72 bytes captured)
IEEE 802.3 Ethernet
Logical-Link Control
ISO 10589 ISIS InTRA Domain Routeing Information Exchange Protocol
    Intra Domain Routing Protocol Discriminator: ISIS (0x83)
    PDU Header Length   : 27
    Version (==1)       : 1
    System ID Length    : 0
    PDU Type            : L1 HELLO (R:000)
    Version2 (==1)      : 1
    Reserved (==0)      : 0
    Max.AREAs: (0==3)   : 0
    ISIS HELLO
        Circuit type            : Level 1 only, reserved(0x00 == 0)
        System-ID {Sender of PDU} : 0192.0168.0002
        Holding timer           : 27
        PDU length              : 51
        Priority                : 64, reserved(0x00 == 0)
        System-ID {Designated IS} : 0192.0168.0002.04
        Protocols Supported (2)
            NLPID(s): IP (0xcc), IPv6 (0x8e)
        IP Interface address(es) (4)
            IPv4 interface address    : 172.16.1.102 (172.16.1.102)
        Area address(es) (4)
            Area address (3): 47.0002
        Authentication (6)
            clear text (1), password (length 5) = ollie
```

Figure 9.2   The simple password authentication used by this IS-IS Hello message carries the password (ollie) in clear text.

Figures 9.3 and 9.4 again show captured OSPF and IS-IS Hellos, but this time MD5 authentication is used. The shared passwords are again stan for OSPF and ollie for IS-IS, but those names are nowhere to be found in the packets. Instead, there are 16-byte (128-bit) message digests that appear to be random numbers.

```
Frame 6 (98 bytes on wire, 98 bytes captured)
Ethernet II, Src: 00:90:27:9d:f1:33, Dst: 01:00:5e:00:00:05
Internet Protocol, Src Addr: 172.16.1.102 (172.16.1.102), Dst Addr: 224.0.0.5
    (224.0.0.5)
Open Shortest Path First
    OSPF Header
        OSPF Version: 2
        Message Type: Hello Packet (1)
        Packet Length: 44
```

```
        Source OSPF Router: 192.168.254.2 (192.168.254.2)
        Area ID: 0.0.0.0 (Backbone)
        Packet Checksum: 0x0000 (none)
        Auth Type: Cryptographic
        Auth Key ID: 0
        Auth Data Length: 16
        Auth Crypto Sequence Number: 0x414764d7
        Auth Data: 79744161070C2FAB6F0BFC85DA5ECB23
    OSPF Hello Packet
        Network Mask: 255.255.255.0
        Hello Interval: 10 seconds
        Options: 0x2 (E)
        Router Priority: 128
        Router Dead Interval: 40 seconds
        Designated Router: 172.16.1.102
        Backup Designated Router: 0.0.0.0
```

Figure 9.3   This OSPF Hello uses MD5 authentication, and the 16 bytes of authentication data reveals nothing about the authentication key.

```
Frame 8 (83 bytes on wire, 83 bytes captured)
IEEE 802.3 Ethernet
Logical-Link Control
ISO 10589 ISIS InTRA Domain Routeing Information Exchange Protocol
    Intra Domain Routing Protocol Discriminator: ISIS (0x83)
    PDU Header Length   : 27
    Version (==1)       : 1
    System ID Length    : 0
    PDU Type            : L1 HELLO (R:000)
    Version2 (==1)      : 1
    Reserved (==0)      : 0
    Max.AREAs: (0==3)   : 0
    ISIS HELLO
        Circuit type             : Level 1 only, reserved(0x00 == 0)
        System-ID {Sender of PDU} : 0192.0168.0002
        Holding timer            : 27
        PDU length               : 62
        Priority                 : 64, reserved(0x00 == 0)
        System-ID {Designated IS} : 0192.0168.0002.04
        Protocols Supported (2)
            NLPID(s): IP (0xcc), IPv6 (0x8e)
        IP Interface address(es) (4)
            IPv4 interface address   : 172.16.1.102 (172.16.1.102)
        Area address(es) (4)
            Area address (3): 47.0002
        Authentication (17)
            hmac-md5 (54), password (length 16) = 0x2e60b26a5c1a5be4050e84318272d91f
```

Figure 9.4   This IS-IS Hello uses MD5 authentication and reveals only the 16-byte cryptographic hash.

Yet another reason for using MD5 authentication is that it provides stronger error detection than either the default OSPF message checksums or the optional IS-IS checksums. See Section 9.2.3 for more information.

Maintaining Effective Authentication

When MD5 was created in 1991, it was thought to be "computationally infeasible" (RFC 1321) to break. But time, powerful PCs, and clever hackers have proven otherwise. You can now download applications such as BAK Scanner, John the Ripper, RainbowCrack, and Cain & Abel that can crack MD5 hashes. These applications use one of two fundamental methods for breaking a hash: brute-force calculations and precomputed tables.

Brute-force methods take repeated guesses at the key, run MD5 against the guessed key, and compare the resulting hash with the intercepted hash. If the hashes match, the program knows the guessed key is correct. These brute-force attacks are often called dictionary attacks because they use an extensive dictionary of common words and names for their guesses.

A crack application using precomputed tables—often called rainbow tables—works similarly to a brute-force program except that it runs through its guesses ahead of time and stores the resulting password/hash pairs in a table. When you try to crack a hash, the program attempts to look the hash up in its table. These programs are faster than brute force, at the expense of using a large amount of memory to store the table.

Fighting this vulnerability in routing protocol authentication means using the same two approaches with your keys that you use to keep any other password-based authentication safe. First, do not use easily guessed keys. If you use a common word or name— even a foreign word or name—a dictionary attack is likely to find it. Use a nonsense word, including a combination of uppercase and lowercase letters, numbers, and punctuation signs.

Second, change your keys regularly. Engineers and operations personnel come and go, leaving more and more people knowledgeable of a "stale" key. Copies of router configurations containing encrypted keys can fall into the wrong hands. And attackers can be adept at "social engineering," tricking someone into revealing a password. I recommend to all of my customers that they change their routing protocol authentication keys at least every three months. Quite a few balk at this, worrying that the benefit of fresh keys does not justify the operational effort of changing keys on a large number of routers. Scripting can ease that effort. Implementations that use keychains—a set of keys that is rotated through periodically and automatically—might reduce the frequency with which you need to change the keys, but even these should be changed regularly.

9.2.2.2 OSPF Authentication

Prior to RFC 2178, OSPF authentication had only an area scope. That is, authentication had to be enabled on all routers and over all links in an area or not at all. RFC 2178 changes that requirement, so that now authentication can be enabled on a link scope; that is, authentication can occur over a single link without having to be enabled on other links in an area. Although authentication is highly encouraged on all links, this change does give you some flexibility in accommodating routers that might not support OSPF authentication. (But that, in turn, raises the question of the wisdom of allowing any OSPF router that does not support authentication into your network.)

The OSPF authentication type and authentication data is carried in the header of every OSPF message (Figure 9.5). The AuType field indicates the type of authentication used:

- **AuType = 0**—Null (no authentication) authentication
- **AuType = 1**—Simple password authentication
- **AuType = 2**—MD5 cryptographic authentication

When Null authentication is used, receiving routers ignore the 64-bit authentication field. Therefore, the field can contain anything; most implementations will set it to all 0s. If simple password authentication is used, the password is carried in the authentication field. Because the field is 64 bits in length, and an ASCII character is 8 bits, the password can be up to 8 characters. If the password is less than 8 characters, 0s are appended to pad the field out to 64 bits.

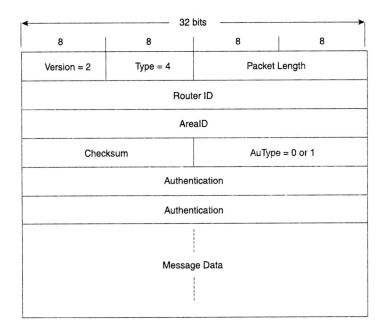

Figure 9.5 The OSPF header format when null or simple password authentication is used.

If MD5 authentication is used, the header format changes as shown in Figure 9.6. The 128-bit message digest (hash) is appended to the end of the message. The Authentication Data length field specifies, in bytes, the length of the appended message digest. Because the hash is always 128 bits (16 bytes), the value of this field should always be 16. The message digest is not considered a part of the OSPF message, and is not accounted for in the Packet Length field of the OSPF header. But as a part of the overall IP packet payload, it is accounted for in the Total Length field of the IP packet header.

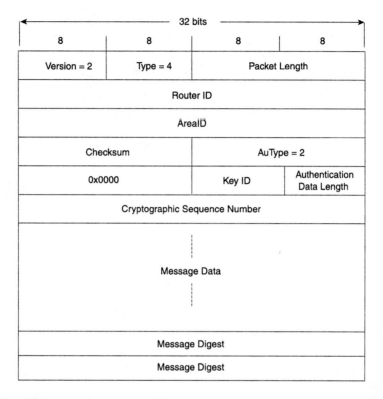

Figure 9.6   The OSPF header format when MD5 authentication is used.

OSPF has a nice feature for changing keys without disrupting the adjacency between neighbors. You can configure multiple keys on an interface and assign each a numeric identifier between 1 and 255. For every message the router sends on the interface, it sends a copy authenticated by each key with the identifier carried in the Key ID field. Neighbors look at the key ID and, if they have a key with the same identifier, use that key for authentication. If there is no matching identifier, the message is dropped. Thus, when you are changing keys, messages continue to be authenticated using the old key. After all neighbors have been configured with the new key, and messages are being authenticated with that key, you can go back and delete the old key.

OSPF MD5 authentication also includes a cryptographic sequence number, which is used to protect against replay attacks. A replay attack is one in which authenticated OSPF packets are copied off of a link and then replayed onto the link at a later time to disrupt or confuse communication between two OSPF neighbors. The cryptographic sequence number is a 32-bit number that the router associates with a neighbor; the router increments the number regularly, and whenever an OSPF message is sent to the neighbor the current value of the number is added to the Cryptographic Sequence Number field. The neighbor, upon receipt of a message, remembers the number. If a subsequent message is received with a cryptographic sequence number less than the current known value, the message is dropped. The idea is that if an OSPF message has been sniffed from the link and replayed at a later time, its sequence number should no longer be valid.

RFC 2328 does not specify a period for incrementing the cryptographic sequence number, leaving that decision up to individual implementers, but it suggests incrementing based on a simple counter or the system clock. A potential problem with this sequence is that there is no provision for a rollover procedure from the maximum value to 0. When a router reaches the maximum value (2^{32}), it resets the number to 0. However, then subsequent messages have values less than the last known number, and the neighbor drops the messages. Because the messages—particularly Hellos—are dropped, the adjacency times out when the RouterDeadInterval expires. When the neighbor changes the router's state to Down, it resets the expected sequence number for the router to 0. Then when the router begins sending messages to reestablish the adjacency, the neighbor will accept them. In reality, rollover should not be a problem in a normally functioning network. With a 32-bit sequence number starting at 0, if the sequence number is incremented once per second it will take more than 135 years to reach the maximum value.

Although cryptographic sequence numbers can prevent some replay attacks, they are not foolproof and in fact can be exploited for a disruptive attack. Notice in Figure 9.3 that the captured packet's cryptographic sequence number, 0x414764d7, is clearly displayed. An attacker could modify the sequence number of a captured message, increasing the number by a significant amount. The message can then be replayed onto the link. The target neighbor will accept these packets with the "more recent" number and begin dropping the legitimate messages, causing the adjacency to fail. When that happens, the attacker can continue to replay the high-numbered messages onto the link, usurping the legitimate messages.

The Authentication Type and Authentication information is stored in the interface data structure (except for the cryptographic sequence number, when used, which is stored in the neighbor data structure). As this implies, you can configure authentication differently on each interface. However, this is usually overkill. Unless you have reason to mistrust a specific neighbor, it is more manageable to use the same authentication key throughout the OSPF domain.

9.2.2.3 IS-IS Authentication

The IS-IS authentication type and authentication data is carried in the Authentication Information TLV (Figure 9.7). The TLV type is 10,[7] and the TLV can be carried in all IS-IS PDU types. ISO 10589 only specifies clear-text password authentication, but because the writers recognized that other authentication methods would be desirable they included an Authentication Type field to specify the method used and a variable Value field that can accommodate a wide range of authentication data.

---

[7] RFC 1195 specifies a TLV type of 133 to support authentication, but no modern IS-IS implementation uses it.

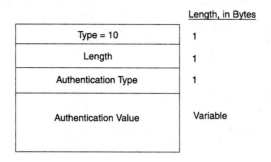

Figure 9.7   The IS-IS Authentication Information TLV.

The currently assigned values of the authentication type field are:

- Authentication Type = 1—**Clear-text password authentication**
- Authentication Type = 54—**HMAC-MD5 authentication**
- Authentication Type = 255—**Routing domain private authentication**

The other possible values of the field are reserved for future use. There is no null or "no authentication" value for IS-IS, as there is for OSPF, because the Authentication Information TLV is optional. If authentication is not configured, the TLV is not included in any IS-IS PDUs. Type 255 authentication is, as the name says, for privately developed authentication mechanisms. When type 1 clear-text password authentication is used, the Authentication Value field carries the ASCII representation of the password. Because the TLV Length field is 1 byte, the maximum length that can be specified is 255 bytes. And because each ASCII character of a clear-text password is 1 byte, the largest password the TLV can carry is 255 characters, although some implementations might limit you to a smaller password length.

IS-IS HMAC-MD5 cryptographic authentication, authentication type 54, is specified in RFC 3567.[8] As with OSPF, the algorithm takes as input the message to be sent and a secret key, and creates a 128-bit cryptographic hash. The hash is carried in the Authentication Value field of the Authentication Information TLV; receiving routers run the same algorithm against the message contents using their own key, and compare the resulting hash with the hash in the Authentication Information TLV. If the originator and receiver have the same key, the hashes should match and the message is authenticated. If the hashes do not match, the message is rejected.

The Checksum and Remaining Lifetime LSP fields are set to 0 by both the originator and the receiver before calculating the hash to negate any influence of a change in either field during transmission might have on the resulting hash. Changing the values of these fields to 0 is only for the authentication algorithm; the actual values of the fields are stored separately.

---

[8]   Tony Li and Ran Atkinson, "Intermediate System to Intermediate System (IS-IS) Cryptographic Authentication," RFC 3567, July 2003.

The total size of the Authentication Information TLV when HMAC-MD5 authentication is used is 19 bytes (a 1-byte type field, 1-byte length field, 1-byte Authentication Type field, and a 16-byte Authentication Value field).

IS-IS HMAC-MD5 authentication does not have a sequencing mechanism like that used by OSPF. So if an attacker can gain physical access to an IS-IS link, it is possible to run a replay attack; IS-IS would then need to rely on fightback characteristics to resist the attack.

IS-IS authentication has three possible scopes:

- Link
- Area
- Domain

When Link authentication scope is enabled, the Authentication Information TLV is carried in Hello PDUs. When Area authentication is enabled, the TLV is carried in all L1 LSPs and SNPs; and when Domain authentication is enabled, the TLV is carried in all L2 LSPs and SNPs. Some IS-IS implementations might not include a separate Link authentication scope, and instead include L1 Hellos in the Area scope and L2 Hellos in the Domain scope.

For each scope supported, you have the option of using the same or separate keys. For example, with the Link scope you can use separate keys on each interface, and with the Area scope you can use separate keys in each area.

All three authentication scopes, and authentication of all IS-IS PDUs, *should* be supported by any implementation, but in reality support can vary. To compensate for this fact some IS-IS implementations will allow you more detailed control over what is authenticated. For example, you might be able to authenticate Hellos, LSPs, and CSNPs but ignore authentication of PSNPs. Juniper Networks JUNOS, for instance, provides the following options that can be enabled for L1, L2, or both:

- no-hello-authentication;
- no-csnp-authentication;
- no-psnp-authentication;

Such intentionally reduced support should be used only when absolutely necessary, to accommodate a system within the domain that does not include full IS-IS authentication. The wisest approach, of course, is to ensure that all systems you install in your network have full HMAC-MD5 authentication support.

Like OSPF, IS-IS allows you to gracefully install or change authentication without breaking adjacencies, but instead of using a key-id scheme it exploits a basic characteristic of the protocol: If an unknown TLV is received, it is ignored. So if an IS-IS router on which authentication is not enabled receives a PDU with a type 10 TLV, the TLV is ignored, and the PDU is accepted. Some implementations therefore allow you to send authenticated IS-IS PDUs while accepting PDUs whether they are authenticated or not. You can enable this option on all routers in the affected scope, enable or change the keys, and then disable the option on all routers so that only authenticated PDUs are accepted. (The Cisco Systems IOS command is **isis authentication send-only** and the Juniper Networks JUNOS command is **no-authentication-check**.) This scheme proves particularly useful for enabling authentication on an operational IS-IS network without scheduling downtime. For changing keys, it appears to be more operationally intense than the OSPF key-id method; but as recommended previously, regular key changes should be performed with scripts, and scripts can easily incorporate this procedure.

9.2.3   Checksums

The OSPF message header (Figure 9.8) includes a Checksum field for helping to verify the integrity of the message. The checksum algorithm is the same one used in most IP headers: The message, except for the 64-bit Authentication field, is divided into 16-bit sections, and the one's complement sum of all these segments is calculated. The one's complement of that sum is then calculated (so that the result is the one's complement of the one's complement sum) and included in the Checksum field before transmission.[9] Receiving OSPF routers make the same calculation and compare the results. Conflicting checksum values indicate that an error has occurred during transmission.

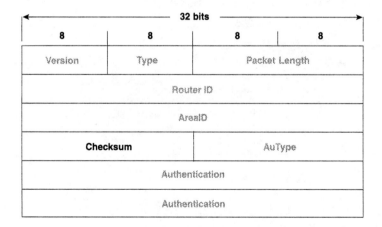

Figure 9.8   The header used by all five OSPF message types includes an IP-style 16-bit checksum field.

This checksum algorithm is weaker than other error-detection algorithms, such as the cyclical redundancy check (CRC) used by some data-link protocols. It cannot, for instance, detect multiple canceling bit errors or the reordering of bytes.

---

[9]   One's complement arithmetic is easily performed, especially by computers. You can learn more from any book on basic binary arithmetic.

Interestingly, the checksum algorithm used with OSPF LSAs is not the IP-style one's complement checksum, but is instead an ISO-style Fletcher checksum.[10] Fletcher checksums are also based on one's complement arithmetic but use a more complicated algorithm than IP-style checksums, producing error detection on par with CRC.

Unlike OSPF, the IS-IS PDU header (Figure 9.9) does not have a Checksum field. So whereas LSPs have a 16-bit Fletcher checksum, Hellos and SNPs must rely on the underlying data-link error detection, if any. To address the concerns about this data-link dependence, RFC 3358 adds an optional checksumming capability.[11] When this option is supported, a Checksum TLV (Figure 9.10) is added to Hellos and SNPs, a 16-bit Fletcher checksum is calculated over the full contents of the PDU, and the result is carried in the Value field of the TLV. The TLV type is 12, and the length of the Value field is 2 bytes.

Intradomain Routeing Protocol Discriminator = 0x83	1
Length Indicator	1
Protocol ID	1
ID Length	1
Type	1
Version	1
Reserved = 0x00	1
Maximum Area Addresses	1

Figure 9.9   The IS-IS PDU header does not have a Checksum field.

Length, in Bytes

Type = 12	1
Length	1
Checksum	2

Figure 9.10   The optional IS-IS Checksum TLV.

If a router supporting the optional checksum capability receives a Hello or SNP with a Checksum TLV and the checksum fails, the router rejects the message. However, if it receives a message that does not contain a Checksum TLV, the router accepts the message. This provides backward compatibility with systems that do not support the option. Systems that do not support the option ignore the Checksum TLV and accept otherwise-valid messages containing them.

---

[10] International Standards Organization, "Information Technology—Protocol for Providing the Connectionless-Mode Internetwork Service: Protocol Specification," ISO/IEC 8473-1:1998, Annex C, 1998.

[11] Tony Przygienda, "Optional Checksums in Intermediate System to Intermediate System (IS-IS)," RFC 3358, August 2002.

If MD5 authentication is used, and a transmission error causes a change to an OSPF or IS-IS message, the authentication check will fail and the receiver will reject the message. MD5 is stronger at detecting errors than either IP-style checksums or Fletcher checksums, providing yet another reason for using MD5 authentication in your OSPF or IS-IS network. Therefore, the standard checksum procedures of OSPF and the optional checksum procedures of IS-IS change when MD5 authentication is enabled. When OSPF MD5 authentication is enabled, the router does not calculate a checksum and sets the checksum field in the header to 0x0000. Similarly, if an IS-IS router supports optional checksums and HMAC-MD5 authentication is enabled, it either sets the checksum value of the Checksum TLV to 0x0000 or it does not include the TLV in the message at all. This procedural change is particularly important for IS-IS because the originator sets the value of the Checksum TLV to 0 before calculating the MD5 hash. Receiving systems that do not support the checksum option will ignore the Checksum TLV and accept the packet, but will include the TLV in the MD5 calculation, causing an authentication failure.

9.2.4 Graceful Restart

One of the first things we all learned about routing is that it consists of two basic processes: path determination and packet forwarding. Modern high-performance routers implement them as separate physical components, with their own processors and memory, as depicted in Figure 9.11 When routing protocol messages are received, the packet forwarding module (of which the router interfaces are a part) sends the messages to the route processing module. The routing protocols running on the route processing module create a routing information database (RIB). The best path to each destination in the RIB is chosen, and this information is used to form the forwarding information database (FIB), which the route processing module sends to the packet forwarding module. The packet forwarding module then forwards according to the information in the FIB without having to directly consult the route processing module.

This delegation of the two basic processes to separate physical components provides performance advantages during times of heavy load: The path determination component can process many routes during times of severe network change without taking resources from the packet forwarding component, and the packet forwarding component can handle peak traffic loads without taking resources from the path determination component.

A side effect of this architecture is that so long as the network architecture does not change the packet forwarding module can continue to forward packets based on the FIB even if the route processing module stops operating. This is the basis of *graceful restart*, also called *nonstop forwarding*: If the routing protocol stops and restarts for some reason, such as a software error causing a protocol reset, a switchover to a backup route processing module, or a manual reset as part of operational maintenance, the router can continue forwarding packets based on the FIB created before the restart. Thus, graceful restart contributes to area stability both by maintaining forwarding paths during a restart and by reducing the LSA/LSP flooding and SPF/FIB churn normally accompanying a router restart. The contingency is that if the network topology changes while the routing protocol is down, the accuracy of the FIB can no longer be assumed and forwarding must stop until the restart is complete.

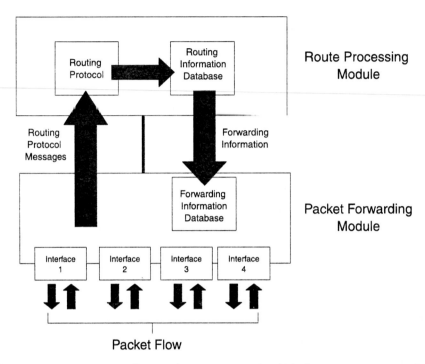

Figure 9.11   A conceptual model of high-performance routers in which discrete components perform route processing and packet forwarding.

Any routing protocol can support graceful restart; this section examines the details for graceful restart for OSPF and IS-IS.

9.2.4.1   OSPF Graceful Restart[12]

Under normal OSPF procedures, when a router restarts, all its adjacencies are broken. If the restart is planned, the router breaks its adjacencies by flushing all LSAs it originated. If the restart is unplanned, the router's neighbors break the adjacencies when they cease receiving Hellos. When a neighbor detects the restart, it refloods its LSAs, indicating that its links to the restarting router are no longer available. With all neighbors following this procedure, traffic is rerouted around the restarting router, avoiding the potential of routing loops or black holes resulting from a loss of synchronization and a possibly corrupted FIB. Graceful restart modifies these procedures so that, for a limited time, the restarting router remains in the forwarding path of any routes that passed through the router before the restart.

---

[12] John Moy, Padma Pillay-Esnault, and Acee Lindem, "Graceful OSPF Restart," RFC 3623, November 2003.

The key conditions that enable OSPF graceful restart are:

- A stable topology during the restart period
- The capability of the restarting router to retain a functioning FIB during the restart period
- The ability of neighbors to revert to the standard OSPF procedures, as described earlier, if a topological change is detected during the restart period

When an OSPF router begins a graceful restart, it sends a Grace LSA that indicates to its neighbors the time, in seconds, that the neighbors should continue to treat the router as fully adjacent (that is, in a state of full database synchronization) and the reason for the restart. During this time, called the *grace period*, the neighbors supporting this graceful restart are called *helpers* and their state is *helper mode*. The helper neighbor is responsible for detecting topological changes during the grace period and responding appropriately.

9.2.4.1.1 Planned Restarts

A planned restart is one in which the OSPF process is administratively restarted. The protocol has the opportunity, in this situation, to notify its neighbors that it is restarting gracefully. The administrator, as a part of the restart request, can specify the grace period or can accept the default grace period. For example, JUNOS has a default OSPF grace period of 180 seconds. The grace period—whether default or specified—should be less than the LSRefreshTime (1800 seconds) so that the LSAs the router originated before restart do not age out of the LS databases.

When a graceful restart is requested, the restarting router first records the cryptographic sequence numbers for each restarting interface. It then issues a Grace LSA to its neighbors on each restarting interface. The router does not flush its LSAs from area databases as it would under normal restart procedures. The router records the grace period, and begins its restart. The graceful restart ends when any of the following occurs:

- The restarting router reestablishes full adjacencies with all neighbors and receives its pre-restart type 1 LSAs from the neighbors (and, if it is the designated router, pre-restart type 2 LSAs).
- The router receives a type 1 LSA from a neighbor that is inconsistent with its pre-restart type 1 LSA, indicating that the neighbor does not support or did not enter helper mode.
- The grace period expires.

When graceful restart ends, the restarting router re-originates its type 1 LSA and (if it is the designated router) its type 2 LSA. It flushes its Grace LSAs, reruns its routing calculations, and updates its FIB. Invalid FIB entries are removed; invalid locally originated LSAs are flushed; and type 3, 4, 5, and 7 LSAs are reflooded as necessary.

In some circumstances, a neighbor will not enter helper mode, even if it is helper capable. For example, if there are LSAs in the neighbor's LS retransmission list for the restarting router other than periodically refreshed LSAs (an LSA change indicates a topological change) the neighbor will not enter helper mode.

A router can act as helper for multiple restarting neighbors, but cannot enter helper mode if it is itself restarting.

A helper neighbor exits helper mode when any of the following occurs:

- The restarting neighbor flushes its Grace LSA, indicating that its graceful restart has successfully terminated.

- The grace period expires.

- A topological change occurs, as indicated by the installation of a new or changed type 1-5 or 7 LSA that would normally require flooding to the restarting neighbor. Periodically refreshed LSAs do not cause an exit from helper mode, because this is a steady-state process that does not result from topology changes.

When a router exits helper mode, it refloods its type 1 LSA. If the OSPF network type of the link to the restarting neighbor is broadcast, the router recalculates the DR and, if it is the DR, it refloods its type 2 LSA.

Note that a neighbor that does not support graceful restart will ignore the Grace LSA. This neighbor will follow normal OSPF procedures, reflooding its type 1 LSA, indicating that the link to the restarting router is no longer available. This changed LSA causes any neighbors of the restarting router that are in helper mode to exit helper mode, and the restarting router to exit graceful restart by the rules stated in the above bulleted lists. This behavior permits backward compatibility, but also means that for graceful restart to be fully effective all routers should support it.

9.2.4.1.2   Unplanned Restarts

Unplanned restarts are the result of such anomalies as routing process failures and unexpected switchover to a backup route processor. Procedures for an unplanned graceful restart are the same as for a planned restart, except that the restarting router sends its Grace LSAs after the restart rather than before. The Grace LSAs must be sent on all OSPF interfaces before Hellos are sent, and with the restart reason set to 0 or 3 (see the following subsection).

An unplanned graceful restart is successful only if the neighbor's RouterDeadInterval does not expire during the restart period. If this timer expires, the neighboring router originates a new LSA, stopping the graceful restart process.

A concern with unplanned restarts is that a software crash causing the restart could corrupt the FIB. As a result, RFC 3623 leaves it to the implementer to decide whether to support unplanned graceful restarts.

9.2.4.1.3 The Grace LSA

The Grace LSA is a type 9 Opaque LSA. (Opaque LSAs are discussed in Section 10.1.2.) This LSA type has link-local scope, meaning it is never flooded beyond a directly connected neighbor. The Opaque Type is 3 and the Opaque ID is 0.

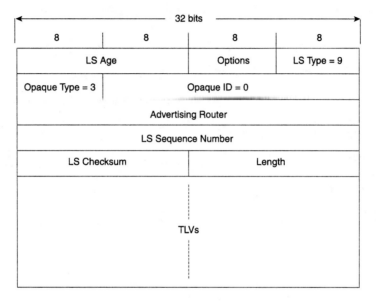

Figure 9.12 The Grace LSA.

Figure 9.12 shows the format of the Grace LSA. The information in the LSA is contained in three TLVs:

- **Grace Period TLV** has a type of 1 and a length of 4. Its Value field specifies the number of seconds a router's neighbors should continue to advertise the originating router as fully adjacent. This value should not exceed the LSRefresh time of 1800 seconds, to prevent the restarting router's LSAs from aging out. The LS age is set to 0 when the LSA is originated, and is incremented normally. The grace period is considered to start when the LSA is originated; if the LS age exceeds the grace period value, the grace period is terminated.
- **Graceful Restart Reason TLV** has a type of 2 and a length of 1. The value field can be 0 through 3, specifying one of the following restart reasons:
  - 0 = Unknown
  - 1 = Software restart
  - 2 = Software reload/upgrade
  - 3 = Switchover to redundant control processor

As mentioned in the previous subsection, an unplanned restart must have a restart reason of 0 or 3. A planned restart can have any of the four reasons.

- **IP Interface Address TLV** has a type of 3 and a length of 4. Its value is the IP address of the interface on which the LSA is originated. This TLV is only needed on multi-access networks (broadcast, NBMA, and point to multipoint), where the helper must identify which of possibly multiple neighbors is restarting.

9.2.4.1.4   Cisco Systems NSF

Cisco Systems signals its Non-Stop Forwarding (NSF) capability as described in the Internet drafts "OSPF Restart Signaling,"[13] "OSPF Link-Local Signaling,"[14] and "OSPF Out-of-Band LSDB Resynchronization."[15] Of these, only the first draft deals directly with NSF. The last two drafts describe mechanisms that can be exploited for support of NSF.

The Internet draft "OSPF Link-Local Signaling" describes an Extended Options TLV for OSPF Hellos. NSF capabilities are signaled between neighbors with a Restart Signal (RS) bit, which is 0x00000002 in the Extended Options TLV. After a route processor switchover, a Cisco Systems router sets the RS bit in its Hellos to inform neighbors that it is restarting in NSF mode (like an unplanned graceful restart) and that it would like the neighbor to preserve the existing adjacency.

When a neighbor supporting the Cisco NSF capability receives a Hello containing an Extended Options TLV with the RS bit set, it ignores the neighbor list in Hellos received from the restarting router. This is to prevent the neighbor from generating a 1-Way Received event, which would normally break the adjacency, if it does not see itself listed in the Hello of a restarting router.

Graceful restart–capable routers that do not support Cisco NSF ignore the RS bit and do not respond in kind. Therefore, Cisco Systems routers treat GR-capable neighbors as non-NSF routers and follow standard OSPF procedures during restarts.

Cisco Systems routers will acknowledge Grace LSAs generated by GR-capable neighbors, but they do not become GR helper neighbors. As a result, GR-capable routers revert to standard OSPF procedures during restart when peered with a Cisco Systems router.

Therefore, although graceful restart and Cisco Systems NSF are not interoperable, their respective signaling causes no difficulties for peering. Further, each router can successfully support the restart of a like neighbor (NSF to NSF or GR to GR) behind the peering.

---

[13] Alex Zinin, Abhay Roy, and Liem Nguyen, "OSPF Restart Signaling," draft-ietf-ospf-restart-01.txt, February 2001.

[14] Alex Zinin, Friedman, Abhay Roy, Nguyen, and Yeung, "OSPF Link-Local Signalling," draft-nguyen-ospf-lls-04.txt, January 2004.

[15] Alex Zinin, Abhay Roy, and Liem Nguyen, "OSPF Out-of-Band LSDB Resynchronization," draft-nguyen ospf-oob-resync-04.txt, January 2004.

9.2.4.2   IS-IS Graceful Restart[16]

The normal reaction of an IS-IS router to a restarting neighbor is similar to OSPF's. When the holding timer associated with the restarting neighbor expires, the router declares the adjacency down and floods LSPs to indicate the adjacency change. The routers in the L1 area or L2 subdomain (depending on whether the broken adjacency was L1 or L2) run an SPF calculation to account for the change. When the router resumes receiving Hellos from the restarting neighbor the adjacency is reestablished, the SRM flags for the link are set on the LSPs in the database; and if the link is point to point, one or more CSNPs are sent to the neighbor. LSPs are again flooded to other neighbors to indicate the adjacency change, and SPF is again run in the area or subdomain.

As with OSPF, IS-IS graceful restart modifies these procedures to exploit a separation of the control and forwarding processors in a router. Defined in RFC 3847, IS-IS graceful restart uses a new TLV, called the Restart TLV and carried in Hellos, to provide the necessary signaling. Similar to the way OSPF graceful restart differentiates between planned and unplanned restarts, IS-IS graceful restart differentiates between *restarting* and *starting* routers:

- A restarting router expects to preserve its FIB and a functioning forwarding module while IS-IS restarts. Therefore, the goal is for the router's neighbors to preserve their existing adjacencies and not reinitialize them.

- A starting router might be starting its IS-IS process for the first time or it might have experienced some uncontrolled (unplanned) restart. In any case, the FIB of a starting router cannot be trusted to be complete or accurate until database synchronization is complete. Therefore, the goal is for neighbors to suppress advertisement of adjacencies to the router until the router's database is synchronized; and if a neighbor has an adjacency to the router left over from a previously existing IS-IS process, that adjacency must be reinitialized.

Although RFC 3847 does not use the terms *helper* and *helper mode*, these OSPF terms can be usefully applied to IS-IS graceful restart. That is, a helper is a router that understands and can support the graceful restart of a neighbor, and the router is in helper mode when it is in the process of supporting a restarting neighbor. RFC 3847 does define *restart mode*, which you might be tempted to equate with helper mode. But there is a difference: Where helper mode refers to the state of a router when it is assisting a gracefully restarting neighbor, restart mode is a neighbor state by which a router views a restarting neighbor.

9.2.4.2.1   The Restart TLV

Any IS-IS router supporting graceful restart capability indicates its support by including a Restart TLV (Figure 9.13) in its Hellos. If a router that does not support graceful restart receives Hellos containing this TLV, the router ignores the TLV.

- The type number of the TLV is 211.
- The **Restart Request** (RR) flag, when set, indicates that the originating router is beginning a graceful restart.

---

[16] Mike Shand and Les Ginsberg, " Restart Signaling for Intermediate System to Intermediate System (IS-IS)," RFC 3847, July 2004.

■ The **Restart Acknowledgment** (RA) flag, when set, indicates that the originating router has received an RR from a restarting neighbor and is willing to enter helper mode.

■ The **Suppress Adjacency Advertisement** (SA) flag, when set, indicates that the originating router is starting (as opposed to restarting) and that the receiving neighbor should not advertise its adjacency to the starting router in its LSPs or include the adjacency in its own SPF calculations, because the starting router's database and FIB cannot yet be trusted to be accurate. This corrects a difficulty inherent in IS-IS, in which two routers are considered adjacent—and the adjacency can be advertised—before their databases are synchronized.

■ **Remaining Time** is used by a router in helper mode to tell a restarting neighbor how long, in seconds, the router will maintain the existing adjacency in the Up state. This time is important for the T3 timer described in the following subsection.

■ **Restarting Neighbor ID** is used by routers sending an RA on a LAN to indicate the SysID of the neighbor that sent the RR. This is so that if more than one router on a LAN has sent a RR, the originator of the RA can indicate which neighbor's restart request it is acknowledging.

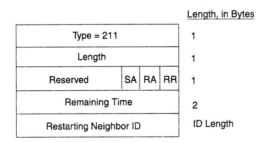

Figure 9.13   The Restart TLV.

9.2.4.2.2 Timers

Three timers are defined by RFC 3847 to manage IS-IS graceful restarts:

■ **T1**—This timer regulates the period that a starting or restarting router waits for an acknowledgement of a restart request before sending another restart request. Because the RRs and RAs are sent and received in Hellos on each interface, a separate T1 is defined for each interface. RFC 3847 suggests a T1 period of 3 seconds.

■ **T2**—This timer regulates the period a starting or restarting router waits to synchronize its database with all neighbors. When the timer expires, the router assumes that the database is synchronized and that it can reliably participate in packet forwarding. The timer is associated with the LS database, and so if a router is L1/L2 there is a separate T2 for each database. RFC 3847 suggests a T2 period of 60 seconds. The T2 timer is used as a protection, so that if two neighbors never synchronize their databases the GR process does not permanently stop.

■ T3—This timer is used only by restarting routers, not by starting routers, and regulates a situation in which a neighbor's holding time expires before database synchronization is complete. The timer is initialized to 65,535 seconds but is then adjusted to the smallest value in the remaining time fields of all RAs received from Up neighbors. If the timer expires before synchronization is complete, it can be assumed that the holding time (from which the remaining time value is derived) of at least one neighbor has expired and that the neighbor has flooded LSPs indicating that the adjacency to the restarting router is down. In this case, the restarting router floods its own LSPs with the OL bit set to indicate that it does not have a fully synchronized database.

9.2.4.2.3 Restarts

When a restart begins, the restarting router sends Hellos on all IS-IS interfaces with the RR flag set and starts timers T1, T2, and T3. When a helper neighbor receives an RR, it knows to attempt to maintain the adjacency to the restarting router. The helper sends a Hello with the RA flag set and the RR flag cleared; the remaining time field set to the present value of its holding timer for the adjacency; and, if the adjacency's interface is LAN, the restarting neighbor ID set to the SysID of the restarting router. This last parameter ensures a restarting router can differentiate an RA meant for it from an RA meant for another restarting router on the same broadcast network. If the interface to the restarting router is point to point, or if the interface is LAN and the helper is the DIS, the helper sends the necessary CSNPs to describe its database.

The restarting router adjusts the period of T3 to the lowest value of the remaining time fields of the received RAs from neighbors indicating an adjacency state of Up to the router. When a CSNP or a complete set of CSNPs and the RA are received, the T1 for the receiving interface is stopped.

When the router has synchronized its database with all neighbors, T2 and T3 are stopped, the router performs its SPF calculations and updates its FIB as needed, and floods its LSPs.

If T1 expires before an RA and CSNP is received on the associated interface, another RR is sent and the timer is restarted. If T3 expires, the restarting router floods its LSPs with the OL bit set to indicate an incomplete database synchronization. If T2 expires, the router runs SPF, updates its FIB as needed, and floods its LSPs. If the LSPs have already been flooded with the OL bit set due to an expired T3, the bit is cleared in the newly flooded LSPs.

Note that the SA flag is not used during restarts, and remains clear throughout the process.

When the restart is complete, the RR, RA, and SA flags are cleared in Hellos sent by the restarted router.

9.2.4.2.4 Starts

A router signals a start by sending on each of its IS-IS interfaces a Hello with the RR and RA flags cleared and the SA flag set to tell its helper neighbors to suppress advertisement of their adjacencies to the starting router. At the same time the SA is sent, the starting router starts timers T1 and T2. T3 is not used during starts.

When the state of an adjacency from the starting router to a neighbor transitions to Up, the starting router sends its LSPs to the neighbor but with the OL bit set. When a CSNP and RA is received from the neighbor, T1 for that interface is stopped. And when either synchronization with all neighbors is complete or T2 expires, the starting router runs its SPF, updates its FIB, and floods its LSPs with the OL bit cleared. Hellos are sent with the SA bit cleared, telling helper neighbors to no longer suppress their adjacencies to the started router.

Notice that the RR flag is not set initially. But if T1 expires, the timer is restarted and Hellos are sent with both the RR and SA flags set.

As with restarts, when the start is complete, the RR, RA, and SA flags are cleared in Hellos sent by the started router.

9.2.4.2.5   Interaction with Neighbors That Do Not Support Graceful Restart

Routers that do not support graceful restart ignore the Restart TLV, and so during starts or restarts proceed with normal IS-IS procedures of transitioning the adjacency state to Down, flooding LSPs, and then attempting to reinitialize the adjacency. When a starting or restarting router receives a Hello with no Restart TLV on a point-to-point interface, indicating that the neighbor does not support graceful restart, it stops the T1 timer for that interface. Normal IS-IS operation means that CSNPs might or might not be received on the interface, so synchronization is considered complete for this neighbor, whether it really is or not.

This does not apply to LAN interfaces, however, where some neighbors might be restart capable and others might not. So if a Hello is received with no Restart TLV, T1 continues running. However if no restart-capable neighbors exist on the LAN link, it would be undesirable for T1 to continually expire and be restarted. Therefore, RFC 3847 recommends that the timer not be restarted after some number of expirations, and normal Hellos be sent after that. The RFC leaves it to the implementers to specify the maximum number of T1 expirations.

9.2.5   Bidirectional Forwarding Detection

Another capability made possible by the architectural separation of route processing and packet forwarding is bidirectional forwarding detection (BFD).[17] This is a simple Hello protocol for verifying bidirectional communication to a neighboring router's packet forwarding module. Specifically, it detects failures to forwarding path next hops. It can detect these failures in the subsecond range and notify routing protocols of the failure, thus augmenting and improving the routing protocols' own failure-detection abilities.

BFD can send and receive its control (Hello) packets in the millisecond range, which provides a useful utility for routing protocols to quickly detect transport failures in the packet

---

[17] Dave Katz and Dave Ward, "Bidirectional Forwarding Detection," draft-katz-ward-bfd-01.txt, August 2003. BFD encapsulation is described separately in Dave Katz and Dave Ward, "BFD for IPv4 and IPv6 (Single Hop)," draft-katz-ward-bfd-v4v6-1hop-00.txt, August 2003.

forwarding module, link, or interfaces. This is particularly important on physical media such as Ethernet that do not provide fast failure detection within the data-link procedures. BFD can also detect unidirectional failures such as can occasionally occur in an Ethernet switch.

Traditionally, attempts are made to decrease failure detection times by reducing the Hello intervals of the routing protocol. But this approach has distinct limitations. The architectural constraints of OSPF, for example, prevent the protocol from detecting loss of 2-way communication with peers in less than 2 seconds. Some IS-IS implementations allow Hello intervals as short as 333 milliseconds, but this is not universally supported. And because routing protocol Hellos are processed in the route processor, significantly reducing the Hello interval can impact the CPU load.

BFD is designed to run on the packet forwarding module. Because of its independence from the route processor and any individual routing protocol, BFD can establish sessions for multiple upper-layer protocols and across multiple connections between peers. This separation from the control plane also means BFD enhances the robustness of graceful restart.

9.2.5.1   BFD Functional Model

BFD has two operating modes and an adjunct function:

- **Asynchronous** mode is the primary operating mode. Independent streams of BFD control packets are sent periodically between devices. If some multiple of sequential control packets are not received, the session is declared Down.

- **Demand** mode is used when neighboring systems have some way to independently verify connectivity. When the BFD session is established, control packets are no longer sent except when a system requests explicit verification of connectivity. This mode proves useful in situations where the overhead of periodic polling might adversely affect performance.

- **Echo** mode is an adjunct function that can be performed in either asynchronous or demand mode. In echo mode, BFD control packets are sent only for parameter negotiation. BFD echo packets are sequentially streamed to the neighboring device, which loops the packets through its forwarding path back to the sender. If a specified multiple of echo packets is not received, the session is declared Down. In this mode the sender is in control of the response times, and can aggressively test both the link and the remote forwarding path. The importance here is that echo mode can compensate for a situation in normal asynchronous mode in which sloppy timers might, through the late transmission of control packets, cause the receiver to falsely declare the link down. In echo mode, the same timer is tied to transmission and reception of the packets, so a late transmission does not cause a false failure detection.

BFD uses a three-way handshake similar to that used by the OSPF Hello protocol to verify bidirectional communication. When the "I Hear You" field of the BFD control packet is non-zero in both directions, bidirectional communication is considered verified and the BFD session is established.

Because multiple BFD sessions can be active on a single link, a discriminator is used to identify and demultiplex control packets for each session.

Three parameters control the exchange of control packets:

- **Desired Minimum Transmit Interval** (bfd.DesiredMinTxInterval) is the minimum interval, in microseconds, that the originating system would like to use between transmitted control packets.

- **Required Minimum Receive Interval** (bfd.RequiredMinRxInterval) is the minimum interval, in microseconds, that the originating system can receive control packets.

- **Detect Multiplier** (bfd.DetectMult) is a nonzero integer multiplier applied to the negotiated transmission interval that specifies the period (the detection time) a system will wait to hear a control packet before declaring the BFD session down.

The two timers and the detection multiplier are continuously negotiated, are independent in each direction, and can be changed at any time. Each system transmits the period it would like to transmit control packets, and the minimum period it is willing to receive control packets. The agreed-upon transmit and receive periods are jittered up to 25 percent to prevent synchronization on multi-access links.

9.2.5.2   The BFD Control Packet

BFD Control packets are encapsulated as appropriate to the transmission link between the neighboring systems. When the packet is encapsulated in IPv4 or IPv6, the TTL (or IPv6 Hop Count) field is set to 255. This helps to prevent attacks against the protocol originating from off the link. The packets are always unicast, and hence BFD sessions are always point to point. Figure 9.14 shows the packet format.

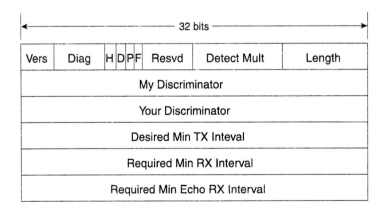

Figure 9.14   The BFD Control packet.

- **Version** is the BFD protocol version. Currently the version is 0.

- **Diagnostic** specifies the reason for a system transition from Up to some other state. The possible transition codes carried in this field are:
  - ◆ 0 = No diagnostic
  - ◆ 1 = Control detection time expired
  - ◆ 2 = Echo function failed
  - ◆ 3 = Neighbor signaled session down
  - ◆ 4 = Forwarding plane reset
  - ◆ 5 = Path down
  - ◆ 6 = Concatenated path down
  - ◆ 7 = Administratively down

- **I Hear You** (H) is cleared (0) if the transmitting system either is not receiving BFD packets from the remote system or is in the process of tearing down the BFD session.

- **Demand** (D) is set if the transmitting system wishes to operate in demand mode.

- **Poll** (P) is set if the transmitting system is requesting verification of connectivity or a parameter change. The bit is used in demand mode.

- **Final** (F) is set if the transmitting system is responding to a control packet in which the Poll bit is set. This bit is used in demand mode.

- **Reserved** bits are cleared (0) and are ignored on receipt.

- **Detect Multiplier** is the multiplier by which the transmitting system calculates the detection time from the negotiated transmit interval when in asynchronous mode.

- **Length** is the length of the BFD control packet in bytes. The control packet is a fixed length, so the value of this field is always 24.

- **My Discriminator** is a unique non-zero value generated by the transmitting system for demultiplexing multiple BFD sessions between the same two systems.

- **Your Discriminator** is the value received in the my discriminator field of the remote system, or is 0 if that value is unknown. When the my discriminator field is reflected back in the your discriminator field, received packets are demultiplexed based on the your discriminator field only. This means that the source address of the packet or the originating interface can change without effecting or disrupting the BFD session.

- **Desired Minimum Transmission Interval** is the minimum interval, in microseconds, that the local system would like to use when transmitting control packets.

- **Required Minimum Receive Interval** is the minimum interval, in microseconds, between received control packets that this system is willing to support.

- **Required Minimum Echo Receive Interval** is the minimum interval, in microseconds, between BFD echo packets this system is capable of supporting. If this field is 0, the originating system does not support the receipt of BFD echo packets.

9.3   Designing for Security and Reliability

The bulk of this chapter focuses on features of and extensions to OSPF and IS-IS that contribute to security and reliability. However, the features and extensions examined here can protect your network only from the potentially negative influences that these two protocols can have. So many other things can go wrong that tightly securing your IGP while ignoring wider vulnerabilities is a bit like locking the door but leaving the windows wide open. Therefore, the remainder of this chapter provides an overview of wider factors to consider for ensuring a secure, reliable network. This section examines good design practices, and Section 9.4 examines good operational practices.

9.3.1   Redundancy

I recently boarded a flight in Taipei bound for Hong Kong. After a noticeable delay on the taxiway, the pilot announced, "Sorry folks, we need to return to the terminal because I'm not happy with the functioning of one of the fuel control systems. Although the system has triple redundancy, I'm not willing to take the chance."

Groans sounded throughout the plane over expectations of missed meetings or missed flight connections, but probably not a single person aboard wished the pilot would go ahead and "take the chance." Even with a triple-redundant system.

Most large enterprises have become dependent on their networks for the functioning of their core business. And if you run a carrier or ISP, the network *is* your business. As a result, designers of large networks must have a streak of pessimism in them, believing that if something can go wrong, it will go wrong. You should be as diligent in designing redundancy into the most vital portions of your network as an aircraft engineer is when designing a vehicle that will carry hundreds of people miles above an ocean. The consequences of failure can be severe.

There are three areas in which to consider redundancy in network design: system components, network links, and network nodes.

The most vulnerable of individual system components is usually the power supply, because of the high heat they generate. All mission-critical routers in your network should therefore have redundant power supplies. And do not make the surprisingly common mistake of connecting both power supplies on the same system to the same power source. They should be on separate electrical circuits with separate circuit breakers.

The second essential system to consider for redundancy on a router is the route processor module—the route processor, routing engine, route controller, control processor, or whatever the individual vendor chooses to call this component. Both heat and complex software code can be culprits in putting these modules at risk. Physical separation of this component from the packet forwarding module, as discussed in Section 9.2.4, makes redundant route processor modules possible. Graceful restart is a particularly important feature to support when using redundant route processor modules, to ensure that an automatic or manual switchover to a backup module does not interfere with packet forwarding.

And because heat is a major contributor to component failure, redundant cooling systems are important. Other router components to consider for redundancy are switching fabrics and clock sources.

Even with a wealth of redundant components, it is still possible for an entire router to fail. Therefore, at the most critical parts of your network, the routers themselves should be redundant. Figure 9.15 shows an example of a common redundant router design typically used in a core access site. Here both the core routers and the aggregation routers behind them are redundant. Such a site architecture provides not only resiliency against a router failure, but also redundancy for one of the most vulnerable parts of the network: the links and interfaces. In this design, no single core or aggregation router failure can isolate the site, nor can the failure of any two links or interfaces connecting the four routers isolate any one of them from the other three.

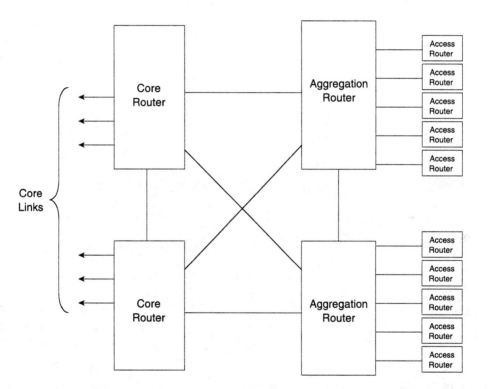

Figure 9.15   Using redundant routers at a core access site.

Because the routers in Figure 9.15 are presumably in the same physical site (and probably in the same or adjoining equipment racks), the links connecting them are likely to be wire or fiber jumpers. As such, they are safer than the usual physical link, but not without risk. Jumpers—particularly the connectors at each end—can go bad. And the biggest risk of all, as usual, is human: The local technician might inadvertently disconnect or break a jumper while working nearby.

However, links connecting core sites to each other and links connecting access sites to the core site—in other words, any link connecting physically remote sites—are among the most failure-prone components of your network. The majority of the physical link is out of your control, and is exposed to human, animal, and natural damage. Redundancy here is crucial, particularly in the core. You have already read, in Chapters 5 and 7, suggestions concerning making your IGP backbone and area connectivity reliable. Figure 9.16 extends those suggestions and shows four general core architectures: fully meshed, partially meshed, ring, and a ring-mesh hybrid.

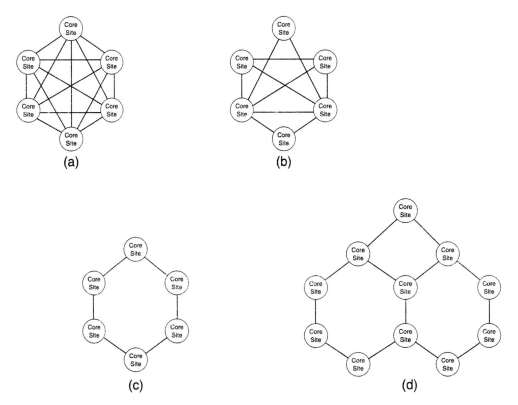

Figure 9.16   Four general core architectures are a full mesh (a), a partial mesh (b), a ring (c), and a ring-mesh hybrid (d).

The full-mesh architecture provides the highest degree of redundancy, but is also the most cost-prohibitive due to the number of links required. The partial mesh is a good compromise, and allows you to add links where you decide that both the risk and the bandwidth demand is greatest. Rings are the most economical of the redundant architectures, but also provide the least resiliency: Any two link failures will partition the network. Rings can also introduce more latency than other architectures because of the average distance between nodes. The ring-mesh hybrid is perhaps the best compromise between redundancy and cost, particularly in large region- or continent-spanning networks. Dual link failures might still isolate some parts of the network, but the mesh element reduces this risk while still requiring a low number of links.

Notice in Figure 9.15 that single links connect the access routers to the aggregation routers. If the access routers are located within the core site, doubling the number of interfaces used easily adds redundancy from each access router to each aggregation router. The consequences of isolating a single access site might well justify the expense of doubling the number of interfaces used. More likely, however, the access routers are located at remote sites—customer sites or field offices, for example. If the remote site is to have redundant connections to the core network, another vulnerability must be considered: A core site is vulnerable to catastrophic loss through fire, weather, flood, massive power outage, riot, or terrorist act. So if a remote access site needs redundancy, consider the technical and economic feasibility of attaching the redundant links to separate core sites.

9.3.2 Protecting the Domain Edge

Always remember that OSPF and IS-IS are IGPs. That is, they are designed to be used interior to an autonomous system. *Never run either protocol to a router outside of your administrative control*; you should always have full control over what crosses the edge of your OSPF or IS-IS domain. Static routes are the preferred means of routing to an external router because you have complete control over the external routes. If dynamic exchange of routes is required, use BGP, which is designed for peering with untrusted routers by supporting complex routing policies.

You must also use packet filters to help regulate what comes into your network. Of particular importance are source filters, which examine the source address of packets and reject any packets with source addresses you do not expect to see from the external peer. This helps prevent source address spoofing, which is a common element of many denial-of-service attacks.

Source address filtering is useful for customer or client peering, where you should know what prefixes the peer network is using. Although this is the most exact method of guarding against address spoofing, in some cases the number of prefixes used by the peer can make a configured source address filter impractical. A somewhat less-exact but still effective alternative supported by a number of router vendors is *Unicast Reverse Path Forwarding* (uRPF). Originally developed to prevent loops in multicast networks, uRPF compares the source address of incoming packets with the unicast routing table. If the route entries indicate that the next hop toward the source address is out an interface different from the interface on which the packet was received, the packet is assumed to have been spoofed and is dropped.

9.3.3   Protecting the Router

When peering to the public Internet, source address filters are impractical, and uRPF is unlikely to be effective. Public peering opens your network to a world of bright, cunning attackers. Just as firewalls and other security devices are necessary to protect hosts and servers exposed to public access, extensive and well-considered measures must be taken to protect your routers from unauthorized access and abuse originating not only from outside of your network but also from within your network.

9.3.3.1   Router Access Policies

One of the holy grails of network attacks is gaining access to a router. An attacker who can control a router can inflict grave harm to your network, or can choose to use covert means to gain even deeper access into your network. Therefore, your first line of defense is to ensure that access to the router is tightly secured.

All commercial routers provide a console port for maintenance access to the router. This port is particularly vulnerable and must be protected by proper physical security of the router. Many network operators provide access to routers through a terminal server or dial-up modem, or both, connected to console ports. Securing these devices is beyond the scope of this brief discussion, but suffice it to say that these devices extend physical access to remote users and therefore represent a significant risk if they are accessible by unauthorized users.

The other means of accessing a router are logical, through a management network or directly from the production network, via a protocol such as Telnet, rlogin, or Secure Shell (SSH). Of these, SSH—particularly SSH version 2—is far more secure. If you have the option on your router, you should use SSH exclusively for logical access and disable Telnet and rlogin. Furthermore, if your router provides the option, you should limit the number of concurrent SSH sessions allowed and the rate of connection attempts. A typical example is a maximum of 10 concurrent sessions and 5 login attempts per minute.

Many routers also support file transport protocols, such as FTP or TFTP for upgrading system software. These protocols should be enabled only when they are needed for system maintenance, and disabled at all other times.

Other protocols that allow packets to reach the CPU of your router, such as Domain Name Service (DNS), Network Time Protocol (NTP), and Simple Network Management Protocol (SNMP), should be authenticated whenever possible. You can further secure protocols such as these, required for normal router operations, by using packet filters to restrict accepted packets to those sourced from one of the few servers that would normally provide these services. Packet filters for router protection are discussed in Section 9.3.3.3.

Of course, you cannot keep everyone out of your routers. Therefore, you need an authentication, authorization, and accounting (AAA) policy to closely control the operations and engineering access required for routine network operations:

- Authentication policies involve requiring anyone attempting to access the router to submit a password or (preferably) a stronger, regularly changing code such as provided by a SecurID system.

- Authorization policies define what a person who has been authenticated is allowed to do on the router. For example, daily operational personnel need to be able to observe the results of various **show** commands, but should have little reason to change the router configuration. Troubleshooting personnel might have all the privileges of operations personnel but can also change a limited number of configuration variables. Senior engineering personnel might have full privileges to execute any command a router supports.

- Accounting policies record what an authenticated and authorized user actually does on the router. An accounting policy should record everyone who accesses the router and when, and should record every command issued on the router, when it was executed, and by whom. This recorded information is useful not only for security but also for troubleshooting: If a mistake is made that is not immediately detected, a later troubleshooter can identify what was done on a router and therefore can more easily understand what corrective actions to take.

AAA policies might be statically defined on a router, but networks of moderate to large size normally use an AAA system such as TACACS or RADIUS. These systems allow policies to be defined on a server rather than on individual routers, making policies uniform across the network and making them easier to change. As with other essential systems, the servers providing these policies should be redundant.

9.3.3.2 Login Banners

Most routers allow you to define a banner that is displayed to anyone logging in to the router. However, the importance of these banners is often overlooked, and the banner (if used at all) might say something like "You have logged into the Acme Anvil Corporation network. If you are not authorized to be here, please log off at once." What the creator of such a banner does not understand is that the banner should be, above all else, a legal document defining an agreement between the user and the network owner.

The login banners should be identical on all routers, and should display a strongly worded message warning of the legal consequences of unauthorized access. Such banners are important when building a successful prosecution case against anyone illegally accessing any of your routers or servers.

A strongly worded login banner should include statements regarding the following:

- Clear prohibition of unauthorized access.
- Clear prohibition of unauthorized use. Some operations personnel might be authorized to access the system but limited in what they are authorized to do. This warns authorized users against stepping outside of the boundaries of their authorization.
- Warning that the system may be monitored. Note that the wording *may be* has important ramifications for successful prosecutions. Do not say the system *will be* monitored.
- Statement that there is no expectation of privacy. This statement ensures that no legal defense can be mounted claiming that you should not have monitored the unauthorized user.
- Statement that results of monitoring may be provided to the appropriate authorities.
- Statement that continued use of the system implies consent to the stated terms and conditions.
- Warning to log off immediately if consent is not given.

Login banners should *not* include any of the following information:

- Information about the device type or software
- Information about the device location
- Contact information
- Administrator information

All of your routers should be configured so that they display the banner at any login, whether remote or local (such as a console login).

An example of a strong login banner is:[18]

```
**********************************************************************
WARNING!

This is a private system, and is the property of Acme Anvil Corporation. Access is
restricted to authorized users and to authorized purposes. Users (authorized and
unauthorized) have no explicit or implicit expectation of privacy.

Any or all uses of this system and all files on this system may be intercepted,
monitored, recorded, copied, audited, inspected, and disclosed to authorized site,
Acme Anvil Corporation, and law enforcement personnel. By using this system, the user
consents to such interception, monitoring, recording, copying, auditing, inspection, and
disclosure at the discretion of authorized site or Acme Anvil personnel.

UNAUTHORIZED OR IMPROPER USE OF THIS SYSTEM MAY RESULT IN ADMINISTRATIVE DISCIPLINARY
ACTION AND CIVIL AND CRIMINAL PENALTIES.
```

---

[18] This banner is based on one used by the United States Department of Energy and is publicly published.

```
By continuing to use this system you indicate your awareness of and consent to these
terms and conditions of use. LOG OFF IMMEDIATELY if you do not agree to the conditions
stated in this warning.

*************************************************************************
```

Although this example banner follows best practice, you should consult legal counsel familiar with local and international telecommunications law for any adjustments to accommodate current local and federal laws.

9.3.3.3 Packet Filtering for Router Protection

Your router simply cannot function usefully without allowing certain packets into the router CPU or route processor module. However, by using packet filters, you can explicitly define what packets are allowed to access the router. The packet filter should define the packets by source and destination address, by protocol, and by port.

A framework for a typical packet filter for protecting a router is:

- Allow any TCP sessions established from this router. This allows BGP sessions the router originates and also allows Telnet or SSH sessions an operator might create from this router to another device.

- If you have an out-of-band management system, allow packets with source addresses coming from this system.

- Allow packets for all routing protocols (OSPF, IS-IS, BGP, and so on) running on this router. You can make this part of the filter much stronger by defining the IP addresses of the router's neighbors and only accepting packets with source addresses from this list. This part of the filter supplements the protocol authentication methods described earlier in this chapter.

- Allow packets from signaling protocols such as Resource Reservation Protocol (RSVP) and Label Distribution Protocol (LDP) that might be running on the router. As with routing protocols, limiting packet source addresses to known neighbors strengthens the filter.

- Allow ICMP messages. ICMP is necessary for routine maintenance, but not all messages are necessary. So, you can make this part of the filter stronger by accepting only the ICMP messages you will need.

- Allow traceroute packets, which are normally UDP packets with destination ports in the range of 33,434 to 33,523.

- Allow packets from operationally necessary protocols such as SNMP, NTP, TACACS or RADIUS, and DNS. List the addresses of the servers providing these services and only accept protocol packets from those sources.

Keep in mind that a filter such as this must be positioned to apply only to packets destined for processing by the router itself. It cannot affect packets transiting the router as part of normal packet forwarding.

9.3.3.4   Rate Limiting

The previous section discussed how you can tighten security on your router by permitting only those packets necessary for the routine operation of the router. But these packets themselves can present a risk. For example, a common denial-of-service attack is to flood the target with more ICMP messages than the target is capable of processing.

If your router supports it, rate limiting of certain packets, particularly ICMP packets, to the route processing module can reduce your exposure to DoS attacks that exploit packet flooding. You should assess for each protocol the maximum rate of packets that might be required for normal operations. You should be liberal with this estimate because a flooding attack can still be expected to far exceed this maximum. For example, in a moderately large network, 500kbps of ICMP and traceroute traffic to a router CPU might be more than sufficient for normal operations; 2Mbps of routing protocol traffic and 5Mbps of SNMP traffic might also be sufficient. Actual numbers, of course, depend on traffic analysis of a specific network. If your router supports it, you should also specify an allowance for small bursts beyond the normal maximum. Any packet rate that exceeds your configured rate limit and burst limit is then considered abnormal, and the out-of-spec packets are dropped.

9.4   Operating for Security and Reliability

Everyone has heard the cliché espoused by combat soldiers, police officers, and firefighters: The job is days of boredom punctuated by moments of sheer terror. Working in the network operations center of a large network can be a bit like that, too. Although there is no risk to life and limb, those occasions when things go very wrong present risks to the profitability and reputation of the business and to the job security of those responsible for the network. The chaos that can ensue during network emergencies can itself represent a long-term risk to the network, as operators "do whatever it takes" to restore service, often moving outside of the boundaries of normal operational practice.

Everyday individualism also adds to long-term degradation of the security and reliability of the network: Different people have different ideas about how routers should be configured and maintained, and no one enjoys the drudgery of documenting their work.

These risks remain unrecognized or unaddressed in a surprisingly large number of networks, including some of nationwide or global scale. This section gets even further away from the particulars of OSPF and IS-IS, but the topic—strong operational policies and procedures—is every bit as important as how you configure those individual protocols. Although the section is divided into three topics—configuration management, change management, and the network lab— in reality configuration management policies and the maintenance of a network lab are a necessary part of strong change management practice.

9.4.1 *Configuration Management*

Although change management is the primary preventive measure against network outages, it is important to recognize that configuration management is an essential prerequisite to effective change management. Configuration management ensures a clear, accurate, and current picture of all existing network elements. Without such reliable information, there can be no confidence that all dependencies have been considered when planning a network change.

A standard procedure must be established for ensuring that all managed configuration elements are updated whenever a move, change, add, or removal occurs in the network infrastructure or logical topology. In some cases, such as the tracking of configuration files, both open-source and commercial automated systems are available that gather and record configuration files from all network devices on a periodic basis. Configuration files should be gathered at least once a day. Other elements, such as physical devices, must be tracked through regular inventory procedures that verify the ongoing accuracy of infrastructure records.

9.4.1.1 *Elements of Configuration Management*

As many physical and logical elements of the network should be tracked and recorded as possible. These elements include but are not limited to:

- Circuits
- Type
- Circuit number
- Physical location of both ends
- Contact information
- Device interface location
- All network devices
- Type
- Physical location (to rack level)
- Access information
- Serial numbers
- Interfaces
- Microcode
- Software version
- Rack diagrams for each network location, indicating all devices
- Wiring diagrams logically indicating all port and interface interconnects
- Configuration files
- Logical diagrams and connection tables
- IP addresses

- BGP peering and route reflectors
- IGP adjacencies and areas
- Routing policies (in pseudocode)
- Logical connections such as ATM or Frame Relay virtual circuits and MPLS label switching paths

9.4.1.2 Conventions and Standards

Established and documented network standards ensure that configurations throughout the network are consistent and well understood by all operations personnel. For example, there can be a standard for locating devices relative to each other in each PoP (a rack design). Naming conventions are important for DNS names and also for device names. Configuration file standards should be established for all features common to all router configurations, such as options to enable or disable, standard security configurations, and standard protocol and interface options.

9.4.1.3 Configuration Repository

A server should be dedicated to storage of configuration documents, with at least one backup server at a different location. All configuration documents should be maintained in "soft" form rather than "hard" (paper) form. Paper documents are easily misplaced and can fall into unauthorized hands, and are not as easily maintained and changed as soft documents. Responsibility for maintaining the repository and ensuring that all documents contained in the repository are current should be assigned to one person or a small team.

9.4.2 Change Management

Typical causes of severe, non-malicious network disruptions include:

- Configuration errors
- Hardware failures
- Hardware/software incompatibilities
- Non-support of features in new software versions
- Software bugs

With the exception of hardware failures, these sources of network disruptions are most commonly encountered during times of network change. It can be argued that even hardware failures are most likely to occur during changes, with failure rates declining when the network is in steady state. Therefore, the most valuable tool for minimizing network outages is a strong change management policy.

The impact of change management policies and procedures on daily network operations is similar to that of security policies and procedures: The stronger the policies become, the more troublesome their enforcement becomes. For both security and change management, at some point the policies and procedures become as disruptive to daily operations as the outages they are designed to prevent. A careful balance must be discovered at which the policies and procedures sufficiently safeguard the continued reliability of the network while not overly burdening operations and without inconveniencing operations personnel to the point that they attempt to circumvent the process.

9.4.2.1 Documentation

Establishing and maintaining standard documentation is key to effective change management. Standard forms must be created and used for:

- Maintenance requests
- Methods and procedures
- Regression and upgrade testing

Larger projects, such as infrastructure migrations and protocol changes, are not as easily documented on standard forms because each project is likely to be unique. Nonetheless, even large projects should be carefully and thoroughly documented using established procedures throughout the planning, design, and implementation cycles.

9.4.2.2 Archives

Change documentation should be archived for future reference. Such archives provide a wealth of experience-based information on past network changes, what worked well, what did not work well, and how future changes can be managed better. The change documentation archive can be located on the same servers as the configuration repository and managed by the same team.

9.4.2.3 Key Administrative Support

Change management policies cannot succeed without understanding and support at all administrative levels. Operations personnel must understand the value of change management to the stability of the network. Mid-level management must ensure that intelligent change management policies are established, and that operational personnel are following the policies. Enforcement of policies also falls under the responsibility of mid-level management. Upper management must be convinced of the financial benefits of strong change management, and provide the corporate policy support to the lower administrative levels.

9.4.2.4 The Change Management Committee

The change management committee is responsible for all aspects of change management, from establishing policies and procedures to evaluating and approving individual change requests. Some members of the committee are permanent, whereas others are appointed to the committee only for the duration of certain projects. The committee should meet on a regular basis, such as once per week, and should also be available on short notice for approval of more urgent maintenance requests. This subsection looks at the individual members of a change management committee and the duties the committee performs.

9.4.2.4.1 The Change Controller

The change controller leads the change management committee and bears ultimate responsibility for seeing that all policies and procedures are followed correctly. The change controller is responsible for justifying the business reasons and financial expenses of network changes to the concerned corporate entities. This should be a permanent, full-time position reporting to the head of network operations.

9.4.2.4.2 The Process Enforcers

One or more process enforcers are directly responsible for evaluating each change request or network project to ensure that all policies and procedures are followed as they apply to a specific task. The process enforcer serves as a liaison between the process owner and the change controller, and must have an understanding of both the change management process and the technical requirements of the specific change. Process enforcers are permanent members of the change management committee, but are not dedicated full-time to the position.

Individual process enforcers should be appointed from the various technical disciplines involved in network operations, such as routing and switching, network management, server management, programming, security, and circuit management. By having representatives from all technical disciplines on the committee, evaluating every change request, there is higher confidence that the impact of a change on all aspects of the network have been considered.

9.4.2.4.3 The Process Owner

The process owner is requestor of a specific network change, and becomes a member of the change management committee only for the duration of the specific project he or she has requested. The process owner holds responsibility for justifying the change request to the committee and gaining their approval for the change, and is responsible for overseeing the change itself. For a simple maintenance change, the process owner might be a single technician or engineer who will conduct the change. For a larger project, the process owner will be the team lead responsible for the project.

9.4.2.4.4 Pre-Change Evaluation

The evaluation process followed by the change management committee is primarily focused on risk assessment and minimization. The issues that must be evaluated before a network change is approved are:

- What is the technical and/or business justification for the change?
- What is the financial cost of the change? Has this cost been approved?
- Who will be performing the individual tasks? Are these individuals properly qualified?

- What physical components and instrumentation are required for the change? Have these components been acquired?

- Is the change documented in sufficient detail?

- When appropriate, have the procedures and configurations been tested under non-operational, laboratory conditions? Have all effects been accounted for, and have the results been properly recorded?

- When is the change to be performed?

- What is the expected duration of each task?

- What are the criteria for evaluating the success or failure of the change?

- What is the back-out plan in the event of failure?

- When are the back-out procedures begun?

9.4.2.4.5 Post-Change Evaluation

Post-change evaluation is a step that is frequently neglected. But performing a "post-mortem" is vital to the success of future changes. Successful procedures should be documented as Methods of Procedure (Section 9.4.2.6), and the causes of failures or inefficiencies should be evaluated and documented for future reference.

9.4.2.5 Maintenance Requests

When relatively small changes are made to the network, such as a routing policy change or a move, add, or removal of an interface or chassis, a Maintenance Request is filed with the change management committee by the process owner. The Maintenance Request is a form standardized by the committee that asks key questions of the process owner, ensures ahead of time that the process owner has considered all variables, and provides sufficient information for the committee to confidently perform a risk analysis.

The committee should establish a standard lead time before the performance of the requested task, by which the Maintenance Request must be submitted—5 to 10 days is a typical lead time. This gives the committee members time to read the request before meeting and formally evaluating the request, and provides time for the process owner to make any required changes.

Of course, not all network changes can be scheduled many days in advance. Network problems can require urgent changes, which must be performed within hours or days, or emergency changes that must be performed immediately. As the lead time for a change decreases, the risk of having the change adversely affect the network or cause a network failure increases. Therefore, the committee should have a well-established set of definitions of normal, urgent, critical, and emergency changes.

Some changes are performed on a daily basis as a part of normal operations. A service provider network, for example, adds and removes connections to customers every day. Although these additions and removals are certainly network changes, they are a part of routine network operations. Having each of these routine changes go through a maintenance request to a change management committee is impractical. They can, however, be regulated and standardized through the use of formalized Methods of Procedure.

9.4.2.6   Methods of Procedure

A Method of Procedure (MoP) is a document stringently describing, step by step, how a particular change activity is performed. A MoP can be specific to a single instance of an activity, such as the change of a particular routing policy for a particular reason, or it can be a generic activity such as the description of the proper way to replace a router interface card. MoPs should also be created for routine network changes such as the addition and removal of customer connections.

For the first year or so after the formation of the change management committee and its associated rules, you should expect that a new MoP will be written to accompany most change requests. Over time a library of MoPs is accumulated, which can be used for similar, subsequent tasks.

The MoP must be a detailed document describing the activity to be performed, including objectives, implementation steps, verification steps, and back-out procedures. If it applies to a unique activity, the MoP serves only as a reference for future similar activities. However, if the MoP describes an activity that occurs on a regular basis—such as the replacement of a component or the addition of a circuit—it should be a fluid document that is changed on a regular basis to include newer and better procedures.

9.4.3   The Network Lab

Building and maintaining a network lab is by far the most difficult challenge to implementing good change management practices, for the simple but inescapable reason that labs are expensive. A good network lab contains enough equipment to accurately mirror all devices in at least two of your network sites, and test equipment to generate and measure network traffic as close to the actual traffic in your network as possible. The cost of such a lab for a large network can easily run into the millions of dollars, and convincing your corporate executives to undertake such an expense is daunting. A network lab plays three key roles in the security and reliability of your network that justify the expenditure:

- Regression testing
- Troubleshooting
- Training

Although many network changes are easily understood and their effects on the network can be confidently predicted, many other changes can have unexpected results. This is particularly true of software and microcode upgrades, routing policy changes, filter changes, the addition of new vendors' equipment, and the addition of new protocols or technologies. In these cases, regression testing is vital for discovering unexpected problems and should be an integral part of change management processes. Regression testing is the practice of simulating in the lab portions of the existing network, verifying that the network operates in a similar manner to the operational network, and then adding the new feature or making the planned change and observing the result. Aside from looking for obvious failures in the simulated network and the correct operation of the new feature, a regression test verifies that all previously functioning features still operate as before and that the new feature does not adversely affect network performance.

A good network lab also allows for safe, thorough troubleshooting of difficult network problems. If performance or stability problems arise, trying potential solutions on the operational network is risky at best. If your troubleshooters can mimic the problem in a lab, they are free to theorize, test, and evaluate potential solutions without worrying about adversely affecting production traffic or customer service.

Finally, a network lab is a key tool for training operations and engineering personnel. The best way to advance knowledge and experience is through hands-on, trial-and-error experimentation. "On-the-job" training on a production network sharply curtails experimentation, and is limited to an unstructured approach of learning only from whatever happens on the network, as it happens.

Review Questions

1. What components or mechanisms of a link state protocol can an attacker target?
2. In what way does the fact that IS-IS is not itself an IP protocol give it a security advantage over OSPF?
3. What is "fightback" behavior?
4. Why is simple password authentication less desirable that MD5 authentication?
5. What is a message digest, and how does it protect the keys used for authentication?
6. What is the benefit of the OSPF Key ID?
7. What is the purpose of the OSPF cryptographic sequence number in MD5 authentication?
8. In what way is IS-IS more vulnerable to replay attack than OSPF?
9. What three authentication scopes are defined for IS-IS? How do the three scopes differ in regard to the carrying of the Authentication Information TLV?
10. How does the enabling of MD5 authentication change the checksum procedures of OSPF and IS-IS?
11. What is graceful restart? What feature of many modern high-end routers makes graceful restart possible?
12. What LSA does OSPF use to support graceful restart?
13. What is the purpose of the restart period?
14. What is a graceful restart helper?

15. What is the difference between a planned and an unplanned restart?

16. What is the purpose of the RR and RA flags in the IS-IS Restart TLV?

17. What is the purpose of the SA flag in the IS-IS Restart TLV?

18. What determines the value of the remaining time field in the IS-IS Restart TLV?

19. What is bidirectional forwarding detection? How does it improve on the Hello mechanisms of routing protocols?

CHAPTER 10

Extensibility

The 1980s and 1990s were the decades of entrepreneurship for the Internet. The World Wide Web changed the Internet from a small community of academics and technophiles into a huge worldwide marketplace. The carriers and ISPs focused on bandwidth, performance, and reliability. By the turn of the century, however, these infrastructure companies began changing their focus. Most offered similar levels of service, so the only way for them to compete with each other was through lower prices. Carriers and ISPs began looking for new service offerings to make up for the lost revenue of increasingly commoditized IP packet transport. Typical of the new services being offered were—and are—voice and video over IP, conference services, and virtual private networks (VPNs).

But underlying all these new services was still plain old best-effort IP. In fact, most service providers began moving services traditionally offered over Frame Relay and ATM to their IP infrastructures to reduce capital and operational expenses. A set of intermediate technologies are required to make the IP infrastructure appear better than best effort—a set of "building blocks" that enable new commercial service offerings. These intermediate technologies include Multiprotocol Label Switching (MPLS), multicast IP, and, increasingly, a new version of IP, IPv6.

Such intermediate technologies require information about the underlying IP network to run correctly, and the best source of that information is the IGP. Rather than inventing a new IGP, designers have added new capabilities to OSPF and IS-IS in recent years. This chapter explores the general concept of extending the protocols to support new capabilities. Chapters 11-13 look at specific extensions to OSPF and IS-IS.

10.1   Extending OSPF

New capabilities are added to OSPF primarily through the addition of new LSAs. You have already encountered in Chapter 7 one example of an LSA that supports an optional capability: The NSSA (type 7) LSA. This chapter and the next three introduce other "extension" LSAs.

10.1.1   The OSPF Extensibility Problem

Two characteristics of OSPF pose problems to extensibility. The first characteristic is that when an OSPF router receives an LSA of an unknown type, it drops the LSA. The influence of this behavior is seen in NSSAs, where all routers in the area must support the NSSA option and understand type 7 LSAs. In this case, the behavior is not a problem because you want all routers in the not-so-stubby area to enforce the rule that no type 5 LSAs are permitted. But there are some cases in which you want only a subset of routers, unrelated to an area or domain, to support an optional capability. For example, you might want only some of your routers to support traffic engineering or IP multicast. In such a case, you must avoid a situation in which some router in your network that does not need to support the option might nonetheless hinder the flooding of the optional LSAs. You can avoid the situation in one of two ways: Either ensure that all routers support the optional capability, regardless of whether you want them to participate in the option; or carefully design your network so that the optional LSAs never need to be flooded through nonsupportive routers.

The second characteristic of OSPF that might hinder extensibility is the inclusion of IPv4 addressing semantics in the LSAs. Take, for example, the most essential LSA: the Router (type 1) LSA, which supplies most of the topological information to the SPF calculation. The format of the LSA, discussed in Chapter 5, is shown again in Figure 10.1. The Link ID and Link Data fields are both 32 bits, and usually contain a 32-bit IP address. If the OSPF network type of the link is broadcast, for instance, the Link ID field contains the IPv4 address of the DR and the Link Data field contains the IPv4 address of the originating router's interface to the link. Similar IPv4-based data is included for other network types.

However, suppose you want OSPF to support other kinds of addresses. Specifically, what if you want to use OSPF to route IPv6, which uses 128-bit addresses? If every IPv6 network was dual stacked—that is, every router interface was assigned an IPv4 address in addition to an IPv6 address—OSPF could support IPv6 through the simple addition of new LSAs to carry the IPv6 addresses. The SPF process would continue to get its information from the type 1 LSAs, which in turn get their link information from the IPv4 addresses. But that defeats one of the objectives of IPv6, which is to overcome some of the limitations of IPv4. OSPF must be capable of routing an IPv6-only network. So the realistic solution to the problem, as discussed in Chapter 12, is a completely new version of OSPF for IPv6 in which the IPv4 address semantics are removed from the LSAs.

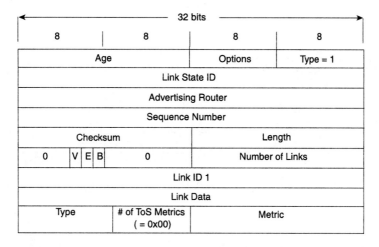

32 bits			
8	8	8	8
Age		Options	Type = 1
Link State ID			
Advertising Router			
Sequence Number			
Checksum		Length	
0 · V E B · 0		Number of Links	
Link ID 1			
Link Data			
Type	# of ToS Metrics (= 0x00)	Metric	

Figure 10.1   The information in the 32-bit Link ID and Link Data fields is, in most cases, based on some IPv4 network address.

10.1.2   Opaque LSAs

One of the difficulties in extending OSPF is that future capabilities cannot always be anticipated. MPLS-based traffic engineering, for example, had not been conceived when OSPF was standardized. It is reasonable to expect that before OSPF reaches the end of its life it will be called upon to support still more as yet unthought-of services.

Opaque LSAs[1] are intended to add flexibility to OSPF, by creating generalized LSAs that can disseminate undefined data from router to router. The data might be used by OSPF for some future capability, or it might be information inserted by some application that utilizes OSPF as a convenient transport but that is not relevant to OSPF route calculations. In this second regard Opaque LSAs serve the same purpose as the route tag fields described in Section 10.3, but with more flexibility.

"Opaque" means something you cannot see through, and this does fit one of the applications of this class of LSAs: to carry information that OSPF does not itself understand or care about. The word also means "obscure" or "difficult to define," which fits the other mission of Opaque LSAs: to support future features that we cannot presently anticipate.

There are three types of Opaque LSA, differing only in their flooding scope (Figure 10.2): link-local, area, and AS. Defining these scopes provides even more flexibility in matching service requirements.

---

[1]   Rob Coltun, "The OSPF Opaque LSA Option," RFC 2370, July 1998.

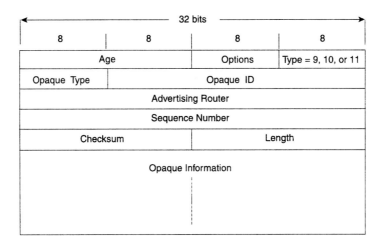

Figure 10.2   The Opaque LSA.

Type is the LSA type, and defines the flooding scope of the LSA:

- **Type 9, link-local scope,** is limited to a single link and is never forwarded by a router to other links.
- **Type 10, area-local scope,** is limited to a single area and is never forwarded by an ABR to other areas.
- **Type 11, AS scope,** is flooded throughout the OSPF domain. Like type 5 LSAs, type 11 LSAs are not permitted in stub areas.

The LSA's 32-bit Link State ID is composed of two parts:

- **Opaque Type,** the first 8 bits, specifies the application of the LSA. Type values of 0 through 127 are allocated by the IANA through the OSPF working group, and type values of 128 through 255 are reserved for private and experimental use. As Table 10.1 shows, as of this writing only four type values have been allocated.
- **Opaque ID,** the last 24 bits, is added to the Opaque Type value to create a unique identifier of the specific LSA type.

Opaque Information is the variable-length field that carries the capability- or application-specific data.

Support of Opaque LSAs is signaled between neighbors during the database exchange process by setting the O bit in the Options field (Figure 10.3) of the Database Description packets. The capability (or lack of it) is recorded in the Neighbor Options portion of the neighbor data structure. A router that supports Opaque LSAs does not flood them to neighbors that do not support the option—that is, Opaque LSAs are not put onto the Link State Transmission list of neighbors that do not indicate support for the option.

Table 10.1 Opaque LSA Type Values

Type Value	Type	Description
1	Traffic Engineering LSA	Used for MPLS-TE, as discussed in Chapter 11.
2	Sycamore Optical Topology Descriptions	Used to communicate details of optical topologies such as switch capabilities and traffic engineering parameters for optical trunk groups and hybrid mesh-ring optical networks. Not discussed in this book.
3	Grace LSA	Used for OSPF hitless restart, as discussed in Chapter 9.
4	Router Information LSA	Used for advertising optional capabilities, as discussed in Section 10.1.3 of this chapter.
5–127	Unassigned	Can be allocated by the IANA through the OSPF working group for future Opaque LSA types.
128–255	Reserved	Set aside for private and experimental use.

*	O	DC	EA	N/P	MC	E	T

Figure 10.3 Support for Opaque LSAs is signaled between neighbors by setting the O bit in the Options field of Database Description packets.

The neighbor table in Figure 10.4 shows the value of the Options field to be 0x42, or binary 01000010, indicating that the O bit is set. Figures 10.5 and 10.6 show a summary of the databases of the neighbor and the router from which the neighbor table was taken, and you can clearly observe the presence of 10 area-local Opaque LSAs.

```
jeff@Juniper6> show ospf neighbor 192.168.7.2 extensive
Address         Interface        State      ID          Pri  Dead
192.168.7.2    fe-0/0/0.0        Full       192.168.254.8  1   35
  area 0.0.0.0, opt 0x42, DR 192.168.7.1, BDR 192.168.7.2
  Up 1w2d 00:47:03, adjacent 1w2d 00:47:03
```

Figure 10.4 The Options (opt) field of this neighbor indicates that it supports Opaque LSAs.

```
Cisco8#show ip ospf database database-summary

            OSPF Router with ID (192.168.254.8) (Process ID 1)

Area 0 database summary
  LSA Type       Count    Delete    Maxage
  Router         4        0         0
  Network        4        0         0
  Summary Net    9        0         0
  Summary ASBR   1        0         0
  Type-7 Ext     0        0         0
  Opaque Link    0        0         0
  Opaque Area    10       0         0
  Subtotal       28       0         0
```

```
Area 20 database summary
   LSA Type       Count   Delete   Maxage
   Router         2       0        0
   Network        1       0        0
   Summary Net    13      0        0
   Summary ASBR   0       0        0
   Type-7 Ext     0       0        0
   Opaque Link    0       0        0
   Opaque Area    0       0        0
   Subtotal       16      0        0

Process 1 database summary
   LSA Type       Count   Delete   Maxage
   Router         8       0        0
   Network        5       0        0
   Summary Net    22      0        0
   Summary ASBR   1       0        0
   Type-7 Ext     0       0        0
   Opaque Link    0       0        0
   Opaque Area    10      0        0
   Type-5 Ext     2       0        0
   Opaque AS      0       0        0
   Total          46      0        0
Cisco8#
```

Figure 10.5   The neighbor table of Figure 10.4 indicates ten area-local (type 10) Opaque LSAs in its database.

```
jeff@Juniper6> show ospf database summary
Area 0.0.0.0:
    4 Router LSAs
    4 Network LSAs
    9 Summary LSAs
    1 ASBRSum LSAs
    10 OpaqArea LSAs
Externals:
    2 Extern LSAs

jeff@Juniper6>
```

Figure 10.6   The router from which the neighbor table of Figure 10.4 was taken also shows type 10 LSAs in its database.

10.1.3   The Router Information Opaque LSA

As the Options field in Figure 10.3 clearly shows, only the leftmost bit remains available for signaling future capabilities. In reality, the first and fifth bits could be redefined, as the ToS and External Attributes capabilities have never come into general acceptance. Nevertheless, the 8-bit Options field represents a limitation on future extensibility.

A proposal has been made, although not yet implemented as of this writing, for a new Opaque LSA called the Router Information (RI) Opaque LSA[2] to advertise optional capabilities. The advantage of this new LSA is that no new bits in the Options field are used (just the O bit to signal support for Opaque LSAs) while providing a way to signal support for up to 32 different capabilities.

Figure 10.7 shows the format of the RI Opaque LSA. The opaque type is 4, and the LSA can have link-local, area-local, or AS scope. The LSA contains one or more TLVs that specify optional capabilities.

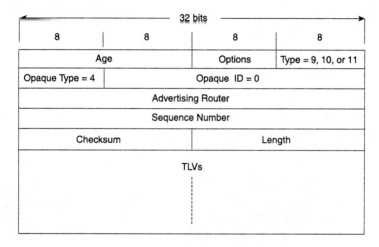

Figure 10.7   The Router Information (RI) Opaque LSA.

The first TLV carried in the RI LSA is the OSPF Router Capabilities TLV, shown in Figure 10.8. This TLV can be followed, depending on the options supported, by other TLVs carrying additional capability information.

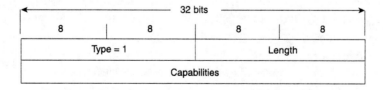

Figure 10.8   The OSPF Router Capabilities TLV.

The type number of the Router Capabilities TLV is 1. The Capabilities field is a 32-bit field that functions similarly to the Options field: It comprises 32 flags indicating, when set, different optional capabilities. Table 10.2 shows what bits represent what options. Although

---

[2] Acee Lindem, Naiming Shen, Rahul Aggarwal, Scott Shaffer, and J.P. Vasseur, "Extensions to OSPF for Advertising Optional Router Capabilities," draft-ietf-ospf-cap-01.txt, October 2003.

it is reasonable to assume that OSPF will never have more than 32 different optional capabilities, the TLV format can be easily extended to support a larger capabilities field.

Table 10.2   Optional Capabilities Specified by Bits of the Capabilities Field of the OSPF Router Capabilities TLV

Bit	Capability
0–3	Reserved
4	OSPF graceful restart capable
5	OSPF graceful restart helper
6	Stub router support
7	Traffic engineering support
8	OSPF point-to-point over LAN
9	OSPF path computation server discovery
10–31	Future assignments

10.2   Extending IS-IS

New capabilities are added to IS-IS through the addition of new TLVs. This section introduces one such added TLV. Chapters 11 through 13 discuss other TLVs that have been added to IS-IS to support optional capabilities.

10.2.1   The IS-IS Extensibility Advantage

IS-IS tends to be easier to extend than OSPF, and this can be observed historically by the timing of vendors' rollouts of new features supported by IS-IS and OSPF. Both MPLS TE and IPv6, for example, were supported in IS-IS production implementations six months to one year before they were supported in OSPF.

The reason for this easier extensibility has to do with the fact that new features are introduced by adding new TLVs to an LSP, while the structure of the LSP itself remains unchanged. This is typically simpler than defining a new LSA for OSPF.

An additional advantage when extending IS-IS is the way the protocol handles unknown TLVs. Unlike OSPF, which drops unrecognized LSAs, IS-IS ignores unknown TLVs in the LSP and passes them on to other neighbors unchanged. This behavior simplifies the introduction of new capabilities into your network, particularly when the capability is to be added only to a subset of all routers in the IS-IS domain.

Finally, the addition of some IP capabilities—particularly support for IPv6—is simpler because IS-IS is not itself an IP protocol. As a result, there are no functional dependencies on IP addressing semantics.

10.2.2   The Protocols Supported TLV

The Protocols Supported TLV shown in Figure 10.9 specifies, as the name implies, what protocols the originating router supports. It lists one or more Network Layer Protocol Identifiers (NLPIDs), which are defined in ISO/TR 9577 and in several extension documents. Because IS-IS was originally designed to route just CLNP, this TLV was added when the protocol was extended to support IP. With it, the originator can advertise whether it supports CLNP only, IPv4 only, or both. With the subsequent extension of IS-IS to support IPv6, as described in Chapter 12, that protocol is also listed in the Protocols Supported TLV when the originator uses IS-IS to route IPv6. The NLPID of IPv4 is 204 (0xcc), and the NLPID of IPv6 is 142 (0x8e).

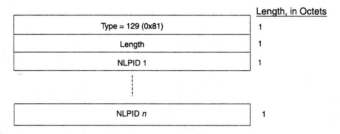

Figure 10.9   The Protocols Supported TLV.

10.3   Route Tagging

Both OSPF and IS-IS allow the association of a value called a *route tag* with external prefixes. You can think of route tags as a protocol extensibility feature in that they enable you to arbitrarily assign some administratively meaningful value to external prefixes to associate them with some group that you define. You can then create routing policies that act on the external prefixes according to their assigned tags. In this, route tags for IGPs[3] serve the same purpose as BGP community attributes.

The Route Tag field is provided in OSPF types 5 and 7 LSAs (Figure 10.10). A Route Tag field is also provided by an IS-IS type 1 sub-TLV (Figure 10.11), which is in turn carried by type 135 Extended IP Reachability TLVs.[4] In both cases, the External Route Tag field is 32 bits, so the tag value can be any number in that range.

---

[3]   RIPv2 and Cisco EIGRP also support route tags.

[4]   Extended IP Reachability TLVs, and hence type 1 sub-TLVs and route tagging, are only supported when wide metrics are enabled on the IS-IS router. Sub-TLVs are explained in more detail in Chapter 11.

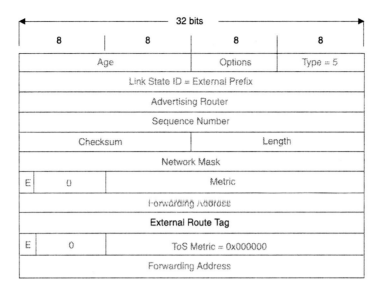

Figure 10.10   The External Route Tag field in OSPF AS-External LSAs allows an arbitrary 32-bit number to be assigned to an external prefix.

	Length, in Bytes
Sub-TLV Type = 1	1
Length	1
External Route Tag	4

Figure 10.11   Sub-TLV 1, carried in Extended IP Reachability TLVs, allows an arbitrary 32-bit number to be assigned to an external prefix.

The most common application of route tags is in complex route redistribution policies. Route tags are used when it is impractical to identify prefixes using prefix lists or route filters, either because there are so many prefixes to be identified that the list would be unmanageably long, or because you are uncertain what prefixes need to be identified. You can tag prefixes at their point of origin—by incoming interface, advertising neighbor, or redistribution point, for example—and then apply polices to the prefixes elsewhere in your network by identifying the tag, rather than individual prefixes.

Figure 10.12 shows an example of where route tags can prove useful. Here, an OSPF domain is the transit network for three external routing domains.[5] The prefixes of each of the three domains are redistributed into OSPF, but must be sorted out when they are re-advertised back to the external domains: Only domain 1 prefixes must be advertised to domain 1, only domain 2 prefixes are advertised to domain 2, and so on.

---

[5]   A key supposition here is that BGP, a protocol far more suited for such policy-based applications, is not and cannot be run in the transit network.

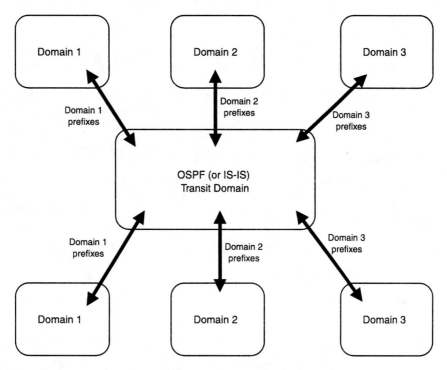

Figure 10.12 The prefixes of each of the three external domains can be distinguished within the OSPF transit domain by tagging them as they are redistributed into OSPF.

As a prefix is redistributed into OSPF, it can be tagged with an identifier that associates it with the proper domain. A policy can then be created that distinguishes the prefixes based on their assigned tags, and advertises only the correct prefixes to each external domain.

Another application for route tags is for leaking prefixes from one IS-IS level to another, in which you want to leak some prefixes but not others. Polices can be used to tag prefixes at their origin, identifying them with administratively defined groups. Other polices can then be implemented at level boundaries that identify the prefix groups, by tags, that are to be leaked and the prefix groups that are to be suppressed.

Review Questions

1. What are some of the challenges in extending OSPF?
2. Why is IS-IS generally easier to extend than OSPF?
3. What are Opaque OSPF LSAs?
4. What are the three types of Opaque LSAs?

5. What is the benefit of the OSPF Router Information Opaque LSA?

6. What is the purpose of the IS-IS Protocols Supported TLV?

7. How is an IGP route tag similar to a BGP community attribute?

CHAPTER 11

Extensions for MPLS Traffic Engineering

As mentioned in Chapter 9, one trend in modern router design is to assign the two fundamental functions of route processing and packet forwarding to separate physical modules. Another way to view this trend is as a separation of intelligence—which is processor-intensive and hence time-consuming—from basic packet forwarding, improving the performance of both. This same trend of separating intelligence from packet forwarding can be seen in large networks as a whole with the increasingly widespread adoption of *Multiprotocol Label Switching* (MPLS). The fundamental idea behind MPLS is to push intelligence to the edge of the network, leaving the core free to do little more than forward packets.

When the predecessors of MPLS, such as tag switching, began appearing in the mid and late 1990s, the motivation of separating intelligence from forwarding was to make the forwarding speeds of routers comparable to those of ATM switches. This was accomplished by adding to packets a fixed-length address, called a *tag* or *label*, that was independent of the data link layer but below the network layer. Routers then switched the packets from incoming interface to outgoing interface based on these "layer 2.5" addresses, the same way ATM or Frame Relay switches on VCI or DLCI labels. Because the labels are a fixed length, and small enough to be able to look them up by indexing into a table, no time-consuming lookups of variable-length IP addresses were necessary. And like ATM or Frame Relay, switching between interfaces is based on a predetermined forwarding table, eliminating the need for complex and time-consuming route processing.

But during the same years that MPLS was evolving, router technology was also evolving. More efficient IP address lookup algorithms were developed, and packet-forwarding functions that had been performed in software began to be implemented in Application-Specific Integrated Circuits (ASICs) and other high-speed hardware components. As a result, shortly before the turn of the century high-end routers routinely had packet-forwarding speeds not just comparable to ATM but exceeding them. High-speed switching ceased to be a motivation for MPLS.

MPLS did not die, however, because the technology offered another similarity to ATM and Frame Relay: The series of forwarding table entries that switched a given packet across a path from an ingress point to an egress point constitutes a *virtual circuit* (VC). And if you can build VCs over your routed network, you can offer services that normally require ATM or Frame Relay without the expense of building and managing an ATM or Frame Relay infrastructure in addition to your routed IP network. The key services currently offered over MPLS networks by service providers are layer 2 and layer 3 *Virtual Private Networks* (VPNs).

Another advantage of being able to create VCs over your router-based network is *traffic engineering* (TE), which provides you with great flexibility in distributing the VCs—and hence your traffic—across your network to bypass trouble spots and better utilize all of your available bandwidth.

Both OSPF and IS-IS have been extended to support TE. To understand those extensions and why they are necessary, it is first necessary to understand the basics of both MPLS and TE.

11.1   MPLS: An Overview

An MPLS VC is called a *Label-Switched Path* (LSP).[1] You can also think of an LSP as a tunnel, in that a packet is encapsulated behind an MPLS header for transport over the LSP. What makes MPLS so flexible is that it is *multiprotocol* both in terms of the data link layer and the network layer. Because it operates above the data link layer, MPLS can run over any kind of data link. And because it runs below the network layer, it can carry any kind of network layer packet.

11.1.1   Labels and Label Switching

An MPLS label is a 20-bit address, normally represented as a simple decimal number. Like ATM VPI/VCIs and Frame Relay DLCIs, it has local significance—that is, it need be unique only between any two devices.

Routers that are MPLS-enabled are called *label-switching routers* (LSRs). These routers have switching tables[2] that map incoming labels with outgoing label/interface pairs. When an MPLS packet is received the label is used as an index to the switching table. The label of the incoming packet is changed (*swapped*) to the mapped outgoing label, and the packet is forwarded out the mapped outgoing interface.

Figure 11.1 shows the label-switching process. A packet with a label of 800003 is received. The label is found in the switching table, which says that the label value is to be

---

[1]   The acronym LSP is, of course, used throughout this book to represent "Link State PDU." This is not the only example of the same acronym representing different terms. In this chapter, you should normally be able to understand which term LSP represents by the context in which it is used. If the context is unclear, the term rather than the acronym is used.

[2]   Depending on the implementation, the switching table is usually just a part of the forwarding table.

swapped to 100056 and the packet is to be forwarded out interface 7. You can readily see that this switching process is similar to what happens in an ATM or Frame Relay switch.

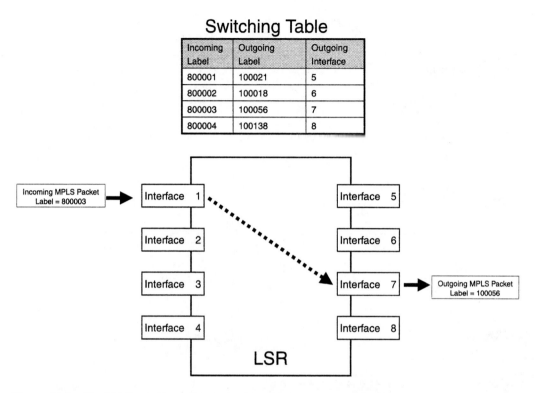

Switching Table

Incoming Label	Outgoing Label	Outgoing Interface
800001	100021	5
800002	100018	6
800003	100056	7
800004	100138	8

Figure 11.1   The MPLS switching table matches incoming labels to outgoing labels and interfaces.

The LSR depicted in Figure 11.1 is a *transit* LSR for the packet shown, traveling along some label-switched path. When a packet is transiting an LSR, the LSR swaps labels as was shown. However, for a given LSP, a router can also be an *ingress* or *egress* LSR. An ingress LSR is the LSR on which an LSP begins; this router *pushes* a label onto a packet and forwards it onto the LSP. The last LSR along the LSP—that is, the router on which the LSP terminates—is the egress LSR for that LSP. An egress router *pops* or removes the MPLS label and then forwards the decapsulated packet by normal network-layer forwarding.

Figure 11.2 illustrates the relationship among LSR types and forwarding actions:

1. The leftmost IP router forwards a packet, using normal IP forwarding, to the ingress router.
2. The forwarding table in the ingress router is instructed, for that packet's destination, to push an MPLS label of 800154 onto the packet and forward it out a given interface. (For readability, the outgoing interface part is not shown in the illustration.)

3. The next router along the path is a transit router, and its switching table is instructed to swap incoming label 800154 for outgoing label 100007.

4. The next transit router swaps incoming label 100007 for outgoing label 0. Label 0 is a special reserved label that tells a receiving router to pop the MPLS label.[3]

5. The egress router, seeing label 0, pops the label and forwards the decapsulated packet using normal IP forwarding.

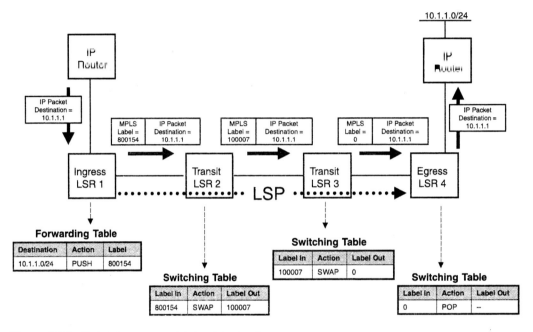

Figure 11.2   Packet flow across a label-switched path.

Figure 11.2 illustrates two important facts. First, LSPs are unidirectional. If MPLS packets are to be forwarded from the rightmost LSR to the leftmost LSR, another LSP must be defined. Of course, if that new LSP flows from right to left, the rightmost LSR is the ingress for that LSP and the leftmost LSR is the egress. This leads to the second important fact: Whether an LSR is ingress, transit, or egress is relative to a given LSP. The transit LSRs in Figure 11.2, for example, might also be ingress LSRs for other LSPs and egress LSRs for yet other LSPs.

---

[3] There is another reserved label, 3, which can be used as an alternative to label 0. Label 3 tells the last transit LSR before the egress LSR—the *penultimate* LSR—to pop the label before forwarding to the egress LSR. This procedure has the wonderful name *penultimate hop popping*.

11.1.2   Forwarding Equivalence Classes and Label Binding

The LSP depicted in Figure 11.2 is, of course, not a physical entity. It is a conceptual entity defined by the series of forwarding and switching table entries from the ingress to the egress. The switching table is, as you saw in the previous section, a set of instructions that identifies incoming packets and classifies them so that they are treated in some predefined way (push, swap or pop some label and forward out some interface). What was not clearly shown in the previous section is that incoming packets with different destination addresses (at an ingress) or different labels (at a transit) or received on different interfaces might be given the same outgoing label and forwarded out the same interface to the same next hop. On any router, the set of packets that the router classifies in such a way that the packets are forwarded identically—for instance, given the same outgoing label, queued the same way, and forwarded out the same interface—belong to the same *forwarding equivalence class* (FEC). All routing involves FECs, but the concept takes on particular importance with MPLS where the router does not "think"; it simply follows the basic set of instructions in the switching table.

When a label is used to identify what FEC a packet belongs to, that label is *bound* to the FEC. Every LSR maintains a pool of free labels. When an FEC is defined, the LSR binds one or more labels from its pool to the FEC. But this binding assumes that upstream neighbors—neighbors forwarding packets to the LSR—know what that bound label value is, so that they can assign that value as an outgoing label. One way of doing this, of course, is to statically define all the switching tables and hence label bindings to create LSPs. The problem with this approach is the same as it is with static routes: It does not scale to a network of any reasonable size. So just as routing protocols are needed to dynamically compute routes, a signaling protocol is needed in MPLS networks to communicate label bindings from one LSR to another.

11.1.3   Label Distribution

Figure 11.3 shows how a signaling protocol might be used to set up the LSP depicted in Figure 11.2. First, when the ingress LSR wants to set up an LSP it looks up the IP address for the LSP endpoint—normally the loopback address of the egress LSR—in its unicast IP routing table. The ingress LSR then can then route a message to the egress requesting that an LSP be set up. Next, the egress router creates a label binding. Because it is the egress, the label binding is simply to a pop function. The egress LSR4 then sends a setup message upstream to LSR3, telling it that it has bound label 0 to the FEC. LSR3 then creates an FEC with outgoing label 0 and the interface on which it received the setup message from LSR4, selects a label from its pool of free labels—in this case 100007—and binds the label to the FEC. LSR3 then sends a setup message to LSR2 with this binding information. LSR2 creates an FEC with the label in the message, selects a label and binds it to the FEC, and sends a setup message to LSR1, the ingress, with the binding information. The LSP is now created, and LSR1 knows that to send any packets over the LSP to LSR4 it encapsulates the packet with a label of 800154 and forwards it out the interface to LSR2.

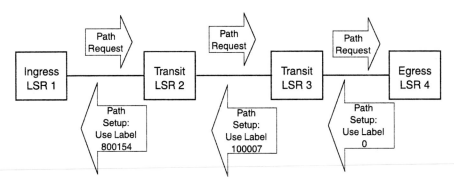

Figure 11.3   An ingress LSR that wants to set up an LSP sends a request message to the egress LSR; the
egress then sends a setup message back upstream to the ingress, so that label bindings can be
created along the path.

The theoretical signaling protocol just described is simplistic and is not the only way to distribute labels, but it gives you an idea of the basic approach to dynamically building an LSP. Three signaling protocols currently are available for distributing labels:

- Label Distribution Protocol (LDP)
- Constraint-Based Label Distribution Protocol (CR-LDP)
- Resource Reservation Protocol for Traffic Engineering (RSVP-TE)

LDP is a lightweight, scalable protocol for distributing labels and is particularly useful in some types of MPLS-based VPN services. However, when LSPs are set up using LDP, they always follow the IGP shortest path as it exists in the network's IP unicast routing tables. As described in Section 11.2, MPLS traffic engineering enables you to set up LSPs over paths other than the ones prescribed by the IGP. Signaling such a path setup requires either CR-LDP or RSVP.

CR-LDP and RSVP-TE are competing and incompatible protocols that do the same thing. Which one you use in your network depends primarily on what vendors you use. Cisco Systems and Juniper Networks, for example, advocate RSVP-TE, whereas Nortel Networks champions CR-LDP.

Describing how any of these three MPLS signaling protocols works is beyond the scope of this chapter; there are plenty of good books and whitepapers available on the subject. For our purposes, it is enough to know that they exist and what they do.

11.1.4 The MPLS Header

MPLS encapsulates packets by adding a 4-byte header to the packet (Figure 11.4). The resulting MPLS packet can then be itself encapsulated by the data link protocol of the link over which it is to be transmitted. Because the MPLS header appears between the network layer header and the data link header, it is sometimes called a "shim" header. Its position between these two headers is also why MPLS is sometimes called a "layer 2.5" protocol.

Figure 11.5 shows the format of the MPLS header. The majority of the header is the 20-bit label.

Data Link Header	MPLS Header	Network Layer Header	Data

Figure 11.4 The MPLS header is added to the front of the network layer packet to be encapsulated, and is then encapsulated by the data link header.

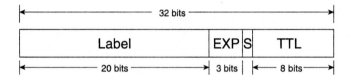

Figure 11.5 The MPLS header.

The Experimental (EXP) field is somewhat unfortunately named, because it now has an explicit use: The value of the 3-bit field specifies how the MPLS packet is to be queued in class-of-service (CoS) applications. The values that can be carried in the field normally correspond to the 3-bit Precedence portion of the Type-of-Service (ToS) field in the IPv4 header.

The Stack (S) bit is used for *label stacking*: Encapsulating an MPLS packet within another MPLS packet. That is, adding another MPLS header in front of an existing MPLS header. Label stacking enables you to tunnel LSPs within other LSPs for scalability. When the S bit is cleared in an MPLS header, it indicates that the next header is another MPLS header. If the S bit is set, it indicates the bottom of the stack: The next header is encapsulated information.

The Time-to-Live (TTL) field is an 8-bit field that functions exactly the same as the TTL field in the IPv4 header and the Hop Limit field of the IPv6 header. It is decremented at each LSR hop, and if it decrements to 0 the MPLS header is discarded. When an IP packet is encapsulated, the value of its TTL field is copied into the TTL field of the MPLS header. The value then continues to be decremented across the LSP. When the packet is decapsulated at the egress LSR, the value of the MPLS TTL field is copied to the TTL field of the IP header. This way the TTL is accurately tracked when an IP packet traverses an MPLS network.

A Useful MPLS TTL Option

An option enables you to disable the operation of writing the value of the MPLS TTL field into the IP TTL field at the egress LSR. The effect of this is that the IP TTL is decremented once at the ingress, before being encapsulated into MPLS, and again at the egress, after being decapsulated from MPLS. As a result, the entire MPLS "cloud" appears to be a single hop.

Many MPLS service providers use this option because many customers regularly track the number of hops through a network on the outdated belief that additional hops add significant latency. (Anyone who has concerns about latency should be tracking actual latency, not router hops.) Therefore, when an LSP is moved for traffic engineering or other reasons, the hop count can change, generating calls to the NOC from customers who mistakenly believe their service is being degraded. Eliminating the MPLS hop count from the IP TTL field prevents a flood of calls from concerned customers every time the service provider makes a traffic engineering change. Customers see a single hop, no matter what the provider is doing internally.

11.2   Traffic Engineering: An Overview

Key to the usefulness of MPLS is that after the LSP is established, your EGP or IGP or both can view the LSP as a traffic path when calculating best paths to a destination. This is again similar to an ATM or Frame Relay VC: Even though the path actually traverses multiple switching nodes, a routing protocol can view it as a single link between the ingress node and the egress node.

The example LSP you have seen so far in Figures 11.2 and 11.3 is too simple to be of practical interest. There is only one physical route from the ingress LSR to the egress LSR, so routing protocols are going to choose it whether an LSP exists or not. But consider the ingress and egress nodes in Figure 11.6. This network contains multiple paths between the ingress and the egress. The IGP in this network will do just what it is designed to do and select the shortest path between ingress and egress based on its given metrics. Assuming that all routers in the network are ingress for some traffic flows and egress for other traffic flows, the traffic might be fairly evenly distributed throughout the network. But suppose much more traffic flows into the one ingress point shown and out of the egress point shown, than anywhere else in the network. The single path chosen by the IGP might become congested while available bandwidth on other paths is underutilized.

Consider also a case in which the network in Figure 11.6 is a multiservice network. You might want to route best-effort traffic between the ingress and egress over longer paths, reserving the bandwidth on the shortest path for delay-sensitive traffic such as voice.

Such requirements are the basis of MPLS traffic engineering. Using MPLS LSPs, you can engineer your traffic loads across the network in such a way that available bandwidth is more efficiently utilized; you can establish different paths for different traffic classes for better multiservice performance; and you can route traffic around trouble spots such as congested links and nodes—congestion that IGPs cannot detect.

Traffic engineering capability has long been a part of ATM and Frame Relay networks. However, before MPLS TE, the only traffic engineering that could be done in IP networks without an ATM or Frame Relay overlay was a crude manipulation of link metrics. Changing a link metric is an all-or-nothing action; the IGP still chooses the shortest path. MPLS

TE enables you to track a number of interface parameters throughout your network and then use these parameters to specify how a path is selected and what packets use what path, permitting much more granularity in regulating traffic flows.

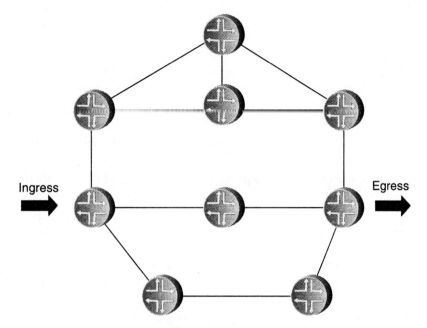

Ingress

Egress

Figure 11.6 The IGP will select only one of the multiple paths between the ingress and egress router in this topology.

11.2.1 TE Link Parameters

As you certainly know, an IGP selects a shortest path based on a metric—some numeric value—assigned to the router interfaces throughout the network. The foundation of traffic engineering is also an assignment of values to interfaces. But because a useful and flexible TE application requires a variety of parameters on which you can base path selection, there must be a variety of values that can be assigned to interfaces that reflect these parameters. Those parameters are:

- Maximum Bandwidth
- Maximum Reservable Bandwidth
- Unreserved Bandwidth
- Traffic Engineering Metric
- Administrative Group

The first three parameters enable a mechanism by which you can specify the bandwidth an LSP can use. For example, an LSP might be required to have 10M available to it. When the LSP is being set up, it can traverse only links between the ingress and egress on which at least 10M of bandwidth is available. That 10M is then reserved on the links and becomes unavailable for use by another LSP. So if a 10M LSP is set up across a link on which there is a total of 15M of available bandwidth, only 5M of reservable bandwidth is left after the LSP is established. If a second LSP is to be set up and also requires 10M, it cannot use this link and must be set up on an alternate path that provides enough bandwidth. If no other path with sufficient reservable bandwidth is available, the second LSP cannot be established.

Maximum Bandwidth is the bandwidth of the interface. It might be the actual bandwidth of the interface or it might be a configured number.

Maximum Reservable Bandwidth specifies how much of the link bandwidth can be reserved by LSPs.

Unreserved Bandwidth is the amount of maximum reservable bandwidth that has not yet been used by LSPs.

Traffic Engineering Metric is a 24-bit value that can be assigned to an interface and is used the same as an IGP metric. The TE metric allows you to set up a metric-based LSP topology that is different from the metric-based IGP shortest-path topology.

Administrative Group, also known as *affinity*, enables you to make an interface a member of one or more of 32 possible administrative groups. Administrative groups are often called *link colors* because you can associate names with each of the 32 administrative groups, and traditionally those names have been the names of colors. For example, you might "color" all of your highest-speed links gold, your medium-speed links silver, and your low-speed links bronze. You could then specify that certain LSPs can only use gold or silver links and other LSPs can only use silver or bronze links. Or instead of specifying what links an LSP can use, you might specify what links an LSP cannot use: For instance, an LSP might use any link except platinum links.

Figure 11.7 shows a Cisco Systems IOS output displaying traffic engineering parameters for an interface. You can observe the TE metric, the maximum bandwidth, the maximum reservable bandwidth, and the administrative groups (affinity bits) to which the interface belongs. Notice that the maximum reservable bandwidth is greater than the maximum bandwidth. Specifying a maximum reservable bandwidth greater than the maximum bandwidth permits oversubscription of the interface.

Of interest in Figure 11.7 are the eight entries labeled "Priority" 0 through 7. The value associated with each of these eight priorities is the unreserved bandwidth. When an LSP is being configured for TE, is can be given a setup and a hold priority, and each of these priorities is a value between 0 and 7. Setup priority is the "strength" the LSP has to preempt another LSP, and the hold priority is the "strength" an LSP has to resist being preempted. If a new LSP has a setup priority higher than the hold priority of an existing LSP, and there are not enough link resources such as bandwidth to support both, the stronger LSP can replace the weaker LSP, and the weaker LSP must find a new path to its egress. So the unreserved bandwidth in Figure 11.7 is allocated separately for each of the eight setup priority levels; 0 is the highest or "strongest," and 7 is the lowest.

```
Cisco7# show ip ospf mpls traffic-eng link
OSPF Router with ID (10.1.1.1) (Process ID 1)
  Area 0 has 1 MPLS TE links. Area instance is 14.
  Links in hash bucket 8.
    Link is associated with fragment 1. Link instance is 14
      Link connected to Point-to-Point network
      Link ID :192.168.5.4
      Interface Address :10.5.0.1
      Neighbor Address :10.5.0.2
      Admin Metric :84
      Maximum bandwidth :150000
      Maximum reservable bandwidth :250000
      Number of Priority :8
      Priority 0 :250000        Priority 1 :250000
      Priority 2 :250000        Priority 3 :250000
      Priority 4 :250000        Priority 5 :250000
      Priority 6 :250000        Priority 7 :212500
      Affinity Bit :0x3
```

Figure 11.7 An IOS output showing the TE parameters associated with an interface.

11.2.2 Constrained Shortest Path First

The calculation of a traffic engineered path takes place only in the ingress router. That means the ingress router must have some way to learn all of the TE parameters assigned to all MPLS interfaces in the network, and it must have a place to store that information. This is where OSPF and IS-IS come in: Both protocols have extensions that allow them to carry the TE interface parameters along with the normal interface parameters such as OSPF or IS-IS metrics and link state. Those extensions, the real topic of this chapter, are detailed in Sections 11.3 and 11.4.

Just as OSPF LSAs and IS-IS LSPs are stored in a link state database, the traffic engineering parameters carried by the extensions to these protocols are stored in a special database called the *traffic engineering database* (TED). Figure 11.8 shows an example of a TED from a Juniper Networks LSR. For each entry, you can observe the administrative groups (called color in this display), the metric, and the bandwidth parameters.

```
jeff@Juniper3> show ted database extensive
TED database: 0 ISIS nodes 6 INET nodes
NodeID: 172.16.229.7
  Type: Rtr, Age: 72166 secs, LinkIn: 1, LinkOut: 1
  Protocol: OSPF(0.0.0.0)
    To: 172.16.229.190-1, Local: 172.16.229.191, Remote: 0.0.0.0
  Color: 0 <none>
      Metric: 100
      Static BW: 1000Mbps
      Reservable BW: 1000Mbps
      Available BW [priority] bps:
        [0] 1000Mbps     [1] 1000Mbps     [2] 1000Mbps     [3] 1000Mbps
```

```
           [4] 1000Mbps      [5] 1000Mbps     [6] 1000Mbps      [7] 1000Mbps
        Interface Switching Capability Descriptor(1):
          Switching type: Packet
          Encoding type: Packet
          Maximum LSP BW [priority] bps:
           [0] 1000Mbps      [1] 1000Mbps     [2] 1000Mbps      [3] 1000Mbps
           [4] 1000Mbps      [5] 1000Mbps     [6] 1000Mbps      [7] 1000Mbps
NodeID: 172.16.229.8
  Type: Rtr, Age: 72161 secs, LinkIn: 1, LinkOut: 1
  Protocol: OSPF(0.0.0.0)
    To: 172.16.229.189-1, Local: 172.16.229.188, Remote: 0.0.0.0
  Color: 0 <none>
      Metric: 100
      Static BW: 1000Mbps
      Reservable BW: 1000Mbps
      Available BW [priority] bps:
       [0] 1000Mbps      [1] 1000Mbps     [2] 1000Mbps      [3] 1000Mbps
       [4] 1000Mbps      [5] 1000Mbps     [6] 1000Mbps      [7] 1000Mbps
      Interface Switching Capability Descriptor(1):
        Switching type: Packet
        Encoding type: Packet
        Maximum LSP BW [priority] bps:
         [0] 1000Mbps      [1] 1000Mbps     [2] 1000Mbps      [3] 1000Mbps
         [4] 1000Mbps      [5] 1000Mbps     [6] 1000Mbps      [7] 1000Mbps
NodeID: 172.16.229.9
  Type: Rtr, Age: 10924 secs, LinkIn: 3, LinkOut: 3
  Protocol: OSPF(0.0.0.0)
    To: 172.16.229.190-1, Local: 172.16.229.190, Remote: 0.0.0.0
  Color: 0 <none>
      Metric: 100
      Static BW: 1000Mbps
      Reservable BW: 1000Mbps
      Available BW [priority] bps:
       [0] 1000Mbps      [1] 1000Mbps     [2] 1000Mbps      [3] 1000Mbps
       [4] 1000Mbps      [5] 1000Mbps     [6] 1000Mbps      [7] 1000Mbps
      Interface Switching Capability Descriptor(1):
        Switching type: Packet
        Encoding type: Packet
        Maximum LSP BW [priority] bps:
         [0] 1000Mbps      [1] 1000Mbps     [2] 1000Mbps      [3] 1000Mbps
         [4] 1000Mbps      [5] 1000Mbps     [6] 1000Mbps      [7] 1000Mbps
    To: 172.16.229.10, Local: 172.16.229.193, Remote: 172.16.229.192
  Color: 0 <none>
      Metric: 100
      Static BW: 155.52Mbps
      Reservable BW: 155.52Mbps
      Available BW [priority] bps:
       [0] 155.52Mbps   [1] 155.52Mbps  [2] 155.52Mbps   [3] 155.52Mbps
       [4] 155.52Mbps   [5] 155.52Mbps  [6] 155.52Mbps   [7] 155.52Mbps
      Interface Switching Capability Descriptor(1):
        Switching type: Packet
        Encoding type: Packet
        Maximum LSP BW [priority] bps:
         [0] 155.52Mbps   [1] 155.52Mbps  [2] 155.52Mbps   [3] 155.52Mbps
         [4] 155.52Mbps   [5] 155.52Mbps  [6] 155.52Mbps   [7] 155.52Mbps
    To: 172.16.229.10, Local: 172.16.229.195, Remote: 172.16.229.194
  Color: 0 <none>
```

```
Metric: 100
Static BW: 155.52Mbps
Reservable BW: 155.52Mbps
Available BW [priority] bps:
 [0] 155.52Mbps    [1] 155.52Mbps   [2] 155.52Mbps   [3] 155.52Mbps
 [4] 155.52Mbps    [5] 155.52Mbps   [6] 155.52Mbps   [7] 155.52Mbps
Interface Switching Capability Descriptor(1):
  Switching type: Packet
  Encoding type: Packet
  Maximum LSP BW [priority] bps:
   [0] 155.52Mbps   [1] 155.52Mbps   [2] 155.52Mbps   [3] 155.52Mbps
   [4] 155.52Mbps   [5] 155.52Mbps   [6] 155.52Mbps   [7] 155.52Mbps
```

Figure 11.8   A JUNOS output showing a traffic engineering database.

When you configure an LSP at an ingress LSR, you specify *constraints* on the LSP: What link colors it can or cannot use, its bandwidth, the maximum number of LSR hops it can traverse, and so on. Using these constraints and the information in the TED, the LSR runs a modified SPF algorithm called *constrained shortest path first* (CSPF), which calculates the shortest path to the egress within the constraints you specified. A specification of the resulting shortest path is then fed to the signaling protocol—RSVP or CR-LDP—which sets up the LSP.

11.3   OSPF Extensions for Traffic Engineering

The role of OSPF and IS-IS in MPLS TE is to communicate TE interface parameters throughout an area to populate the traffic engineering database. In this, the role of these protocols is the same as their role for IGPs; in fact, this is just an extension of basic link state IGP behavior. The OSPF extensions for TE are specified in RFC 3630.[4]

OSPF carries TE interface parameters in Traffic Engineering LSAs (Figure 11.9), an adaptation of type 10 Opaque LSAs. As first discussed in Section 10.1.2, Opaque LSAs are general-use LSAs intended for future extensions; the extension-specific information is carried in TLVs in the payload portion of the LSA.

This LSA performs essentially the same function as Router (type 1) LSAs: It identifies the originating router, the router's neighbors, and characteristics—in particular the TE parameters—of the links to those neighbors. Because the necessary TE parameters are carried in this LSA for interfaces to both point-to-point and multi-access links, there is no need or a special "TE version" of Network (type 2) LSAs. The existing type 2 LSAs are sufficient for the CSPF calculations.

The *Opaque Type* of the TE LSA, as shown in Figure 11.9, is 1.

---

[4]   Dave Katz, Kireeti Kompella, and Derek M. Yeung, "Traffic Engineering (TE) Extensions to OSPF Version 2," RFC 3630, September 2003.

Instance[5] differentiates this LSA from other TE LSAs. Because this field is 24 bits (unlike a regular LSA ID field, the Opaque type takes up the first 8 bits) there can be a maximum of $2^{16} = 16,777,216$ TE LSAs in a given traffic engineering area.

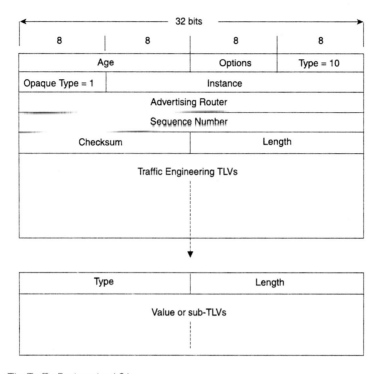

Figure 11.9   The Traffic Engineering LSA.

The payload portion of the TE LSA is one or more TLVs of one of the following types:

- **Router Address TLV** (TLV type 1) carries in its value field an always-reachable IPv4 loopback address of the originating router. This address is normally also the RID of the originator, but of more importance here is that the address serves as the endpoint of any LSP egressing the originator.
- **Link TLV** (TLV type 2) describes the TE parameters of a single link. The value of this TLV is a set of sub-TLVs. The format of a sub-TLV is the same as any other TLV; it is a sub-TLV only by virtue of the fact that it is in the value field of another TLV.

---

[5] Recall from Section 10.1.2 that this field in the general Opaque LSA format is called the Opaque Type field and is defined as an identifier specific to the LSA application.

The sub-TLVs of the Link TLV, and their types, are as follows:

- **Link Type** (type 1) carries as its value a 1-byte field that specifies the type of link being described: point to point (link type 1) or multi-access (link type 2).

- **Link ID** (type 2) serves the same purpose, and uses the same semantics, as the Link ID in Router LSAs: It identifies the LSR at the other end of the link. If the link type is 1 (point-to-point link), the link ID is the RID of the neighbor. If the link type is 2 (multi-access), the Link ID is the interface address of the DR.

- **Local Interface IP Address** (type 3) specifies the IP address of the originator's interface to the link. This sub-TLV can carry multiple IP addresses if the interface has more than one address.

- **Remote Interface IP Address** (type 4) specifies the IP address or IP addresses of the neighbor's interface to the link, if the link is point to point. If the link is multi-access, the value of this sub-TLV is 0.0.0.0 or, alternatively, the sub-TLV is not included at all.

- **Traffic Engineering Metric** (type 5) carries a 4-byte TE metric as described in Section 11.2.1.

- **Maximum Bandwidth** (type 6) carries the maximum bandwidth as described in Section 11.2.1. This is a 4-byte value specifying the bandwidth in bytes (not bits) per second.

- **Maximum Reservable Bandwidth** (type 7) carries the maximum reservable bandwidth, as described in Section 11.2.1. This is also a 4-byte value specifying the bandwidth in bytes per second.

- **Unreserved Bandwidth** (type 8) carries the unreserved bandwidth for each of the eight setup priority levels 0 through 7, as described in Section 11.2.1. You can observe these values in Figures 11.7 and 11.8; they are listed in the sub-TLV in order from 0 to 7. Because each bandwidth size is described by a 4-byte number (again in bytes per second), the total length of the value field of this sub-TLV is 32 bytes.

- **Administrative Group** (type 9) specifies the administrative group (link color) or groups to which the link is assigned. The value is a 32-bit field, with each of the bits representing one of 32 possible administrative groups. If a bit is set, the link belongs to the group corresponding to that bit position. The most significant bit corresponds to administrative group 31, and the least significant bit to group 0. In Figure 11.7, the value of that link's affinity bit (yet another name for administrative group) is 0x3, so the link belongs to administrative groups 1 and 0 (and hence to whatever "colors" the network administrator has associated with those two numbers). In Figure 11.8, this same TLV value is labeled as "color," and the value of 0 indicates that the links in the database do not belong to any administrative groups.

Every Link TLV must have a Link Type and Link ID sub-TLV, but the other sub-TLVs might or might not appear in the Link TLV depending on whether the TE parameter is specified.

A significant point is that type 10 Opaque LSAs, on which the TE LSAs are built, have area flooding scope. That means that when you design a TE domain using OSPF, its boundaries must correspond to the boundaries of an OSPF area. Typically, because a TE domain is in the core of a network, the domain boundary corresponds to OSPF area 0.

And because the TE LSAs flood throughout the area they are originated in, all routers in the area, whether they individually participate in TE or not, must recognize and flood these LSAs.

11.4   IS-IS Extensions for Traffic Engineering

The IS-IS extensions for traffic engineering support are specified in RFC 3784.[6] Semantically, the extensions are the same as those for OSPF: The same TE parameters are communicated, the same value ranges are used (such as 4 bytes for the maximum bandwidth parameter), and the values are represented the same (such as bandwidth values in bytes per second). And, as with OSPF, sub-TLVs—TLVs nested within the value fields of other TLVs—are used to carry the TE parameters.

The sub-TLVs carrying TE parameters are carried in the Extended IS Reachability (type 22) TLV, which was introduced in Section 5.5.7[7] and is shown again in Figure 11.10. Of particular note is that in another similarity to OSPF TE extensions, the TE parameters are carried in sub-TLVs. For each of the sub-TLVs supported by the Link TLV in OSPF TE LSAs, an analogous sub-TLV is supported by the IS-IS type 22 TLV. So rather than repeat their identical functions, they are listed in Table 11.1 next to their OSPF counterparts.

IS-IS TE extensions also have a TLV that is analogous to the OSPF Router Address TLV described in the previous section: the Traffic Engineering Router ID TLV. This TLV type is 134, and it carries the 4-byte RID of the originating router. For both OSPF and IS-IS, this address is configured on a loopback interface and serves as the endpoint for egress LSPs. Because it exists on the loopback interface, it is independent of any instability on a single physical interface. It is a stable endpoint as long as it is reachable through some physical interface.

The OSPF Router Address TLV and the IS-IS Router ID TLV also serve a purpose in TE domains where both OSPF and IS-IS are running. If a router advertises its link TE parameters in both OSPF TE LSAs and IS-IS Extended IS Reachability TLVs, it should also originate both an OSPF Router Address TLV and an IS-IS Router ID TLV containing the same address.

---

[6]   Henk Smit and Tony Li, "Intermediate System to Intermediate System (IS-IS) Extensions for Traffic Engineering (TE)," RFC 3784, June 2004.

[7]   The relevance of the Extended IS Reachability TLV in Section 5.5.7 is its support for wide metrics. The implication here is that when IS-IS support for traffic engineering is enabled, support for wide metrics is enabled because both use the same TLV.

A router building a single TED from both OSPF and IS-IS TE TLVs can identify, based on the identical address in the Router Address TLV and the Router ID TLV, that the OSPF and IS-IS information come from the same router rather than separate routers.

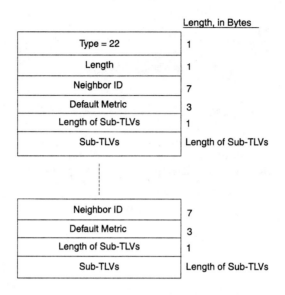

Figure 11.10   IS-IS communicates TE link parameters in the Extended IS Reachability TLV.

Table 11.1   Sub-TLVs Carried in IS-IS Extended IS Reachability TLVs or TE Support

Sub-TLV	Type Number	Length (Bytes)	Corresponding OSPF Sub-TLV
Administrative Group (Color)	3	4	Administrative Group
IPv4 Interface Address	6	4	Local Interface IP Address
IPv4 Neighbor Address	8	4	Remote Interface IP Address
Maximum Link Bandwidth	9	4	Maximum Bandwidth
Reservable Link Bandwidth	10	4	Maximum Reservable Bandwidth
Unreserved Bandwidth	11	32	Unreserved Bandwidth
TE Default Metric	18	3	TE Metric

Review Questions

1. Why is MPLS called *multiprotocol?*
2. What is an MPLS LSR?
3. What is an MPLS LSP?
4. How is an MPLS label like a Frame Relay DLCI?
5. What is an FEC?
6. What are the EXP bits in the MPLS header used for?
7. What are some benefits of MPLS traffic engineering?
8. What is the purpose of a signaling or label distribution protocol? What three protocols are available for MPLS signaling?
9. Why is LDP not used for traffic engineering?
10. What role does OSPF or IS-IS play in MPLS TE?
11. What is the TED?
12. What is CSPF?
13. What is a sub-TLV?
14. What type of Opaque LSA does the Traffic Engineering LSA use? What is the design implication of using this LSA type?
15. What two top-level TLV types can the TE LSA carry, and what is the purpose of each?
16. What IS-IS TLV carries TE sub-TLVs?
17. What significance do the OSPF Router Address TLV and the IS-IS Router ID TLV have in mapping OSPF and IS-IS TE topologies?

CHAPTER 12

Extensions for IPv6

One of the more significant differences between OSPF and IS-IS—a difference that you have already observed in the previous three chapters—is that IS-IS is much easier to extend to support new features and capabilities than is OSPF. This difference is nowhere more striking than in the two protocols' support for IP version 6. IS-IS is extended to support this "next generation" of IP through the simple definition of two new TLVs. OSPF, on the other hand, requires an entirely new version: OSPFv3.

12.1 IPv6: An Overview

In its infancy, what we now call the Internet was a research and development network; Chapter 1 tells the story of these early years. There was little if any expectation that this internetworking of academic, military, and corporate networks would have the phenomenal commercial success it has since enjoyed. As a result, great blocks of IP addresses were taken by universities, companies, and government organizations involved in this internetwork with the assumption that the IPv4 address space was fairly inexhaustible. The vast majority of those early address allocations were made in the United States, where most of the early research and development was taking place.

You know the rest of the story. Many university students exposed to this internetwork understood its potential and went on to build companies to exploit that potential. The World Wide Web became the first of the "killer apps" that popularized the Internet with the general public and caused an explosion of new users. Suddenly, what was once assumed to be a vast supply of available IP addresses was quickly becoming depleted. In the mid-1990s, a number of analyses predicted that based on existing allocation trends, the IPv4 address space would be used up in a few short years.

The solution to IP address exhaustion was to develop a new version of IP, with a larger address space. That solution, which was first called IPng (ng for "next generation") and eventually became IPv6, quadrupled the size of the address to 128 bits. This larger address size means an exponentially larger number of available addresses—you will see how much larger in the following section. But it was understood that a short-term solution was needed to slow IP address exhaustion while the long-term IPng was being developed. The short-term solution was to create "private" IP addresses, as defined in RFC 1918, and a mechanism that allowed many of these non-unique private addresses to share one or a few globally unique IP addresses: Network Address Translation, or NAT.

NAT and dynamic private IP addresses have become so widely accepted that they are a part of most modern networks, from small multi computer home networks to large enterprises. And the mechanism has been so successful in slowing the depletion of IPv4 addresses that as of this writing many question the need for IPv6 in the near future. But NAT is increasingly viewed as an inhibitor to innovation in application development. Peer-to-peer applications, for example, are made more difficult if not impossible when the end systems are hidden behind NAT devices. Likewise, VoIP, security, quality-of-service, and multicast applications are more difficult when run from behind NAT. Moving NAT back to what it was originally intended to be—a short-term solution to the IP address exhaustion problem—and moving the IP world to IPv6 will re-energize the innovative thinking of the earlier Internet and result in new and unexpected kinds of applications.

The early push for widespread adoption of IPv6 has been in Asia, with its large consumer electronics industries. These industries, and the governments that back them, understand that to continue selling new network-enabled devices and services a large pool of readily available, globally unique IP addresses is needed. Additionally, Asia is aggressively building new Internet infrastructures. However, because large portions of the IPv4 address space were allocated in the United States in the early days of the Internet, acquiring the addresses necessary to support the burgeoning Asian Internet is increasingly difficult. In India, you can find hierarchical NAT architectures five layers deep to compensate for that lack of IP addresses.

A single fact clearly explains the Asian interest in IPv6: Some 65 percent of the total IPv4 address space has been allocated, leaving approximately 1.3 billion globally unique addresses still available. The population of the Peoples' Republic of China is also, it turns out, about 1.3 billion. So by giving a single IPv4 address to each person in China, all of the remaining IPv4 addresses would be used up.

Which is not to say that IPv4 addresses *will* be used up, by China, India, or anyone else. The reality is that the IPv4 address space will never be completely depleted. Can you imagine the justification required to get the last IPv4 address?

Already, stringent guidelines are in place to ensure that globally routable IPv4 addresses are not given out frivolously. If you are a service provider or enterprise network operator, you must provide careful justification for the address space you request. If you run a small business or home network, you likely have to pay your service provider for static IP addresses, if you can get them at all. As the number of available IPv4 addresses continues to shrink, they will become increasingly more difficult and expensive to obtain. It is predicted that at some point those companies and institutions that acquired a surplus of address space in the early days of the Internet will recognize their spare IPv4 addresses as a valuable commodity, and a private market for IPv4 addresses will spring up. So, this is the true driver for IPv6: a new, plentiful source of easily obtainable IP addresses.

Asian governments—particularly those of Japan, South Korea, Taiwan, and China—see IPv6 as essential to the security and continued growth of their technology-based economies. Similar interest is growing in Europe for much the same reason. And in North America, where the relative wealth of IPv4 addresses has until recently kept enthusiasm for IPv6 low, government interest—particularly from the military—is expected to drive development of new IPv6 applications that will in turn drive commercial deployment.

This section does not come close to providing a complete treatment of IPv6. Instead, it provides a brief overview of its most important characteristics before we delve into how OSPF and IS-IS are extended to route this new version of IP.

12.1.1   IPv6 Features and Functions

The most understood feature of IPv6 is its 128-bit address size. This larger address means a total address space that is almost incomprehensibly larger than that of IPv4: some 340 trillion trillion trillion addresses, as opposed to 4.3 billion IPv4 addresses. To put the relative sizes of these two address spaces into some perspective, suppose each IPv4 and IPv6 address weighed 1 gram. If so, the entire IPv4 address space would weigh approximately one-seventeenth the weight of the Empire State Building.[1] In contrast, the IPv6 address space would be 56.7 billion times the weight of planet Earth![2]

In addition to the larger address size, several significant features of IPv6 are:

- A neighbor discovery protocol
- The ability of nodes to statelessly autoconfigure their interface addresses
- A simplified header format
- The use of extension headers to add information to the header
- Integrated authentication and encryption

Subsequent sections briefly examine each of these new features. But first, we look more closely at IPv6 address format and representation.

---

[1] According to www.gibnet.org/heavy.htm, the Empire State Building weighs 365,000 tons, or 328.5 billion grams.

[2] According to www.howstuffworks.com/question30.htm, the Earth, based on gravitational measurements, weighs 6.00e + 27 grams. My gratitude to Brian McGehee, from whom I shamelessly stole this example.

12.1.2   IPv6 Address Format

There are three basic types of IPv6 address, defined in RFC 3513:

- **Unicast** addresses specify a single interface.
- **Multicast** addresses identify a group of interfaces. A packet with a multicast destination address should be delivered to all members of the multicast group.
- **Anycast** addresses also identify a group of addresses. The difference between an anycast address and a multicast address is that a packet with an anycast destination address is delivered to only one member of the group—normally the member closest to the source. Anycast addresses are used, for example, to create redundant routers.

Unlike IPv4, IPv6 does not have a broadcast address.

Figure 12.1 shows the format of the IPv6 global unicast address. Like the IPv4 address, the IPv6 address includes a host part (identifier) and a network part (location). However, the IPv6 address format is much more rigid, making address management easier. The host part in IPv6 is called the Interface Identifier, and with few exceptions is 64 bits long. Preceding the Interface ID is the Subnet ID. Unlike IPv4, where the subnet portion of the address always uses a part of the host portion of the address and can be of variable length, the IPv6 Subnet ID is a part of the prefix and is usually 16 bits long.[3] Having a fixed 16-bit Subnet ID might seem wasteful to you. After all, only the largest networks are likely to have anything close to the 65,535 subnets this field can represent, yet if you get an IPv6 prefix you are likely to get exactly that. The rationale, like that of the Interface ID, is that the simplified manageability associated with fixed address fields is worth the tradeoff.

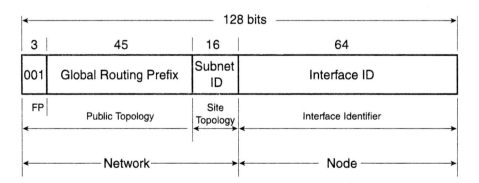

Figure 12.1   The IPv6 global unicast address format.

---

[3] The 16-bit subnet field is recommended by RFC 3177 for the majority of allocations. However, a 17-bit field (leaving 47 bits of prefix) might be assigned to a very large enterprise, and an allocation with no subnet ID field at all (64-bit prefix) might be assigned when only one subnet is needed.

The 48 bits preceding the Subnet ID is the globally unique prefix. The first 3 bits of this and other IPv6 address types make up the Format Prefix field. For currently assigned global unicast addresses, these 3 bits are always 001.

You might have seen diagrams of the global unicast IPv6 address in which the global routing prefix divided into Top-Level Aggregate (TLA), Next-Level Aggregate (NLA), and Subnet-Local Aggregate (SLA) sections. This earlier format was defined in RFC 2374, but has been obsoleted in favor of the format in Figure 12.1 in RFC 3587.

In addition to the global unicast address, which is of course globally unique, there are other scopes of uniqueness:

- **Link-local** unicast addresses are unique only within the scope of a single link. Packets with link-local addresses are therefore never forwarded by routers to other links. The first 10 bits of link-local addresses are always 1111111010 (FE80::/10).

- **Site-local** unicast addresses are unique only within a specified site. In this, their function is similar to that of private IPv4 addresses defined in RFC 1918. The first 10 bits of site-local addresses are always 1111111011 (FEC0::/10).[4]

Figure 12.2 shows the format of an IPv6 multicast address. The first 8 bits of this address are always all 1s (FF00::/8). The next 4 bits are flags, and at present only the last flag is used. This T flag specifies whether the address is a permanently assigned ("well-known") multicast address such as those used by OSPFv3, or a transient multicast address. The next 4 bits specify the scope of the address, and the remaining 112 bits identify the multicast group.

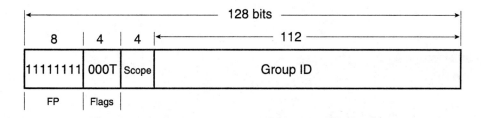

Figure 12.2   The IPv6 multicast address format.

Anycast addresses are defined by application, rather than a format. In this, they are indistinguishable from unicast addresses. However, the node to which an anycast address is assigned must know that the address is anycast, to avoid the erroneous generation of duplicate address errors.

---

[4] At this writing, there is an argument within the IETF IPv6 working group about whether to deprecate site-local addresses, and it appears at this time that the deprecation will happen.

12.1.3   IPv6 Address Representation

IPv4 addresses, as you know, are written in four decimal segments, each representing 8 bits and separated by dots (dotted decimal). IPv6 addresses are written in eight hexadecimal segments, each segment representing 16 bits and separated by a colon. For example:

```
3ffe:3700:1100:0001:0210:a4ff:fea0:bc97
```

Such an address is, of course, hard to write and almost impossible to remember. Fortunately, many IPv6 addresses contain strings of 0s, and there are two rules for using those strings to reduce the size of the address. The first rule is that you can leave off leading 0s in any 16-bit segment. Consider the following address:

```
fe80:0210:1100:0006:0030:a4ff:000c:0097
```

By leaving off the leading 0s in each segment, the address can be written:

```
fe80:210:1100:6:30:a4ff:c:97
```

Note that only the leading 0s can be "compacted." If trailing 0s were also left off, you could not tell where the 0s belong.

The second rule for compacting IPv6 addresses is that if one or more complete 16-bit segments consist entirely of 0s, you can represent one entire string with a double colon. For example, the address:

```
ff02:0000:0000:0000:0000:0000:0000:0001
```

Can be written:

```
ff02::1
```

An address of all 0s—which is called the unspecified address, and is used in several link-local operations such as neighbor discovery—can be represented simply as:

```
::
```

However, you can only use the double colon once in an address. If it is used more than once, the length of the 0 strings becomes ambiguous. Take, for instance, the following address:

```
2001:0000:0000:0013:0000:0000:0b0c:3701
```

This can be written in one of two ways:

```
2001::13:0:0:b0c:3701
```

Or

```
2001:0:0:13::b0c:3701
```

But the address cannot be written like this:

```
2001::13::b0c:3701
```

This last case is illegal because it is not clear where all the 0s go. It could represent any one of the following three addresses:

```
2001:0000:0000:0013:0000:0000:3701
2001:0000:0000:0000:0013:0000:3701
2001:0000:0013:0000:0000:0000:3701
```

12.1.4   The Neighbor Discovery Protocol

Just as ICMP is the core maintenance protocol for IPv4, ICMPv6 (RFC 2463) is the core maintenance protocol for IPv6. Many of the functions and messages are the same between these protocols, such as:

- Destination unreachable
- Packet too big
- Time exceeded
- Parameter problem
- Echo request
- Echo reply

Five new messages have been defined for ICMPv6 that enable the IPv6 Neighbor Discovery Protocol (RFC 2461):

- Router Solicitation (RS)
- Router Advertisement (RA)
- Neighbor Solicitation (NS)
- Neighbor Advertisement (NA)
- Redirect

As the names of these messages suggest, using the Neighbor Discovery Protocol a node can solicit information about a neighbor or router. A neighbor or router can also advertise unsolicited information about itself. In all cases, these messages have a link local scope and are not forwarded by any router.

Redirects are just as you understand them for IPv4, but are redefined under the Neighbor Discovery Protocol for IPv6 because IPv6 hosts build default gateway lists based on the information learned from Router Advertisements.

Neighbor Discovery also takes over functions performed by other protocols in IPv4. For example, IPv6 does not have ARP. Instead, NS and NA messages are exchanged for a similar link-layer address resolution.

The major functions performed by Neighbor Discovery are:

- Link-layer address resolution
- Router discovery
- Local prefix discovery
- Address autoconfiguration
- Link parameter discovery
- Next-hop determination
- Neighbor and router reachability detection
- Duplicate address detection
- Redirects

Although all of these functions are of interest, most are beyond the scope of this book. The functions that are important for our discussion are address autoconfiguration and duplicate address detection, as described in the next section.

12.1.5   Stateless Address Autoconfiguration

IPv6 addresses can be configured on hosts manually, of course. But more importantly, they can be automatically configured either statefully or statelessly. Stateful address autoconfiguration happens with IPv6 just as it does with IPv4, using DHCP,[5] and is useful when you want strong control over local host address allocation. Stateless address autoconfiguration, using the Neighbor Discovery Protocol, eliminates the need for DHCP servers and simplifies mobile IP infrastructures.

A host statelessly autoconfigures its address in four steps:

1. Determine the Interface ID (the last 64 bits of the IPv6 address).
2. Determine the link-local IPv6 address.
3. Determine whether there are other hosts using the derived address (duplicate address detection).
4. Determine the global IPv6 address.

---

[5]   IPv6 uses DHCPv6, specified in RFC 3315.

If a host's interface has a MAC address (which almost all hosts do nowadays), it uses a simple procedure called MAC-to-EUI-64 conversion to derive an Interface ID that should, in most cases, be universally unique. The MAC-to-EUI-64 conversion changes the 48-bit MAC address into a 64-bit Interface ID by inserting the 16-bit value 0xFFFE between the first three octets and the last three octets of the MAC address, and then setting the Universal/Local (U/L) bit to a value of 1 to give the address universal scope.

For example, take the MAC address:

```
000a:958b:3cba
```

Inserting 0xFFFE into the middle, the address changes from 48 bits to 64 bits:

```
000a:95ff:fe8b:3cba
```

The U/L bit is the seventh bit in the MAC address. Flipping that bit from 0 to 1 results in an address of:

```
020a:95ff:fe8b:3cba
```

This is the resulting Interface ID.

Next, the host must determine its link-local address. Recall that link-local addresses always have the first 10 bits set to FE80::/10. By adding this well-known prefix to the previously derived Interface ID, the host now has its link-local address:

```
fe80::20a:95ff:fe8b:3cba
```

The host now has an IP address that can be used to communicate with any other device on the local link. However, before going further, the host must verify that no other device on the link uses that address. Although unusual, it is possible for another interface to have the same MAC address and therefore derive the same link-local address. So, the host performs a duplicate address check. In a nutshell, the host multicasts a Neighbor Solicitation message on the link that includes its new link-local address. If another device has the same address, it responds with a Neighbor Advertisement including the disputed address. The host must now fall back to some other procedure, such as manual configuration, to solve the problem.

If the host verifies that no duplicate address exists on the link, it sends a Router Solicitation message to the well-known All-Routers multicast address FF01::2. Assuming there is at least one router on the link, that the router's interface has been configured with at least one IPv6 address, and that Neighbor Discovery Protocol has been enabled on its interface, the router will respond to the host's RS with a Router Advertisement that includes (among other things) the prefix assigned to the link. The host can then add that prefix onto its Interface ID and has a global (or perhaps site) IP address. For example, suppose the router's interface has an assigned IPv6 address of:

```
3ffe:2650:1200:15::116/64
```

When the host receives the RA containing the 64-bit prefix, it adds the prefix to the Interface ID for a resulting IPv6 address of:

$$3ffe:2650:1200:15:20a:95ff:fe8b:3cba$$

Neighbor Discovery has other options that allow flexibility in how the address is auto-configured. For example, the RA contains flags that allow the router to tell the host to go to a DHCP server for all its parameters, or to take the prefix from the RA but go to a DHCP server for other address parameters.

12.1.6   IPv6 Header Format

Figure 12.3 shows a side-by-side comparison of the IPv4 and IPv6 header formats.[6] The most interesting detail, and probably the first thing you noticed, is that although the IPv6 source and destination addresses are each four times as large as the IPv4 source and destination addresses, the IPv6 header is not much larger than the IPv4 header. The reason, as you can also see in Figure 12.3, is that there are fewer fields in the IPv6 header.

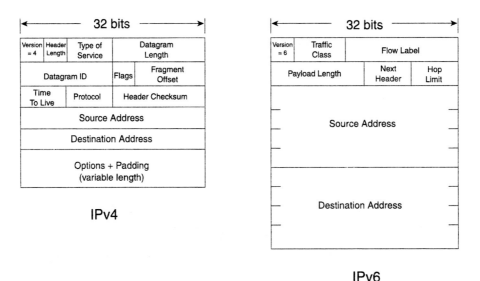

Figure 12.3   IPv4 and IPv6 headers.

The fields in the IPv6 header (not including the Address fields, which are self-explanatory) are:

Version is the same 4-bit field as in the IPv4 header, except that of course its value is 6 instead of 4.

---

[6]   You can read a more comprehensive coverage of the IPv6 header and extension headers in RFC 2460.

Traffic Class is an 8-bit field that is to be used for differentiated services (DiffServ). In recent usage the bits of the IPv4 header's Type-of-Service (ToS) field have been redefined to support DiffServ. So in this regard, the IPv6 Traffic Class field can be said to correspond to the IPv4 ToS field. You can read more about DiffServ code points in RFC 2474.

Flow Label is the only field in the IPv6 header that has no similar field in IPv4. This new 20-bit field is intended to identify packets belonging to a single communication stream, so that they can forwarded differently than default best-effort service. That is, the Flow Label field is intended to enable quality-of-service (QoS) forwarding. Although there has been much discussion about how the Flow Label field might be used, as of this writing no consensus has been reached. The field might eventually be applied as is, or it might be modified in some way in the future. You can read more about the original plans for the Flow Label field in RFC 1809.

Payload Length is a 16-bit field whose value, obviously, specifies the length of the payload (in octets) encapsulated by the header. This field serves as something of a replacement for the IPv4 Header Length and Datagram Length fields, but does not correspond directly. The IPv4 Options field makes the IPv4 header variable length, so machines determine the payload length by subtracting the header length value from the datagram length (payload + header length) value. The IPv6 header, in contrast, is always a fixed length of 40 octets, so the payload length can be specified directly.

Next Header is an 8-bit field that corresponds directly to the IPv4 Protocol field. So for example, if a UDP header immediately follows the IPv6 header the next header value is 17, if OSPF the value is 89, and so on. The reason for the name change is that in IPv6 the next header is not always that of an upper-layer protocol. It might be an IPv6 extension header, as described in the next section.

Hop Limit is an 8-bit field that performs the same function as the IPv4 Time-To-live (TTL) field. The only reason for the name change is, as Christian Huitema says, for "truth in advertising." The original intention of the TTL was that as a packet is queued in a router during transport to its destination, the TTL value would be decremented once each second. The reality is that no router does this. Routers just decrement the TTL once as the packet passes through, no matter how long it is queued. If the TTL reaches 0, the packet is discarded. So the TTL value has always been a hop limit, and is named accordingly in IPv6.

Figure 12.4 illustrates the corresponding fields we have been discussing, and shows the IPv4 fields that have no directly equivalent field in the IPv6 header in gray. As you can see, those fields (in addition to the Header Length and Datagram Length fields we have already mentioned) are the Datagram ID, Flags, Fragment Offset, and Options fields.

Elimination of these IPv4 fields simplifies the IPv6 header, but what happens when the functions they support are needed? Datagram ID, flags, and fragment offset are needed whenever the packet is fragmented, and Options is needed for functions such as source routing and route recording. IPv6 supports these and other functions with *extension headers*.

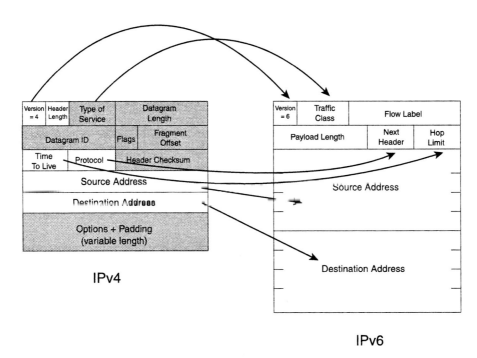

Figure 12.4   IPv4 fields that have functionally corresponding fields in IPv6, and fields that have no equivalent function in IPv6.

12.1.7   Extension Headers

IPv6 keeps its packet header simple by including only fields that are always used.[7] When some optional function must be supported, IPv6 adds an extension header that contains whatever information the function requires. Like the IPv6 header, every extension header has a Next Header field so that multiple extension headers can be inserted between the IPv6 header and the upper-layer protocol header. Table 12.1 lists the extension headers that have been defined as of this writing, along with their assigned next header values and a description of what each header does.

Figure 12.5 illustrates the use of extension headers. The first packet shown contains no extension headers—a TCP segment is encapsulated behind the IPv6 header. In this case, the value of the Next Header field in the IPv6 header is 6 (the TCP protocol number). In the second packet, the originator is using authentication. Notice that the next header value in the IPv6 header is 51, indicating that the next header is the authentication header. The authentication extension header carries an NH value of 6, indicating that the following header is TCP. In the third example, the originator is both authenticating and fragmenting the packet. Here the NH value in the IPv6 header is 44 (fragment extension header), the NH

---

[7]   The flow label field is currently an exception to this, but if it ever becomes used as intended the field will need to be in the packet header for efficient processing.

value in the fragment header is 51 (authentication), and the NH value of the authentication header is 6. In the last example, the originator is performing a route trace, so the routing extension header (NH value 43) is used. Because a route trace is the only reason for sending the packet, no other data is encapsulated. The NH of the routing header is set to 59, a value that indicates no further headers.

Table 12.1   Defined Extension Headers for IPv6

Extension Header	NH Value	Description
Hop-by-hop options	0	Options that must be processed by every node along the forwarding path, such as Jumbo Payload and Router Alert
Destination options	60	Information to be examined either by the ultimate packet destination or by some specific node along the forwarding path
Routing	43	Source routing and route recording
Fragment	44	Information required to reassemble fragmented packets
Authentication	51	Information that allows nodes to authenticate each other before beginning communication
Encapsulating security payload (ESP)	50	Data encryption and decryption (IPSec)

IPv6 Header NH = 6	TCP Header + Data

IPv6 Header NH = 51	Authentication NH = 6	TCP Header + Data

IPv6 Header NH = 44	Fragment NH = 51	Authentication NH = 6	TCP Header + Data

IPv6 Header NH = 43	Routing NH = 59

Figure 12.5   Extension headers, when used, are inserted between the IPv6 header and the upper-layer protocol header.

Extension headers have two distinct advantages. First, as you have seen, they allow simplification of the IPv6 header. Optional information is added to IPv6 packets only when it is needed. Second, new types of extension headers can be easily defined in the future, as new optional capabilities are needed, greatly adding to the extensibility and overall flexibility of the protocol.

IPv6 and Packet Fragmentation

Because Fragmentation extension headers have been mentioned, I want to point out another significant difference between IPv4 and IPv6. As you likely know, IPv4 packets can be fragmented by routers anywhere along the path, when a link is encountered whose MTU is smaller than the size of the packet. IPv6 discontinues this practice. It is up to the originating IPv6 node to decide whether to fragment a packet; if an IPv6 router receives a packet that is larger than the MTU of the link over which the packet must be forwarded, the router drops the packet.

A host can adhere to this new rule in two ways. First, the host can perform MTU path discovery (PD), as defined in RFC 1981. A host sends packets and watches for ICMPv6 Packet Too Big error messages. If any error messages are received, the host adjusts the packet size downward or fragments its packets until the errors are no longer received.

The second way to adhere to the new rule is to take advantage of known MTU rules. RFC 2460, Section 5, specifies that every IPv6-capable link must have an MTU of at least 1280 bytes (1500 is recommended). Knowing this, hosts that do not want to perform MTU PD can simply ensure that they do not send packets larger than 1280 bytes (by size limitation or fragmentation).

12.2   OSPFv3

IPv6 introduces an interesting opportunity that is not at first expected or intended. That is, as long as we are transitioning our networks (from IPv4 to IPv6), we might as well transition several long-standing but acknowledged poor networking practices. Chief among these practices are the way we do multihoming and the way we do security. Although discussion of these changes is beyond the scope of this book, pointing out this opportunity is important because the same thinking has been applied to OSPF. That is, in developing a new version of OSPF to accommodate IPv6, the opportunity exists to apply lessons learned and improve the protocol itself. This has in fact happened, and OSPFv3 is improved over OSPFv2 for reasons that have nothing to do with IPv6.

12.2.1   IPv4 and IPv6 Compatibility in OSPF

OSPFv3 is specified in RFC 2740. The basic mechanisms, databases, data structures, and algorithms remain the same as OSPFv2. However, OSPFv3 is not backward compatible with OSPFv2. In other words, OSPFv3 supports only IPv6. So if you want to route both IPv4 and IPv6 in the same network with OSPF, you must run both OSPFv2 and OSPFv3, as shown in Figure 12.6. In this example, OSPFv2 is configured just as you have seen in previous examples: AIDs and the interfaces running in each of the areas are specified. Notice that the OSPFv3 configuration (JUNOS keyword **ospf3**) looks exactly the same. The reason identical configurations are possible is because the AIDs used by OSPFv3 remain 32 bits. In fact, AIDs, RIDs, and LSA IDs all remain 32 bits in OSPFv3. The chief advantage of this is that if you want to run an OSPFv3 topology that is identical to an existing OSPFv2 topology, you can use the same identifiers for both. You can, of course, use separate identifiers if you so choose.

```
[edit]
jeff@Juniper3# show protocols
ospf {
    area 0.0.0.0 {
        interface so-1/0/0.0;
    }
    area 192.168.51.0 {
        interface ge-0/0/0.0;
    }
    area 192.168.3.0 {
        interface ge-0/0/1.0;
        interface ge-0/0/2.0;
    }
}
ospf3 {
    area 0.0.0.0 {
        interface so-1/0/0.0;
    }
    area 192.168.51.0 {
        interface ge-0/0/0.0;
    }
    area 192.168.3.0 {
        interface ge-0/0/1.0;
        interface ge-0/0/2.0;
    }
}
```

Figure 12.6   If you want to route both IPv4 and IPv6 with OSPF, you must run both versions 2 and 3.

12.2.2 Differences from OSPFv2

The most advantageous improvements to OSPFv3 over version 2 are in the LSAs, described in Section 12.2.3. But a number of other functional and procedural differences exist, some of which are improvements and others of which are just necessitated by the need to support IPv6 addresses. You can find a more complete description of these differences in Section 2 of RFC 2740.

■ **Removal of addressing semantics**—You have already seen an example of this change in the example configuration of Figure 12.6 in the preceding section. That is, by keeping the AIDs, RIDs, and LSA IDs 32 bits, these values are not IPv6 addresses. They are not IPv4 addresses either, of course, but they have traditionally been expressed in the same dotted-decimal format and are, in OSPFv2, often derived from them. The advantage here is that if you want to overlay an OSPFv3 domain on an OSPFv2 domain, the same RIDs and AIDs can be used for both. Removal of addressing semantics also means that IPv6 addresses are not found in OSPF packets other than the LSAs of Update packets. There are also changes to the way network addresses are advertised in LSAs, as you will learn in the next section.

■ **Addition of a link-local flooding scope**—OSPFv2 has area and domain (AS) flooding scopes, as you already know. Certain LSAs, such as Router and Network LSAs, can be flooded only within an area, whereas other LSAs such as AS-External LSAs can be flooded throughout the OSPF domain. OSPFv3 retains these two scopes, but adds a third scope that encompasses only a single data link. LSAs with this link-local flooding scope can then only be flooded to routers sharing the same link. You will see—again, in the next section—how OSPFv3 applies this scope to a new LSA type to add a bit of efficiency to its flooding operations.

■ **Removal of OSPF authentication**—IPv6 has authentication and encryption support built in. So rather than duplicate efforts by adding separate authentication mechanisms to OSPFv3, the protocol just uses the existing capabilities of IPv6.[8]

■ **Support for multiple instances per link**—In some cases, multiple OSPF routers share a common link, but should not run a common process. For instance, suppose there are six routers connected to a single Ethernet link. Routers 1 and 2 link two OSPF subdomains and should form an adjacency to connect their subdomains. Likewise, routers 3 and 4 should form an adjacency to connect their subdomains, and routers 5 and 6 should form an adjacency. However, there should be no other adjacencies. In other words, the six subdomains should comprise three separate OSPF domains, with no communications between them. You can accomplish this with OSPFv2 by manipulating authentication, but OSPFv3 supports it by including an Instance ID field in its packet header.

■ **Per-link protocol processing**—OSPFv2 defines interfaces as connected to subnets. Therefore, an OSPFv2 process runs per subnet, as defined by the IPv4 subnet address. IPv6 changes this semantic, so that interfaces are connected to a link rather to a subnet. This removes the address dependency, so that two routers can share OSPFv3 packets over a link with multiple defined subnets, even if the two routers are not on the same subnet. This is in keeping with the IPv6 capability of supporting multiple addresses per interface.

---

[8]   At the time of this writing, procedures for authenticating OSPFv3 using the IPv6 AH/ESP extension header are described in an Internet Draft: Mukesh Gupta and Nagavenkata Suresh Melam, "Authentication/Confidentiality for OSPFv3," draft-ietf-ospf-ospfv3-auth-03.txt, August 2003.

■ **More flexible handling of unknown LSA types**—One of the operational difficulties of OSPFv2 is that it throws away unknown LSA types, making network changes and transitions more complex. OSPFv3 treats unknown LSAs more similarly to the way IS-IS treats unknown TLVs, forwarding them rather than discarding them. The result can be, in some cases, simplified network changes—particularly as they apply to stub areas.

■ **Neighbors are always identified by RID**—OSPFv2 is inconsistent in its neighbor identification. Neighbors on point-to-point and virtual links are identified by RID, whereas neighbors on broadcast, point-to-multipoint, and MBMA links are identified by their IPv4 interface addresses. OSPFv3 neighbors are always identified by RID, on all link types.

12.2.3 OSPFv3 LSAs

The OSPFv3 LSA header, shown in Figure 12.7, looks almost identical to the OSPFv2 LSA header. The only difference is that the LS Type field is now 16 bits in the space where there was an 8-bit Options field and an 8-bit LS Type field in the version 2 header.

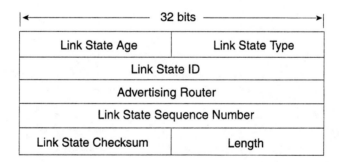

Figure 12.7 The OSPFv3 LSA header.

This longer LS Type field, shown in Figure 12.8, begins with 3 new bits. The U bit tells receiving routers how to handle the encapsulated LSA, if the router does not recognize the LSA type. If the bit is cleared (0), the router treats the LSA as if it had link-local flooding scope. In other words, the LSA is not flooded beyond the receiving router. If the U bit is set (1), the router stores the LSA and floods it as if the LSA type were recognized.

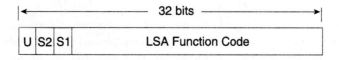

Figure 12.8 Details of the Link State Type field in the OSPFv3 LSA header.

The S2 and S1 bits together indicate the LSA's flooding scope. The possible flooding scopes, and the corresponding values of the S bits, are shown in Table 12.2.

Table 12.2   Flooding Scopes Indicated by the S bits in the LS Type Field

S2	S1	Flooding Scope
0	0	Link-local scope (flooded only on the link the LSA is originated on)
0	1	Area scope (flooded to all routers in the area the LSA was originated in)
1	0	AS scoping (flooded to all routers in the OSPFv3 domain)
1	1	Reserved

The last 13 bits comprise the LSA function code, which as the name implies indicates the function of the encapsulated LSA. In this regard, the LSA function code serves the same purpose as the complete OSPFv2 LS Type code. Table 12.3 lists 10 OSPFv3 LSAs and the LS Type values that correspond to them. You can see from the Hex Type values that all 10 have the U bit set by default to 0. The S bits of all LSAs except two, the AS-external LSA and the Link LSA, are set to area scope. The AS-External LSA has AS flooding scope, and the Link LSA has link-local flooding scope.

Table 12.3   OSPFv3 and OSPFv2 LSA Types

OSPFv3 LSAs		OSPFv2 LSAs	
Type	Name	Type	Name
0x2001	Router LSA	1	Router LSA
0x2002	Network LSA	2	Network LSA
0x2003	Inter-Area Prefix LSA	3	Network Summary LSA
0x2004	Inter-Area Router LSA	4	ASBR Summary LSA
0x4005	AS-External LSA	5	AS-External LSA
0x2006	Group Membership LSA	6	Group Membership LSA
0x2007	Type 7 LSA	7	NSSA External LSA
0x0008	Link LSA	*	
0x2009	Intra-Area Prefix LSA	*	
0xa00a	Intra-Area-TE LSA	*	

* No equivalent LSA type

Also shown in Table 12.3 are the OSPFv2 LSAs that correspond to the OSPFv3 LSAs. Some OSPFv3 LSAs have the same names as OSPFv2 LSAs, but differ significantly in the information they carry. Other OSPFv3 LSAs are functionally the same as their OSPFv2 counterparts, but have been renamed. And two entirely new OSPFv3 LSA types contribute greatly to the overall improvement of the protocol. We will look at each LSA in a bit more detail next.

12.2.3.1   Link LSA

The first of the new LSAs is the Link LSA, which is used for communicating information that is significant only to two directly connected neighbors. The link-local scope of the LSA ensures that it and its information are not flooded beyond the link on which they originated. OSPFv2 has no corresponding LSA. If information relevant only to neighbors sharing the same link is to be sent, it must be enclosed in version 2 Router or Network LSAs (practical application normally dictates the latter). Because these LSAs have area flooding scope, the link-local information is inefficiently carried throughout the area of origin, to routers that have no use for the information.

A router originates a separate Link LSA (Figure 12.9) on each of its attached links belonging to an OSPFv3 domain, and a receiving router, because of the link-local flooding scope, never forwards the LSA to any other link. The LSA performs three functions:

- It provides the originating router's link-local address to all other routers attached to the link.
- It provides a list of IPv6 prefixes associated with the link.
- It provides a set of Option bits to associate with Network LSAs originated on the link.

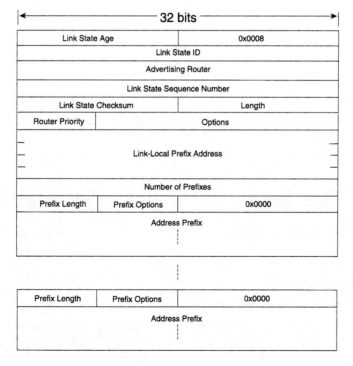

Figure 12.9   The OSPFv3 Link LSA.

Router Priority specifies the router priority assigned to the interface of the originating router.

Options specifies the options bits that the originating router would like to set in the Network LSA that will be originated for the link. This is the same 24-bit Options field carried in OSPFv3 Hello and DD packets, and in a number of OSPFv3 LSAs. The Options field is detailed in Section 12.2.4.

Link-Local Prefix Address specifies the 128-bit link-local prefix of the originating router's interface attached to the link.

Number of Prefixes specifies the number of IPv6 prefixes contained in the LSA, as described by the following Prefix Length, Prefix Options, and Address Prefix fields.

Prefix Length, Prefix Options, and *Address Prefix* describe one or more IPv6 prefixes associated with the link by the originating router. This set of fields is used not only in the Link LSA, but also the Intra-Area Prefix, Inter-Area Prefix, and AS-External LSAs. The advertised prefix can be any length between 0 and 128. When the prefix is not an even multiple of 32 bits, it is padded out with 0s to fit the 32-bit boundaries of the Address Prefix field. The Prefix Length field specifies the length of the unpadded prefix, in bits. The Prefix Options field, shown in Figure 12.10, specifies optional handling of the prefix during routing calculations.

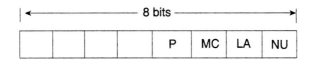

Figure 12.10   The Prefix Options field.

The *Propagate* (P) bit is set on NSSA area prefixes that should be re-advertised at the NSSA area border.

The *Multicast* (MC) bit, when set, specifies that the prefix should be included in multicast routing calculations.

The *Local Address* (LA) bit, when set, specifies that the prefix is an interface address of the advertising router.

The *No Unicast* (NU) bit, when set, specifies that the prefix should be excluded from unicast route calculations.

12.2.3.2   Intra-Area Prefix LSA

The second new LSA is the Intra-Area Prefix LSA. Recall from Chapter 8 that one of the factors limiting the size of OSPFv2 areas is the fact that prefixes must be carried in Router and Network LSAs. To recap, some networks such as access service providers can have routers with large numbers of links, which tend to change frequently because of normal customer service activity. The problem is that every time a link is added or deleted, or otherwise fluctuates due to instability or an address change, the link's associated prefix must be advertised or withdrawn. With OSPFv2, this means originating a new Router or Network LSA. But a new

Router or Network LSA triggers a new SPF calculation in all the routers in the area, because its primary function is to identify the location of a router or pseudonode in relation to its neighbors on the SPF tree.

OSPFv3 removes the prefix information from its Router and Network LSAs, and carries it in Intra-Area Prefix LSAs. Now, when a link or its prefix changes, the connected router originates an Intra-Area Prefix LSA to flood the information throughout the area. This LSA does not trigger an SPF calculation; the receiving routers simply associate the new prefix information with the originating router. Router and Network LSAs, in OSPFv3, serve only to provide topological information. As a result, this new LSA should make OSPFv3 significantly more scalable for networks with large numbers of frequently changing prefixes. Figure 12.11 shows the format of the Intra-Area Prefix LSA.

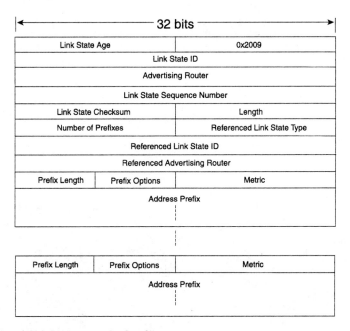

Figure 12.11   The OSPFv3 Intra-Area Prefix LSA.

Number of Prefixes specifies the number of prefixes contained in the LSA.

Referenced Link State Type, *Referenced Link State ID*, and *Referenced Advertising Router* identify the Router or Network LSA with which the contained prefixes should be associated. If the prefixes are associated with a Router LSA, the referenced link state type is 1, the referenced link state ID is 0, and the referenced advertising router is the RID of the originating router. If the prefixes should be associated with a Network LSA, the referenced link state type is 2, the referenced link state ID is the interface ID[9] of the link's DR, and the referenced advertising router is the RID of the DR.

---

[9]   The interface ID used in this and other OSPFv3 LSAs should not be confused with the 64-bit Interface ID portion of an IPv6 address. This field is a 32-bit value distinguishing this interface from other interfaces on the originating router. RFC 2740 suggests using the MIB-II IfIndex for the interface ID value.

Each prefix is then represented by a Prefix Length, Prefix Options, and Address Prefix field, as described previously for the Link LSA. Added to these three fields is *Metric* field, which is the cost of the prefix.

12.2.3.3   Router LSA

Figure 12.12 shows the OSPFv3 Router LSA compared to the OPSPFv2 Router LSA. You can readily see that the format, although the two LSAs retain the same name, is significantly different. The primary reason for this difference, as you just read, is the elimination of prefix information in the OSPFv3 Router LSA. The OSPFv3 Router LSA now describes just the originating router, its attached links (not prefixes) and directly connected neighbors, and its only purpose is to represent the originating router in the SPF calculations.

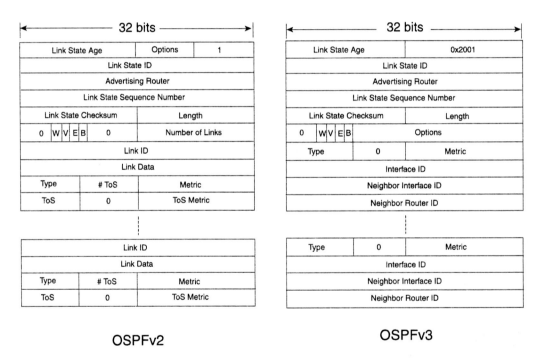

Figure 12.12   Comparison of the OSPFv2 and OSPFv3 Router LSAs.

Options, although in a different position within the LSA format and a longer length (24 bits) than the OSPFv2 Options field, performs the same function of identifying optional capabilities. The Options field, carried in several packets and LSAs, is described separately in Section 12.2.4.

Following the Options field is a set of fields that can appear multiple times, to describe each of the attached interfaces.

Type specifies the interface type. Table 12.4 lists the possible interface type values.

Table 12.4 Interface Types in OSPFv3 Router LSA

Type	Description
1	Point-to-point connection to another router
2	Connection to a transit network
3	Reserved
4	Virtual link

Metric specifies the outbound cost of the interface.

Interface ID is a 32-bit value distinguishing the interface from other interfaces on the originating router.

Neighbor Interface is the Interface ID advertised by neighbors on the link in their Hellos or, in the case of type 2 links, the Interface ID of the link's DR.

Neighbor Router ID is the neighbor's RID or, in the case of type 2 links, the DR's RID.

12.2.3.4 Network LSA

The OSPFv3 Network LSA is, as shown in Figure 12.13, similar to the OSPFv2 Network LSA. Functionally, it is identical to the OSPFv2 Network LSA (originated by the DR to represent a pseudonode, 0 cost to attached neighbors is assumed, and so on). The only significant differences are the location of the Options field and the elimination of the Network Mask field (which has no meaning in IPv6).

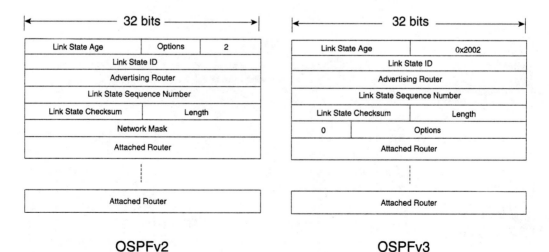

Figure 12.13 Comparison of the OSPFv2 and OSPFv3 Network LSAs.

12.2.3.5   Inter-Area Prefix LSA

The Inter-Area Prefix LSA performs the same function as the OSPFv2 type 3 Summary LSA—ABRs originate them into an area to advertise networks that are outside the area but inside the OSPF domain—it just sports a different, and more accurately descriptive, name. An ABR originates a separate Inter-Area Prefix LSA for each IPv6 prefix that must be advertised into an area. An ABR can also originate an Inter-Area Prefix LSA to advertise a default route into a stub area.

Figure 12.14 compares the formats of the two LSAs. Once again, the Prefix Length, Prefix Options, and Address Prefix fields completely describe the advertised prefix. The 24-bit Metric field performs the same function—specifying the cost to the destination—in both LSAs.

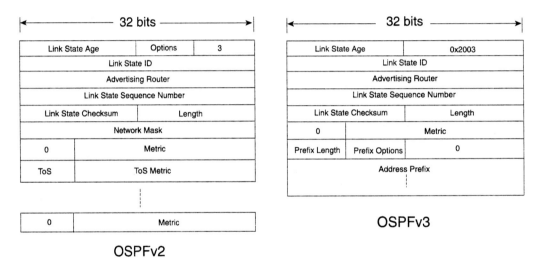

Figure 12.14   Comparison of the OSPFv2 Network Summary and the OSPFv3 Inter-Area Prefix LSAs.

12.2.3.6   Inter-Area Router LSA

The Inter-Area Router LSA performs the same duties for OSPFv3 as the type 4 Summary LSA performs for OSPFv2. An ABR originates an Inter-Area Router LSA into an area to advertise an ASBR that resides outside of the area. The ABR originates a separate Inter-Area Router LSA for each ASBR it advertises.

Figure 12.15 compares the Inter-Area Router LSA with the OSPFv2 type 4 Summary LSA. Although the OSPFv2 type 3 and type 4 Summary LSAs have the same formats, you can see by comparing Figures 12.14 and 12.15 that the Inter-Area Network and Inter-Area Router LSAs are different. The fields are self-descriptive: Options specifies optional capabilities of the ASBR, Metric specifies the cost to the ASBR, and Destination Router ID is the ASBR RID.

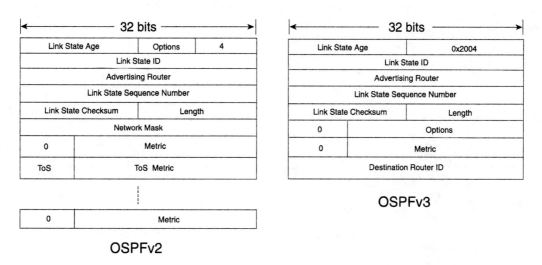

Figure 12.15   Comparison of the OSPFv2 ASBR Summary and the OSPFv3 Inter-Area Router LSAs.

12.2.3.7   AS-External LSA

Prefixes exterior to the OSPF domain are advertised by both OSPFv2 and OSPFv3 in AS-External LSAs. And with both protocols, an individual AS-External LSA must be generated for every external prefix to be advertised. Therefore, all the same warnings about redistributing large numbers of external prefixes (almost always from BGP) into the domain that apply to OSPFv2 also apply to OSPFv3.

Although the names and functions are the same, Figure 12.16 shows that the formats of the AS-External LSAs vary significantly between OSPFv2 and OSPFv3.

The *E* flag performs the same function in the OSPFv3 LSA as in the OSPFv2 LSA. If set, the metric is a type 2 external metric. If the bit is cleared, the metric is a type 1 external metric.

The *F* flag indicates, when set, that a forwarding address is included in the LSA.

The *T* flag indicates, when set, that an external route tag is included in the LSA.

Metric, of course, specifies the cost of the route. Whether it is type 1 or type 2 depends on the value of the E flag.

Prefix Length, *Prefix Options*, and *Address Prefix* completely describe the enclosed prefix, as described earlier in this section.

Forwarding Address, if included, is a fully specified 128-bit IPv6 address representing the next-hop address to the destination prefix. It is included only if the F flag is set.

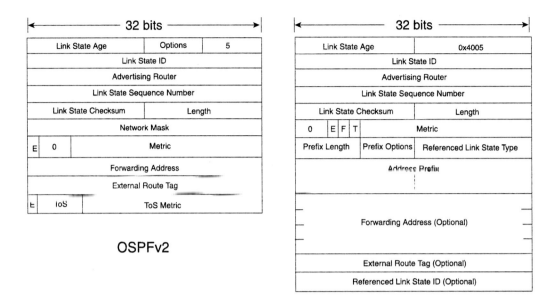

Figure 12.16   Comparison of the OSPFv2 and OSPFv3 AS-External LSAs.

External Route Tag, if included, performs the same function as the External Route Tag field in the OSPFv2 AS-External LSA. It is included only if the T flag is set.

Referenced Link State ID and *Referenced Link State Type*, if used, allow additional information about the prefix to be included in another LSA. These two fields describe the Link state ID and the type of the LSA carrying the additional information. The Advertising Router field of the referenced LSA must also match the value of the Advertising Router field in the AS-External LSA. The additional information has, as with the External Route Tag, no relevance to OSPF itself but is used to communicate information across the OSPF domain between border routers. If this function is not used, the Referenced Link State Type field is set to all 0s.

12.2.3.8 Other LSAs

Although they are not illustrated here, you can see from Table 12.3 that OSPFv3 also supports MOSPF with a Group Membership LSA and Not-So-Stubby areas with the Type 7 LSA. The table also lists an Intra-Area-TE LSA, which is a proposed LSA for support of traffic engineering in OSPFv3.[10] As of this writing, the LSA is not yet supported by the large router vendors. Such support is likely to be in place, however, by the time you are reading this book. Such are the difficulties of book publishing in the face of fast-evolving technology.

---

[10] Kunihiro Ishiguro and Toshiaki Takada, "Traffic Engineering Extensions to OSPF Version 3," draft-ietf-ospf-ospfv3-traffic-01.txt, August 2003.

12.2.4   *The Options Field*

You have seen in the previous section that a 24-bit Options field, specifying optional capabilities of the originating router, is carried in Router, Network, Inter-Area Router, and Link LSAs. As the next section shows, this field is also carried in the Hello and Database Description packets. Figure 12.17 shows the format of the Options field. As of this writing, only the 6 rightmost bits are defined as options flags, and most of those are the same flags you are familiar with from OSPFv2. OSPFv3 routers ignore unrecognized options flags.

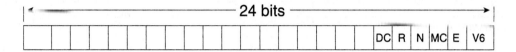

Figure 12.17   The OSPFv3 Options field.

DC specifies support for demand circuits capability.

R indicates whether the originator is an active router. When this bit is cleared, routes transiting the originating node cannot be computed. The R flag therefore adds a capability similar to the IS-IS Overload bit.

N specifies support for NSSA LSAs.

MC specifies support for MOSPF.

E specifies how AS-External LSAs are flooded, for the formation of stub areas.

V6, if clear, specifies that the router or link should be excluded from IPv6 routing calculations.

12.2.5   *OSPFv3 Packets*

OSPFv3 uses the same five packet types as OSPFv2, and the mechanisms and functions associated with the packets are also essentially the same. Just as OSPFv2 packets are identified by IP protocol number 89, OSPFv3 packets are identified with next header number 89. And OSPFv3 packets use the same multicast procedures as OSPFv2. For IPv6, the AllSPFRouters multicast address is FF02::5, and the AllDRouters multicast address is FF02::6.

Unlike the LSAs, which must vary considerably from version 2 to support both IPv6 prefixes and modified link state processing procedures, the packet formats of OSPFv3 differ little from those of OSPFv2. Most of the differences are in the packet headers and in the Hello packets.

Figure 12.18 compares the OSPFv2 and OSPFv3 packet headers. The values used in the Type field of the OSPFv3 header are identical to the type values used by OSPFv2, because the same five packet types are used. The most noticeable difference between the two headers is the elimination of the authentication fields in OSPFv3. As mentioned earlier in this chapter,

OSPFv3 has no authentication procedures of its own but instead relies on the authentication procedures built into the IPv6 packets.

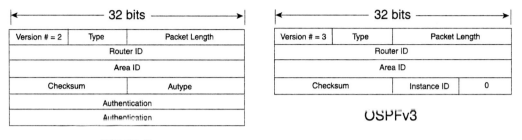

OSPFv2

OSPFv3

Figure 12.18   Comparison of the OSPFv2 and OSPFv3 packet headers.

The other difference is the *Instance ID* field in the OSPFv3 header. This field enables the support of multiple OSPFv3 instances on the same link, a capability that OSPFv2 does not have. As discussed earlier in this chapter, multiple instance support means that a set of routers can share a multi-access link while at the same time belonging to separate OSPFv3 domains. Although you can achieve similar results by manipulating OSPFv2 authentication, the resulting implementation is inefficient. As routers in one subset reject Hellos from routers in other subsets, authentication failure messages are being generated at a rate equal to the Hellos generated by all those "outside" routers.

The Instance ID must be unique only to the local link.

Figure 12.19 compares OSPFv2 and OSPFv3 Hello packet formats. The Network Mask field of the OSPFv2 Hello is not included in the OSPFv3 Hello, because IPv6 has no need for it. Beyond that, the same fields (below the header) appear in both packets. The Options field increases in size to 24 bits, and the router dead interval is decreased from 32 bits to 16 bits. The implication of this second field is that the theoretical maximum router dead interval is decreased from 4.3 billion seconds to 65,535 seconds. This change has little or no bearing on operational networks. The maximum configurable router dead interval on the most common OSPF implementations has long been 65,535 anyway, and intelligent OSPF designs do not approach even this maximum.

The OSPFv3 Database Description packet, shown in Figure 12.20, differs from its OSPFv2 counterpart only in the repositioning of the Options field to accommodate its greater length. OSPFv3 Link State Request, Link State Update, and Link State Acknowledgement packets are identical in their format, beyond the header, to their OSPFv2 counterparts and are therefore not illustrated in this chapter.

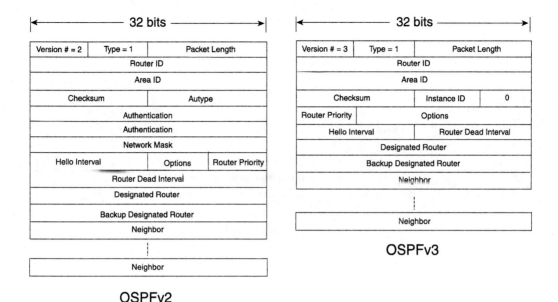

Figure 12.19 Comparison of the OSPFv2 and OSPFv3 Hello packet formats.

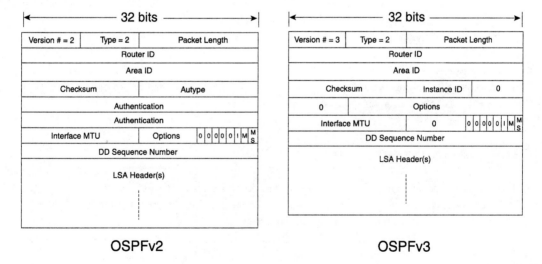

Figure 12.20 Comparison of the OSPFv2 and OSPFv3 Database Description packet formats.

12.2.6 Future Extensions to OSPFv3

I began the discussion of OSPFv3 by stating that the protocol includes several improvements over OSPFv2 that have nothing to do with IPv6. The natural question to ask, then, is: If it is a better protocol, why shouldn't it be extended to support IPv4? At the time this chapter is being written, discussion is ongoing within the IETF's OSPF working group concerning the practicality of such an extension. The key limitation here is that OSPFv3 is designed to run over IPv6. That means that the protocol cannot run in an IPv4-only environment. Having said that, there are no serious roadblocks to using OSPFv3 to carry IPv4 prefixes as long as the underlying network is IPv6-enabled. The Link LSAs can easily accommodate IPv4 prefixes. The focus of the WG discussions is more on how to implement such support. Is it better to have integrated IPv4/IPv6 processing, so that only one SPF tree is calculated within an area and no duplicate adjacencies are needed? Or, is it better to use the Instance ID to define separate OSPF instances for IPv4 and IPv6, trading some processing efficiency for the case of managing and troubleshooting a separate link state database for IPv4 and IPv6?

An Internet Draft proposes the support in OSPFv3 not just of IPv4, but of multiple address families.[11] The proposal is to use multiple instances, and to reserve Instance ID ranges for address families: 0 through 19 for IPv6 unicast, 20 through 39 for IPv6 multicast, 40 through 59 for IPv4 unicast, and 60 through 79 for IPv4 multicast (and reserving 80 to 255 for future address families). The draft also proposes a new flag, the AF flag, in the Options field for signaling router support of multiple address families. Whether such an extension to the protocol is ever developed depends largely on whether users demand it. By the time you are reading this book, perhaps that question will be answered.

There is also a proposal before the OSPF WG for carrying OSPFv2 Opaque LSAs in OSPFv3. These LSAs (types 9, 10, and 11 in OSPFv2) have proven useful in extending new capabilities to OSPFv2, and so their utility is desirable for OSPFv3. The three Opaque LSAs are made OSPFv3-capable by adding an OSPFv3 LSA header. In the Type field, the LSA function code (see Figure 12.8) is the version 2 type value, the U bit is 1, and the S2/S1 bits are set to reflect the flooding scope of the original version 2 LSAs. As with IPv4 support, whether this extension is adopted is yet to be seen.

12.3   IS-IS Extensions for IPv6

RFC 2740, specifying OSPFv3, is 80 pages long. And the bulk of this chapter is devoted to just a high-level description of the protocol. In contrast, the Internet Draft describing the extension to IS-IS for support of IPv6 is a mere seven pages long,[12] reflecting the relative simplicity of the extension. Although the Internet Draft has yet to become an RFC, the extension is supported by all major router vendors and in most cases was implemented before OSPFv3.

The extension involves adding two new TLVs to the existing protocol: the IPv6 Reachability TLV and the IPv6 Interface Address TLV. These are merely IPv6 counterparts to the IPv4 TLVs added to IS-IS well over a decade ago. When an IS supports IPv6, it advertises

[11] Sina Mirtorabi, Abhay Roy, Michael Barnes, Acee Lindem, Quaizar Vohra, and Rahul Aggarwal, "Support of Address Families in OSPFv3," draft-mirtorabi-ospfv3-aff-alt-00.txt, August 2003.

[12] Christian E. Hopps, "Routing IPv6 with IS-IS," draft-ietf-isis-ipv6-05.txt, January 2003.

that capability by including the IPv6 NLPID value of 142 (0x8E) in its Protocols Supported TLV.

The IPv6 Reachability TLV, shown in Figure 12.21, advertises IPv6 prefixes and their associated metrics. It performs the functions that the IP Internal Reachability and IP External Reachability TLVs perform for IPv4 by including a flag designating the prefix as internal or external. The TLV also has provisions for carrying sub-TLVs, should such a capability be required in the future.

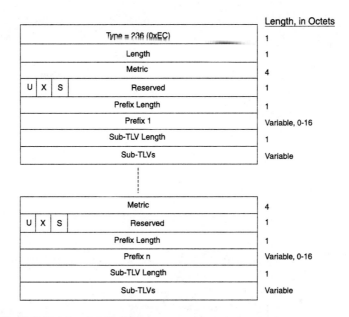

Figure 12.21   The IS-IS IPv6 Reachability TLV.

The TLV type, as shown in the illustration, is 236.

Metric is the cost assigned to the prefix. You can see in the illustration that the TLV uses the newer wide (32 bit) metrics, discussed in Chapter 8.

U is the Up/Down bit, used for preventing looping between L1 and L2, as discussed in Chapter 7.

X (External) designates whether the prefix originated internally (0) or externally (1) to the IS-IS domain.

S indicates, when set, that sub-TLVs are included in the TLV. If the bit is 0, the sub-TLV length and sub-TLVs fields do not exist in this TLV.

Prefix Length specifies the length, in bits, of the prefix.

Prefix is the IPv6 prefix, packed into an even number of octets. The number of octets containing the prefix can be calculated from the value of the Prefix Length field:

```
prefix octets = integer of ((prefix length + 7) / 8)
```

The IPv6 Interface Address TLV (Figure 12.22), the IPv6 counterpart of the IP Interface TLV, advertises the IPv6 addresses assigned to the interface from which it originates. Note that while the IP Interface Address TLV can carry up to 63 four-octet IPv4 interface addresses, the IPv6 Interface Address TLV can carry a maximum of 15 IPv6 interface addresses. This is a function of the 8-bit length field, which in both TLVs specifies the length of the remaining TLV (the value part) in octets, and the fact that IPv6 addresses are 16 octets each.

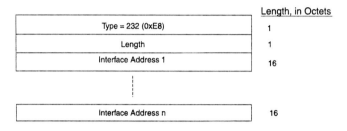

Figure 12.22   The IS-IS IPv6 Interface Address TLV.

The type of addresses carried in the IPv6 Interface Address TLV depends on the PDU in which the TLV is contained. If the TLV is in a Hello PDU, the interface addresses are only the link-local addresses of the originating interface. If the TLV is in an LSP, the interface addresses are only the non-link-local addresses of the originating interface.

Review Questions

1. What is the length, in bits, of an IPv6 address?
2. What is the difference between an anycast address and a multicast address?
3. What is the normal length of the Interface ID portion of an IPv6 address?
4. What is the normal length of the Subnet ID field of an IPv6 address?
5. What three scopes are defined for unicast IPv6 addresses?
6. What is the scope of the IPv6 address FE80:10:1::50? How do you know?
7. What type of IPv6 address is FF02::D? How do you know?
8. Can the leading or trailing 0s in one 16-bit segment of an IPv6 address be compacted?

9. What does a double colon in an IPv6 address signify? Why can a double colon appear only once in a given IPv6 address?

10. How does the MAC-to-EUI64 process change a 48-bit MAC address into a 64-bit IPv6 Interface ID?

11. How is a given Interface ID used to create a unique link-local IPv6 address?

12. In what two ways is the Neighbor Discovery Protocol used during IPv6 address autoconfiguration?

13. What is the length of an IPv6 packet header?

14. What is the difference between the IPv6 Hop Limit field and the IPv4 Time-to-Live field?

15. Why does IPv6 use a Next Header field instead of a Protocol field as in IPv4?

16. What is the advantage of using extension headers?

17. Can OSPFv3 support routing of IPv4?

18. Why is there no support for authentication in OSPFv3?

19. How does OSPFv3 differ from OSPFv2 in the handling of unknown LSA types?

20. How does OSPFv3 differ from OSPFv2 in the identification of neighbors?

21. What is the purpose of the OSPFv3 Link LSA?

22. What is the purpose of the OSPFv3 Intra-Area Prefix LSA? How can it increase the scalability of an OSPF area?

23. What are the OSPFv3 functionally equivalent LSAs to the OSPFv2 type 3 and type 4 LSAs?

24. What is the purpose of the Instance ID field in the OSPFv3 packet header?

25. What two TLVs are added to IS-IS to extend the protocol for IPv6 support?

CHAPTER 13

Extensions for Multi-Topology Routing

Within the past few years, carriers and service providers have been reassessing their service offerings because "plain" IPv4 packet transport has become commoditized and unprofitable. Carriers and service providers worldwide recognize that to create new revenue streams, they must provide new services to their customers, and they must implement these new services economically by leveraging a single router-based infrastructure and eliminating traditional "overlay" ATM, Frame Relay, and telephony networks. The services themselves are seldom unique: voice and video transport, virtual private networks, and group-collaboration applications have been around for a long time. What is unique is offering them over a single IP infrastructure rather than over separate—and hence expensive—single-purpose infrastructures. *Multiservice* and *next-generation* are the current networking buzzwords.

Many of the intermediate or enabling technologies required for multiservice networks, such as MPLS, IP multicast, and IPv6, require extensions to OSPF and IS-IS; Chapters 11 and 12 explored those extensions. However, there is one more requirement for multiservice networks: Although running on the same IP infrastructure, some or all of these services might require different routing topologies. Your IPv6 topology might be a subset of your IPv4 topology (and in the not-so-distant future, your IPv4 topology might be a subset of your IPv6 topology). Similarly, your multicast topology might be a subset of your unicast topology. And your inband management network might be routed independently of your customer services.

The extensions to OSPF and IS-IS for support of multiple topologies (MT) are simple and surprisingly similar:

- Each logical topology is assigned a *multi-topology identifier* (MT ID).
- Each OSPF or IS-IS interface is assigned one or more MT IDs to designate what topologies run on that interface.
- Adjacencies are established with all neighbors as usual.
- LSAs and LSPs are tagged with the appropriate MT IDs.

- A separate SPF algorithm is run for each topology.

- The route entries resulting from the topology-specific SPF calculations are stored in separate routing information databases (RIBs).

You can create multiple OSPF and IS-IS topologies without the MT extensions by enabling a separate routing protocol instance on each router, if your protocol implementation supports multiple instances, for each desired topology. Authentication is then used to create adjacencies within each instance that follow the desired topology. The problem with this approach is inefficiency. Each protocol instance on a router maintains its own database, its own adjacencies, and sends its own Hellos. The MT extensions use a single database and maintain single adjacencies across a given link, no matter how many topologies actually use the link. Only the SPF calculations and the RIDs are maintained separately for each topology.

13.1   OSPF Extensions for Multi-Topology Routing

At the time of writing of this chapter, the first Internet Draft proposing Multi-Topology OSPF (MT-OSPF)[1] is only a few months old, and MT-OSPF has not yet seen general deployment. By the time you read this, the extensions are likely to be on vendors' development roadmaps, if not in production code.

Although some extensions to OSPF have required new LSAs or even a new version of the protocol, MT-OSPF support is implemented simply by exploiting unused fields in modern OSPF LSAs. You might recall from Chapter 5 that OSPF was originally specified to support type-of-service (ToS) routing but that the option was never implemented commercially. Conveniently, the LSAs were designed to carry multiple ToS metrics. So, MT-OSPF redefines the ToS fields to carry MTIDs and their associated metrics. But before examining the changes to LSAs in Section 13.1.2, we will look at the OSPF procedure changes needed to support multiple topologies.

13.1.1   MT-OSPF Procedures

A Router (type 1) LSA originated by an MT-OSPF router lists, as usual, all OSPF links for that router and all the router's neighbors. The difference is that the LSA indicates for each link what topologies the link belongs to and a metric for the link that is specific to the topology. Type 3, 4, 5, and 7 LSAs are also modified to advertise not only prefixes (or in the case of type 4 LSAs, ASBRs) but what topologies the prefixes belong to and their metric in each topology. For each MTID listed by the LSAs in the link state database, a separate SPF calculation is run, and the results are recorded in a separate RIB.

There is always a *default topology*, signified by a MTID of 0, which consists of all routers and links in the OSPF domain. Because OSPF routers that are not MT-aware ignore the ToS fields in the LSAs, and because the MTIDs and MT metrics appear in what were ToS

---

[1] Peter Psenak, Sina Mirtorabi, Abhay Roy, Liem Nguyen, and Padma Pillay-Esnault, "MT-OSPF: Multi-Topology (MT) Routing in OSPF," draft-ietf-ospf-mt-00.txt, October 2004.

fields, MT-OSPF is compatible with non-MT-OSPF—assuming, of course, that all nondefault topologies consist of MT-OSPF routers. In other words, MT-unaware OSPF routers interpret MTID 0 as ToS 0, which is the normal OSPF procedure.

The default topology is the foundation structure of the domain, and all other topologies—signified by MTIDs between 1 and 127—are subsets of the default topology. Hellos are sent on all OSPF links regardless of the topologies the link belongs to, and the adjacencies between neighbors are not specific to any topology.

An OSPF interface can only be configured to reside in a single area. Therefore, a link is in the same area regardless of what—or how many—topologies use it. This implies that although a non-default topology might use only some of the routers and links of the default topology, it cannot have different area boundaries.

The DR/BDR election process is independent of individual topologies, so a multi-access link has the same DR and BDR no matter what or how many different topologies it belongs to. Recall that Network (type 2) LSAs do not carry any link or metric information; they serve only to represent a broadcast network as a pseudonode on the SPF calculation. Therefore, type 2 LSAs need no modification to be used in MT-OSPF. The SPF calculations for each topology use the type 2 LSAs for any multi-access link included in the topology.

Finally, if a link state changes for any topology—whether a metric change or a change in its availability—the routers attached to the link must flood a new type 1 LSA indicating the change, even if the state change affects only one topology and not all topologies to which the link belongs. Similarly, if a prefix or ASBR changes, the appropriate type 3, 4, 5, or 7 LSA must be flooded to indicate the change, even if the change applies to only one topology.

13.1.2   MT-OSPF LSAs

The Router LSA, extended for MT-OSPF, is shown in Figure 13.1. Comparing it to the standard Router LSA in Figure 5.14, you can easily see how the ToS fields have been reused as MT fields. The LSA lists all OSPF-enabled links attached to the router by Link ID and Link Type, and includes link data for each link that varies according to the Link Type. All links belong to the default topology (MTID = 0), so the standard link Metric field applies to this topology. Then for each additional topology to which the link belongs, the MTID and the MT metric for that topology is listed. The field that in standard OSPF is the Number of ToS Metrics field has become the Number of MTIDs field to indicate how many MTIDs are listed for the link. Backward compatibility is accomplished because an OSPF router that does not support MT likely also does not support ToS and ignores those fields, using only the Metric field in its SPF calculations.

As discussed in the previous section, no modification of the Network LSA is necessary. Referring back to the diagram of the Network LSA in Figure 5.16 shows why: No links or metrics are listed in the LSA, only attached routers, and the cost to the attached routers is always 0. And the DR on the link is the same for all topologies. So if the Router LSA indicates that a given multi-access link belongs to a given topology, the relevant Network LSA is used in the SPF calculation for that topology. If the multi-access link does not belong to a given topology, the Network LSA is irrelevant to the topology and is not used in the SPF calculation.

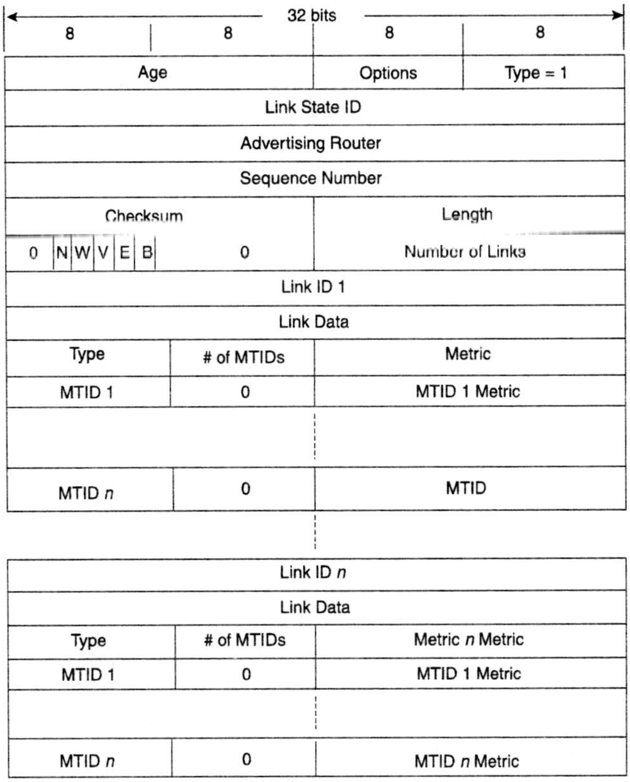

Figure 13.1   The MT-OSPF Router LSA.

Figure 13.2 shows the format of the MT-OSPF Network Summary and ASBR Summary LSA. (Remember that the formats of the type 3 and type 4 LSAs are identical; only the information in the Link State ID varies according to type.) These LSAs advertise a single destination: either a prefix outside of the area in which the LSA was originated or an ASBR. Again, the standard Metric field applies to the default topology for backward compatibility, and then the MTIDs and associated metrics are listed for each topology to which the prefix or ASBR belongs. Notice that the MTID metrics, like the default metric, are 24 bits long in these LSAs (and in the type 5 LSAs discussed next) rather than the 16-bit metrics used in type 1 LSAs, to accommodate potentially longer inter-area paths.

Figure 13.3 shows the MT-OSPF AS-External or NSSA LSA. Comparing the format with that of the standard type 5 LSA in Figure 5.23 or type 7 LSA in Figure 7.22, you can again see the reuse of the old ToS fields. The LSA advertises a single prefix external to the OSPF domain, the standard Metric field is used for the default topology, and the MTIDs are listed for each topology to which the prefix belongs. Separate Metric, Forwarding Address, and External Route Tag fields are also included for each topology, as is an E bit to indicate whether the metric for that MTID is E1 or E2. The inclusion of this bit also explains why the MTID must be between 0 and 127: Because of the bit there are only 7 bits available for the MTID in this LSA, even though the MTID field is 8 bits in type 1, 3, and 4 LSAs.

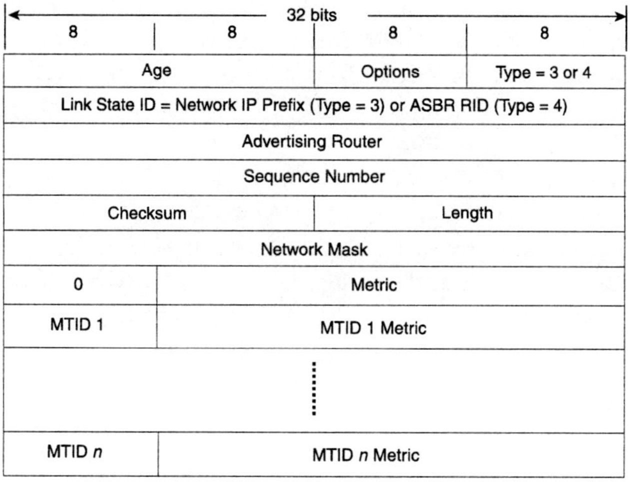

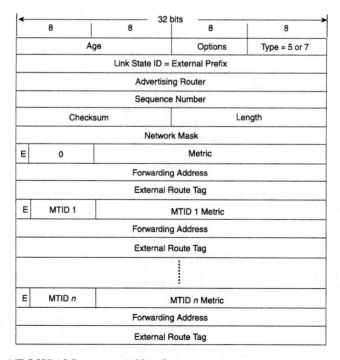

Figure 13.2   The MT-OSPF Network or ASBR Summary LSA.

Figure 13.3   The MT-OSPF AS-External or NSSA LSA.

13.1.3   Link Exclusion

As MT-OSPF has been described so far, all routers and links in an OSPF domain belong to the MTID 0 default topology. But a link might be required to belong to some specialized topology only and be excluded from the default topology. A link can be excluded from the SPF calculation for the default topology, but only if all routers in an area know to exclude it. A new parameter is defined for the MT-OSPF area data structure called MTRoutingExclusionCapability. If this parameter is disabled, the router can form adjacencies with any other OSPF router. If MTRoutingExclusionCapability is enabled, the router can only form an adjacency with other MT-OSPF routers supporting the link-exclusion capability.

The link-exclusion capability is advertised in Hello packets. Once again, the unused ToS capability is exploited by redefining the T (ToS) flag in the Options field as the MT flag (Figure 13.4). If the MTRoutingExclusionCapability parameter in the area data structure is enabled, the MT bit is set in Hellos; the router then forms adjacencies only with neighbors that also send Hellos with the MT bit set. If the MT bit is cleared in a received Hello while the MTRoutingExclusionCapability parameter is enabled, the Hello is dropped.

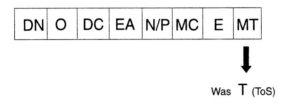

Figure 13.4   The bit originally defined as the T bit in the Options field has been redefined as the MT bit for indicating support of MT-OSPF link exclusion capability.

When the neighbors on a link support link exclusion and the link is configured to be excluded—that is, the default topology for that link is disabled—the routers advertise the link with the default Metric field set to infinity (0xFFFF). When SPF is run for the default topology, links with this cost are ignored.

13.2   IS-IS Extensions for Multi-Topology Routing

At the time of writing of this chapter, support for Multi-Topology IS-IS (MT-ISIS)[2] is in the early stages of adoption. As a result, support differs from vendor to vendor. Cisco Systems, for example, supports MT-ISIS for IPv4 and IPv6 unicast topologies, whereas Juniper Networks supports MT-ISIS for IPv4 and IPv6 unicast and multicast topologies. By the time you read this, both vendors likely will support more diverse topology types.

---

[2] Tony Przygienda, Naiming Shen, and Nischal Sheth, "M-ISIS: Multi Topology (MT) Routing in IS-IS," draft-ietf-wg-multi-topology-07.txt, June 2004.

13.2.1 MT-ISIS Procedures

IS-IS is extended to support multiple topologies by defining a new MT Intermediate Systems TLV and new MT Reachable IPv4 and IPv6 Prefixes TLVs that serve the same functions as the Extended IS Reachability TLV (type 22) and Extended IPv4 and IPv6 Reachability TLVs (types 135 and 236), respectively, but which have additional fields for MTID information. Table 13.1 lists the MTIDs defined by the MT-ISIS draft.

Table 13.1 MTIDs Defined for MT-ISIS

MTID Value	Topology
0	Standard (default) topology (IPv4 unicast routing topology)
1	IPv4 in-band management
2	IPv6 unicast routing topology
3	IPv4 multicast routing topology
4	IPv6 multicast routing topology
5–3995	Reserved for IETF consensus
3996–4095	Reserved for development, experimental, and proprietary features

The table shows that like MT-OSPF, MTID 0 signifies the default or, in MT-ISIS terms, *standard* topology. Again, this topology consists of all routers and links in the IS-IS domain and helps with backward compatibility. Any router that does not advertise MT capability, or which uses types 22 and 135 TLVs rather than the MT TLVs is considered by MT-ISIS routers to belong to the default topology. At the same time, MT-ISIS routers can use type 22 and 135 TLVs to advertise their membership in the default topology, and use MT TLVs to advertise membership in topologies other that MTID 0. Routers that do not support the MT extensions accept the type 22 and 135 TLVs as usual and ignore the MT TLVs.

When an MT-ISIS router originates a Hello on an interface, it includes in the Hello a set of Multi Topology TLVs, one for each topology that the originating interface belongs to. When the router originates its LSPs, it uses MT Reachable IS TLVs to list the topologies the router belongs to and the neighbors belonging to the same topologies. If a neighbor's Hellos indicate that it belongs to a topology that the receiving router does not, or that the neighbor does not belong to a topology that the receiving router does, the router does not associate the neighbor with that topology when it originates its LSPs.

If a neighbor does not include any MT TLVs in its Hellos, the receiving router includes the neighbor only in the default topology. Adjacency behavior is a bit different between point-to-point and broadcast interfaces: If two neighbors have no topologies in common on a point-to-point interface, no adjacency is formed; but an adjacency is formed between two or more neighbors on a broadcast interface even if they do not have any topologies in common. This is because, as with DRs and MT-OSPF, the DIS election is independent of the MT-ISIS extensions. So because a router that does not support MT extensions can be elected DIS, all routers on a broadcast network must be adjacent at the same level.

There are two more similarities to MT-OSPF: If a router detects a change in a topology to which it belongs, it must reflood a new LSP to advertise the change. And, level boundaries are the same for all MT-ISIS topologies, just as area boundaries are the same for all MT-OSPF topologies. The NET of each router also applies to all topologies to which the router belongs.

Although NETs and level boundaries must be consistent, a router can set the Overload bit separately for each topology to which it belongs. And a router can be an L1/L2 router for some topologies and not for others; as a result, an L1/L2 router can set the Attached bit separately per topology.

13.2.2   MT-ISIS TLVs

The Multi Topology TLV (type 229) is shown in Figure 13.5. The TLV lists the MTIDs, up to 127, to which the originating router belongs, and is carried in both Hellos and LSPs. The MTID for MT-ISIS is 12 bits, rather than the 7-bit MTID that MT-OSPF uses. An Overload (O) bit and an Attached (A) bit is associated with each MTID listed, so that overloading and L2 attachment can be advertised separately for each topology. The R bits are reserved.

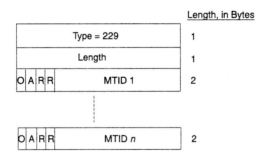

Figure 13.5   The MT-ISIS Multi Topology TLV.

Figure 13.6 shows the MT Intermediate Systems TLV (type 222). This TLV serves the same purpose as the Extended IS Reachability TLV shown in Figure 5.33: It describes the originating router's links to neighboring routers and the cost of those links, and so serves as the fundamental information for the SPF calculations. The difference is that the MT IS TLV associates the listed neighbors with a specific MTID. (The 4 bits preceding the 12-bit MTID are reserved.) The format of the TLV, aside from the added MTID field, is identical to the Extended IS TLV. This TLV can appear multiple times, according to the number of MTIDs the originator supports.

Similarly, the MT Reachable IPv4 Prefixes TLV (Figure 13.7) has the same function as the Extended IP Reachability TLV shown in Figure 5.34: It advertises internal and external prefixes and their metrics, but associates the prefixes with a specific MTID. The type of the TLV is 235, and it can appear multiple times according to the number of topologies supported by the originating router.

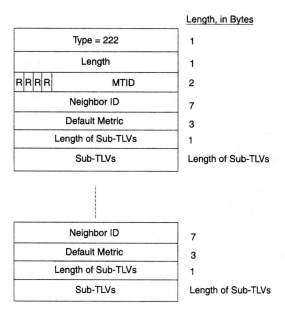

Figure 13.6 The MT-ISIS MT Intermediate Systems TLV.

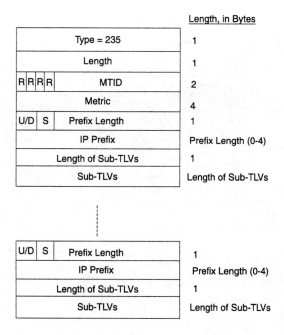

Figure 13.7 The MT-ISIS MT Reachable IPv4 Prefixes TLV.

Finally, the MT Reachable IPv6 Prefixes TLV (type 237) shown in Figure 13.8 is an MT version of the IPv6 Reachability TLV shown in Figure 13.21: It advertises IPv6 prefixes, but like the MT Reachable IPv4 Prefixes TLV, it lists the IPv6 prefixes relevant to a specified MTID. One difference with this TLV and the related IPv4 MT TLV is that "regular" type 236 IPv6 Prefix TLVs and these type 237 MT IPv6 Prefix TLVs cannot be mixed. An IS-IS domain should use one type or the other, but not both.

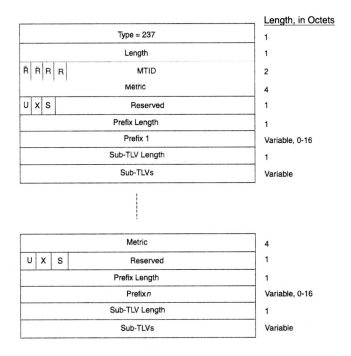

Figure 13.8   The MT-ISIS MT Reachable IPv6 Prefixes TLV.

Review Questions

1. What is multi-topology routing?
2. What is an MTID?
3. What is the default topology, and what is its MTID?
4. Which of the first five LSA types does not require any changes for MT-OSPF support, and why?
5. What is MT-OSPF link exclusion, and how is support for it signaled between neighbors?

6. Can an MT-ISIS router advertise separate overloading and L2 attachments for each topology?

7. If two IS-IS neighbors on a point-to-point link have no MTIDs in common, do they become adjacent? What about two neighbors on a broadcast link with no MTIDs in common?

8. How does an MT-ISIS router interpret a neighbor that does not include any MT TLVs in its Hellos?

The Future of Link State Protocols

OSPF and IS-IS are both almost 20 years old, and are based on a mathematical algorithm that is almost 50 years old; in Internet years, this is nearly prehistoric. They were designed in the days when processors were slow, memory was expensive, and each router added significant latency to the network. As a result both protocols have features and characteristics that no longer matter, meant to solve problems that no longer exist. The 32-bit alignment of all OSPF data units for orderly processing and the original 6-bit IS-IS metric for faster processing are just two examples. Although the operational experience gained from the original link state protocol used in the ARPANET led to some key design differences in OSPF and IS-IS—such as the use of linear rather than circular sequence number spaces—some of the problems the protocols were designed to address were speculative rather than tied to practical experience. And a few features originally intended for one purpose have since been utilized for another purpose. The IS-IS overload (OL) capability is a good example: The original intent was to signal memory overload in a router. Today, memory limits are not a serious issue, but the OL function is used to prevent the blackholing of packets during BGP convergence. This practice has become so common that a capability similar to the IS-IS overload has been added to OSPF.

As the change in application of overloading would indicate, modern changes to OSPF and IS-IS are no longer motivated by speculative problems but instead driven by practical experience. Throughout the 1990s, the challenges were to enhance the scalability and reliability of the protocols to keep pace with the enormous increase in the size of IP networks. This growth continues, and beginning in the late 1990s the increasing interconnectedness of IP networks added security to the list of issues OSPF and IS-IS must address. Also beginning in the late 1990s and continuing to the present day are new capabilities in IP networks requiring extensions to OSPF and IS-IS such as IP multicast, IPv6, and MPLS.

Some of the newest networking capabilities being developed spring from experience with MPLS. MPLS separates the control and signaling functions of networks from the switching and forwarding functions, so that control and signaling can be isolated to the network access nodes. That is, MPLS keeps the "intelligence" of the network at the edges. The benefit of MPLS, as discussed in Chapter 11, is that you can use it to build virtual circuits across IP networks, thereby providing what appears to be a connection-oriented service over a connectionless network. These virtual circuits, called label switched paths (LSPs), can be used for traffic engineering, QoS, and for building various kinds of virtual private networks (VPNs). The concept has been successful enough that MPLS is being extended to create LSPs across not only packet switched networks but also time domain networks such as SONET/SDH, wave domain networks such as lambda switching, and special domain networks such as fiber switches. A version of MPLS called Generalized MPLS (GMPLS) extends a common control plane not only to label switching routers and ATM switches but also to the lower-level elements of a network such as DWDM systems, optical cross-connects, and add-drop multiplexors (ADMs). OSPF and IS-IS are being extended to support traffic engineering capabilities in GMPLS as they presently do for MPLS.

Given the age of link state protocols in general, and OSPF and IS-IS in particular, one must ask whether link state protocols will be replaced in the future by some newer, better algorithm. It is true that new algorithms are proposed in academic papers from time to time. But no algorithm has stimulated widespread interest either among the operators of large-scale networks or among the router vendors that supply these operators. So although some new, improved algorithm might eventually supplant link state protocols, this will not happen in the foreseeable future.

And although growing and evolving IP networks produce new network capabilities and applications, engineers usually prefer to hold on to what is familiar and proven whenever possible. Hence, OSPF and IS-IS continue to be extended to support these new network technologies. The arc of engineering and operational experience invested in these two protocols over the past 20 years, and their ongoing extensibility, indicate that OSPF and IS-IS will continue to be the preferred routing protocols for large IP networks for many years to come.

INDEX

V

values
   Circuit Type, 94
   TLVs. *See* TLVs
VC (virtual circuit), 68, 374
vector protocols
   BGP, 37
   characteristics of, 28-29
   convergence, 27-28
   EIGRP, 35
   overview of, 25
   routing loops, 29-35
virtual circuit. *See* VC
virtual links
   IS-IS, 270
   OSPF, 241-248
VPNs (virtual private networks), 374

W-Z

Washington University (St. Louis), 7
wide metrics, 157
windowing transmission rates, 136

Zinky, John, 18

Register
Your Book

at www.awprofessional.com/register

You may be eligible to receive:

- Advance notice of forthcoming editions of the book
- Related book recommendations
- Chapter excerpts and supplements of forthcoming titles
- Information about special contests and promotions throughout the year
- Notices and reminders about author appearances, tradeshows, and online chats with special guests

Contact us

If you are interested in writing a book or reviewing manuscripts prior to publication, please write to us at:

Editorial Department
Addison-Wesley Professional
75 Arlington Street, Suite 300
Boston, MA 02116 USA
Email: AWPro@aw.com

Visit us on the Web: http://www.awprofessional.com